Portrait of Humanity
Vol 2

Portrait of Humanity Vol 2

First edition

Copyright © Hoxton Mini Press 2020
All rights reserved

All images © The Photographers
Cover image by Eric Demers
Introduction by Gemma Padley
Sequence by Friederike Huber
Design by Daniele Roa
Copy editing by Gemma Padley
and Faith McAllister
Production by Anna De Pascale

With special thanks to Shaz Madani for
the design work of *Portrait of Britain*
which informed the design of this book.

Images shortlisted from Portrait of
Humanity 2020, created by 1854 Media

A CIP catalogue record for this book
is available from the British Library

ISBN 978-1-910566-73-2

First published in the United Kingdom
in 2020 by Hoxton Mini Press

Printed and bound by: Livonia, Latvia

To order books, collector's editions
and signed prints please go to:
www.hoxtonminipress.com

Portrait of Humanity
Vol 2

HOXTON MINI PRESS

Note from the Publisher

Everything has gone to shit.

Or has it?

As I write this, alone in an office with hand gel by my side, London is at peak lockdown. The Tube is empty, Boris is only just getting his breath back and those of us who are not baking or cleaning or coughing, are questioning what it means to live in a society. If you are reading this without a mask or gloves on, please tell me, did we find a vaccine?

At the very least, a new humanity is shining through. We smile at strangers, we speak more to our relatives, we appreciate the little of the outdoors that we are allowed to enjoy. Social distancing is, perversely, helping us to find some long-lost intimacy.

Looking through this year's edition, I'm more touched than ever by the stories included. Of course, I would say that, wouldn't I? But, still, there is a resonance here. The stories of shared pain and love and hope, mostly taken before the Corona storm, seem to hint at the power of a collective humanity that may, just, take us out of it.

Or is this just my hope? No, surely, it's all of ours. Thank you to the *British Journal of Photography* for once again, bringing this book together. If we don't find a vaccine soon, then maybe this book, in a very small way, is a temporary antidote to our collective troubles.

Stay well everyone.

Martin Usborne
Co-founder, Hoxton Mini Press

Foreword

It is more than a century since Lenin famously said 'there are decades where nothing happens; and there are weeks where decades happen'. That sentiment has never seemed more relevant than at this moment in time, during which people all over the world are locked down and separated from each other, and from the normality we all (used to) take for granted.

A year ago, I wrote in the foreword of the first edition of this book that '*Portrait of Humanity* was [intended to] provide an antidote to the negativity and animosity that we hear about relentlessly in mainstream media and international politics'. Just 12 months later, it seems surreal that major items on the news agenda like Brexit, impeachment and climate change are barely mentioned – their importance not diminished, but completely overshadowed by the Coronavirus epidemic.

The cover image by Eric Demers, of Greta Thunberg addressing half a million climate change demonstrators in Montreal, is a reminder of the importance of these major issues. But while our planet is responding well to its break from humanity, this pandemic has proven to be a leveller for its most advanced inhabitants, ignoring all cultural, economic and geographic boundaries.

In writing this foreword I have had to question whether releasing this book now is appropriate. Whether curating a photographic exhibition and book may even be viewed as frivolous, given what is happening around the world. But I can't get away from the notion that this serves as an important and timely reminder that while we are literally, physically, apart, we have a shared humanity. The 200 portraits in this book are an unashamed celebration of that humanity, with images from all around the world that do not elevate or promote any one particular culture, religion, sex, gender, age or ability, over another.

The exhibition on Clear Channel screens along with the physical touring show will make this the most viewed photographic exhibition on the planet. And this

year we will be broadcasting our message
of peace and unity beyond – exhibiting
the images high in the stratosphere
against the extraordinary backdrop of
space. The images will then be translated
into binary code and travel unimpeded
through the solar system and ultimately
through the universe at the speed of
light. These messages could continue
on an infinite journey for the rest of
time – or perhaps until another
civilisation receives and decodes them.
I wonder what they will make of us...

The twist in all of this is that it has
brought us together, in our millions.
From small, friendly gestures and
celebrations of frontline healthcare
workers in the streets, to unprecedented
support by governments, businesses
and organisations the world over, we
are seeing the best in us. The humanity
in us.

Will we remain closer and more tolerant
when this is all over? I don't know,
but would like to think so. What I do
know is that right now, more than ever,
we need a reminder that we are not alone.
The 200 portraits in this book may be
just the ticket.

Marc Hartog
Founder and CEO, 1854 Media

Introduction

Photography has been and continues to be by humanity's side, recording our greatest moments, our most terrible, and everything in between. In photography's almost 200-year history, the camera has accompanied humans into war, borne witness during unimaginable suffering and been present as we start over, time and time again. Occasionally, as W. Eugene Smith pointed out, it moves us in profound ways. 'Photography,' he wrote, 'is a small voice, at best, but sometimes – just sometimes – one photograph or a group of them can lure our senses into awareness.'

Whether we are the one taking the picture, being photographed or looking at an image, photography invites us to pause and think about what makes us human, to celebrate our differences and to remember that we are not all that different after all. Looking through the images in this second edition of *Portrait of Humanity*, it's heartening to see so many examples of the best of humanity captured through photography's ever shifting lens. The images in this collection whisk us off on a journey through 21st century life where we experience the entire gamut of human emotion and experience. There are displays of courage, love, tenderness, defiance, camaraderie and strength; there is eccentricity, playfulness, loss, companionship, despair, laughter, faith, hope and new life. Each image is like a portal into a world where for the briefest of moments we connect with the person or people depicted and share something of their experience in a very visceral, intimate way.

And what sobering experiences they are. Celina (p.45) lost her family to Ebola and wants to be a doctor so she can help others. She has not been cowed by the disease, rather she defiantly meets our gaze amid the ramshackle surroundings of Magazine Wharf, one of the largest slums in Sierra Leone's capital, Freetown. Elsewhere, Grace (p.199) has chosen to use alternative therapies to treat her tumour and like her name she is the epitome of humility and dignity as she stands submerged in water. Carol Anne Mayer (p.48) survived a house fire and has rebuilt her life; now she voluntarily counsels burns victims. These women, like many others in the book, have come through or are coping with huge challenges, but they refuse to be beaten. Their remarkable resilience is deeply humbling.

There are the people boldly adapting to a changing world or who keep on keeping on even as their way of life is increasingly threatened. A Tibetan girl adopts an almost heroic pose (p.71) as we learn that the life she and her family lead may disappear because the Chinese Government wants to see nomads settled. Or there is the little girl whose family lives on the remote Arctic Archipelago of Svalbard (p.304) where the signs of climate emergency are rapid and profound: waters are warming, sea ice is melting. Beneath a threatening sky she plays on a trampoline as any child plays anywhere in the world.

There are those who have found great comfort through photography such as the mother who took pictures to cope with the challenges of caring for her ailing father and young son (p.77), or the photographer who began a portrait project with her mother who has depression (p.197).

And there are those who come together for what they believe in and to effect change: the Birmingham swimmers literally standing side by side to protest against the closure of their local swimming pool (p.293), or the performance artists-activists at Extinction Rebellion's spring uprising in April 2019 who use art to confront the seminal issue of our time head on (p.89).

In times of extreme crisis, art becomes more vital, more necessary, more urgent than ever. As the novelist Olivia Laing has written in the *Guardian:* 'novels, films and paintings [and we might add photography to this list] offer more than escapism – they provide hope'. It is hope that gives us the courage to pick ourselves up and carry on when everything around us is spiralling out of control.

Hope and courage can be found in abundance across the following pages, from Pakistan to Tanzania, Bolivia to Greenland. And while art (in this context, photography specifically) can't solve the problems facing humanity outright, it can, as Laing aptly puts it, 'serve as an antidote to times of chaos. It can be a route to clarity, and it can be a force of resistance and repair, providing new registers, new languages in which to think'. It calls upon us to pull together and begin again.

Gemma Padley
London, 2020

Portraits

Camaraderie
by Nicole Osula
London, UK

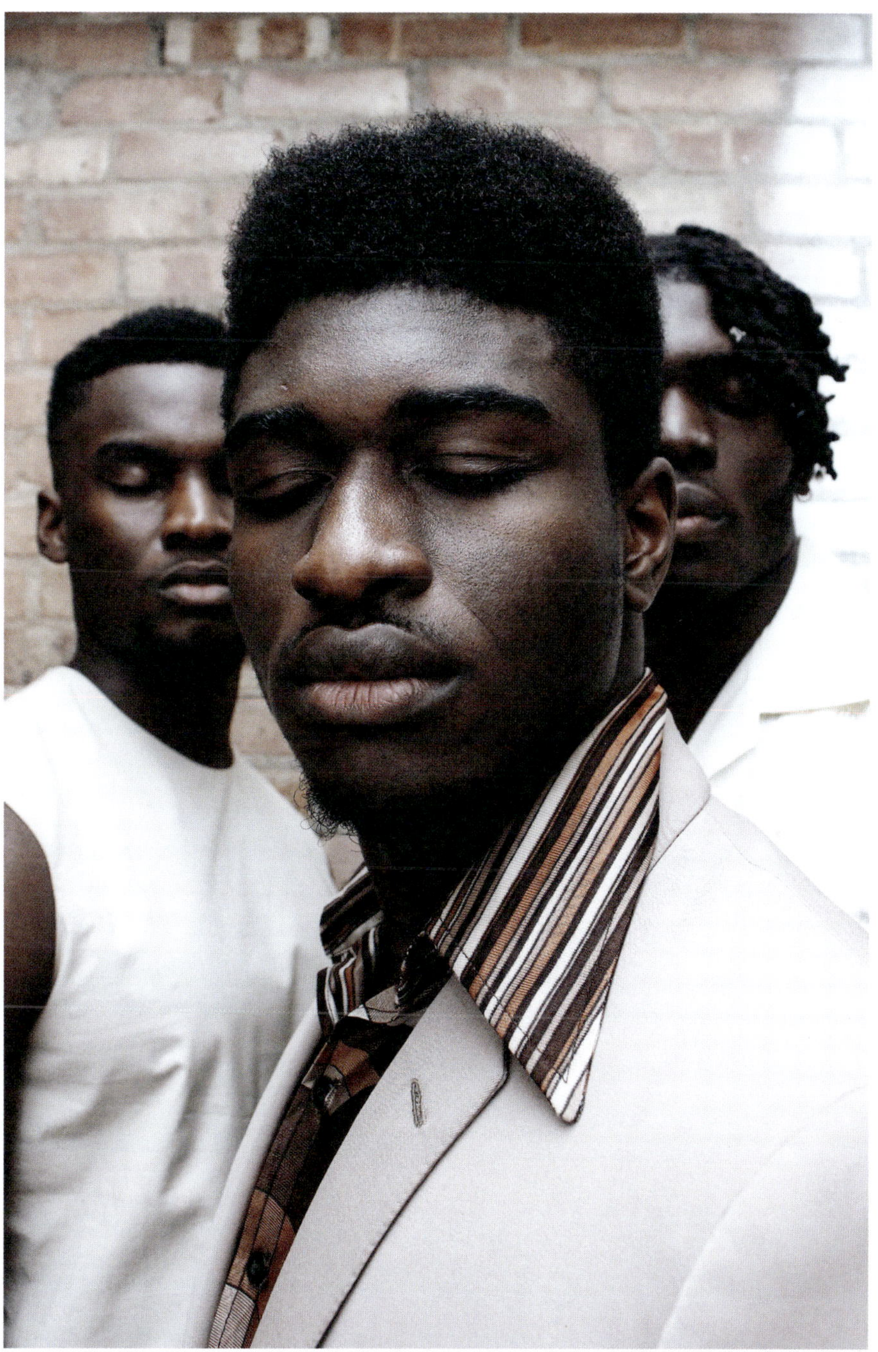

Cat Grace
by Kristina Varaksina
New York City, New York, USA

Yana Dobroliubova is a Russian model. I met her
on a photoshoot and was struck by her unusual beauty
and the way she moved like a cat.

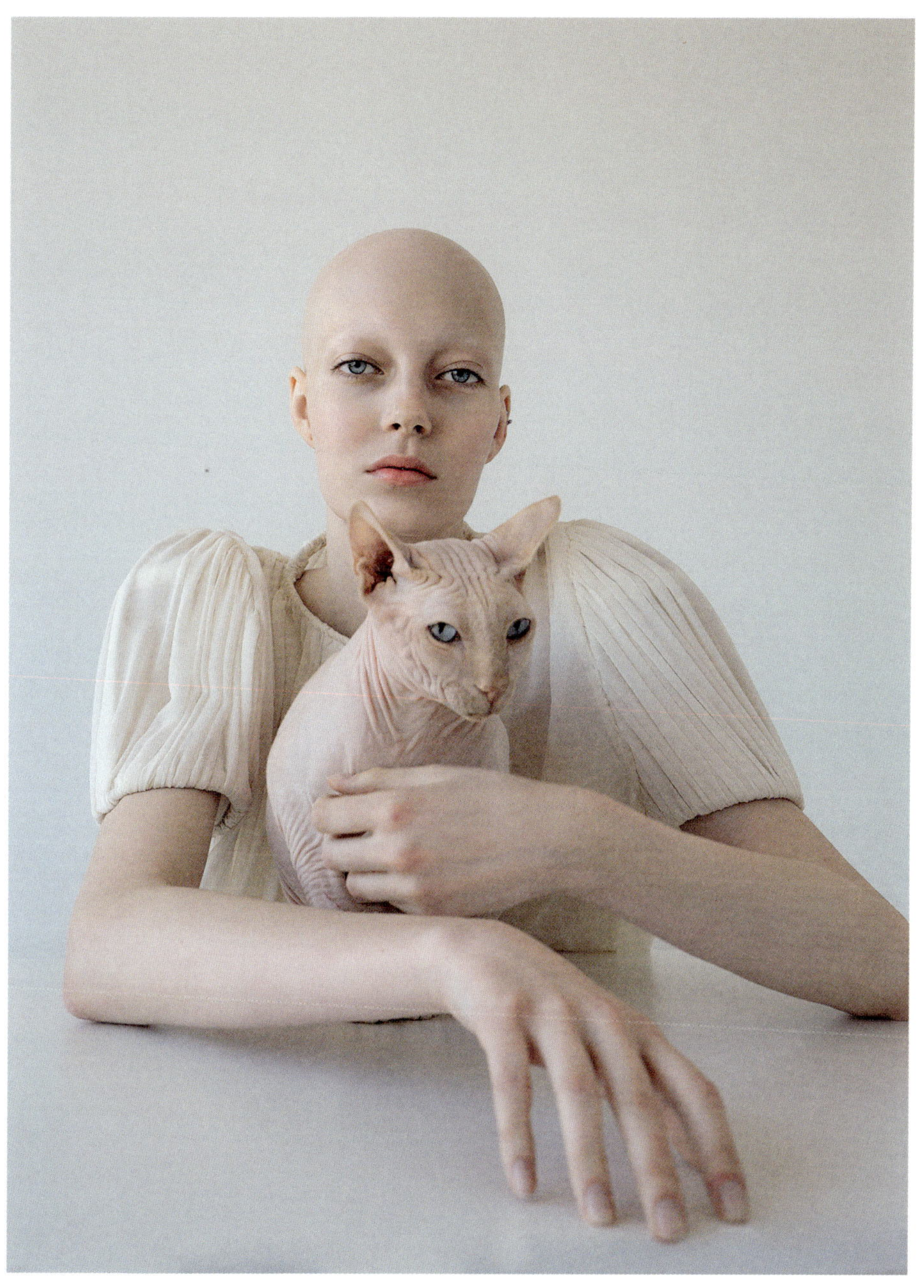

Young Indigenous Hunters
by Annie Sakkab
Ontario, Canada

Olivia Hilldercach, 7, holds her gun during
duck hunting season in Tyendinaga Mohawk Territory,
a reserve on the Bay of Quinte in southeastern Ontario.
When I asked Olivia why she hunts, she replied:
'When I hunt I feel happy for other people because
we give them food.'

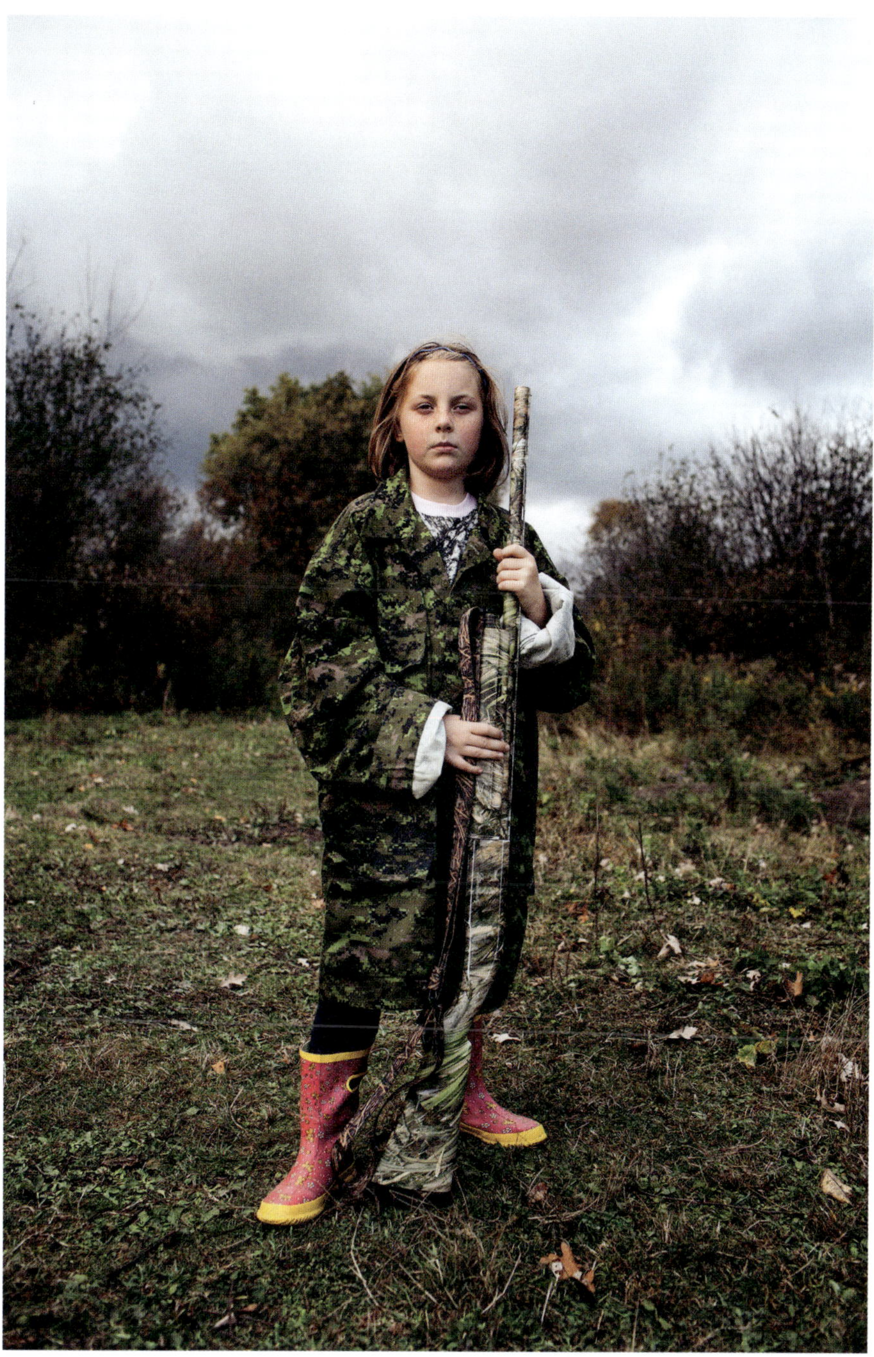

Ayanda
by Joey Carrapichano
Cape Town, South Africa

Ayanda is my niece. She is so full of life and
has an amazing energy. 'I feel proud inside and
beautiful and great. When we took the picture
I felt a bit scared, but I was brave and did it.'
– Ayanda Mlalazi Carrapichano

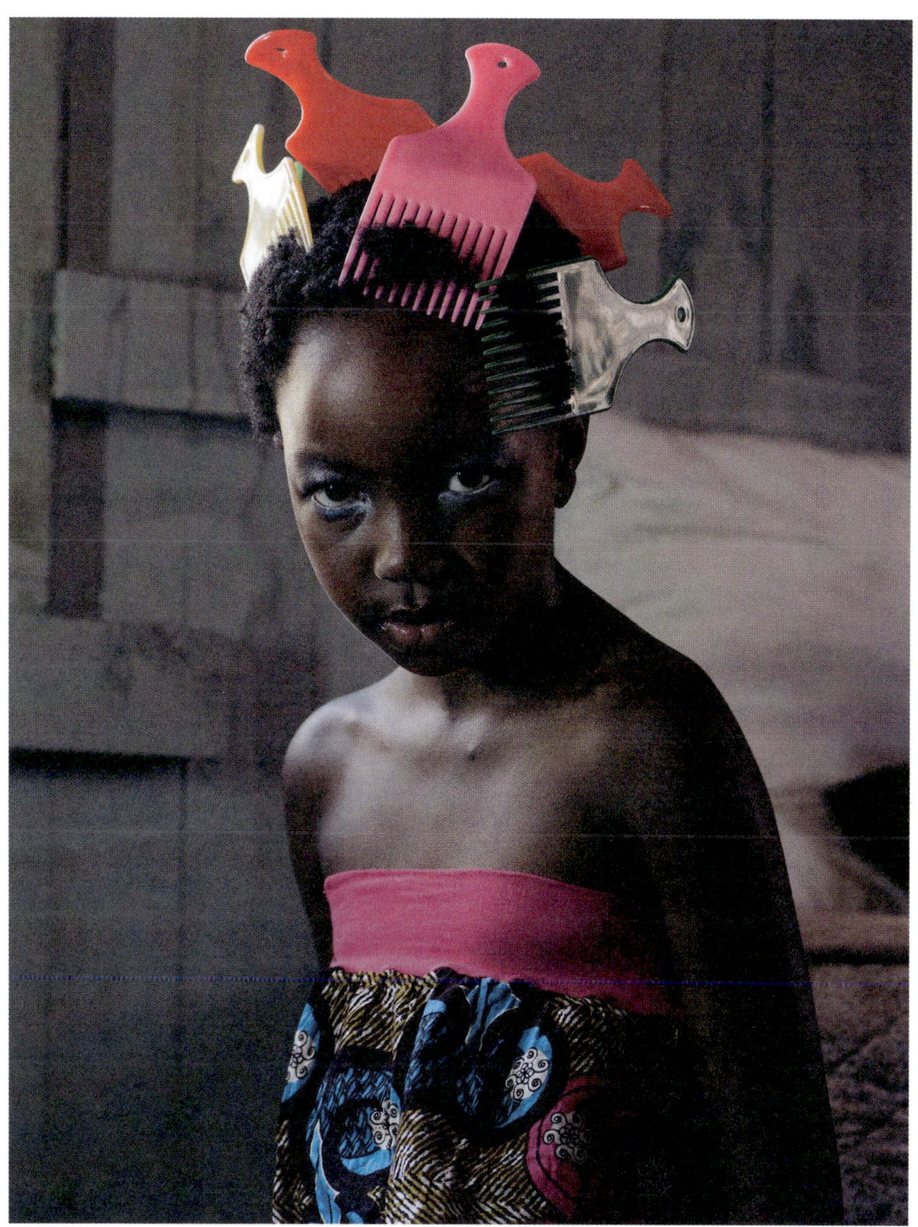

Hendrick
by Aron Klein
Hasvik, Norway

Hendrick belongs to the next generation of
the Sámi tribe, an indigenous Finno-Ugric people.
For thousands of years they have coexisted with
reindeer herders and each year make the journey
from the island's lush summer pastures to
the mainland's tundra, following the reindeer.
Hendrick peers out from the family's goahti, the
traditional teepee-like structure that will be
their home for the two months that the migration
lasts. The goahti is a strong symbol of the Sámi
people and one of the oldest architectural
structures still in use.

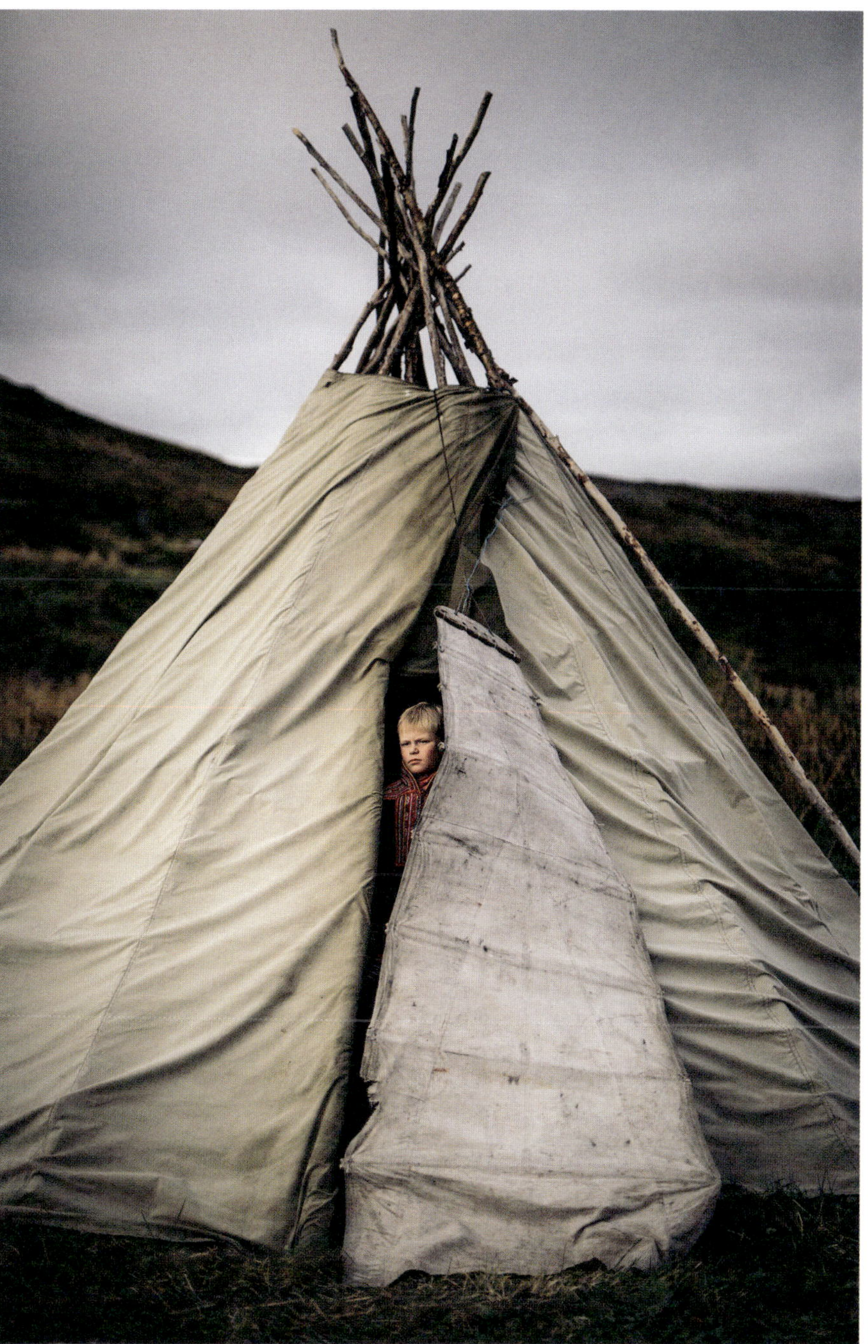

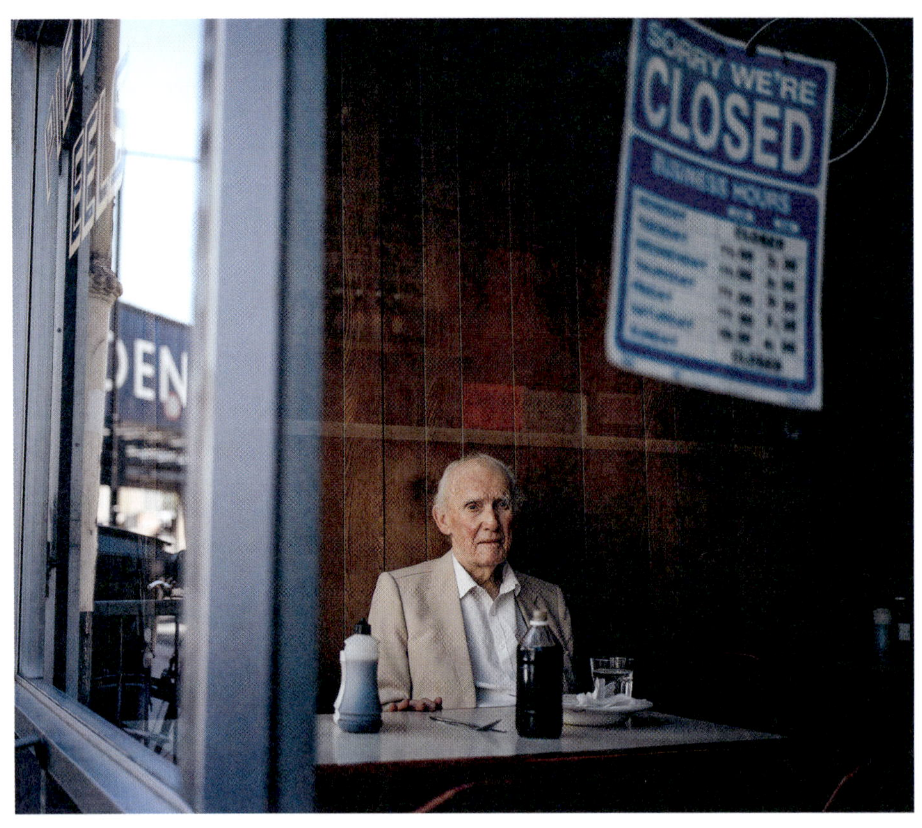

Patsy

by Sam Gregg
London, UK

I regularly bump into 93-year-old Patsy at
Castle's Pie & Mash shop, one of Camden's oldest
family-run businesses. Patsy is emblematic of
my project 'Blighty' as he belongs to an era I'm
trying to capture before it disappears.

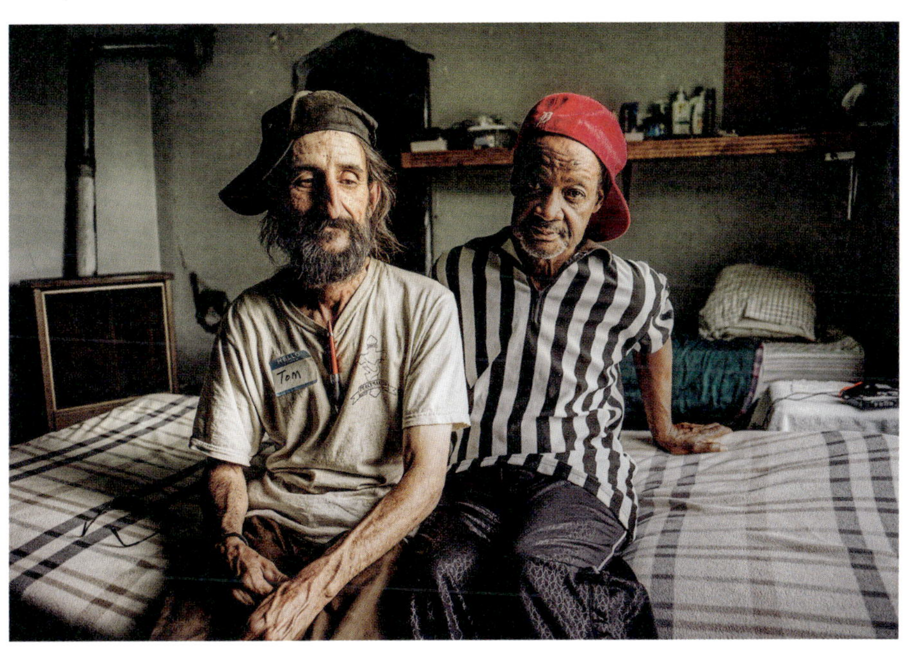

Tom and Harris
by Eric Smith
Detroit, Michigan, USA

Tom and Harris are members of a homeless
shelter run by the church and charitable organisation,
Peacemakers International. Both were former addicts.
They met at the outreach centre and
became best friends.

Twins
by Chiara Luxardo
Yangon, Myanmar

Martha and Mary are six-year-old twins.
Their mother died during childbirth and the father
brought them to this Christian orphanage.
Martha would like to become a soccer player or
a boxer (boxing is very popular in Myanmar)
while Mary wants to be a singer or an actress. Something
about their firm expressions caught my attention.

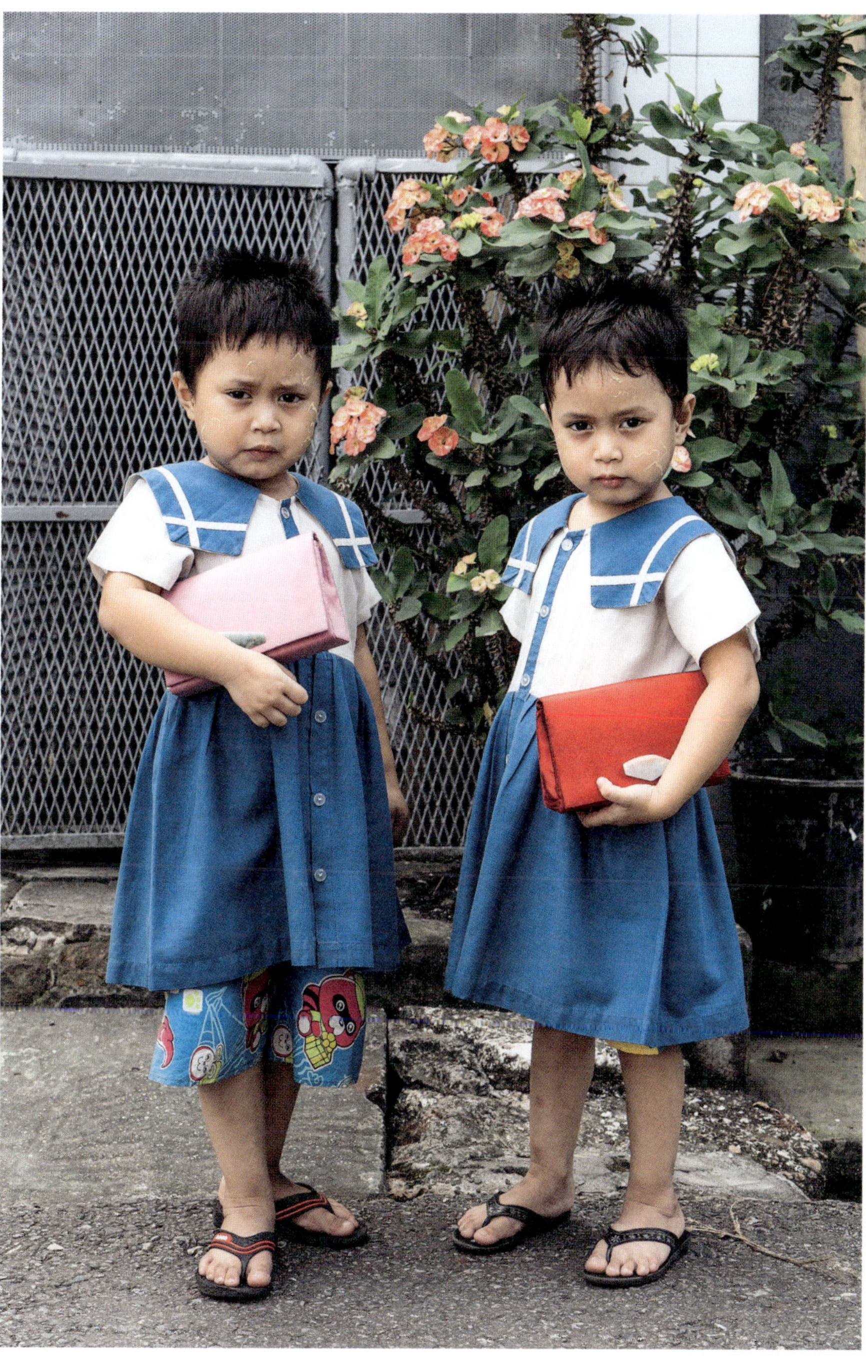

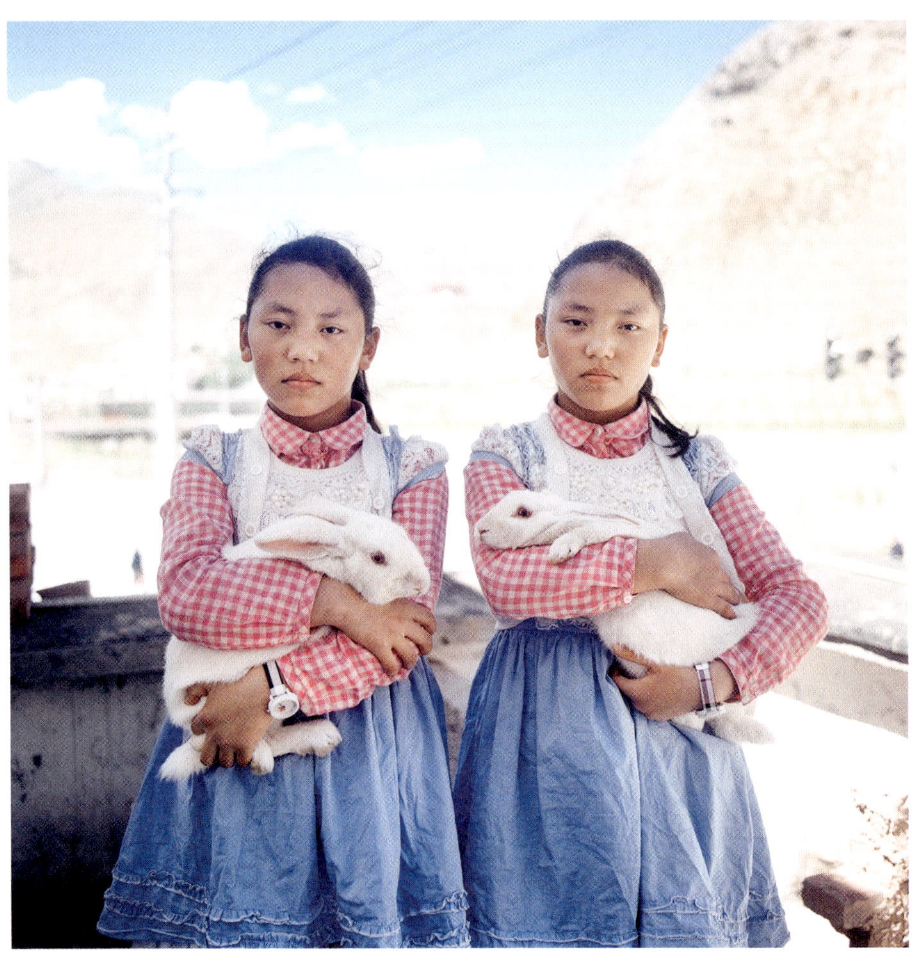

Lhamo Tsertso and Lobsang Chödron
by Rinchen Ato
Kham, Northeast Tibet

I have been photographing my friend's twin
daughters since they were toddlers and have watched
them change each year.

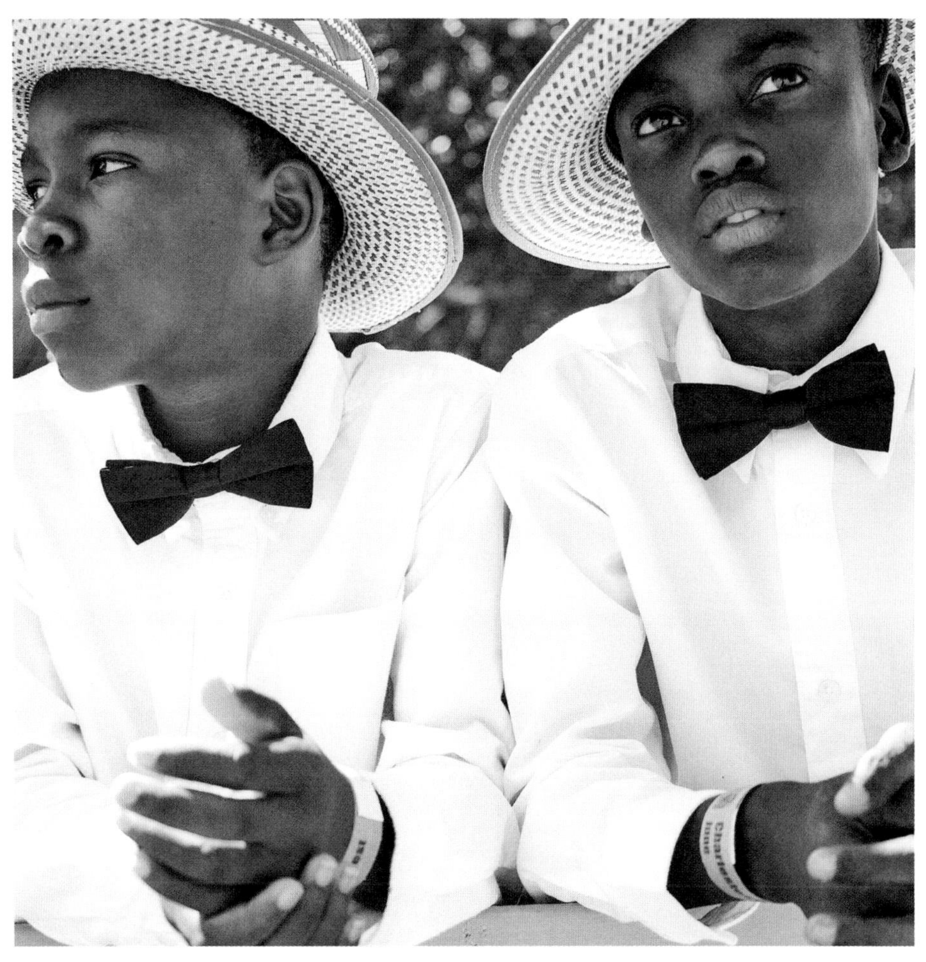

Haitian Orphan Choir
by Michael Campina
Charleston, South Carolina, USA

Maiko Jean Baptiste and Davidson Fils are part
of an orphan choir. Twenty-five of the 30 children are sole
survivors of the 2010 earthquake that destroyed Haiti.
They lost everything, including their families.

My Grandmother On Her Bed
by Lidewij Mulder
Haren, The Netherlands

My 82-year-old grandmother feels more like
a friend to me. She is very youthful and
mischievous and has taught me how to be an
independent woman. My grandmother has been
fighting for equality since she was a kid.

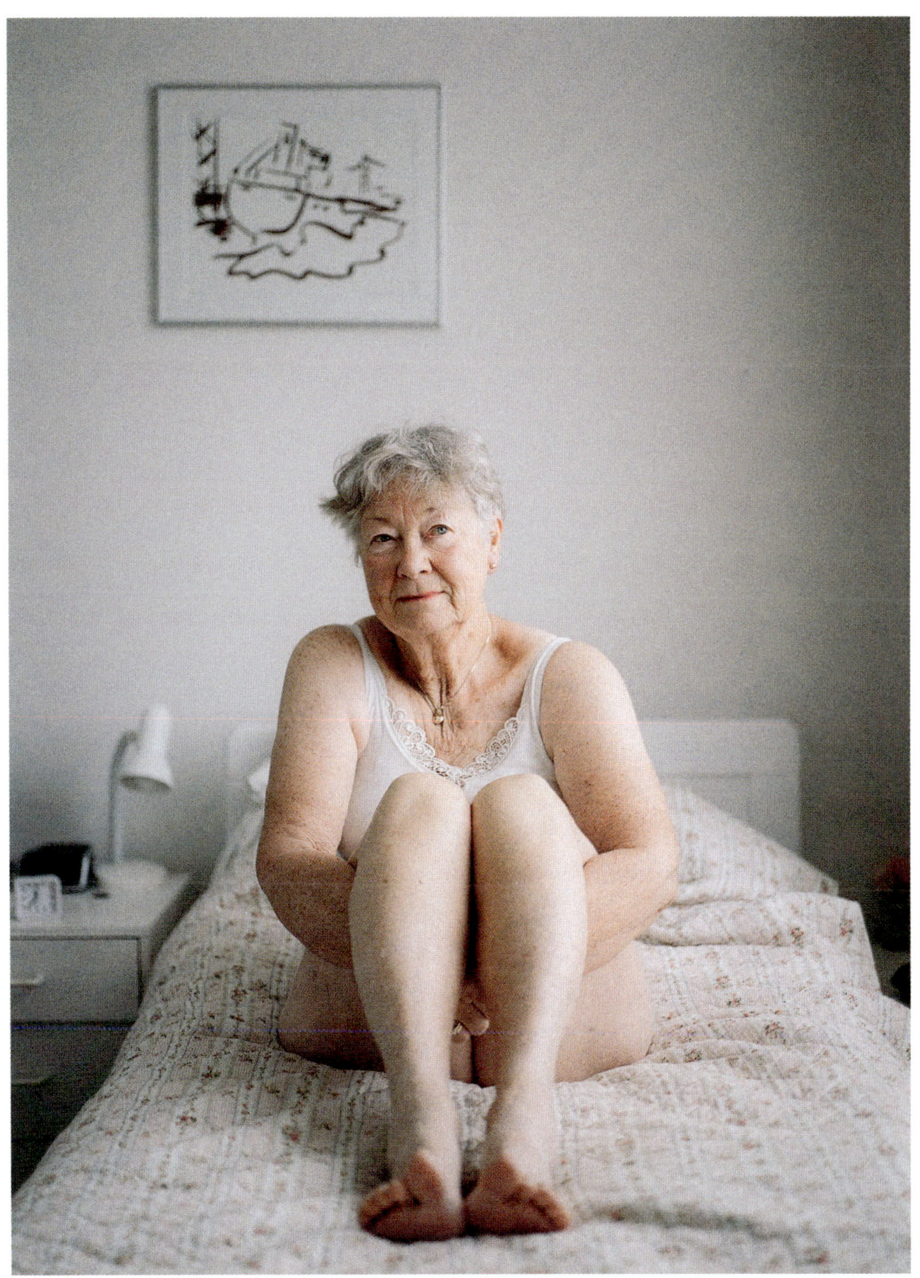

Scott
by Simon Murphy
Glasgow, UK

Scott runs the Jagged Edge tattoo studio in
Govanhill on Glasgow's Southside. It's not easy to
miss Scott – he often stands outside the shop smoking
or drinking a cup of coffee. The word 'family' above
his right eye stood out to me. 'What does family mean to
you?' I asked. 'Life is family and family is life,'
he replied.

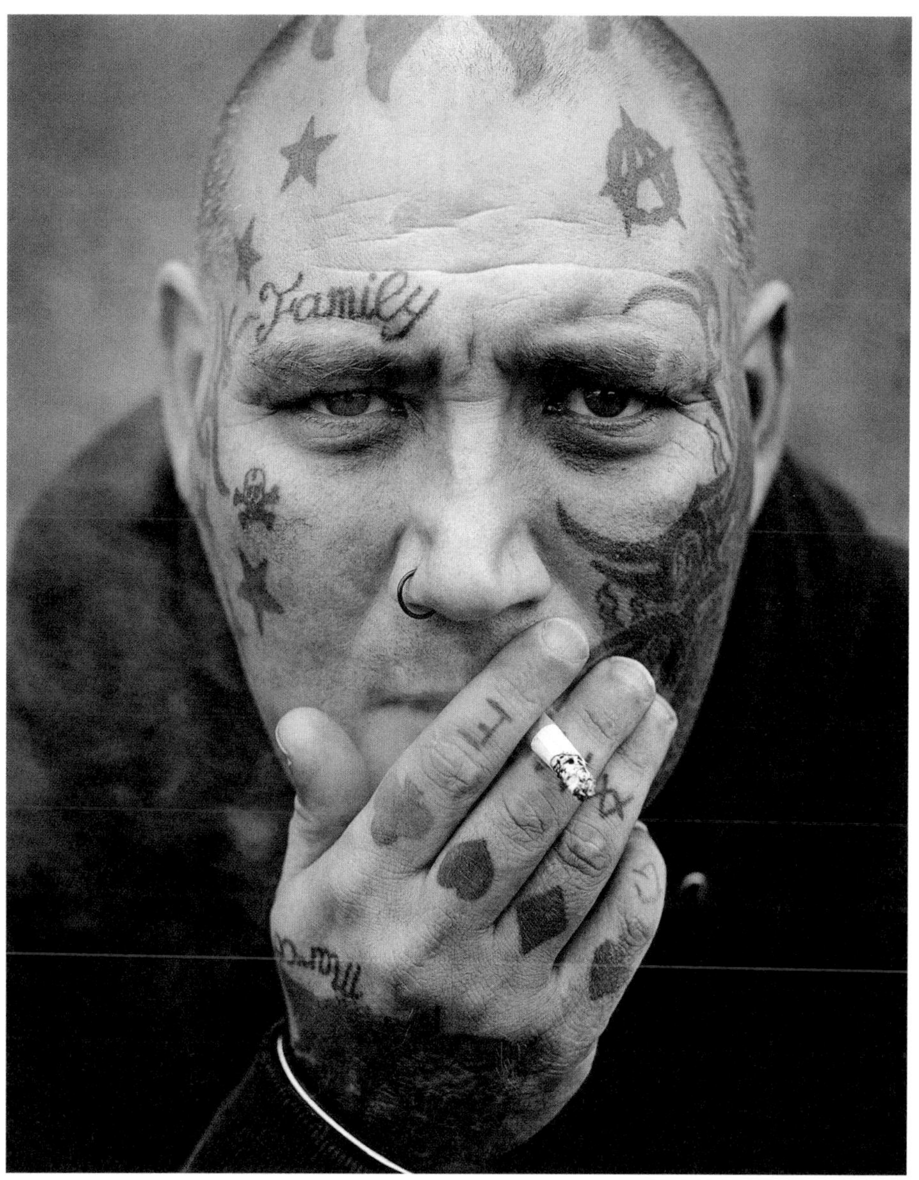

Tina de Groot
by Wouter le Duc
Utrecht, The Netherlands

Tina is a Dutch illustrator. We met through
social media and I photographed her in beautiful
sunlight in her house. We talked about what
it's like to be an artist and the struggles
we have to overcome.

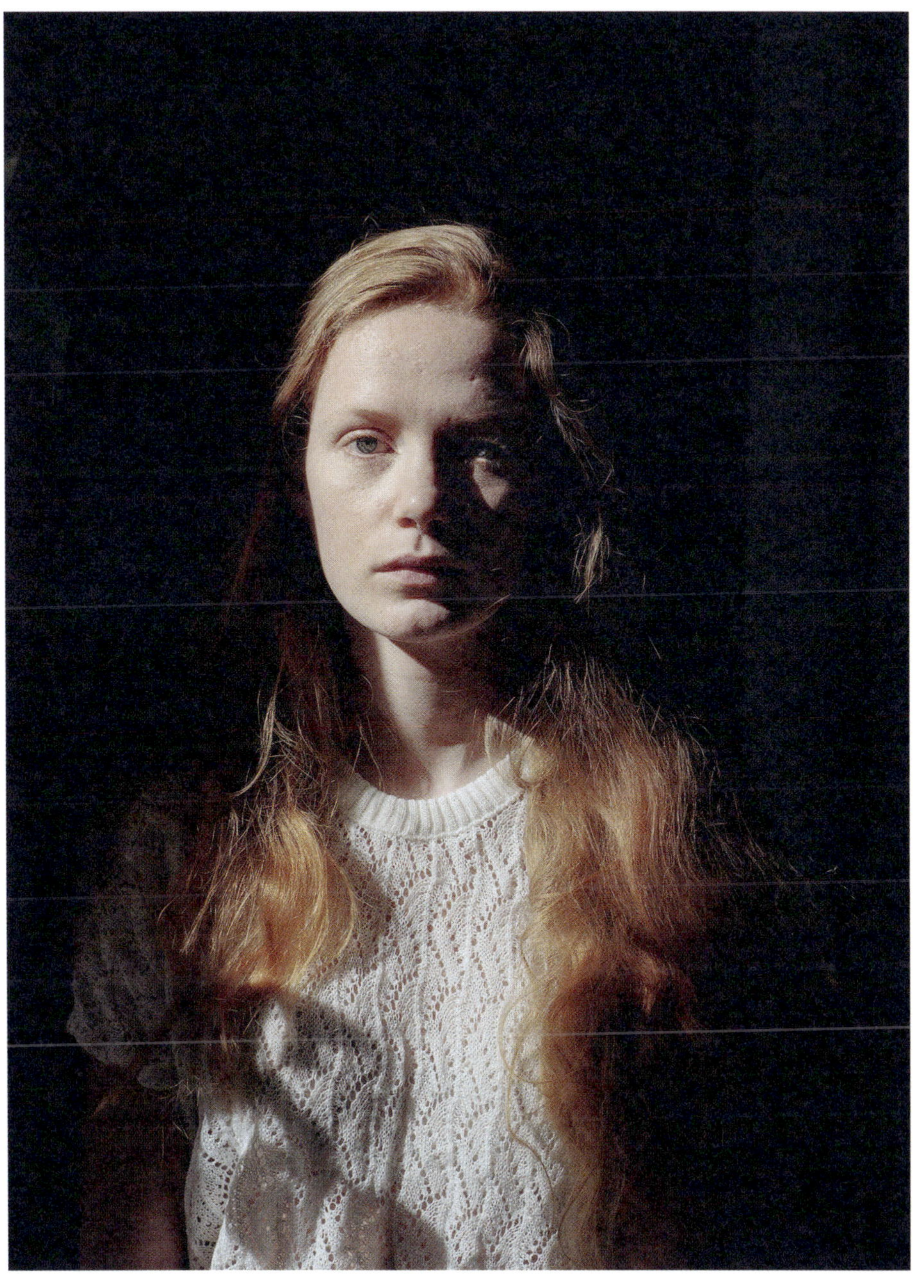

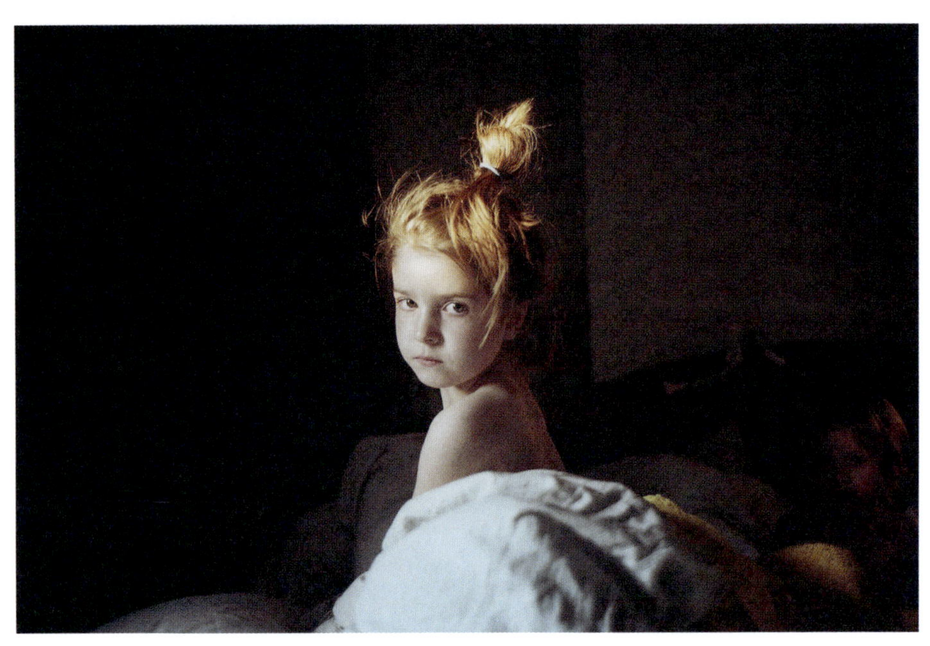

L. and E.
by Sipke Visser
London, UK

Whenever there is great light I run for my
camera and ask my daughters to pose, which is
getting trickier as they get older, but they are
learning how beautiful light can be.

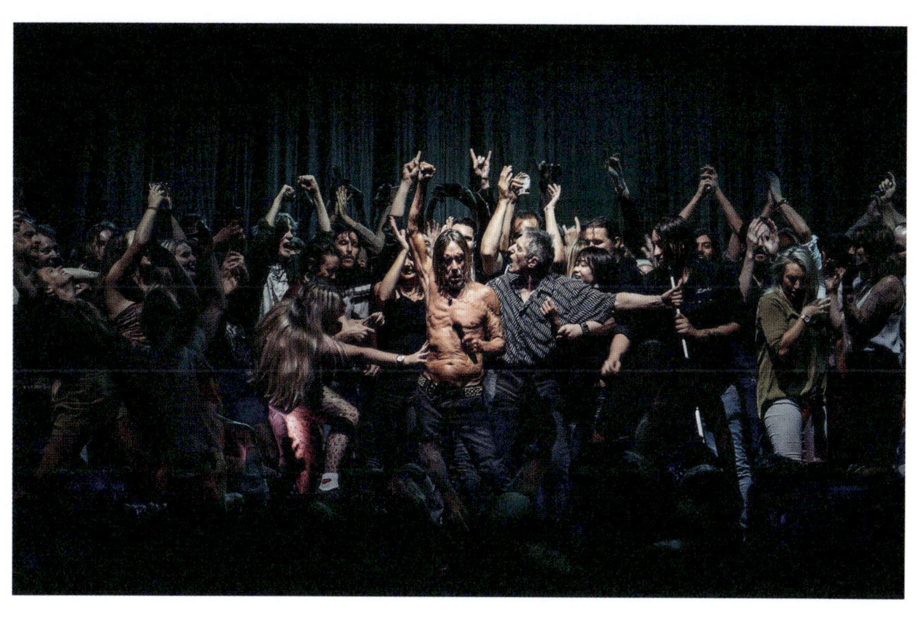

Iggy Pop
by Antoine Veling
Sydney, Australia

Punk icon Iggy Pop performs at the Sydney
Opera House amid adoring fans who gladly accepted
his invitation to dance with him on stage.

After the Medicine
by Daniel Fernández
Bogotá, Colombia

I was invited to a private ayahuasca or
'yagé' ceremony conducted by the well-known
indigenous Taita Eustorgio Payaguaje from
Putumayo, the Amazon region of Colombia.
After the ceremony I spoke with Eustorgio about
humility. I remember his words clearly:
'I am not a master. I am an imperfect human
being like all of us.'

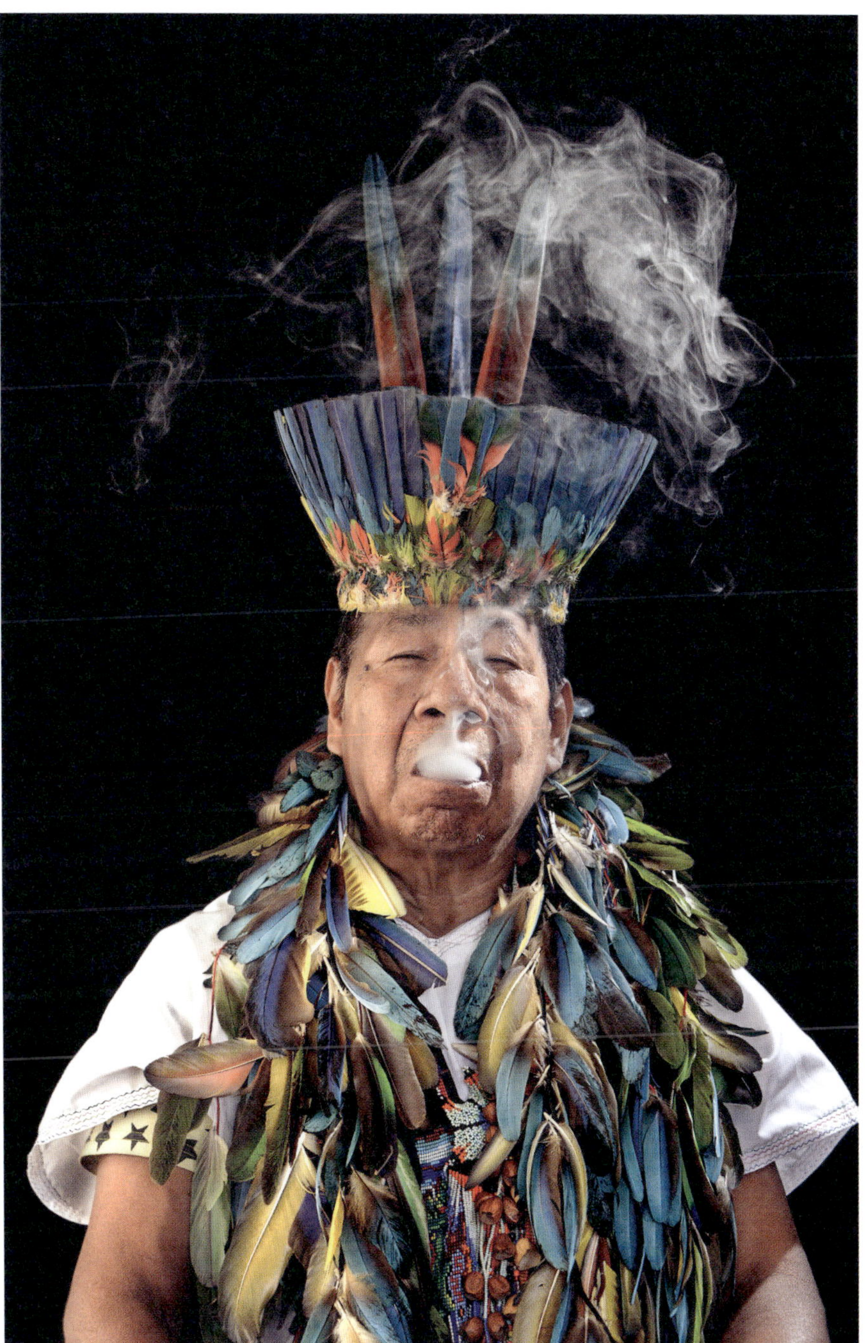

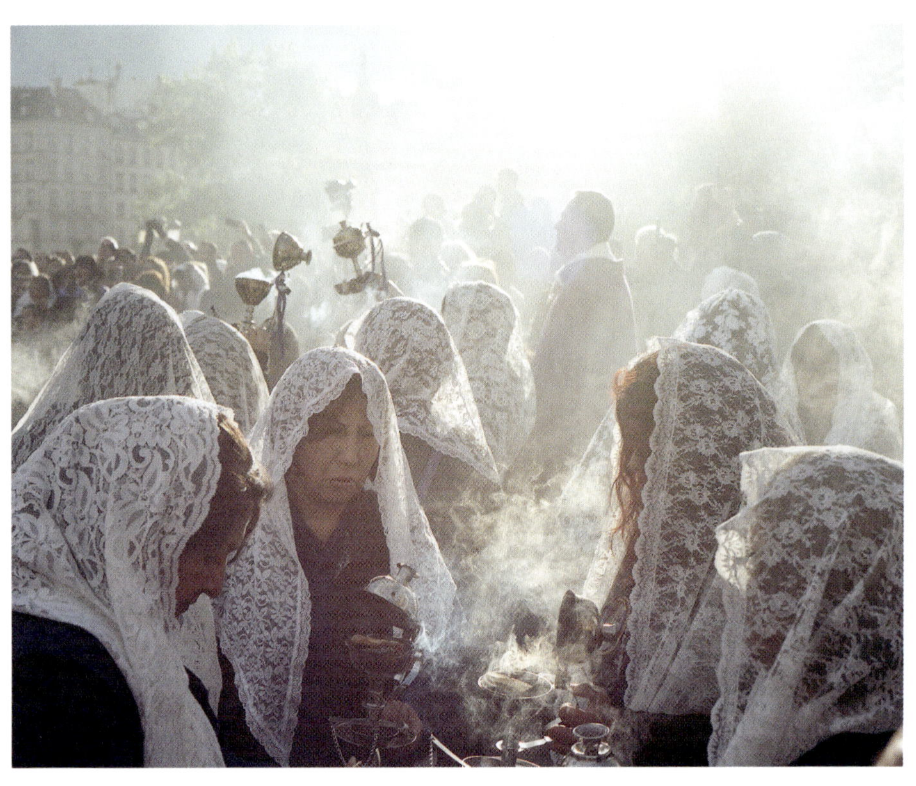

Untitled

by Daniel Loveday
Paris, France

I took this image on a cold winter's day in Paris.
As we turned the corner into the square
outside Notre-Dame, the clouds broke apart and
the sun shone through onto women who were
performing a religious ceremony.

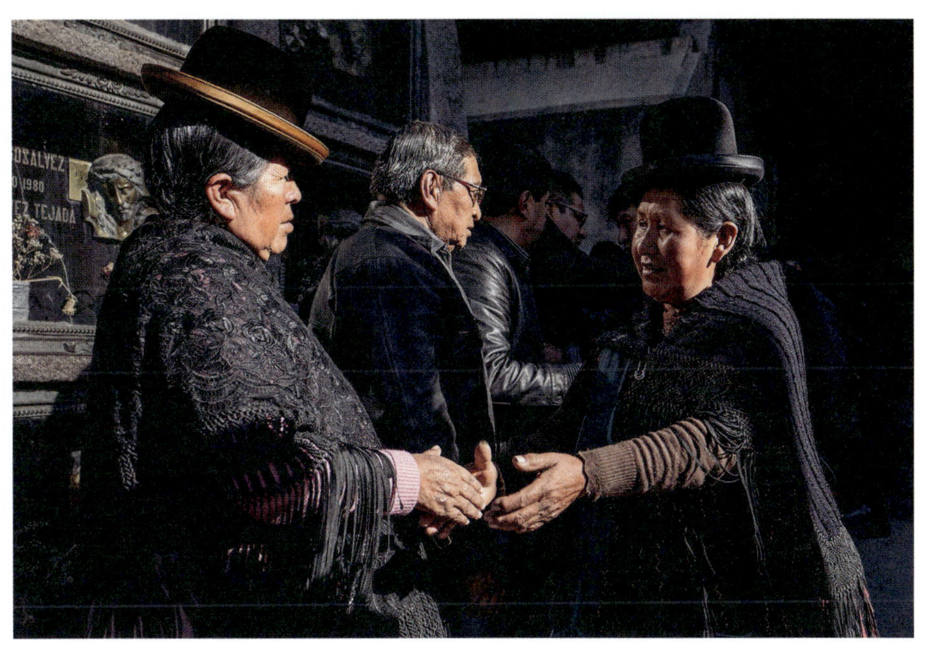

Condolences

by Ivan Ferrer
La Paz, Bolivia

After a burial, mourners stand in a line and pass
by the bereaved, offering their sympathies. The women are
wearing traditional hats worn by Bolivia's indigenous
'cholitas', a group that has been discriminated against in the
past but is now a symbol of the country.

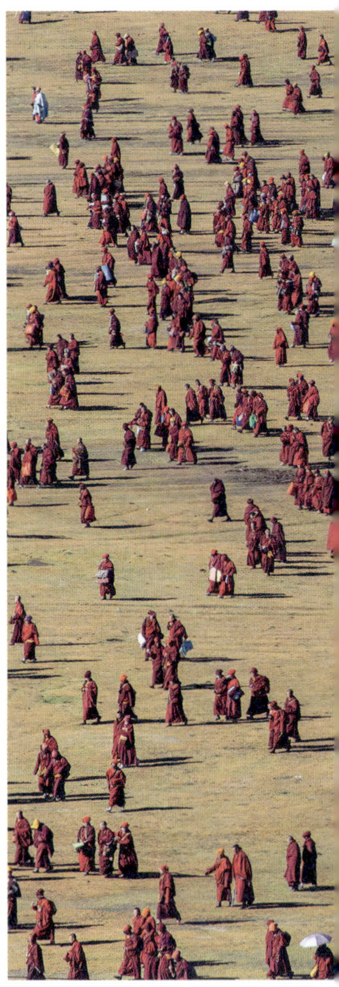

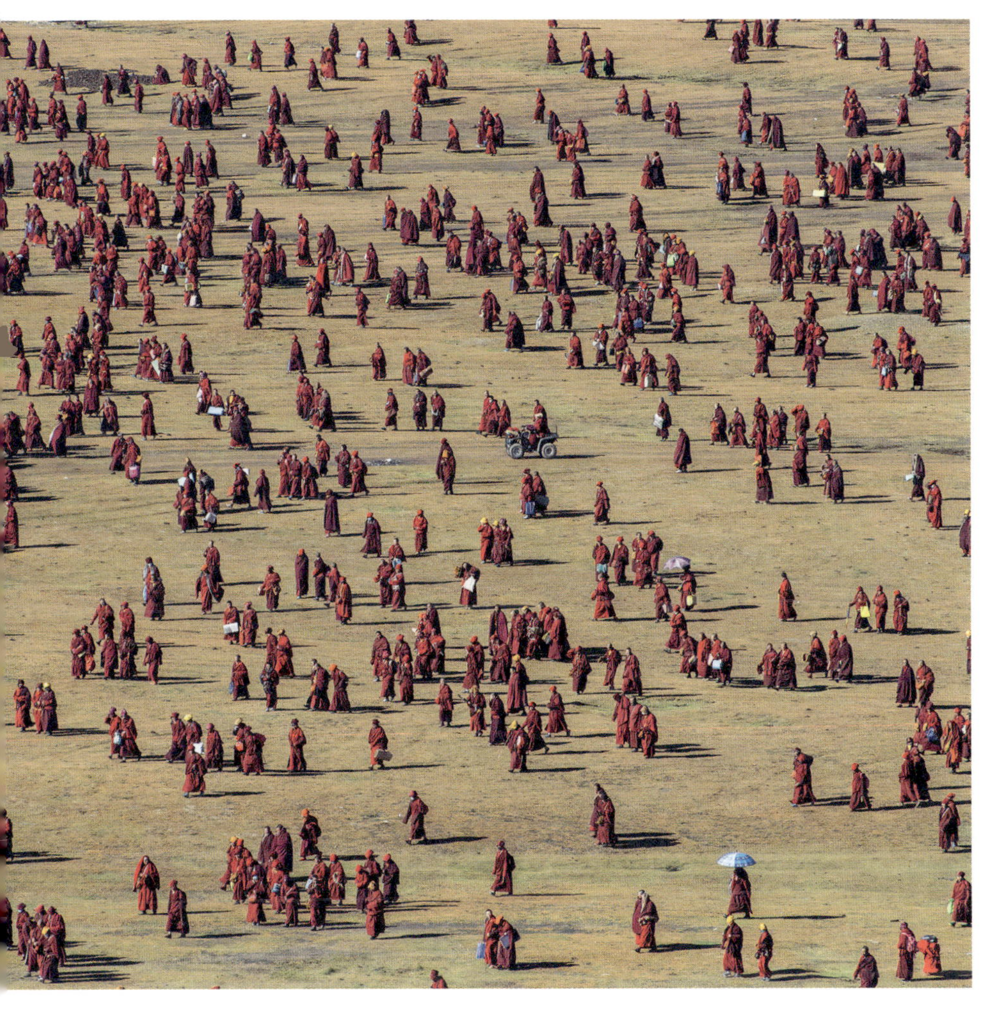

Pattern of Grassland
by Shinya Itahana
Ganzi, Tibet

Tibetan Buddhist nuns and monks walk on grassland in an
isolated valley 4,000m above sea level. As the red dots spread
across the earth I sensed the emergence of life.

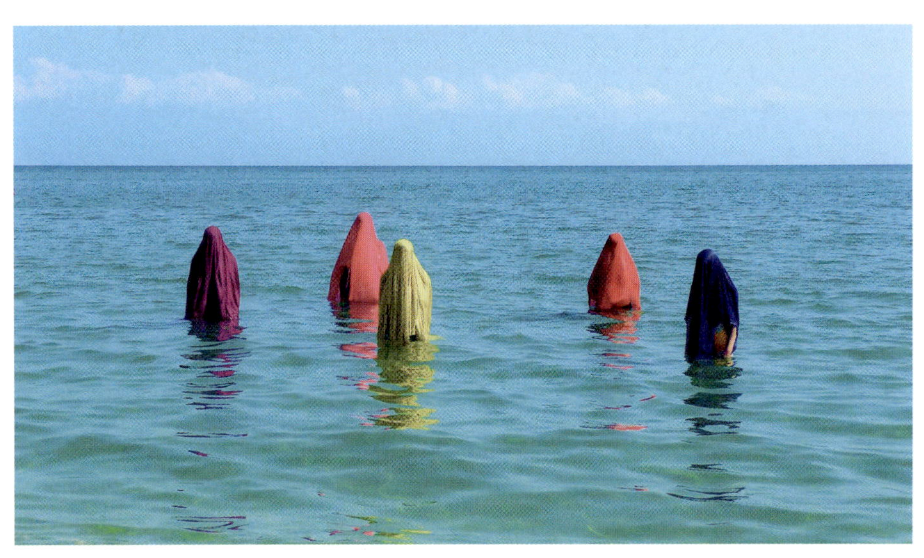

Threshold
by Jojo Taylor
Yumurtalik, Turkey

During an artist residency I made a short film off
the coast of Yumurtalik, not far from the Syrian border.
This is a still from the film.

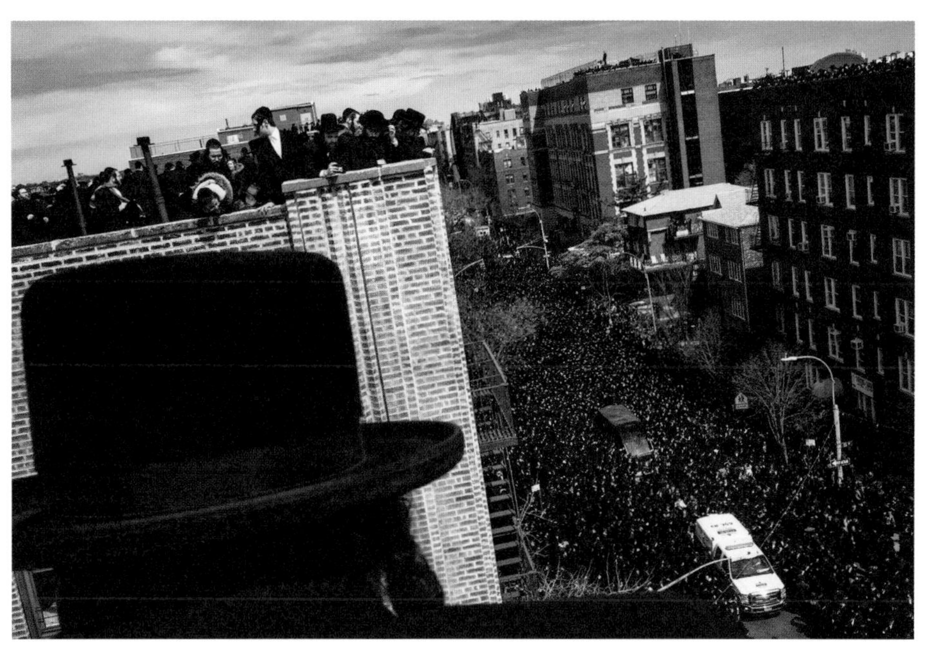

The Great Procession
by Lori Hawkins
New York City, New York, USA

Mourners watch as the casket of 95-year-old
Rabbi Yisroel Avrohom Portugal, a popular Brooklyn
rabbi who survived the Holocaust, passes by
in Borough Park, New York, on its way to Monsey,
New Jersey. He was the last American Rebbe
to be born in pre-war Europe.

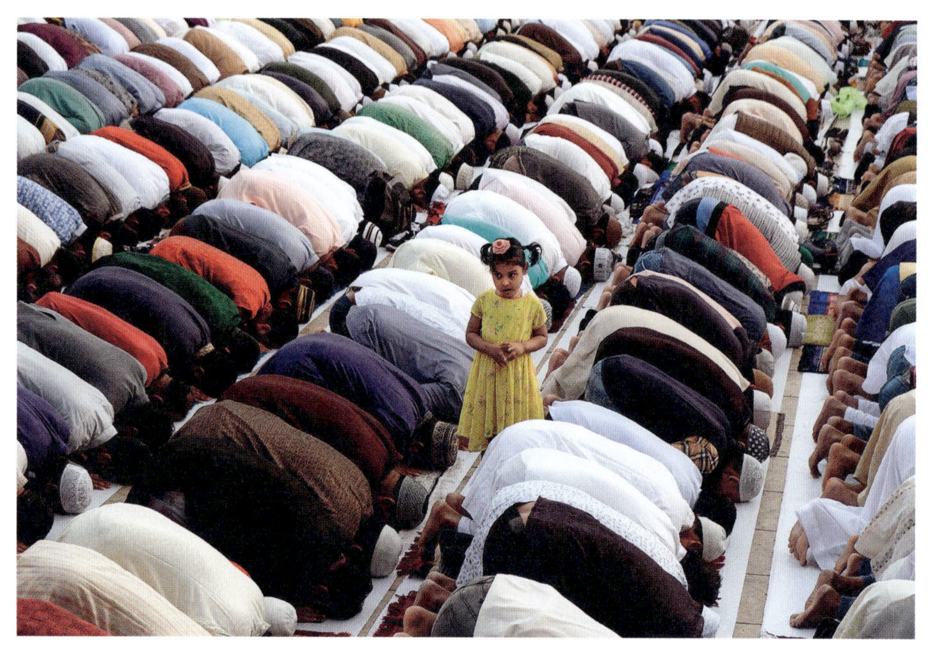

Girl in the Middle of Praying Men
by Filipe Bianchi
Lisbon, Portugal

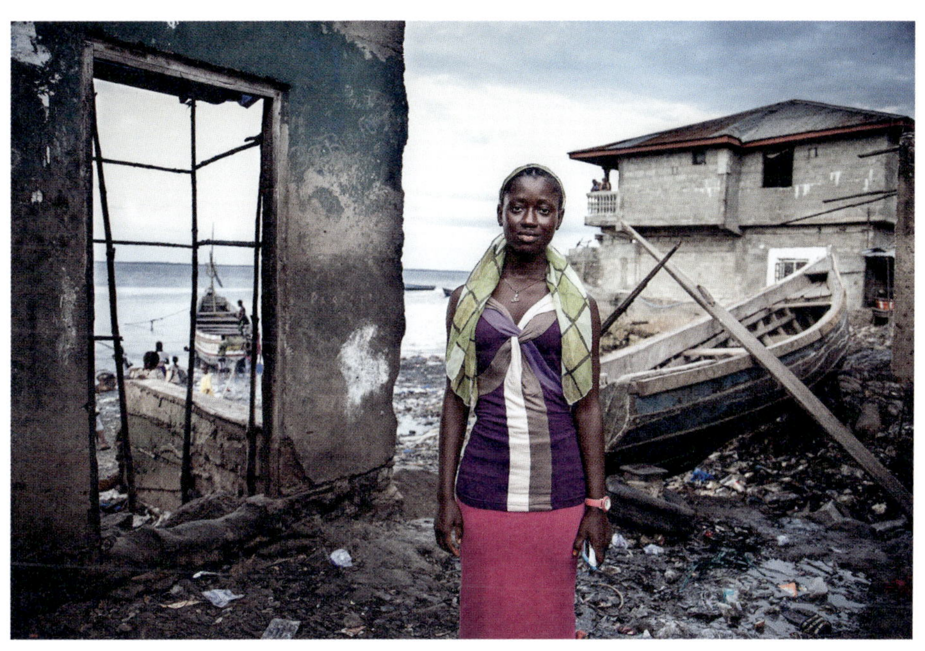

Ebola Survivor Celina Kamanda
by Simon Davis
Magazine Wharf, Freetown, Sierra Leone

Despite losing her entire family to Ebola, Celina is
quietly resolute. I met her five days before Sierra Leone
was declared Ebola-free. Thanks to the charity
Wharf Kids she is back in school. 'I would like to be
a doctor,' she says. 'When I was in the treatment
centre I saw people suffering. Now I want
to look after others.'

Evening Swim
by Pascal Vossen
Dalarna, Sweden

At a lake near Tommy's home town of Kåtilla,
he and his one-year-old son Harley share a loving
moment. Earlier that day he was released
from prison having been incarcerated for 22 months.
He took his family for a swim that evening on
what was possibly the last warm day of the year.
Tommy has no education and three young children with
two different women. I have been documenting
his journey of coming to terms with fatherhood
and his troublesome past since 2015.

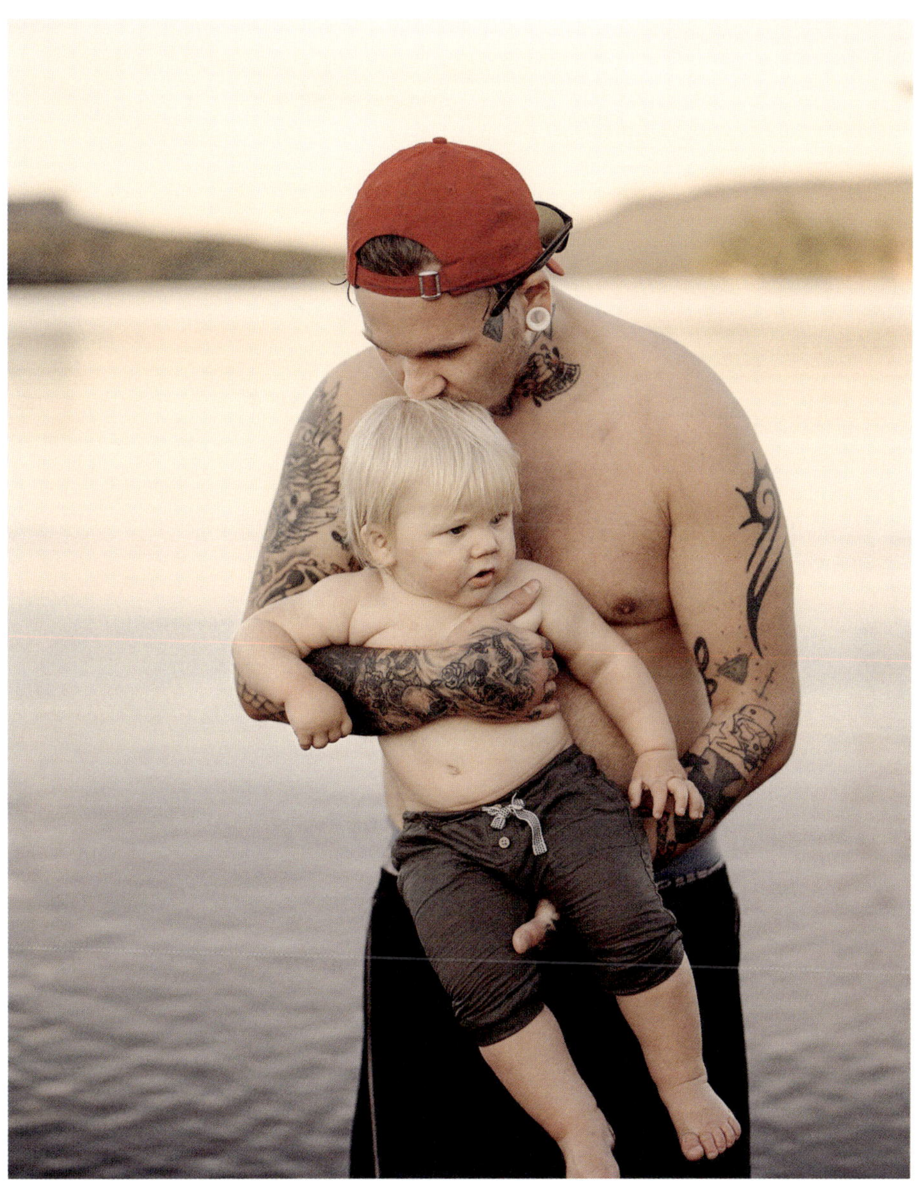

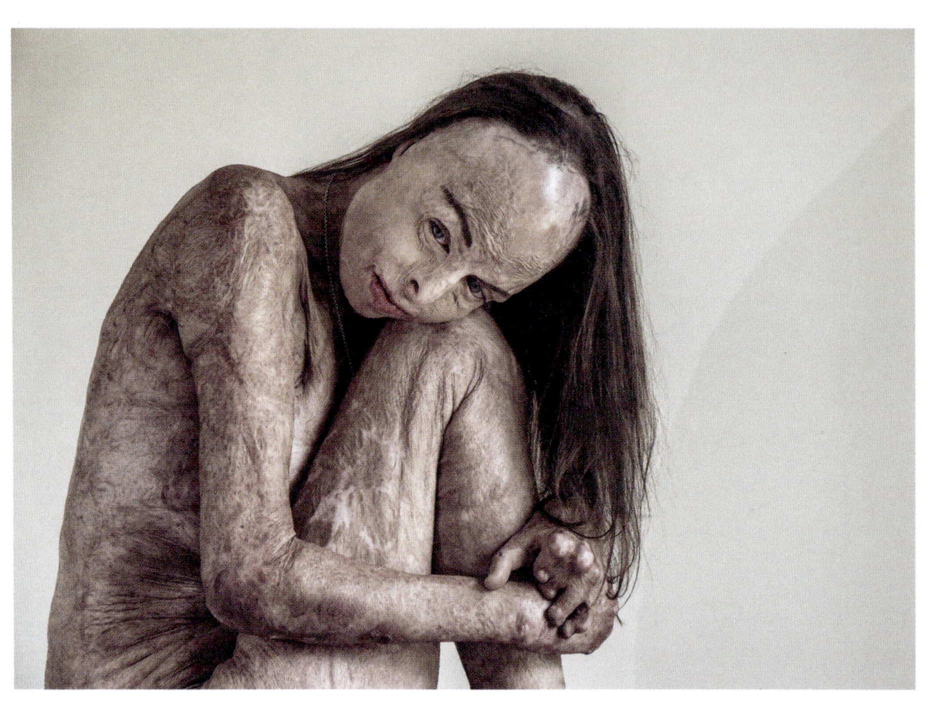

The Skin I'm In
by Brian Cassey
Cairns, Australia

Carol Anne Mayer was badly burnt in a house
fire over a decade ago. Her family was told she would
not survive, but she did. Now Carol gives her time
voluntarily to counsel other burns victims.

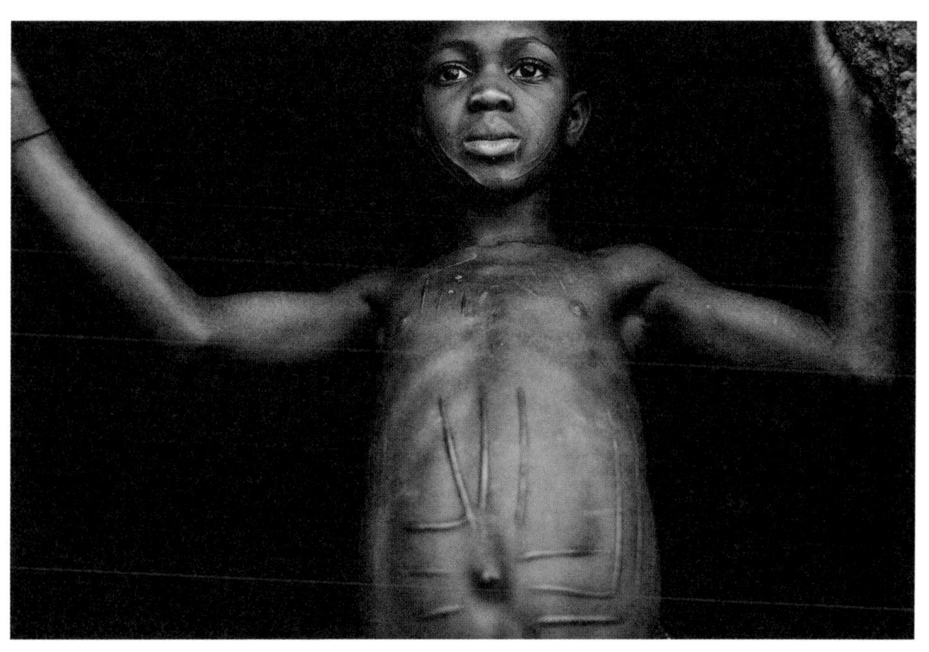

The Son of a King
by Ingetje Tadros
Atakora Mountains region, Benin

This boy lives in the Taneka villages of northern
Benin, home to a group of ethnic minorities that settled
there generations ago to escape the slave trade.
His father is a king and he and his family have different
marks on their skin to other families.

Takayuki Suzuki
by Christopher Owens
Newcastle upon Tyne, UK

UK-based Japanese Paralympic swimmer
Takayuki Suzuki has congenital limb deficiency.
He was left at the hospital by his biological parents
at birth. A Paralympian gold and silver medalist,
Takayuki has never considered himself disabled.
I wanted to make a picture that forces the viewer to
consider the concept of disability. We see the
abnormality of his limbs but at the same time
are confronted by his physical strength.

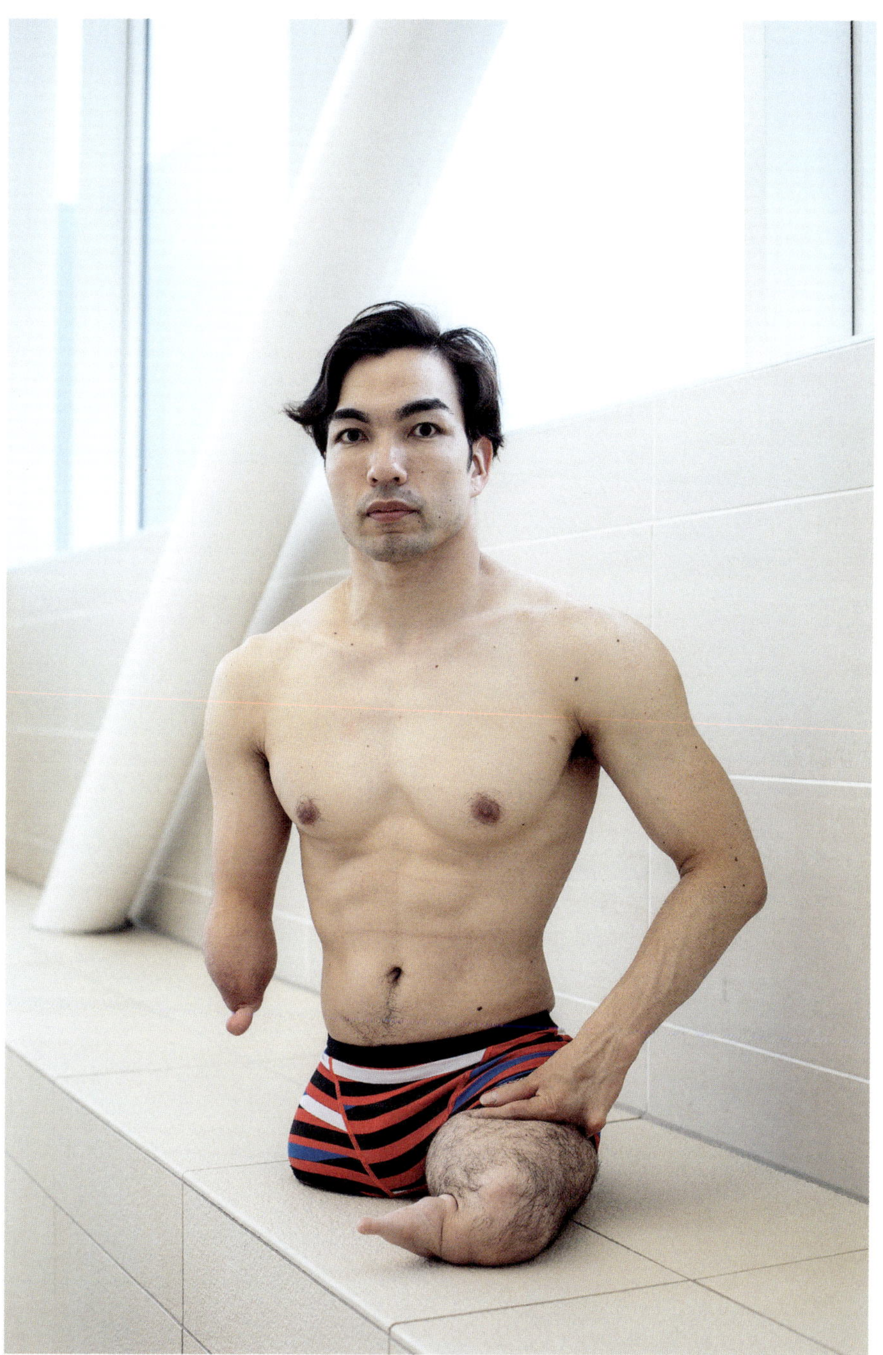

Jordan and Jermaine
by Alexander Ikhide
London, UK

I wanted to capture a sense of the community
and bonding I witnessed at the UK's annual Black Pride
celebration. This was my first time at the event.
As a black gay person myself, I don't often see others like me
represented in the mainstream LGBT media in
the UK. I feel that more spaces like this should
be created for LGBT people to feel safe and proud
of who they are without fear of prejudice
or discrimination.

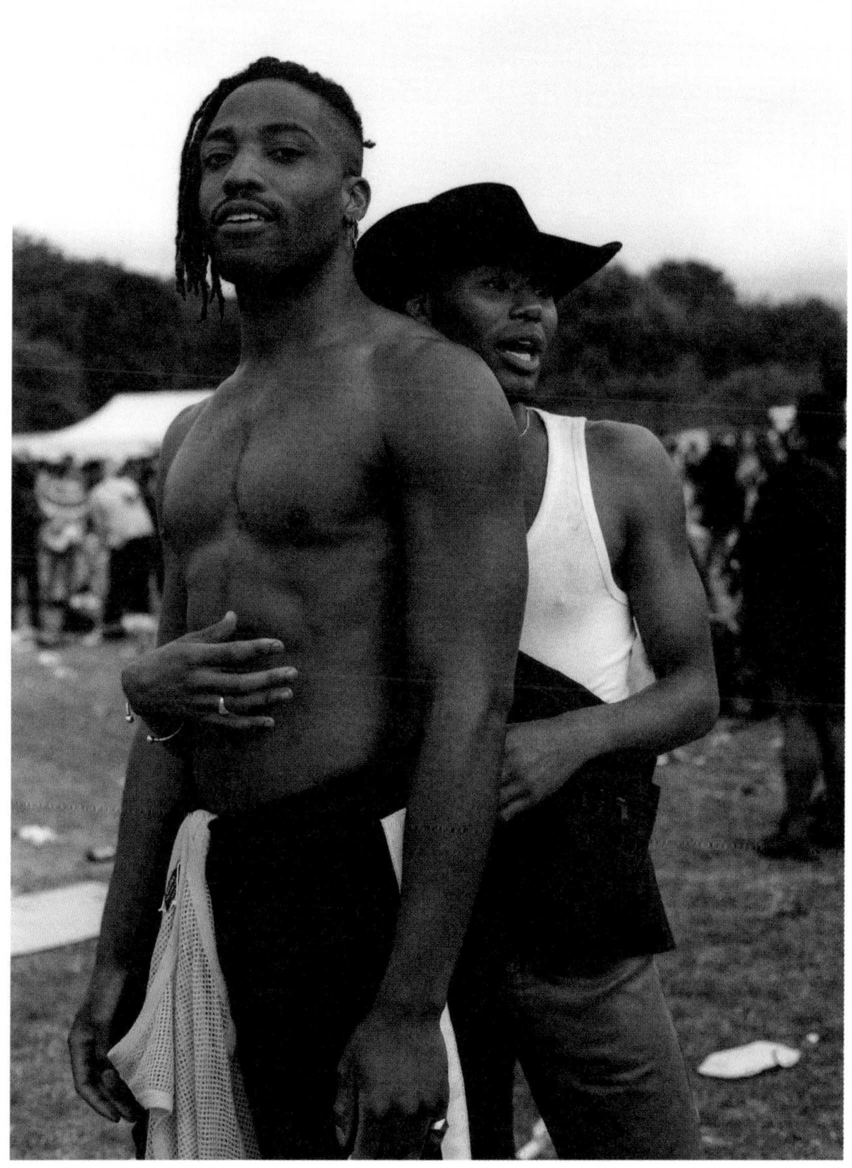

Maisie, Summer 2019
by Tim Smyth
London, UK

Maisie is a photographer and visual artist.
Here she is seven months pregnant with our daughter.
Our garden faces south and has wonderful
light throughout the day. Maisie asked me to take
her portrait while she was pregnant to show our
daughter when she is older. It is a record of our time
in our first home together preparing for
the arrival of our first child.

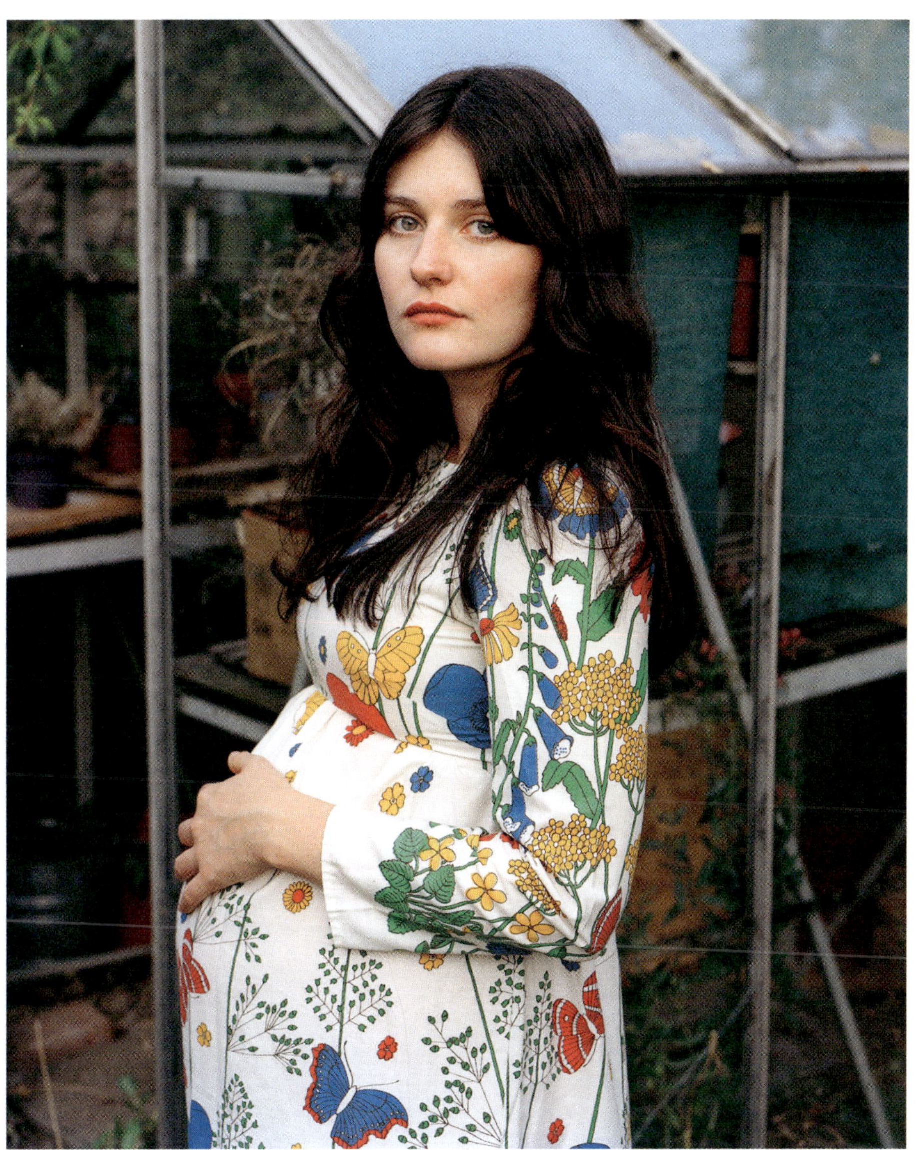

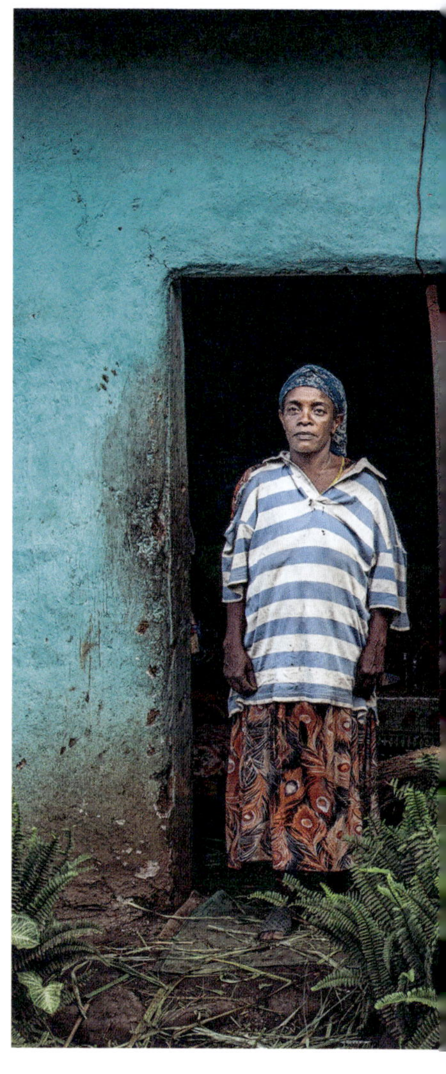

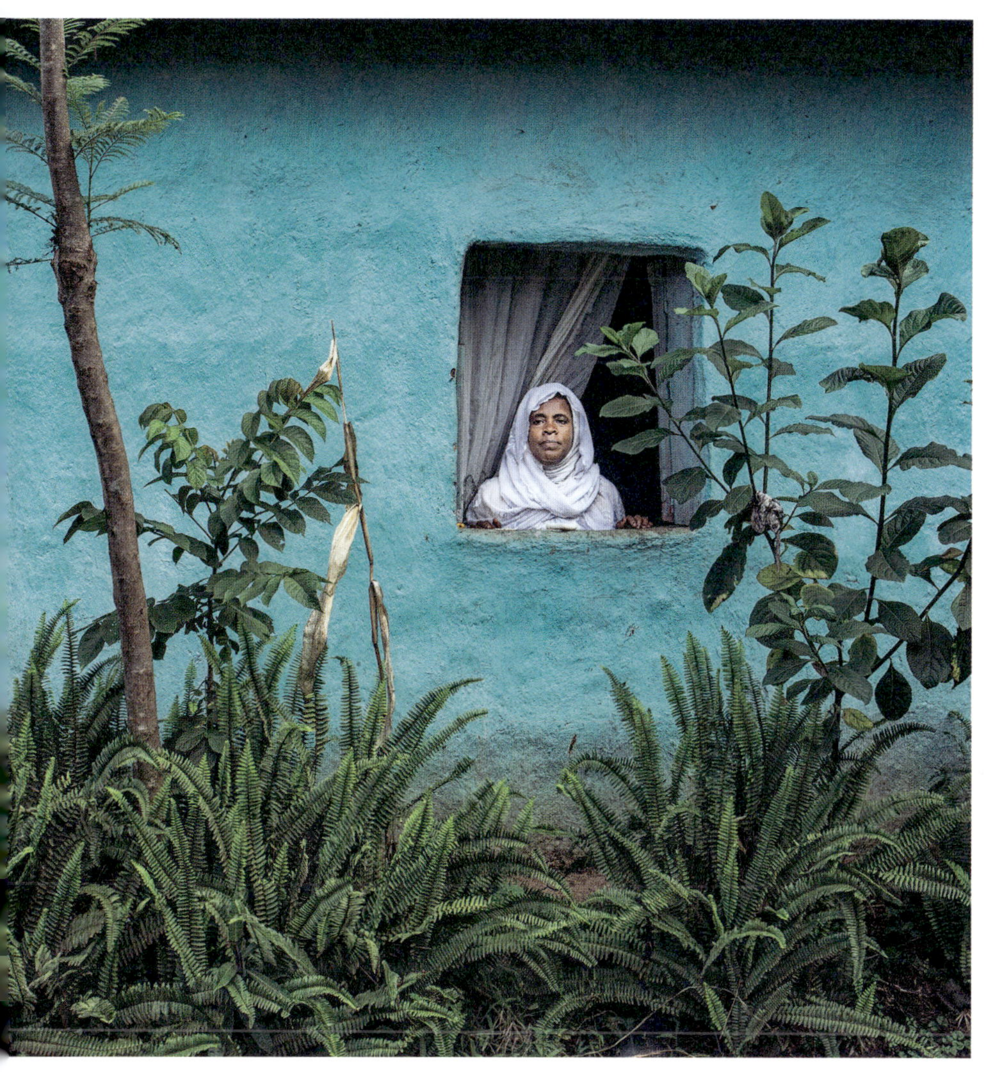

Mother and Daughter
by Margarita Mavromichalis
Omo Valley, Southern Ethiopia

Marina Getting Baptised
by Natalia Shaidenko
Montreal, Canada

My daughter, her godfather and a Russian
Orthodox priest. Even though my daughter was born
Canadian it was important for us to observe
tradition and baptise her in a Russian Orthodox
Church. We move around quite a bit and so I hope
my child will learn about her heritage no
matter where she ends up living.

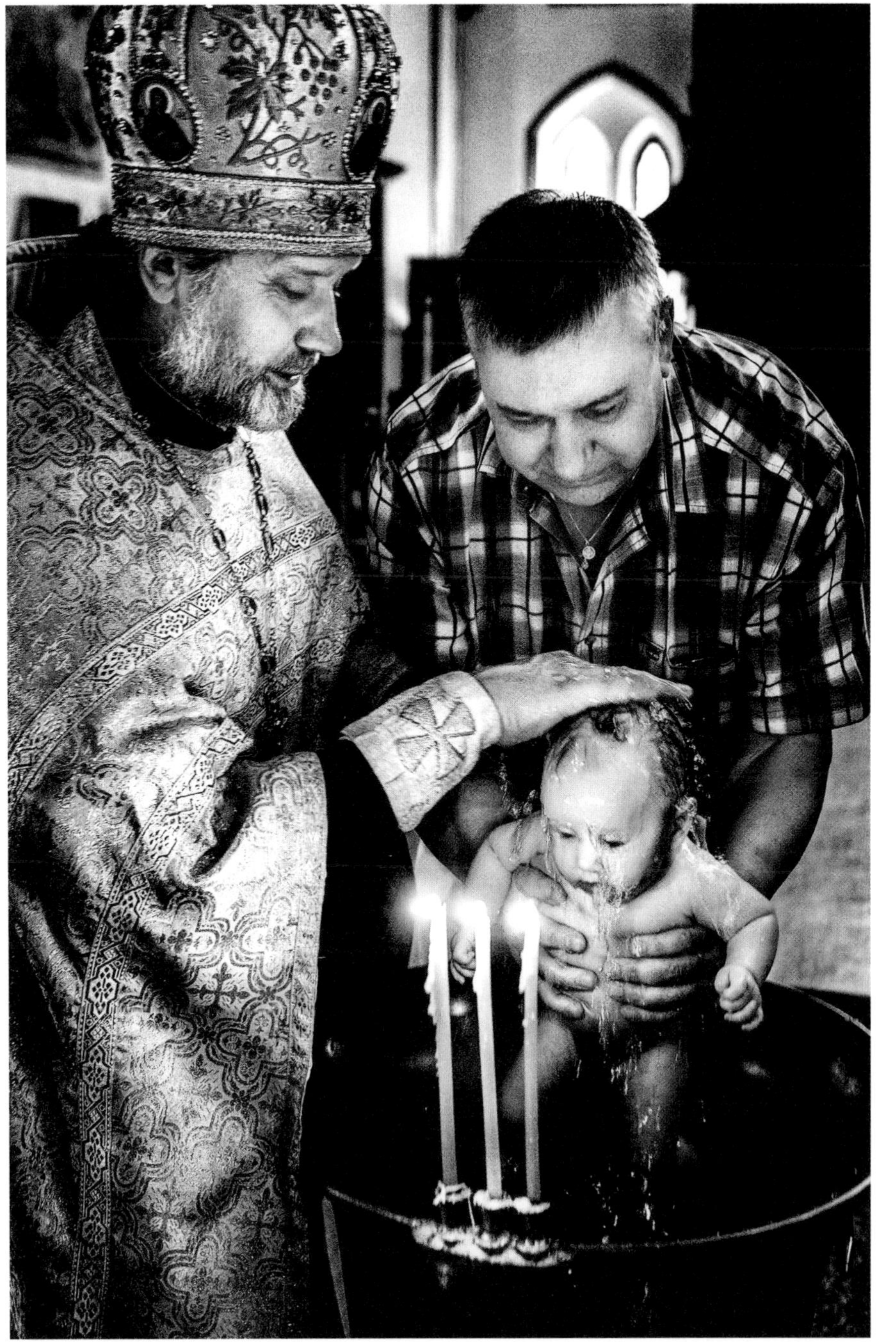

Akodessawa #01
by Francesco Merlini
Lomé, Togo

Inside Akodessawa Fetish Market, the world's
largest voodoo market, Bertin, who has a stand there,
plays with a python. Snake teeth are commonly
pulverised and injected into newborns to protect
against snake bites.

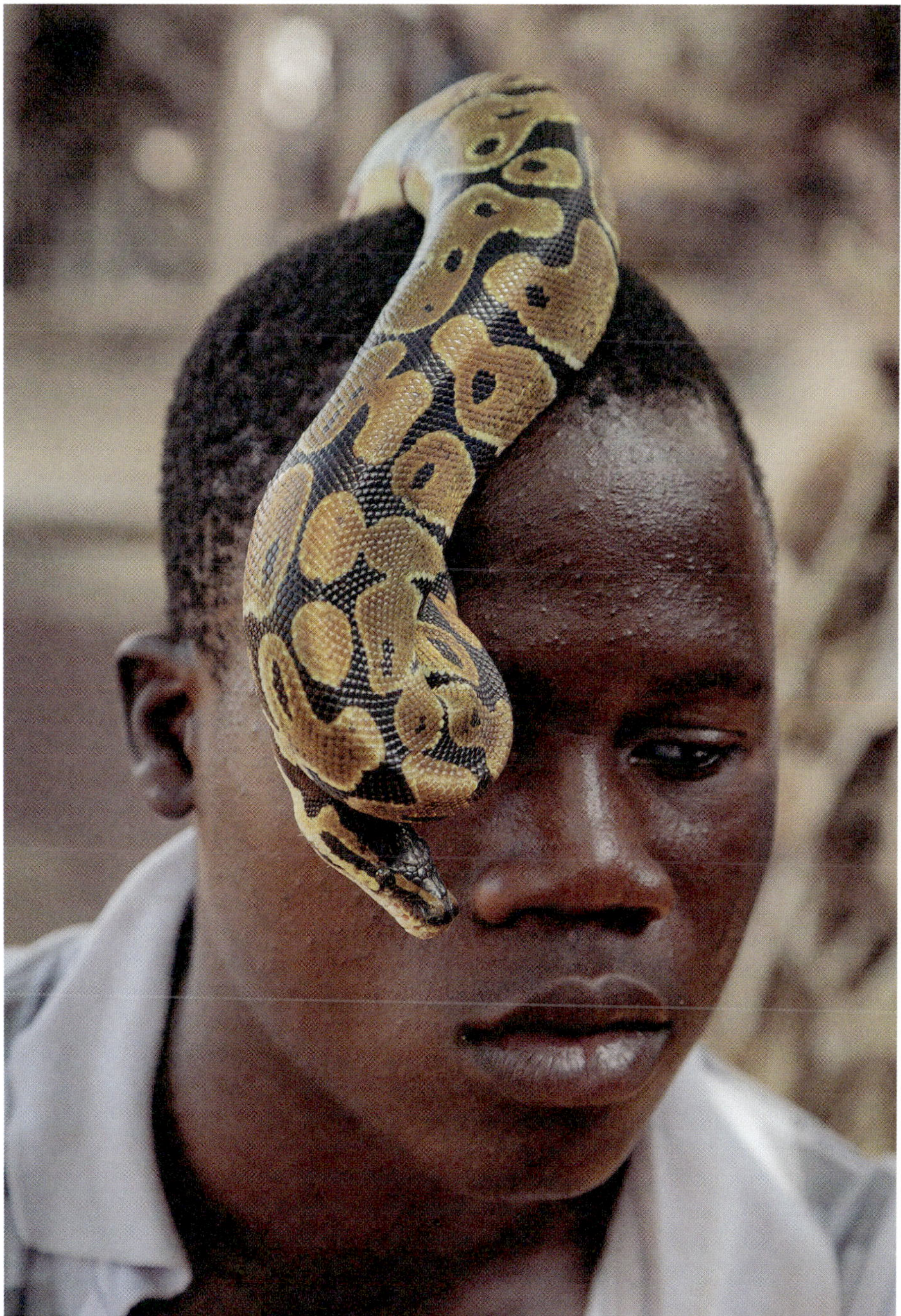

George Tongariro
by Simon Dixon
Porirua, New Zealand

George, a friend and colleague of mine, is of
Māori/European descent. Facial tattoos, also referred
to as Mataora-Tä Moko, are important in
Māori culture. 'This is my birthright, and to receive
and wear the Mataora is an honour and
a privilege,' says George.

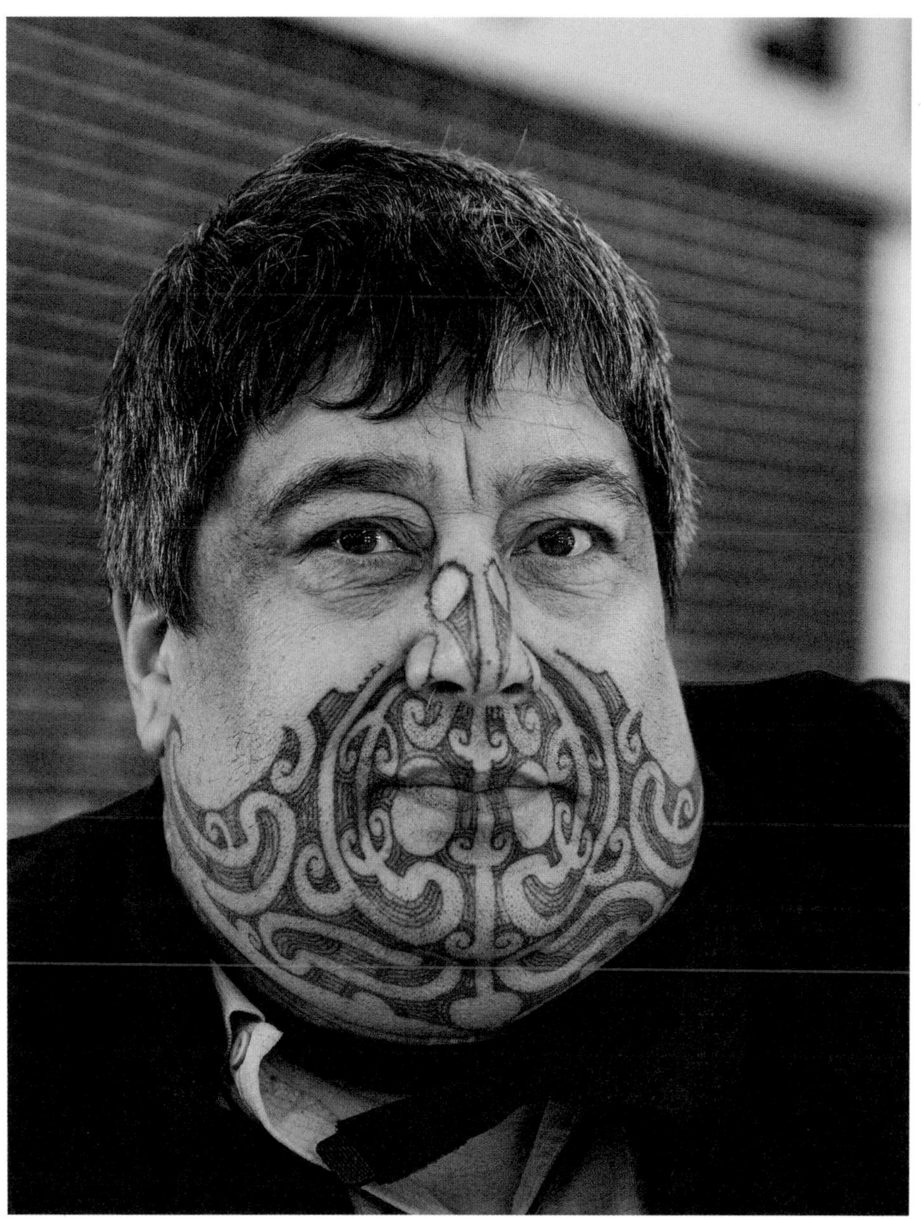

Amber

by Justine Tjallinks
Diepenbeek, Belgium

This is 13-year-old Amber Vanderweert. She has
progeria, an extremely rare condition that causes the
body to age very rapidly. Amber is 1.15m tall
and weighs just 15kg. She is wise beyond her years
and remarkably bright. Shortly after my mum died at
a relatively young age, I watched a documentary
that featured Amber. Her situation got under my skin,
so I contacted the family and asked if I could
make a portrait.

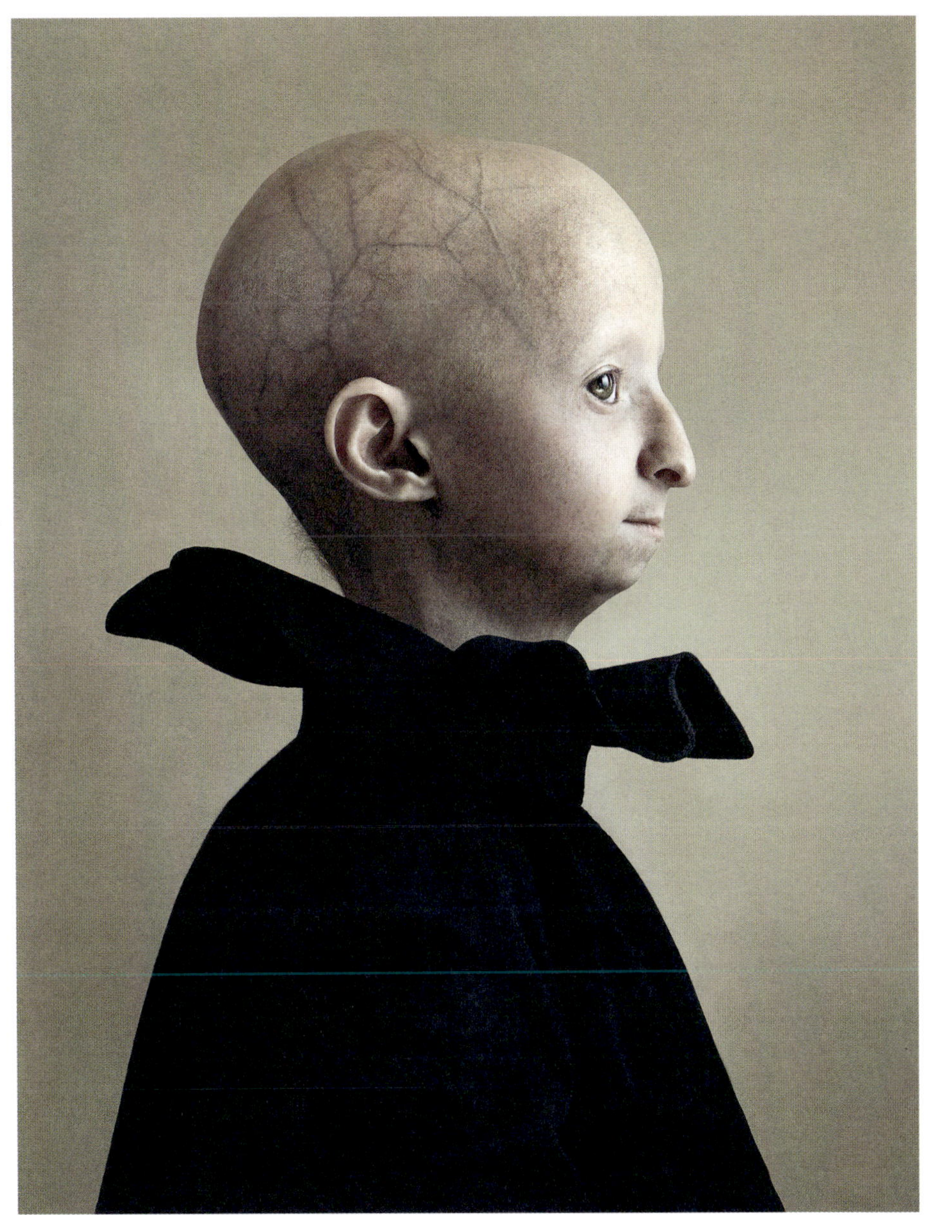

Manny and Courtney
by Maria Sturm
Fayetteville, North Carolina, USA

Manny is a young Native American man
who identifies as a member of the Lumbee Tribe.
Courtney doesn't identify as Native American
but is a strong supporter of Manny's dancing and
drumming. She accompanies him to as
many events as she can.

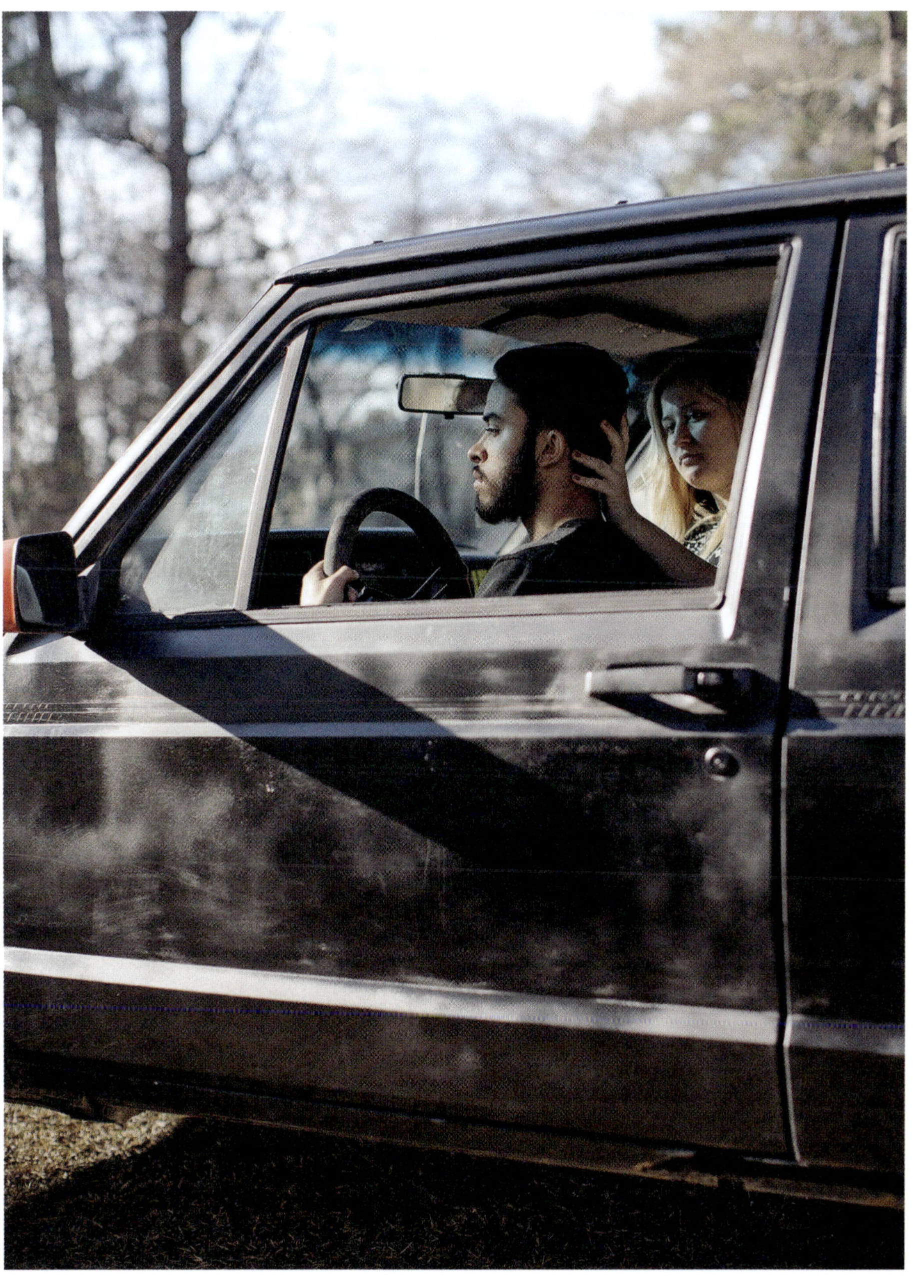

Boys of Volta #1
by Jeremy Snell
Lake Volta, Ghana

The trafficking of children into child labour
in this region is rife. Boys as young as six years old,
including this boy, are often forced to fish on
the lake. Life on the water is hard and it is all these
kids have known. The beauty of Lake Volta
juxtaposed with this harsh reality is quite sobering.

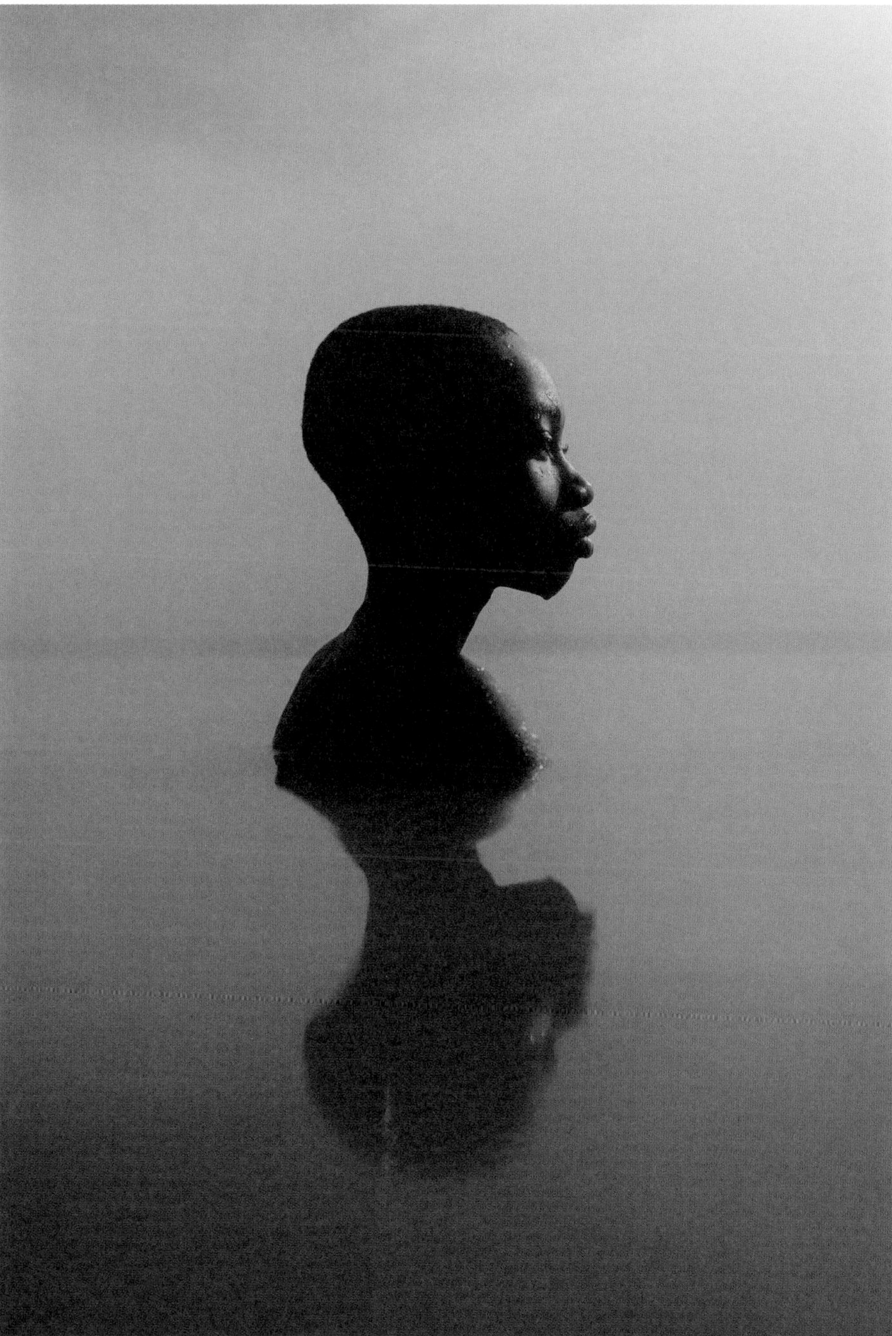

Nomadic Life
by Naomi Goddard
Lhagang Grassland, China

A Tibetan girl holds sprigs that she will use
to light a fire. With no specific place to call home, her
family is led by their yak herd, chasing fresh grass
to feed their animals and themselves. Many nomads
fear that the traditional Tibetan way of life will
disappear as the Chinese government urges them
to resettle in permanent housing communities
away from the grasslands.

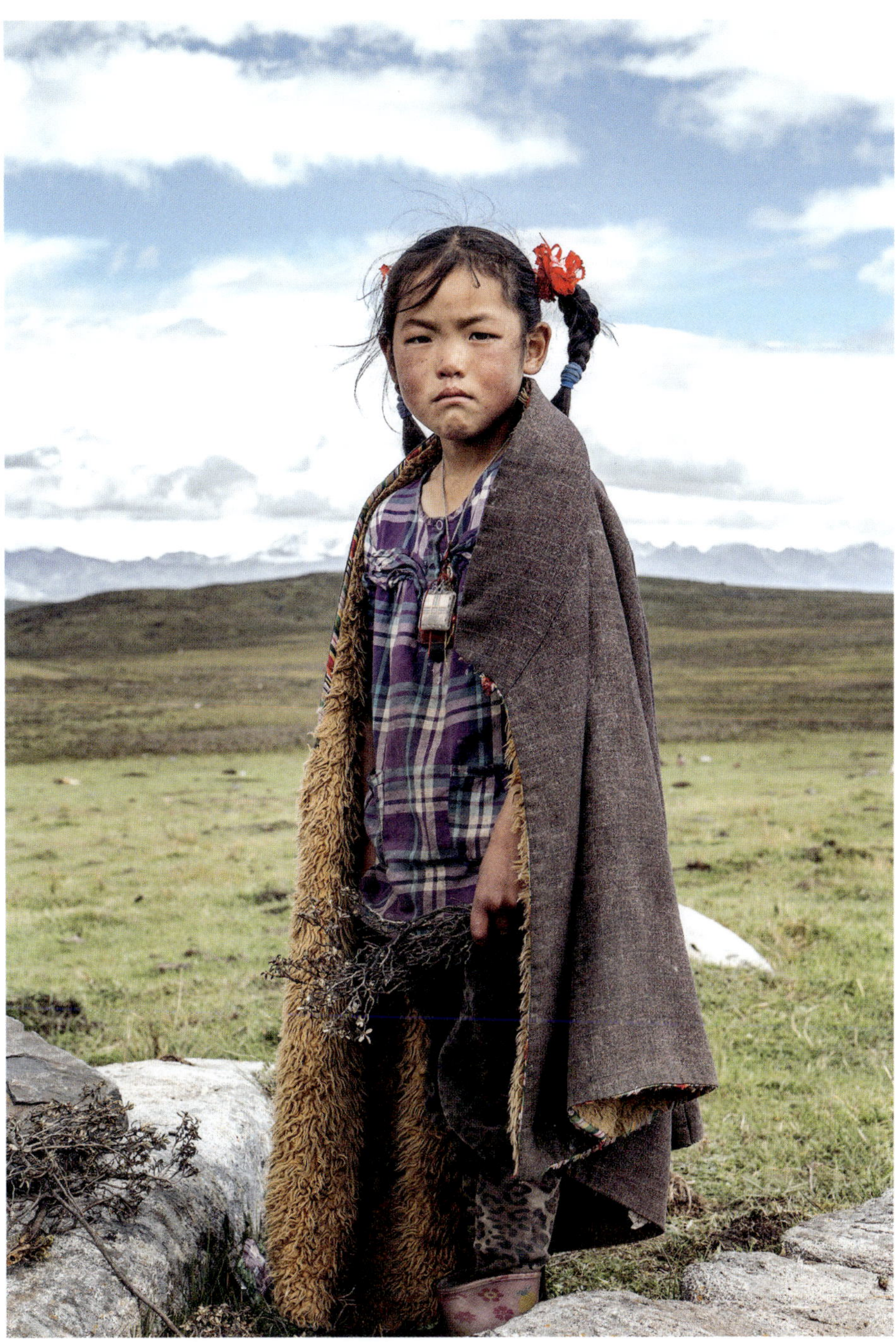

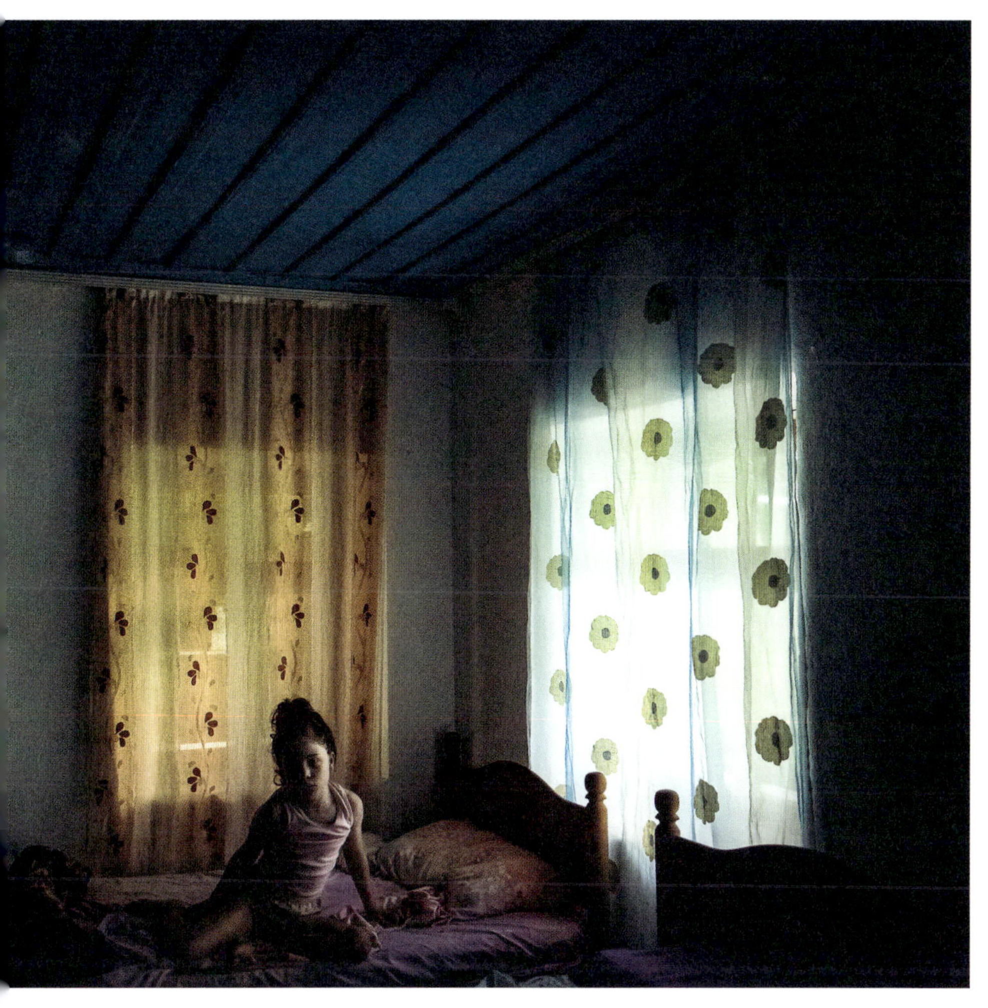

Foreign Places
by Cathy Ronalds
Berisha, Albania

My daughter is shy but sometimes she lets me take her
picture. I took it while my family and I, who live in Australia,
were travelling through Albania.

The Shallow End
by Miles Kiernan
Pueblo Nuevo, Panama

A woman in a remote Ngäbe community
in Panama had just done some laundry while
her granddaughter played in the water.
The community relies on the river for washing
clothes and bathing. It is also a place where people
congregate in the mornings and evenings.

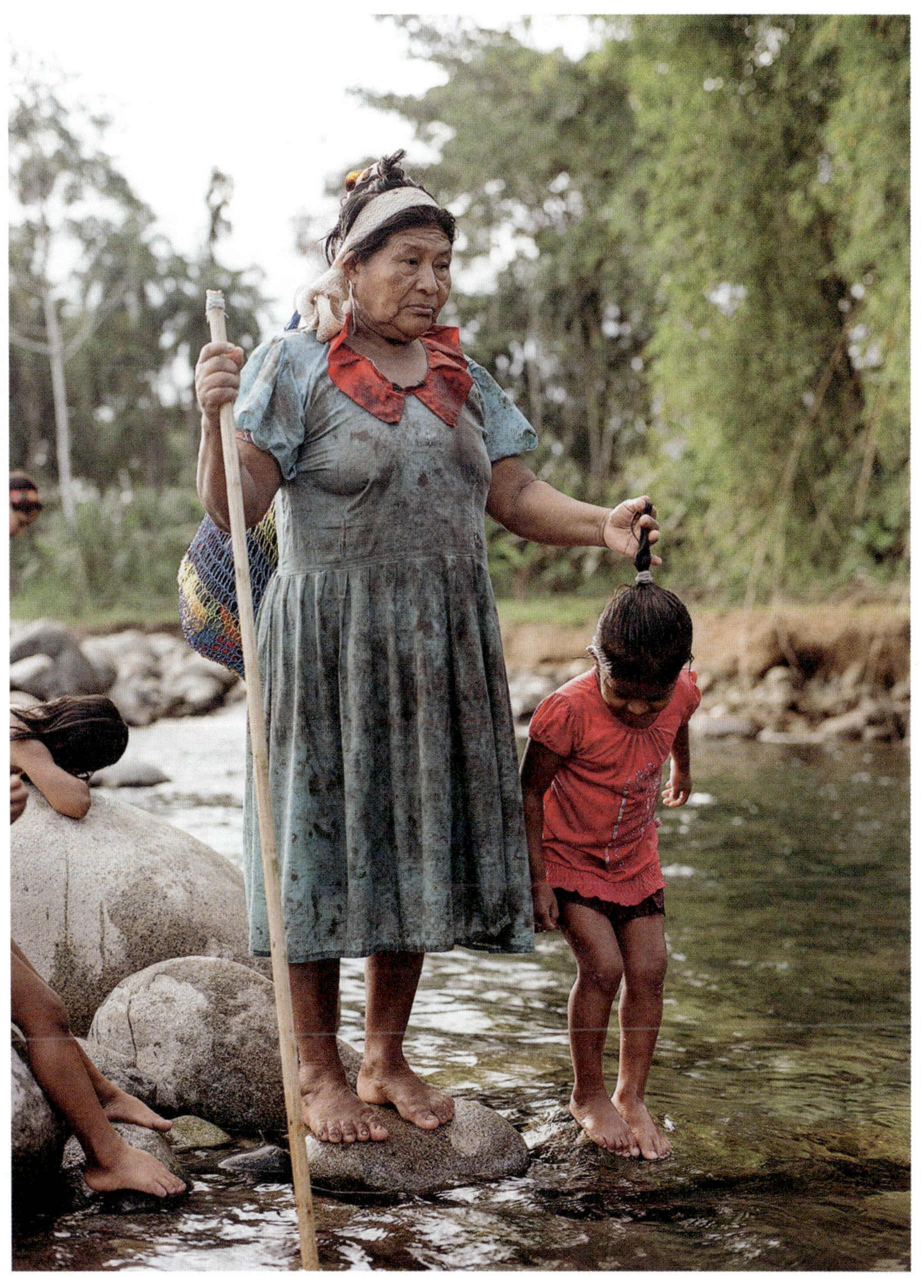

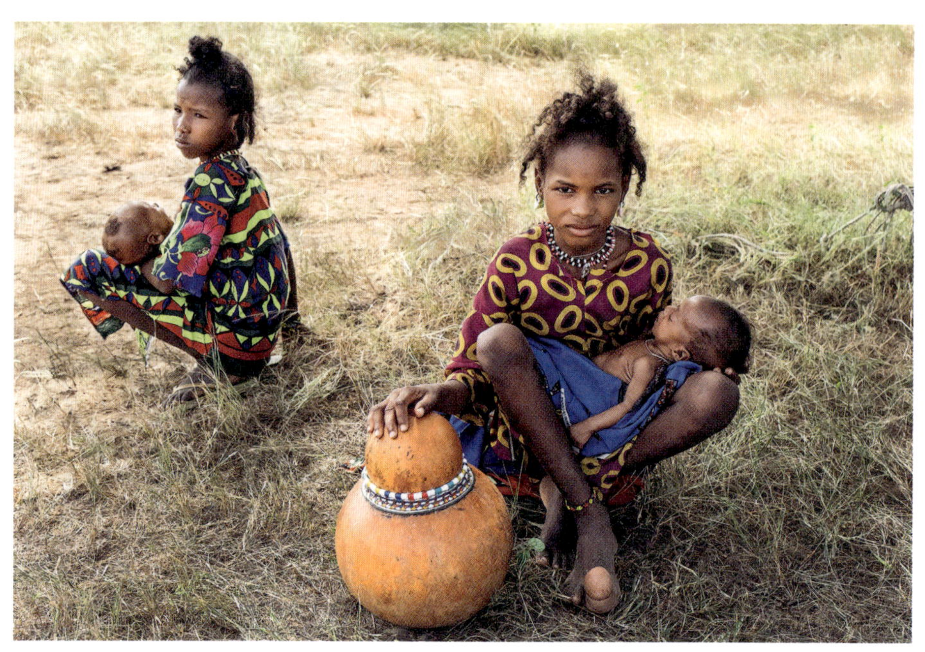

Wodaabe Babysitters
by France Leclerc
Sahel, Chad

These two young girls belong to the Wodaabe,
a nomadic tribe of cattle herders who live in small clans
and roam all year so they can feed their cattle.
From a very young age, girls help the women in many
ways including by dealing with younger siblings.
The girl's deformed foot is possibly a
congenital malformation.

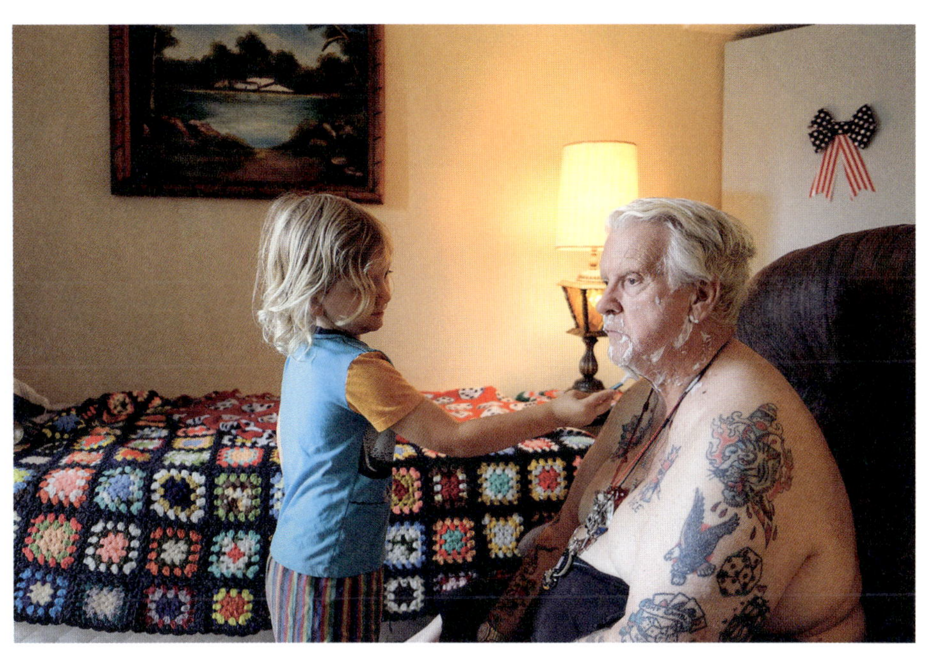

Shaving Grandpa

by Julie Grace Immink
San Gabriel, California, USA

My son helps me to shave my dad who was
diagnosed with dementia when my son was born.
He helps with many daily tasks. Overwhelmed
by having to care for the needs of my father and
a bouncing toddler, I turned to photography as an outlet.
The pictures I made explore the trials of ageing, mental
health and how community shapes our identity.

Bridesmaid of Kosmach
by Stijn Hoekstra
Kosmach, Ukraine

A girl dressed in traditional clothing is
a bridesmaid at a Hutsul wedding. Hutsuls is
an ethnic group living in western Ukraine.
The wedding was in the house of the bride's parents.
I photographed the bridesmaid as she took
a short break from all the festivities.

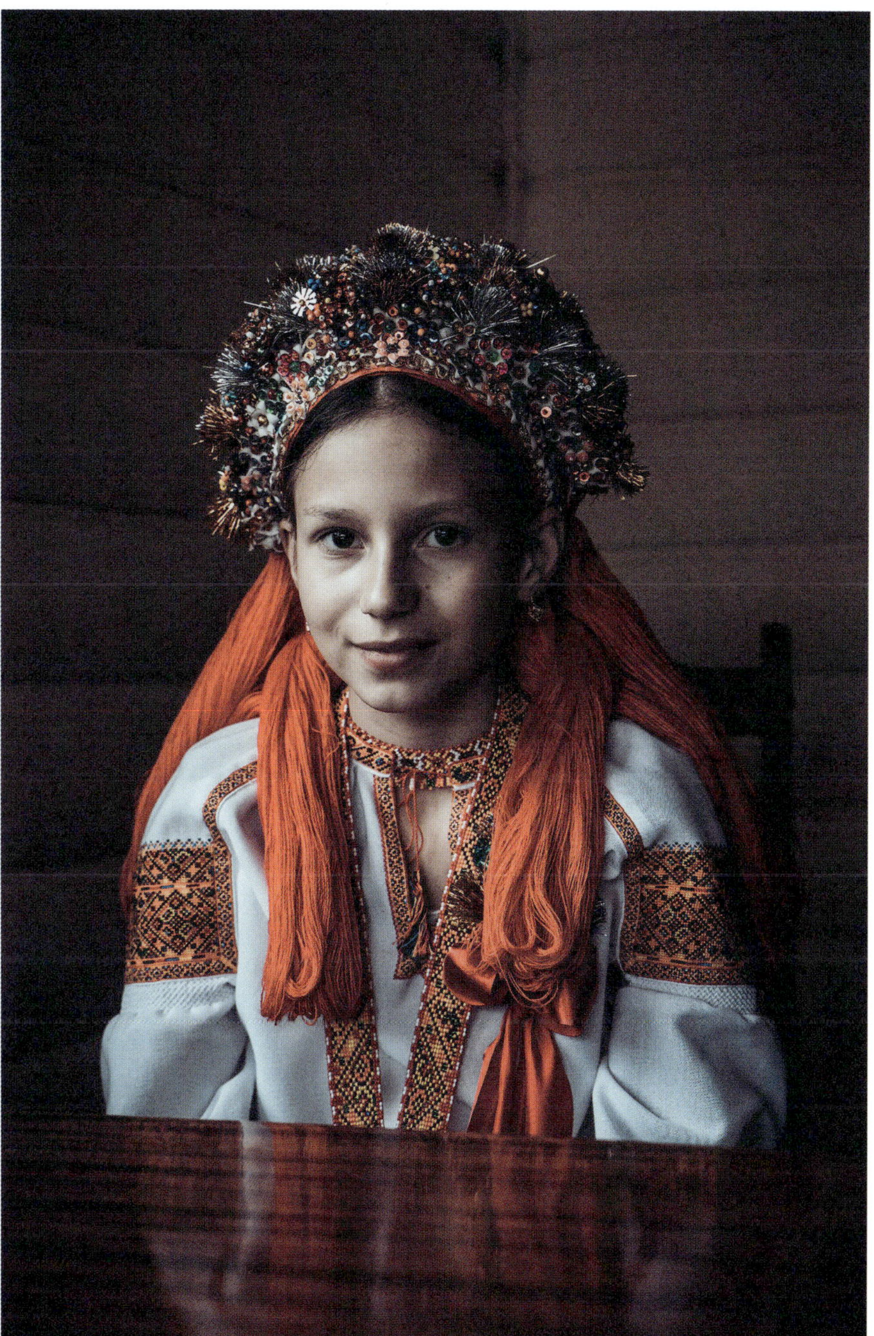

Jayde
by Whitney Hayes
Fair Haven, New Jersey, USA

Jayde, who is 14, and her family came to my
shore home, my favourite place to shoot, to make
a series of images. She has a casual confidence
that I found compelling.

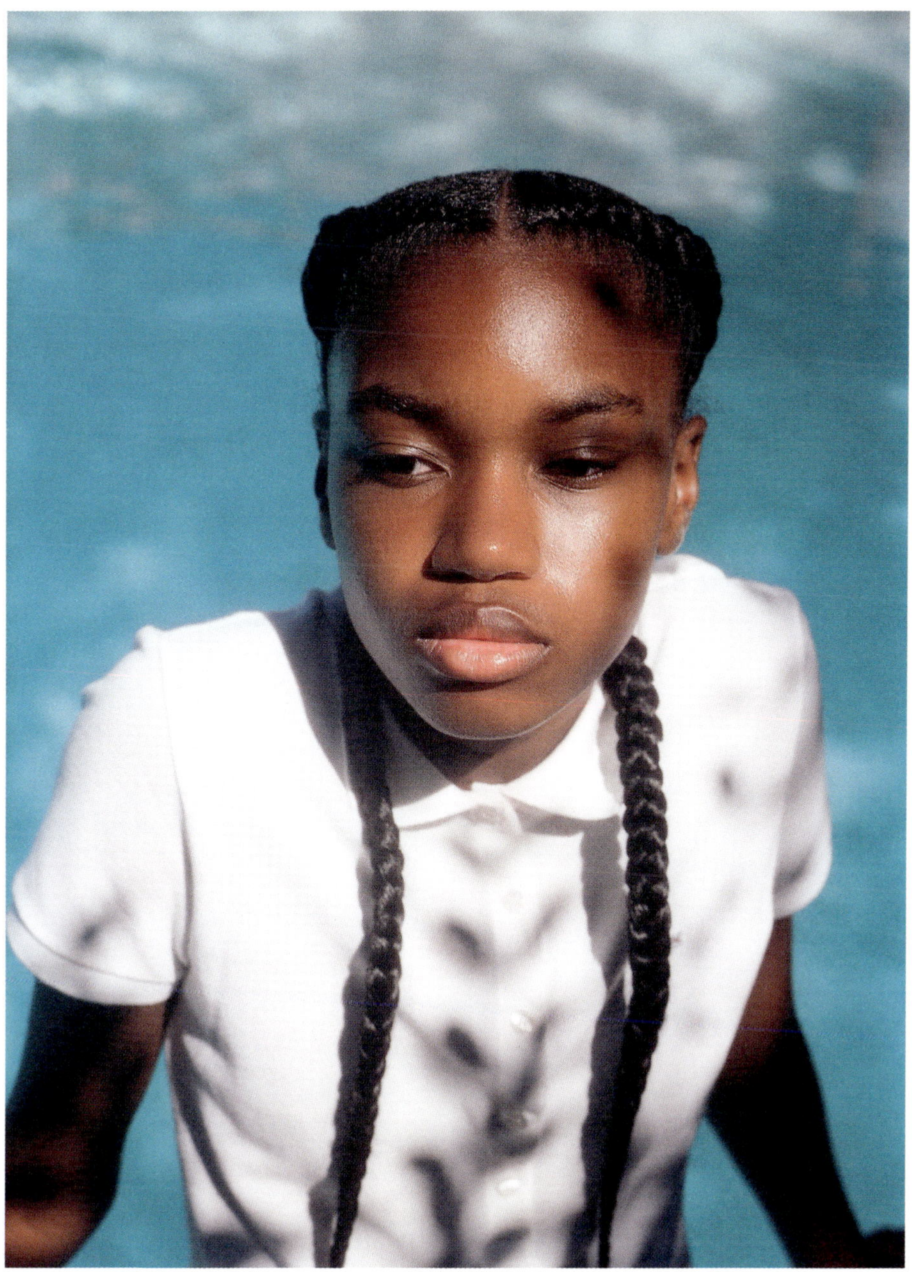

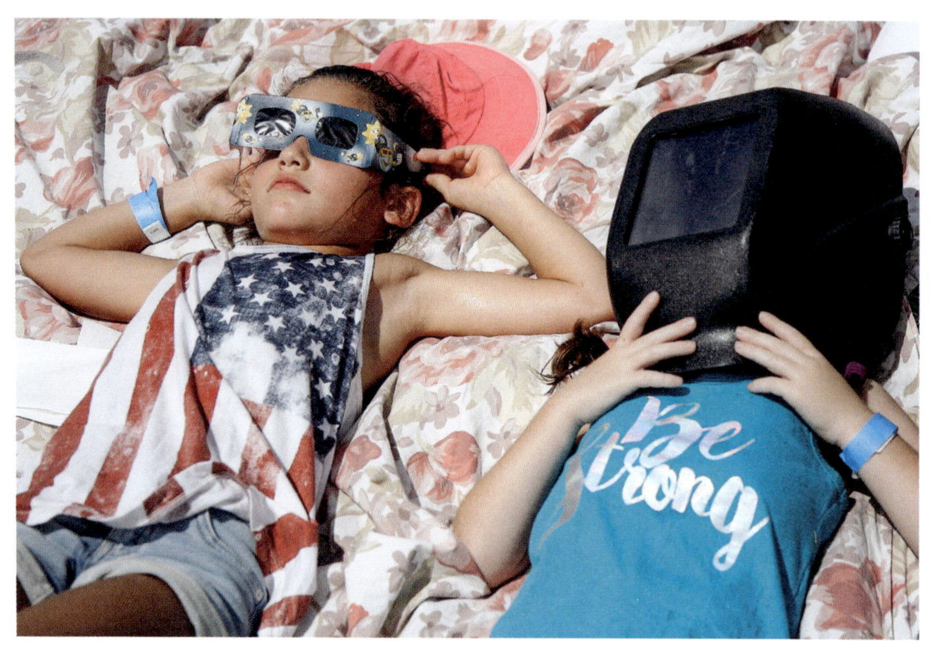

Eclipse
by Michael Campina
North Charleston, South Carolina, USA

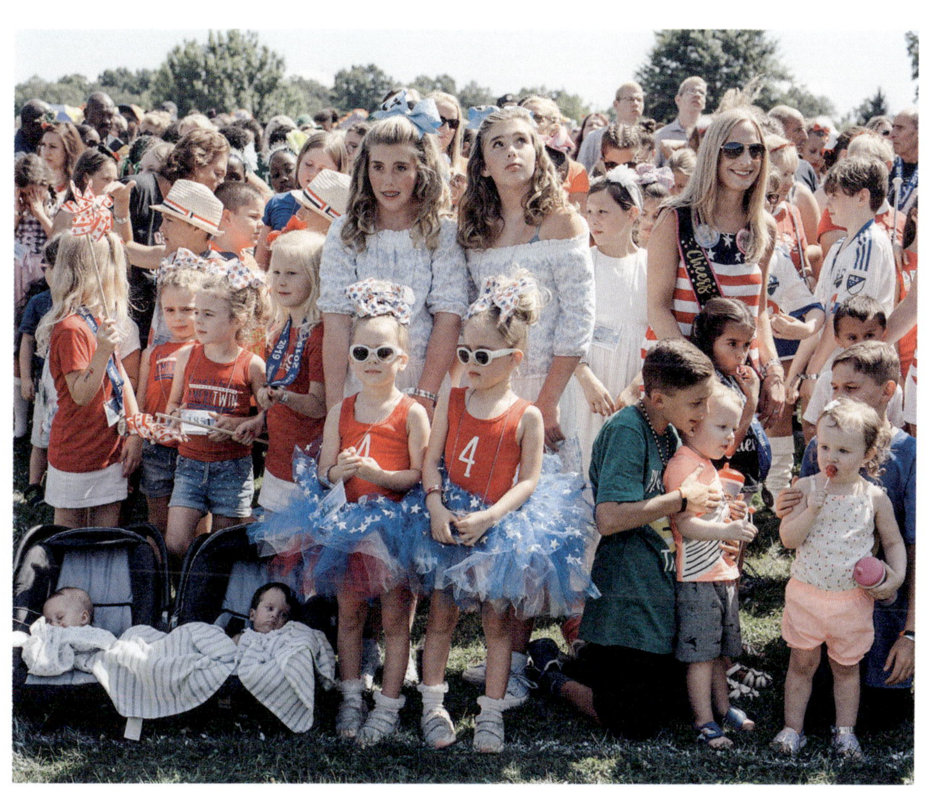

Twinsburg

by Josie Gealer-Ng
Twinsburg, Ohio, USA

Young Amish Twins
by Josie Gealer-Ng
Twinsburg, Ohio, USA

Identical twins Lorelle and Lauren had travelled
from Pennsylvania Amish Country to attend
the Twins Days Festival, the largest annual gathering
of twins and multiples in the world. Members of
the Amish community do not like having their picture
taken but the twins were happy to be photographed
in the spirit of the festival.

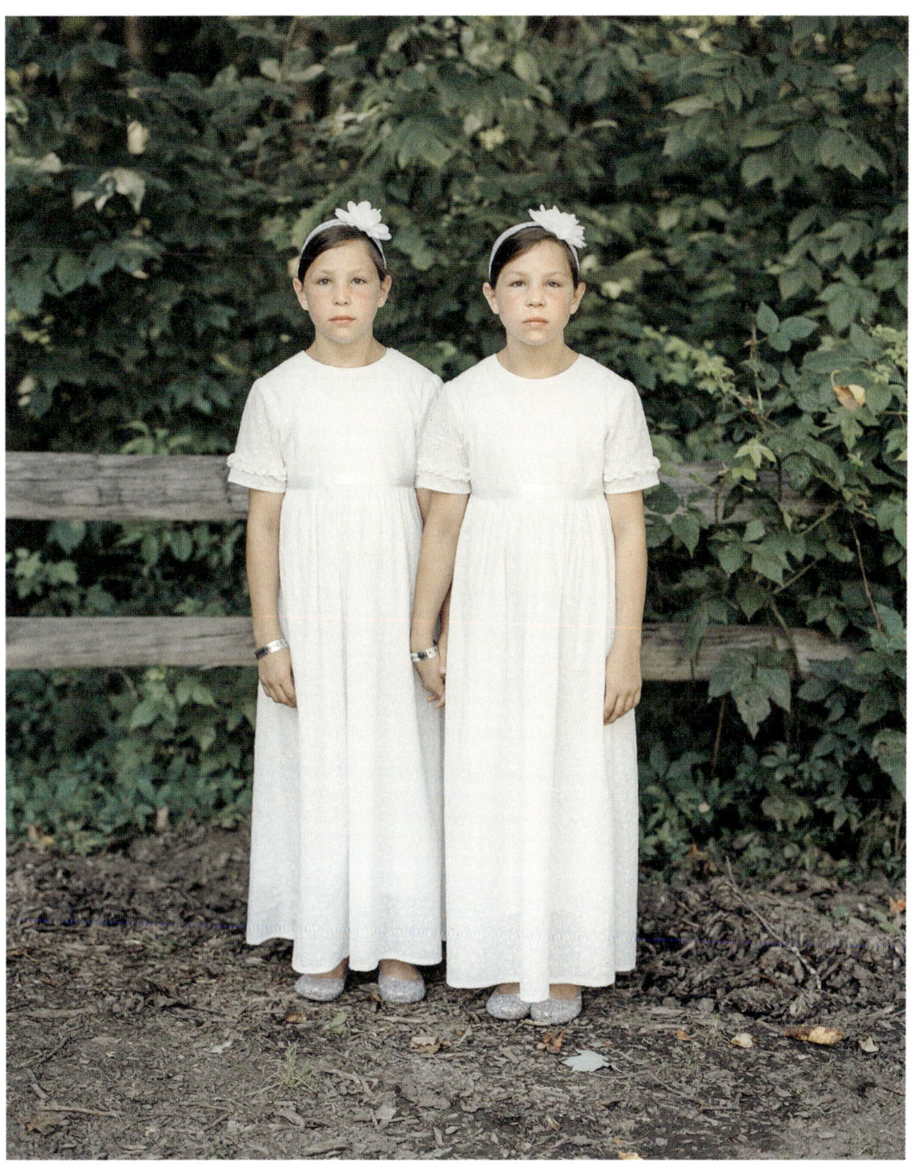

Sara
by Simon Murphy
Glasgow, UK

Sara is a young Roma girl. Govanhill is one
of Scotland's most deprived areas but it is also one of
the most diverse and vibrant parts of Glasgow.
I spotted Sara sitting on the pavement outside her home.
It's rare to see children on the streets today. As
a child I would be out until all hours, kicking a
football about or playing by the river. Sara reminded
me of a happy time when the streets were
our playgrounds.

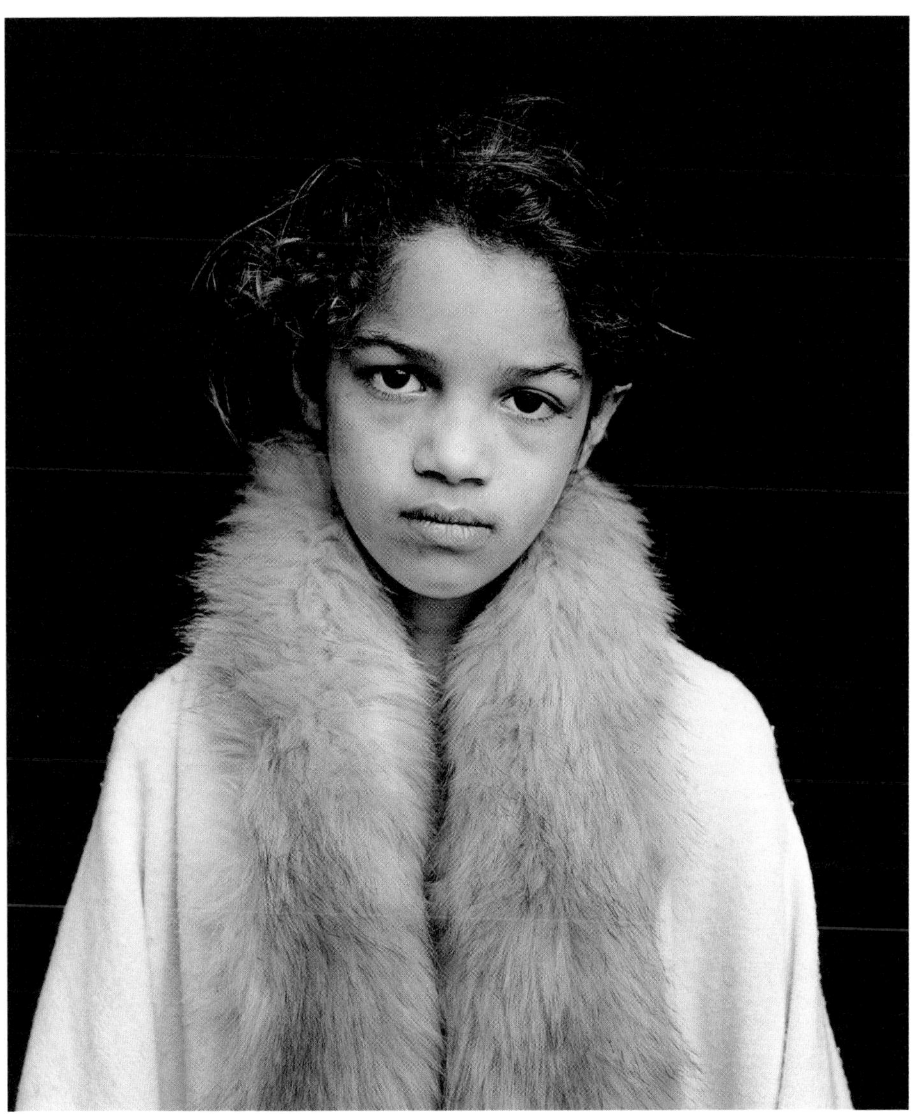

For You
by Peter Brooks
London, UK

The Extinction Rebellion Red Rebel Brigade
operates at the intersection of art and activism.
'There's something incredibly powerful especially in
volatile, chaotic and high-tension protest
situations about inviting people to slow down and
connect with their hearts. Performing with the
Red Rebel Brigade leads to a beautiful forgetting of
the self, a melting into each other as we become
part of a deep and often forgotten interconnectedness.'
– Red Rebel Brigade member

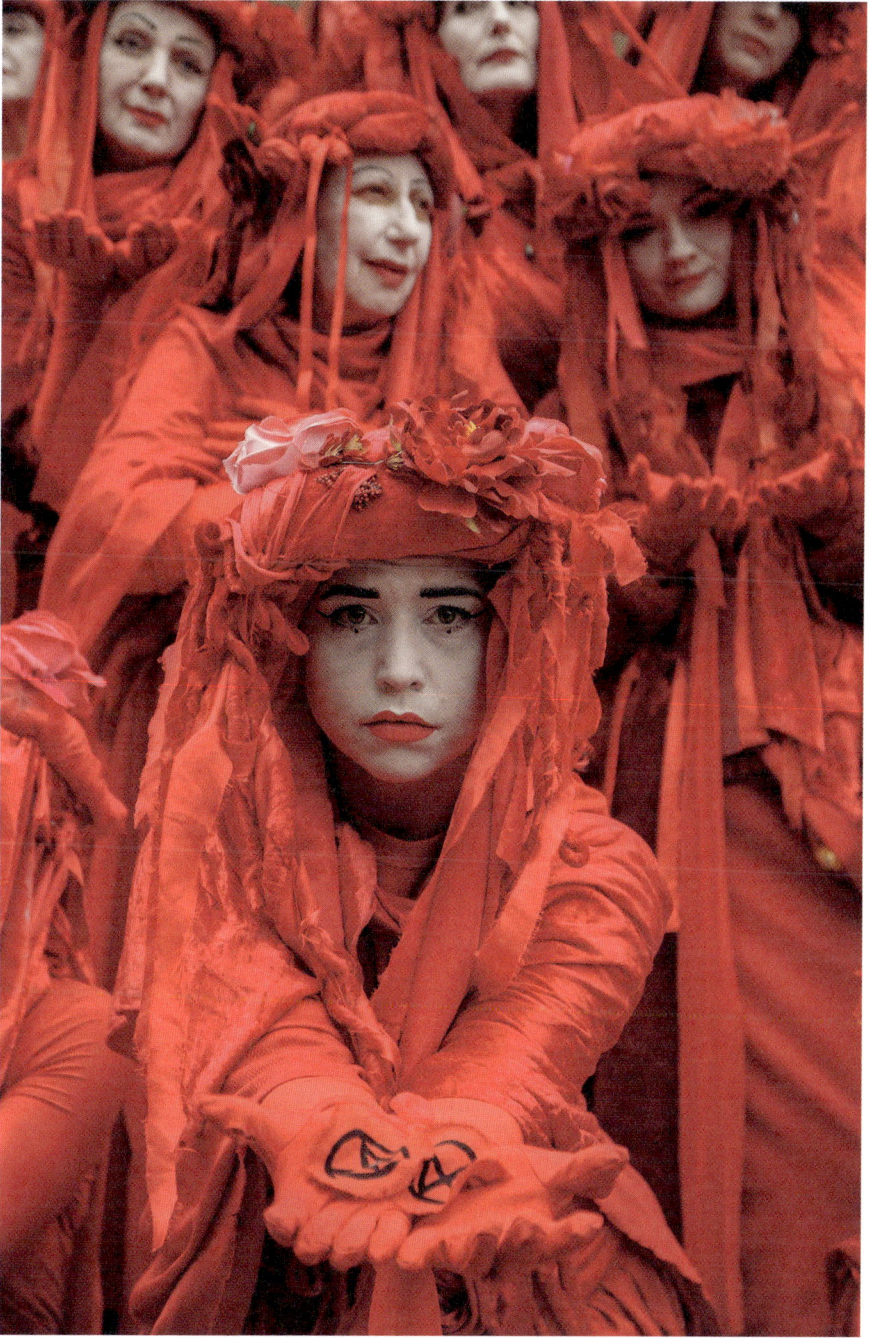

Cougars, Fort Lauderdale
by Edouard Jacquinet
Fort Lauderdale, Florida, USA

These girls belong to the cheerleading team,
Cougars. They were standing in front of their school
waiting for their teacher to take a picture.
I was in Fort Lauderdale for an assignment and
noticed the girls as I was driving past.
I was struck by their unity.

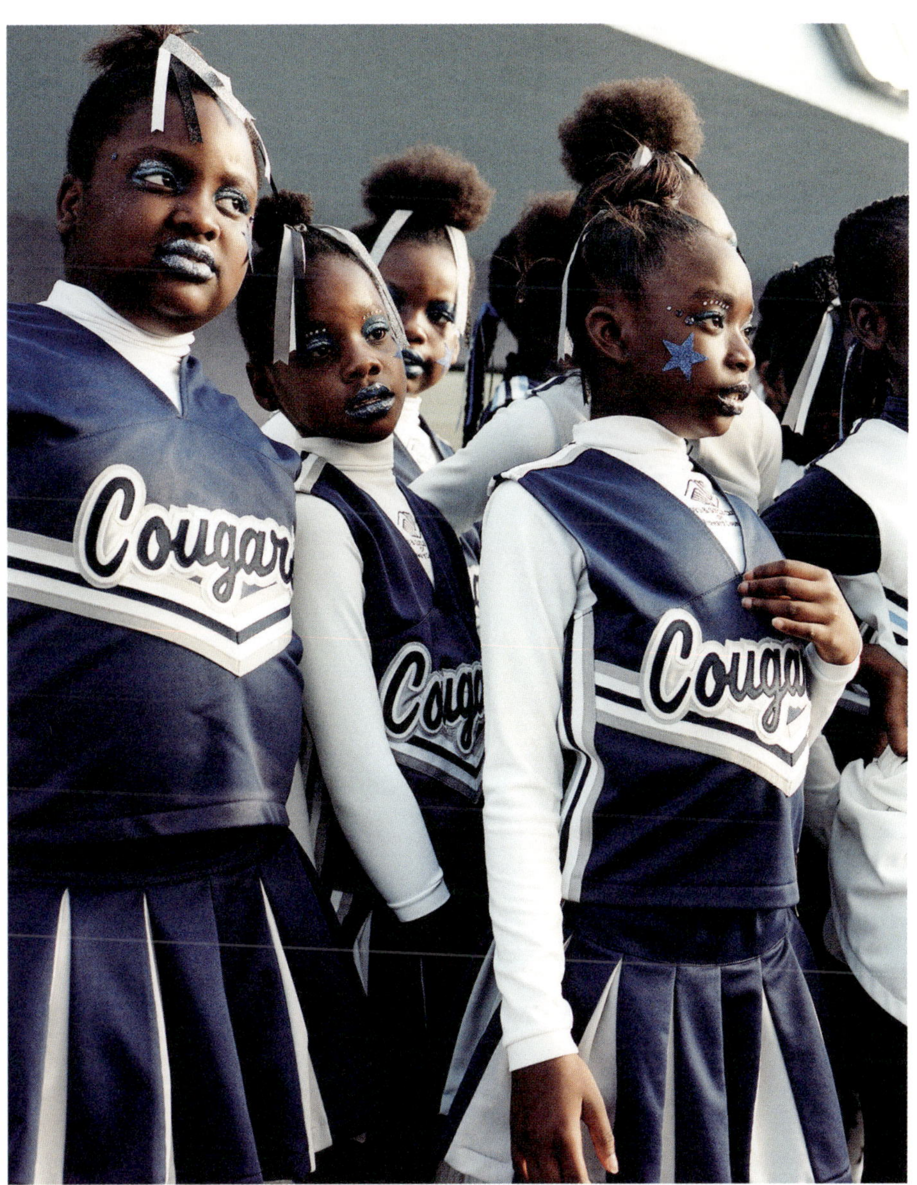

Brett and Billy
by Claudia Leisinger
London, UK

Brett *(right)* and Billy enjoy a cigarette after
work at Billingsgate Market. I met Brett on my first
visit to the market in 2011. He was curious,
generous and thoughtful. His enthusiasm is a big part
of what gave me access to this unique world.
Brett's dad also worked at the market, and his
grandfather too. Brett's ambition was to
become a fully-fledged porter, like his grandad.
Billy is Brett's close friend. I only ever
saw him with Brett.

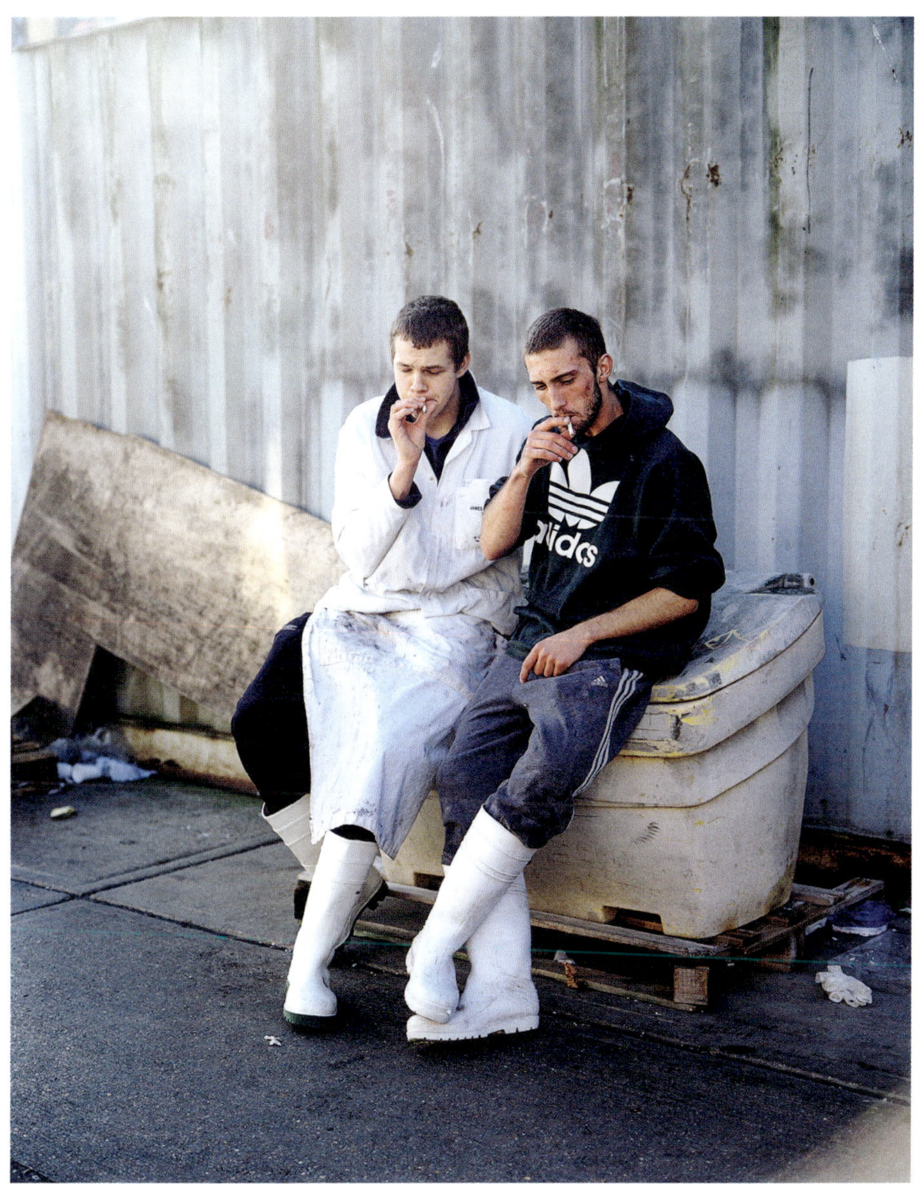

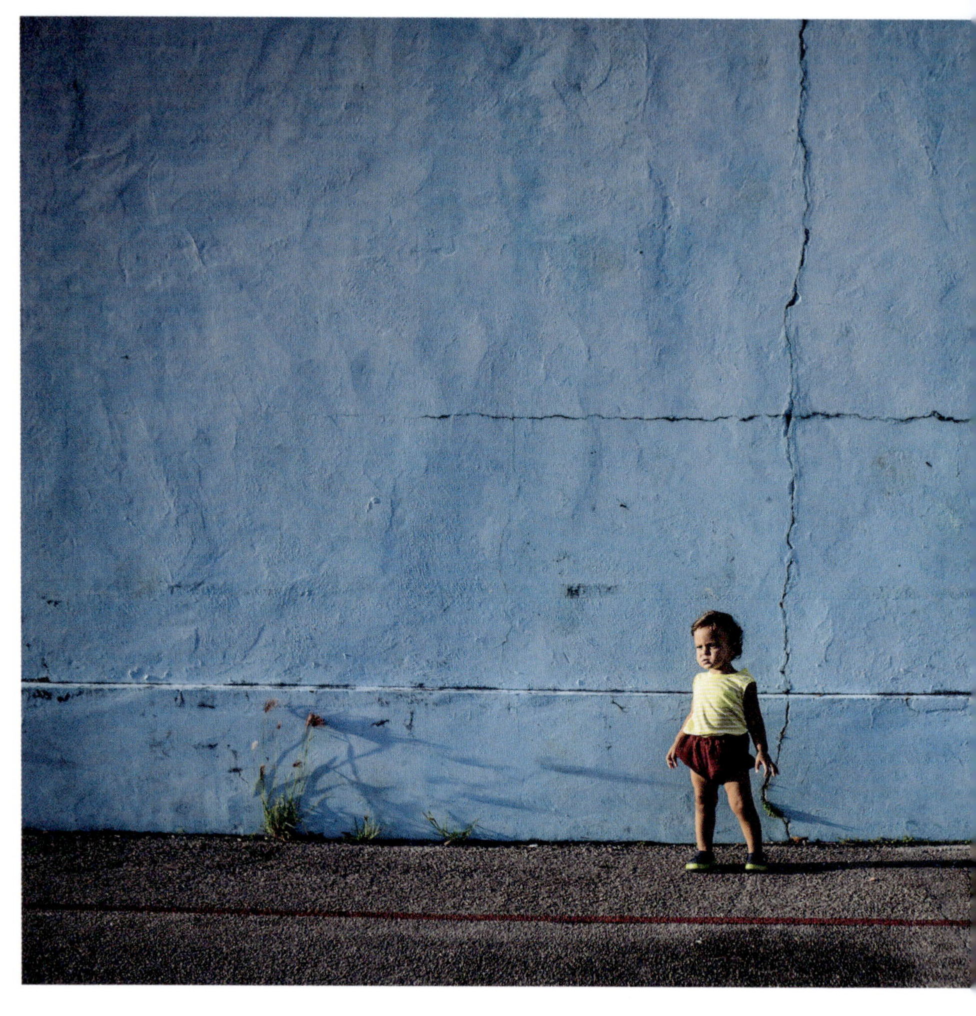

Otis and Blue
by Aniya Emtage Legnaro
St. John, Barbados

My one-year-old son Otis and his sisters, who are 14
and 15, are extremely close. He is always looking around for
them. The girls are playing volleyball outside of the frame.

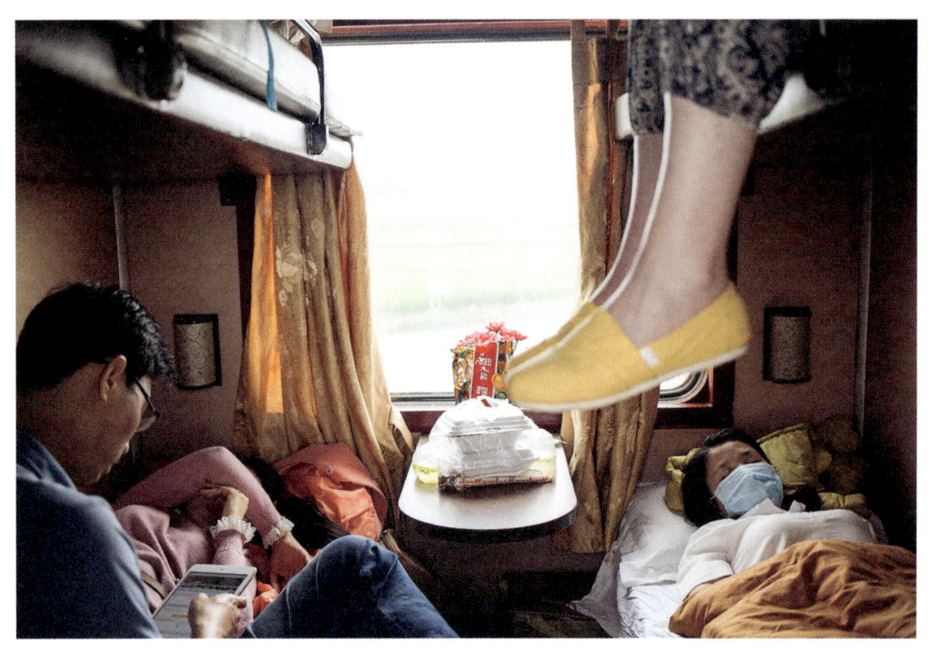

Train

by Charlotte Sverdrup
Train from Hoi An to Ho Chi Minh, Vietnam

My friend and I travelled in a shared sleeper
carriage and spent more than 20 hours on the train
from Hoi An to Ho Chi Minh. My friend's
feet dangled over the edge of the top bunk as
I took the picture from the hallway.

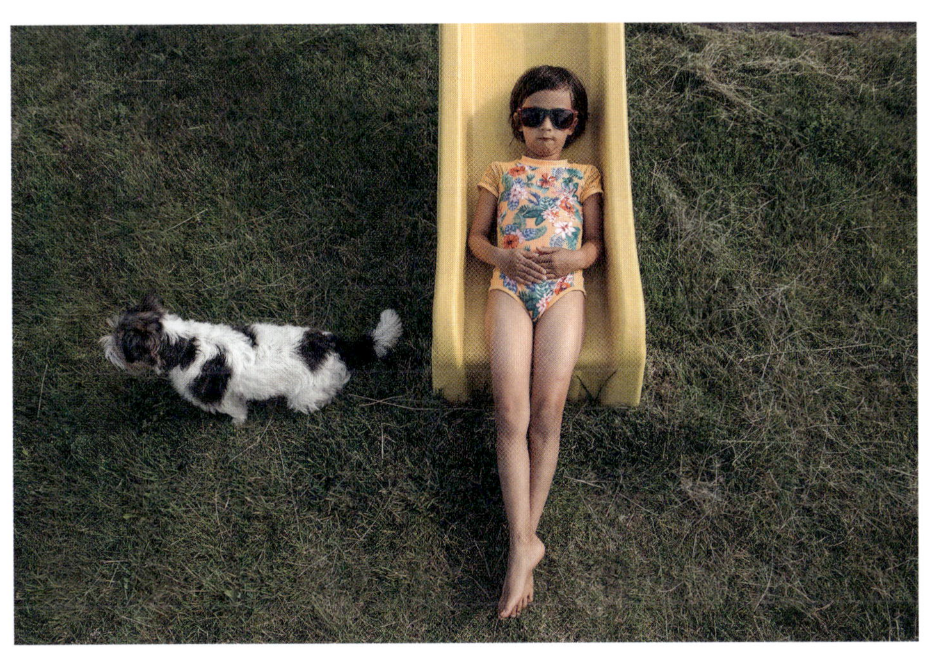

Portrait of Her First Girl Swimsuit
by Margaret Albaugh
Spokane, Washington, USA

My oldest daughter was born assigned male.
As she got older and we realised who she really was,
we honoured that. At the age of seven, we let her
choose her own swimsuit and she immediately picked
this one. I wanted to photograph her in the first
swimsuit she chose. The neighbour's dog would not
leave the picture.

Untitled
by Krisztián Éder
Moat Peam, Cambodia

This little girl was silently sitting on a moped
when I took this image during the dry season. The area
is usually underwater. At this time of year the
people, who mostly make their living from fishing,
struggle because of the lack of opportunities.

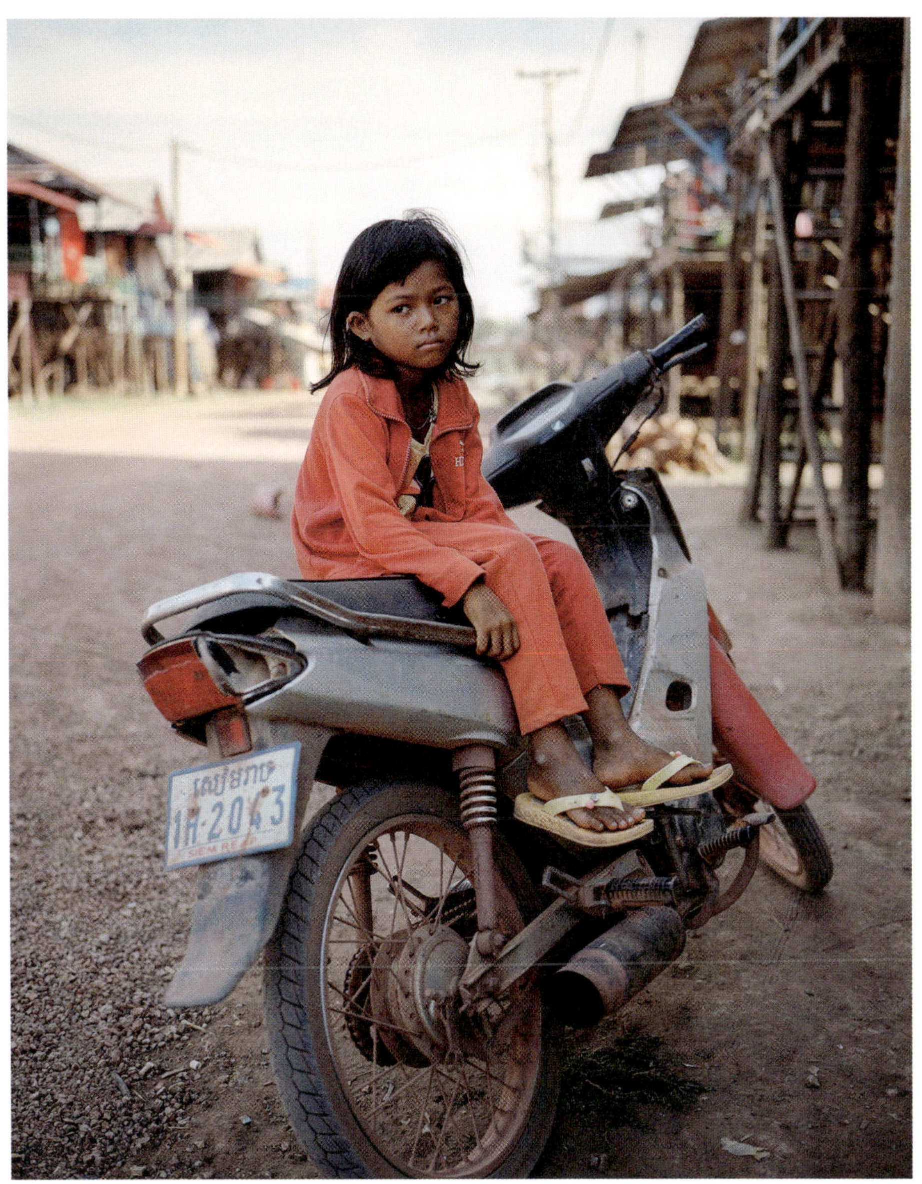

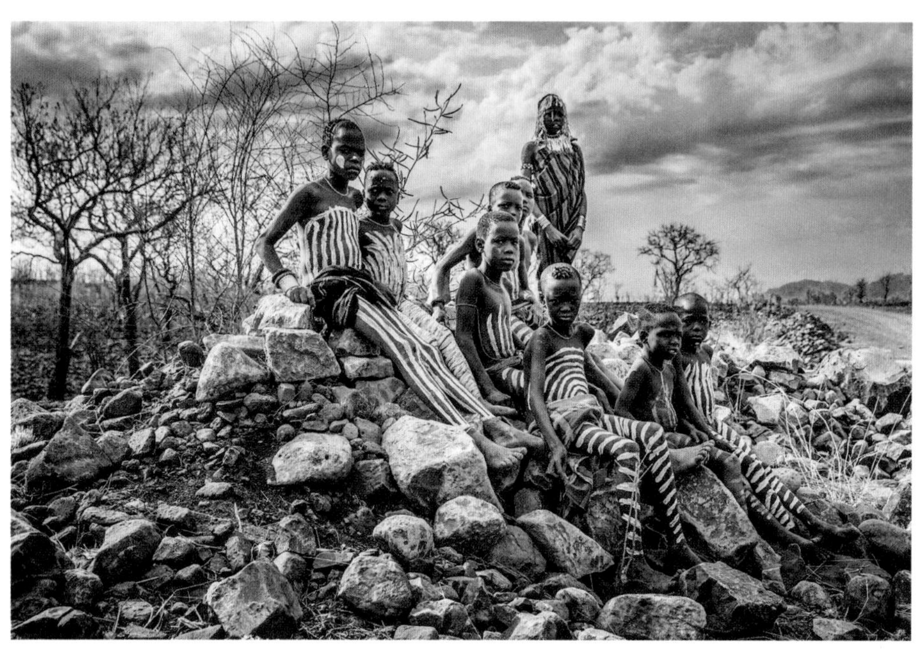

Painted Stripes
by Georgia Darlow
Lower Omo Valley, Ethiopia

I met this group of children during my travels
around Ethiopia. They were playing by the roadside as
a storm rolled in. The Mursi people use their bodies
as canvases. They decorate themselves with piercings,
through scarification and paint. The tradition is
a form of self-expression and ritual. They also use body
art to connect to their natural environment.

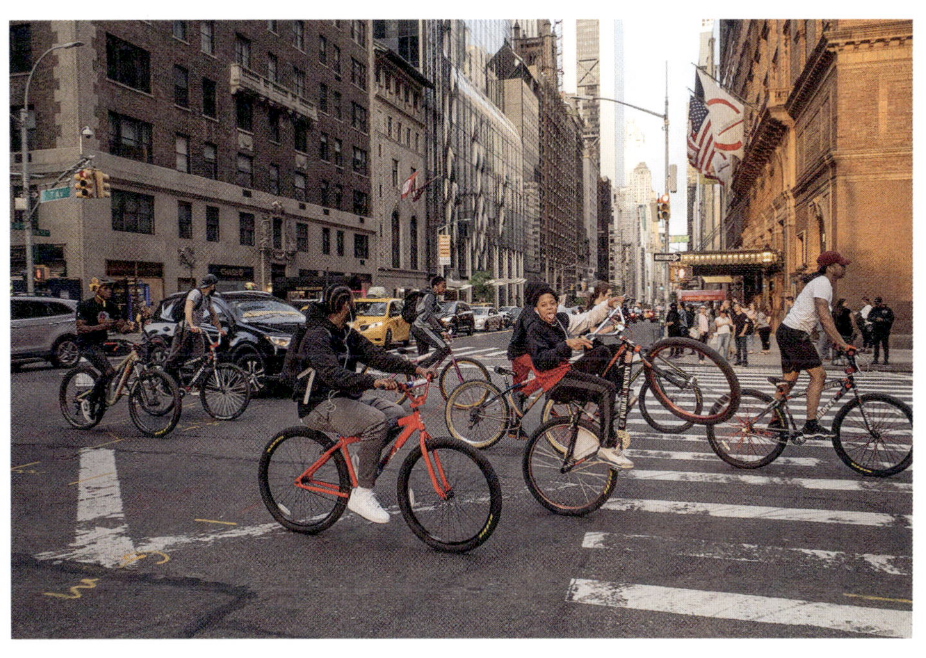

Cycling Kids of NYC
by Orlando Figueiredo
New York City, New York, USA

I was walking along Eighth Avenue one afternoon
when I saw this group of kids. When they noticed me
taking pictures they started waving and showing off.

Maxim
by Vivek Vadoliya
London, UK

Sixteen-year-old Maxim joined Ebony Horse Club
in Brixton five-and-a-half years ago. He had no prior
experience with horses. The club provides
invaluable opportunities for disadvantaged young
people. You could tell how dedicated Maxim is
to the place; he comes several times a week to help out.
There is a beautiful family vibe at the club. Everyone
is so lovely and patient with the kids. They teach
them about discipline and structure. The horses
seem to help with the kids' mental health.

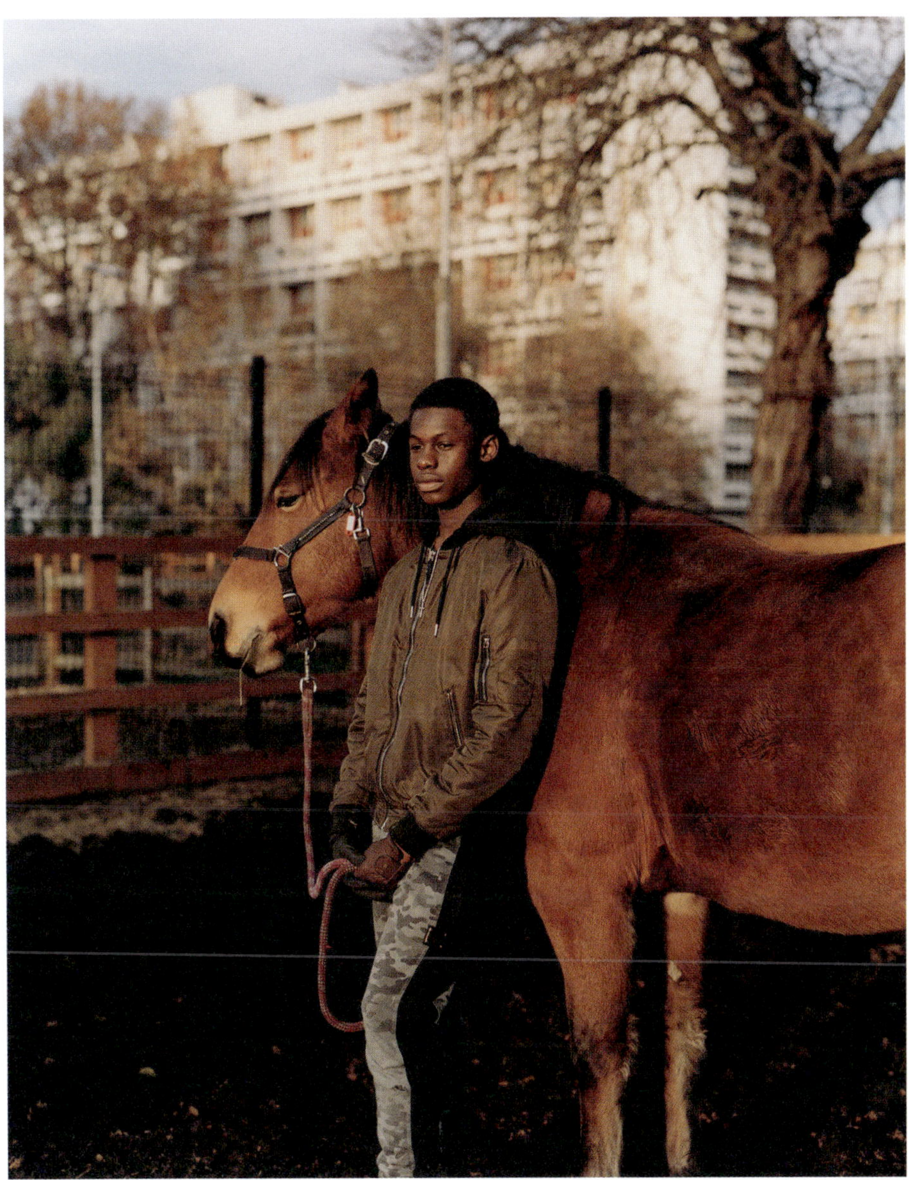

Suresh Kumar

by Aiyush Pachnanda
Dera Baba Nanak, Punjab, India

Suresh Kumar is a soldier who works on
the border between India and Pakistan. He introduced
me to his dog Mani and instructed her to show me
a trick. 'I love her,' he said. 'She makes my days better.'

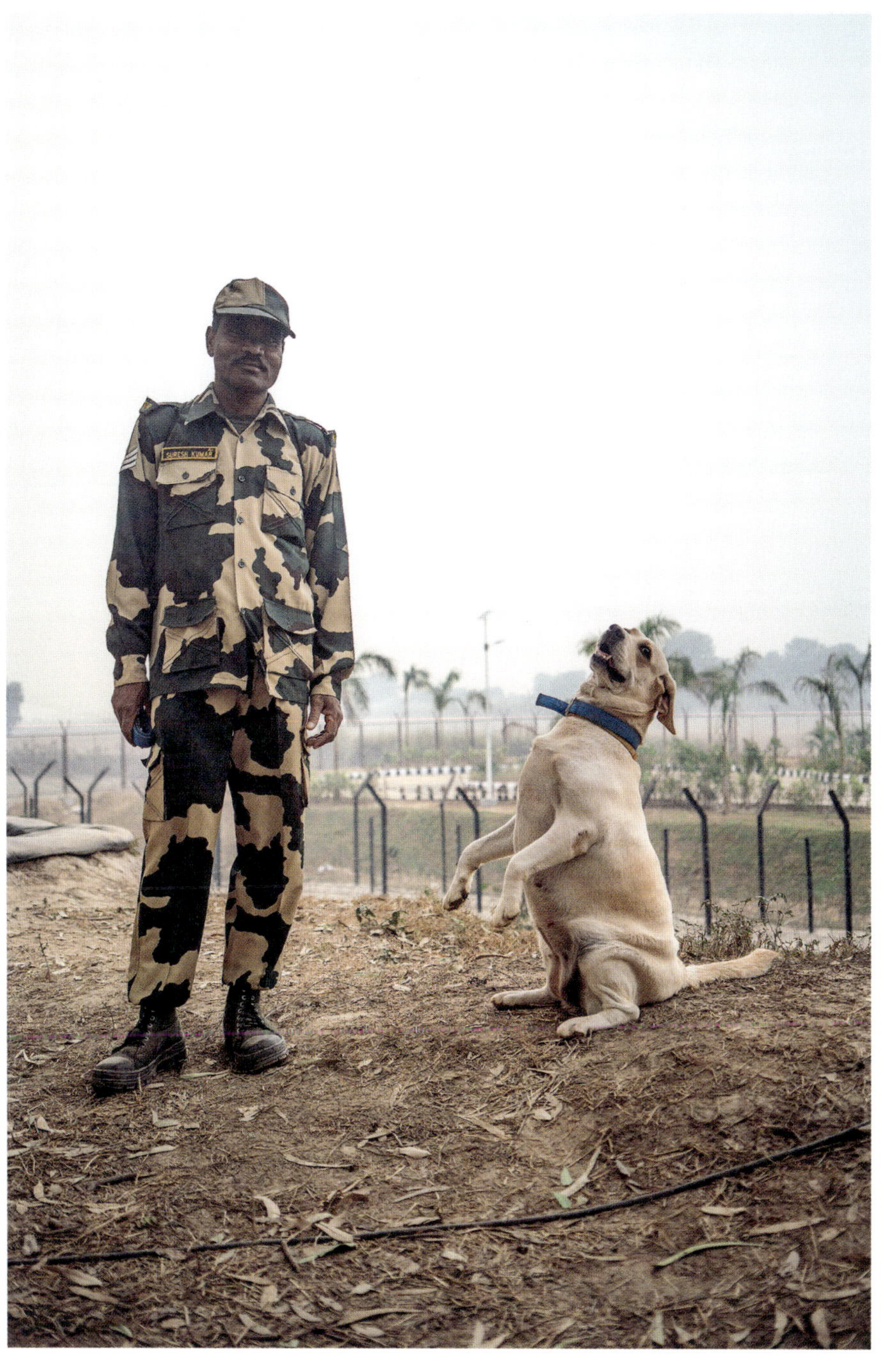

Bill Murray
by Nate 'Igor' Smith
New York City, New York, USA

I had the chance to photograph the cast of
the movie *Isle of Dogs* with rescue puppies to help
raise awareness of Best Friends Animal Society.
It has to be the best job I have ever had and is probably
my favourite photo I have ever taken. I mean,
it's Bill Murray with a tiny puppy!

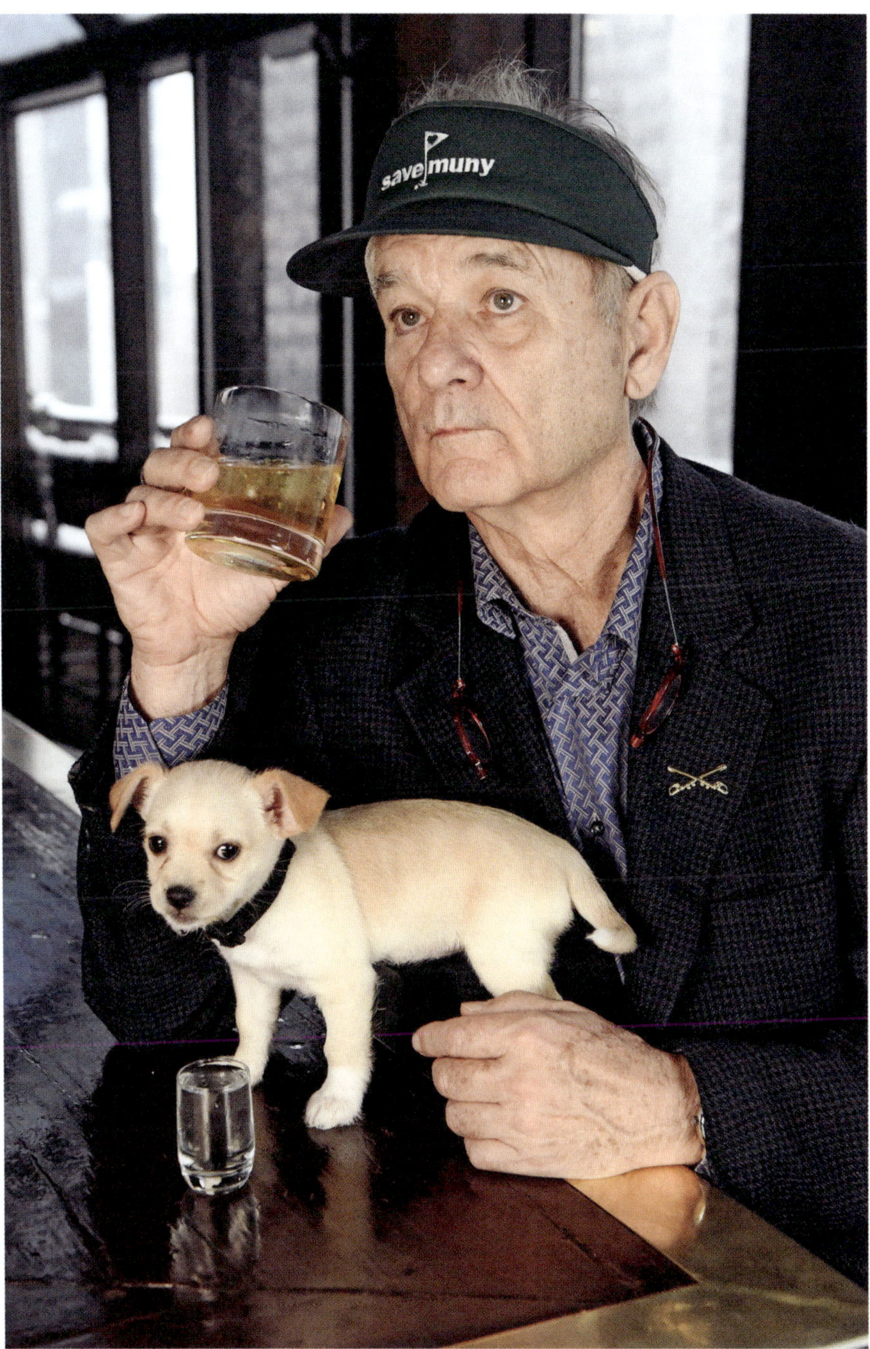
save muny

Hans-Georg and Kriemhilde Vogt
by Arne Piepke
Silbach, Germany

Hans-Georg and Kriemhilde Vogt celebrate
50 years of being the 'Queen' and 'King' of their
local marksmen's club during a marksmen festival in
the Sauerland. Every year, from May to September,
marksmen festivals are held in the region.
The three-day festivals consist of marches, processions,
dances and a shooting competition. I have been
visiting the festivals since childhood, which led me
to reflect on the tradition.

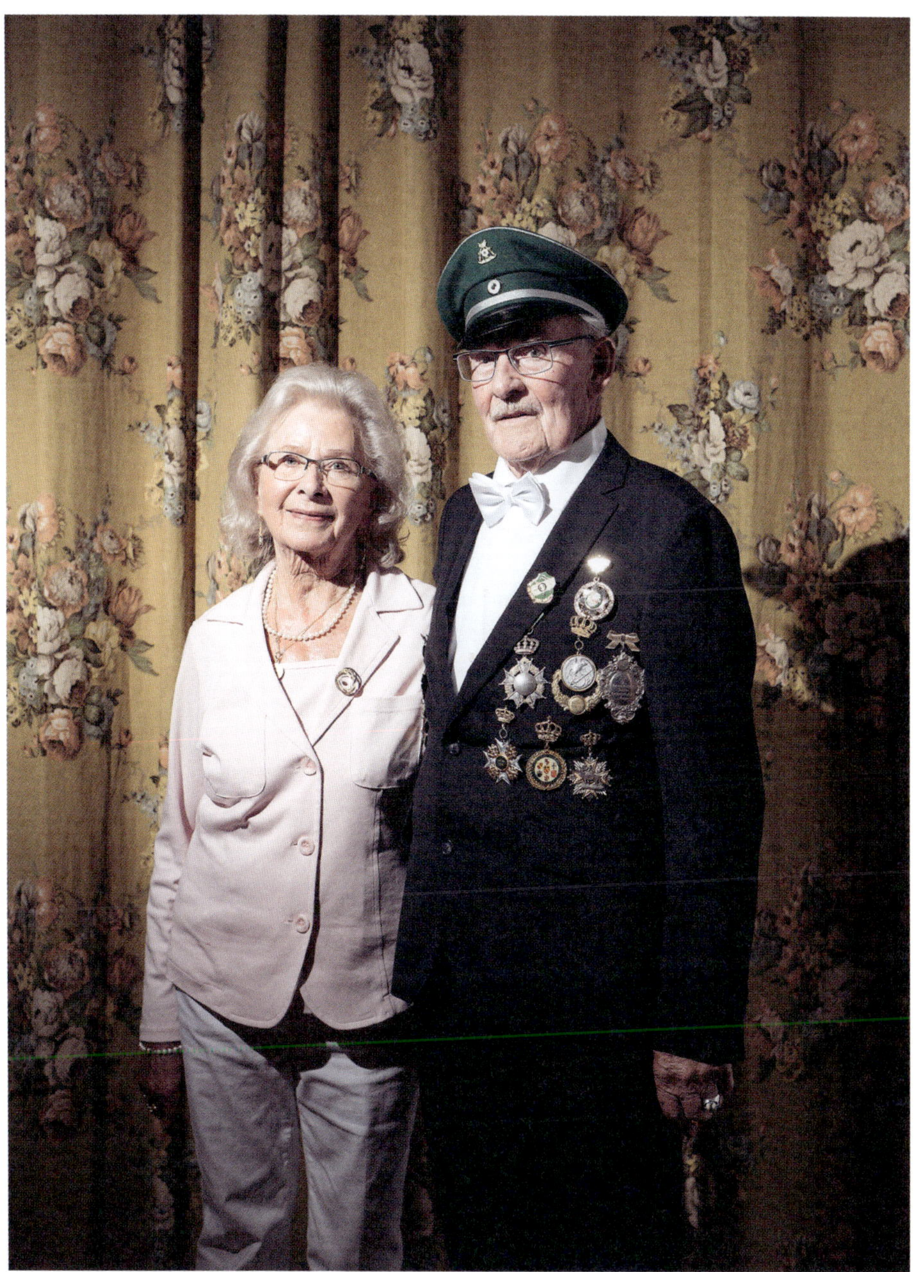

Akodessawa #03
by Francesco Merlini
Lomé, Togo

Gibodja Kake rests and protects himself from
the sun while waiting for customers in front of his
stand at Akodessawa Fetish Market, the world's
largest voodoo market. Behind a rusty iron gate lies
a sandy yard with two big metal awnings to
protect from the scorching sun. Men, women and
children lie and sit on benches, waiting
for customers to buy their wares that include
talismans, skulls, bones, horns, paws, shells, herbs
and feathers.

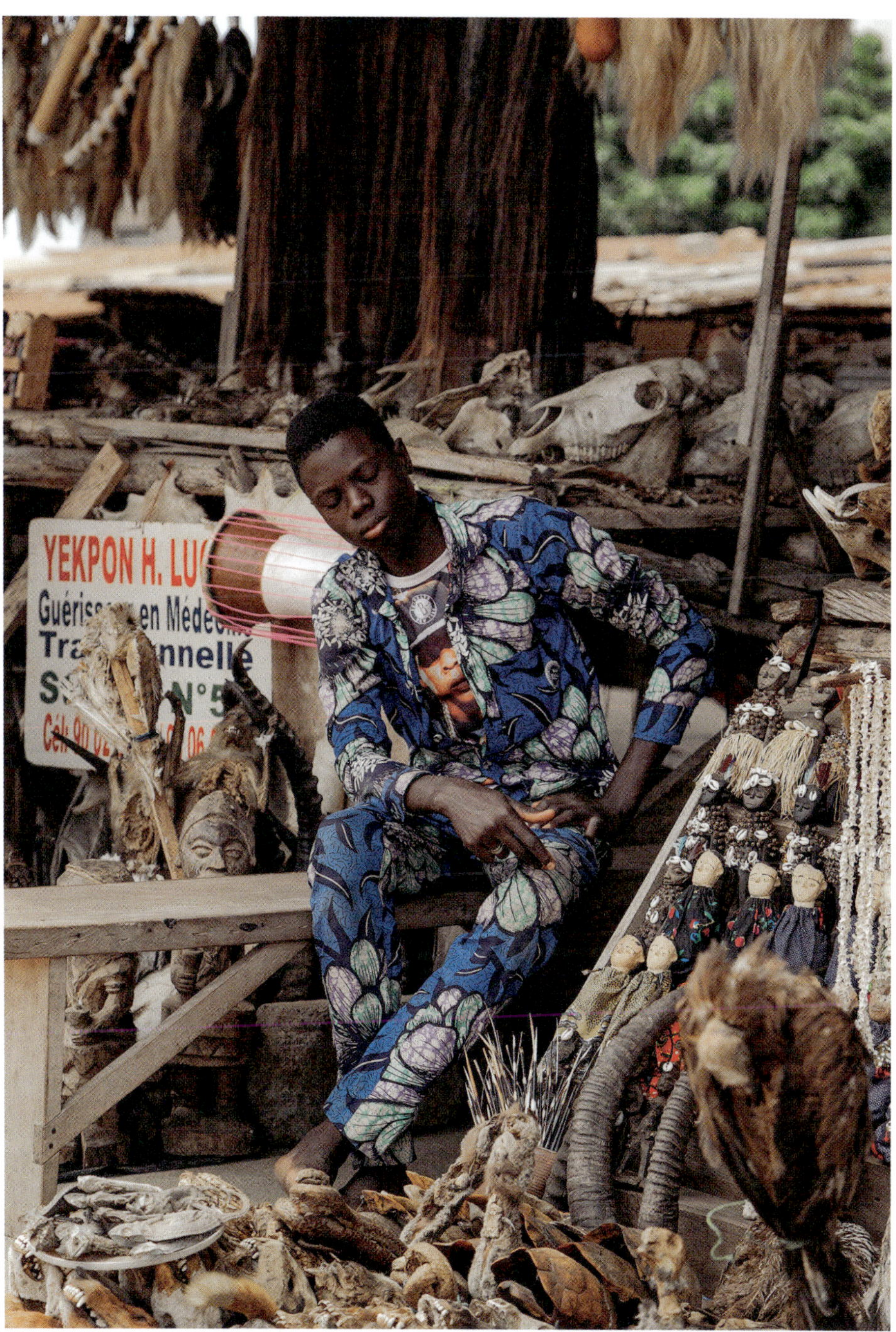
YEKPON H. LUC
Guérisseur en Médecine
Traditionnelle
S   N° 5
Cél 90 02   06

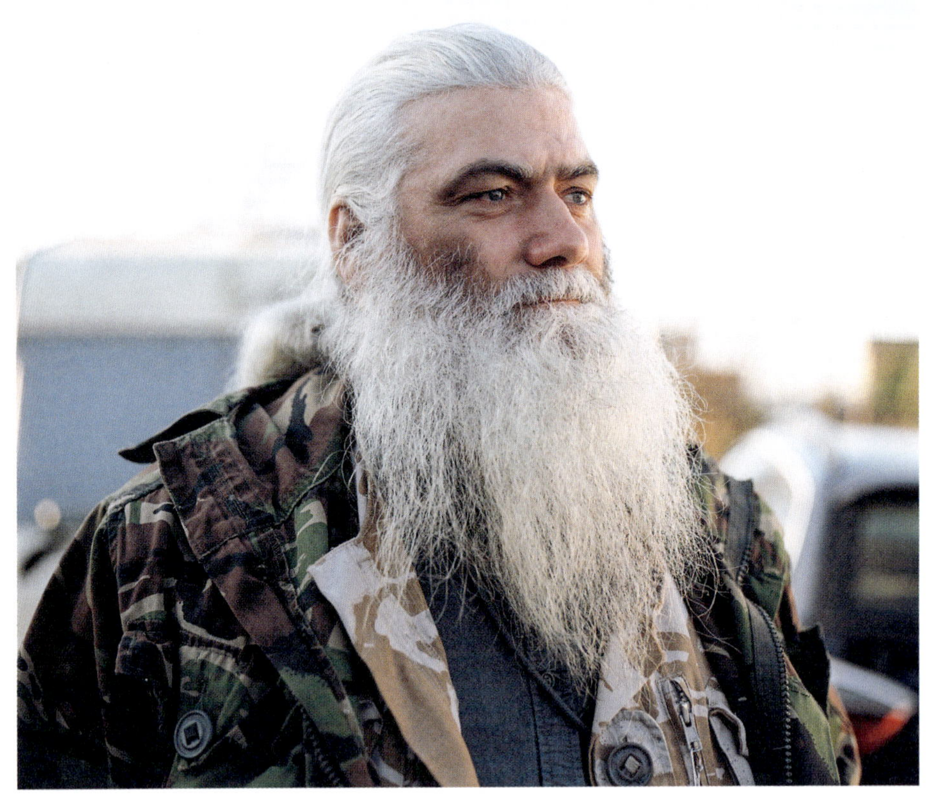

Jasper
by Theodore Tennant
Sittingbourne, UK

Jasper is a Romani Gypsy. We spent half an hour
together and instantly connected. I was struck
by his stillness and how, despite a harsh life lived outside,
beneath the white hair he had the appearance
of a younger man.

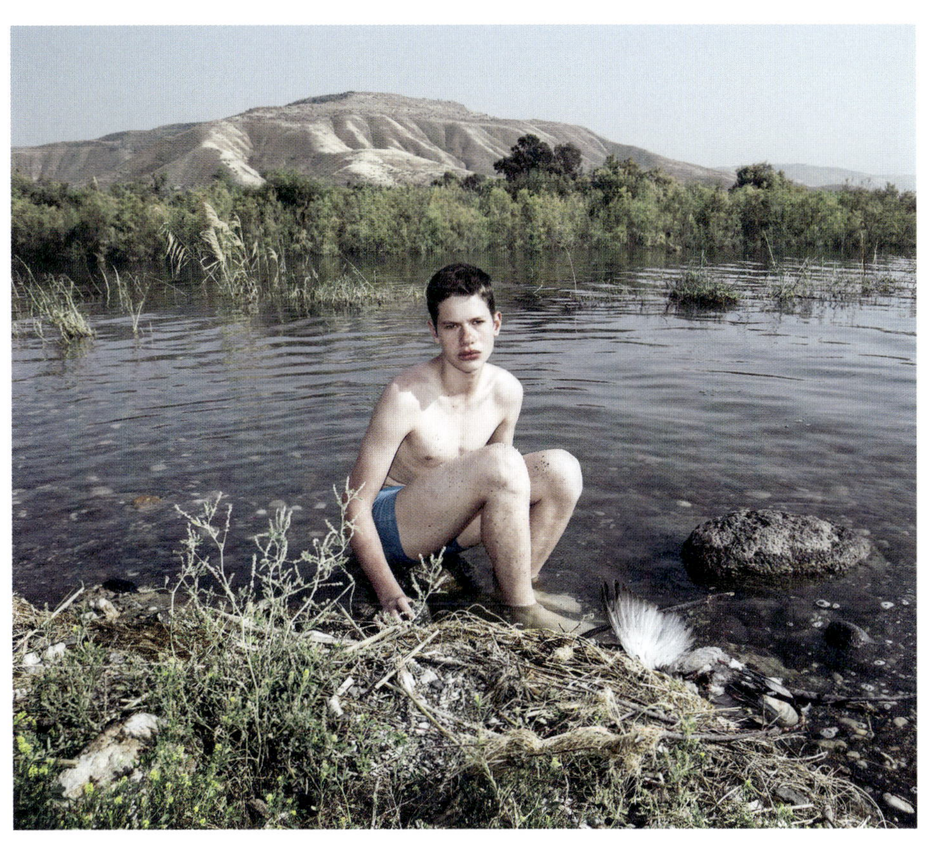

My Brother
by Itamar Freed
Sea of Galilee, Israel

This is my teenage brother just before
he joined the army. To me he represents the current
generation of young Israelis who are dealing
with the daily reality of conflict.

The Little Girl on the Horse
by Sandra Mickiewicz
Dereham, UK

I saw this girl standing alone in front of a
caravan at Dereham Horse Fair. I was fascinated by
her beauty and light curly blonde hair. Suddenly
she spoke with an older man who was her grandfather.
He put the girl on a horse tied to the caravan.
The girl was really scared at first but when she heard
her grandfather's voice, she felt safe and posed
for the picture.

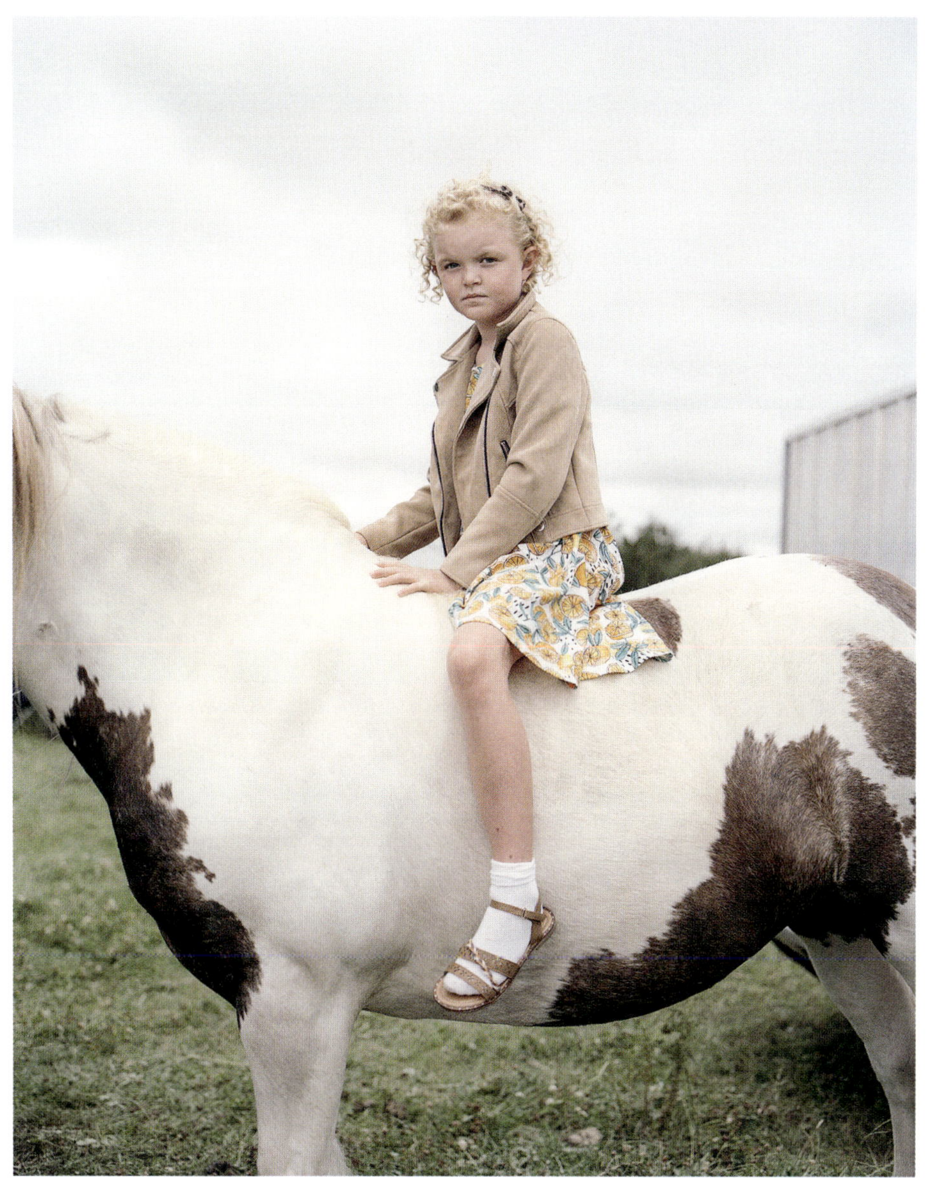

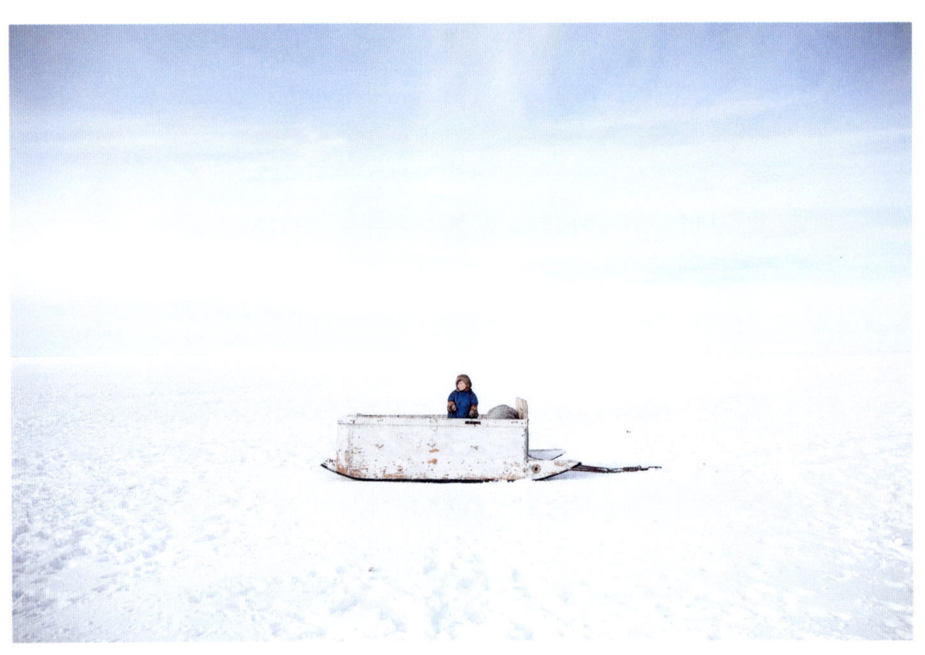

Rosebud

by Oded Wagenstein

Yamalo-Nenets Autonomous Okrug, Russia

Three-year-old Nyadma Serotetto, who belongs
to the nomadic Nenets tribe of the Siberian Arctic, stands
on his family's wooden sleigh during their migration
across the frozen Ob River. During his lifetime, Nyadma
will travel thousands of miles with his family in one
of the most extreme environments on earth.

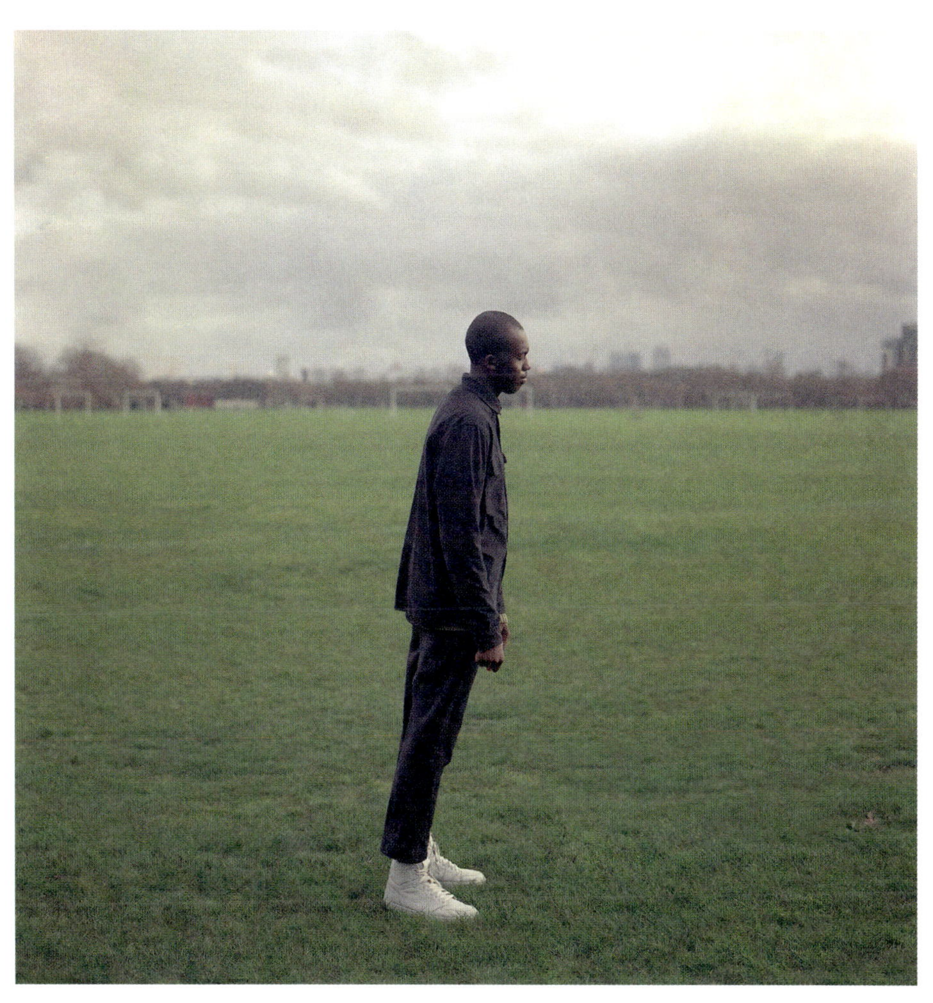

Lean Into It

by Dean Idoniboye
London, UK

Tolu is my closest friend. We took a walk in Hackney
Marshes on an incredibly windy day and I asked Tolu to
lean into the wind, which seemed to echo our conversation
about facing and pushing through criticism.

Untitled
by Jordie Hennigar
Victoria, British Columbia, Canada

I met Tendai while I was searching for
interesting people to photograph. She was very
quiet and a little hesitant but striking.

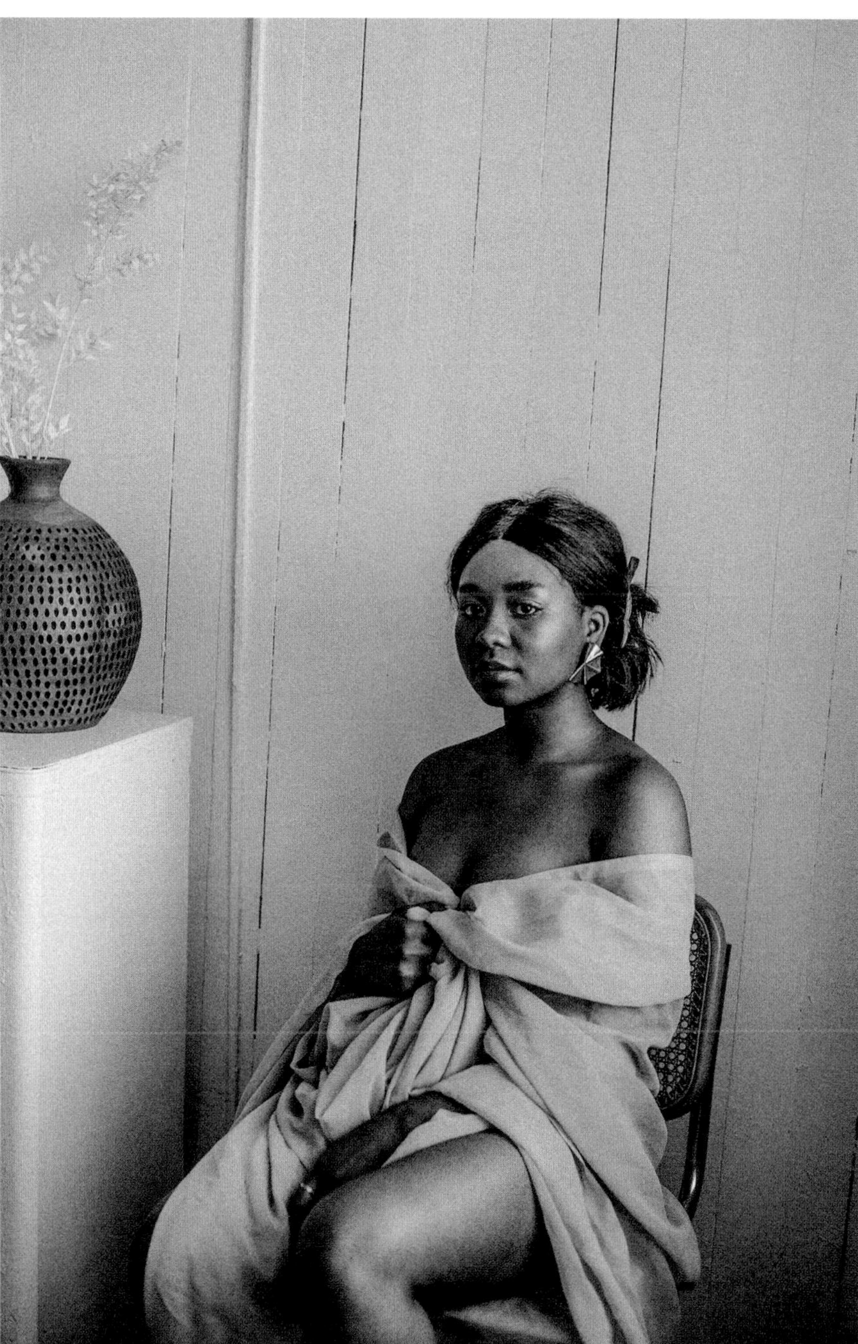

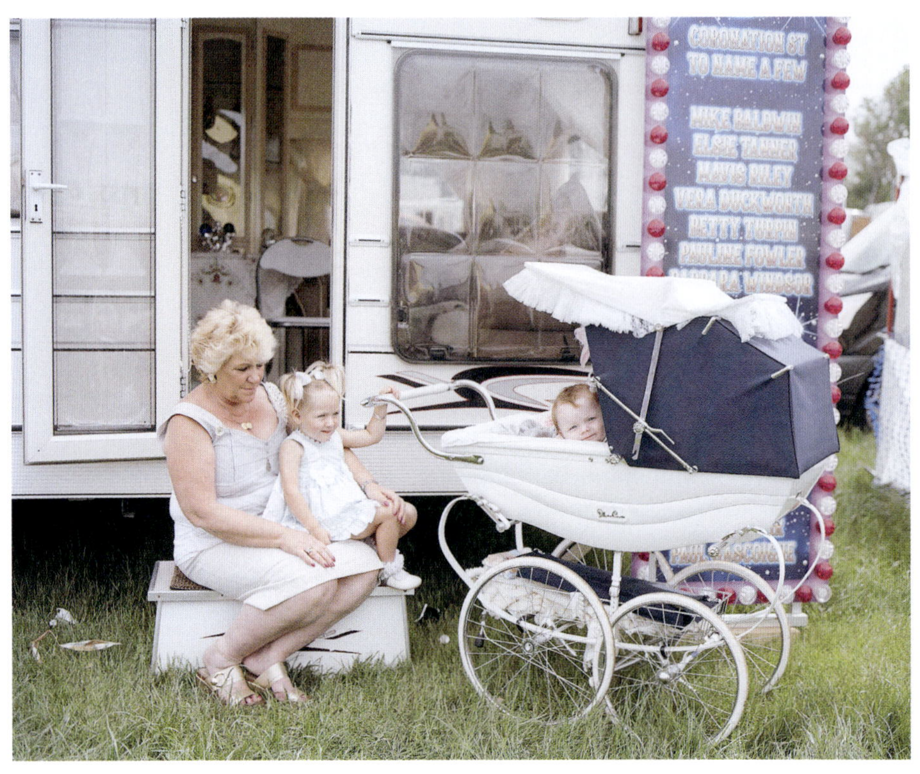

Kookie with her Grandchildren

by Sandra Mickiewicz
Appleby-in-Westmorland, UK

Kookie came to Appleby Horse Fair with her family.
The event is very popular among Gypsies and
Travellers. She sat on a step with her older grandchild
and when I moved back the youngest child
suddenly looked out of the pram.

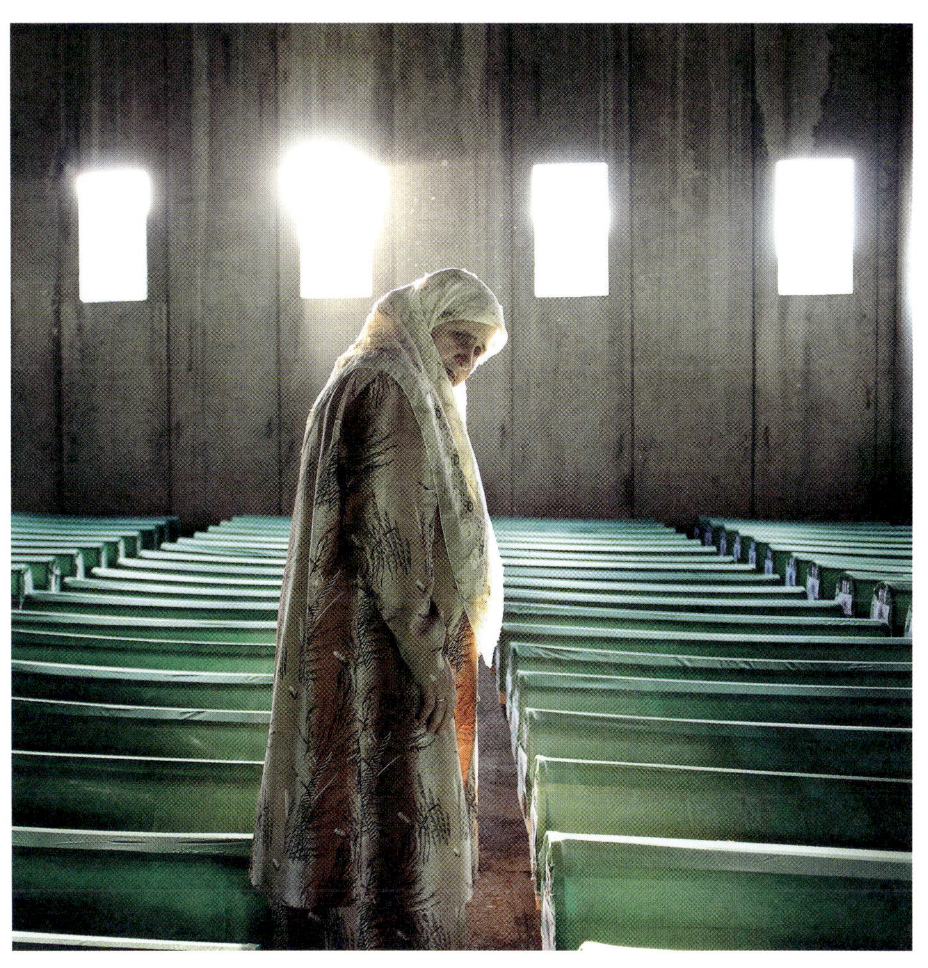

Remembering Srebrenica
by Lara Ciarabellini
Srebrenica, Bosnia and Herzegovina

The Bush Man
by Haley McHaffie
Great Ocean Road, Victoria, Australia

This is my father, Monty. It's true what they say
about time: before too long you run out of it. This was
the problem Monty and I had. We'd never spent
time together and we knew very little about each other.
I didn't want to live my life not knowing who
I really am or where I came from. Monty is half of
me and I needed to know which half. Living in
the Bush with him would help me find out.

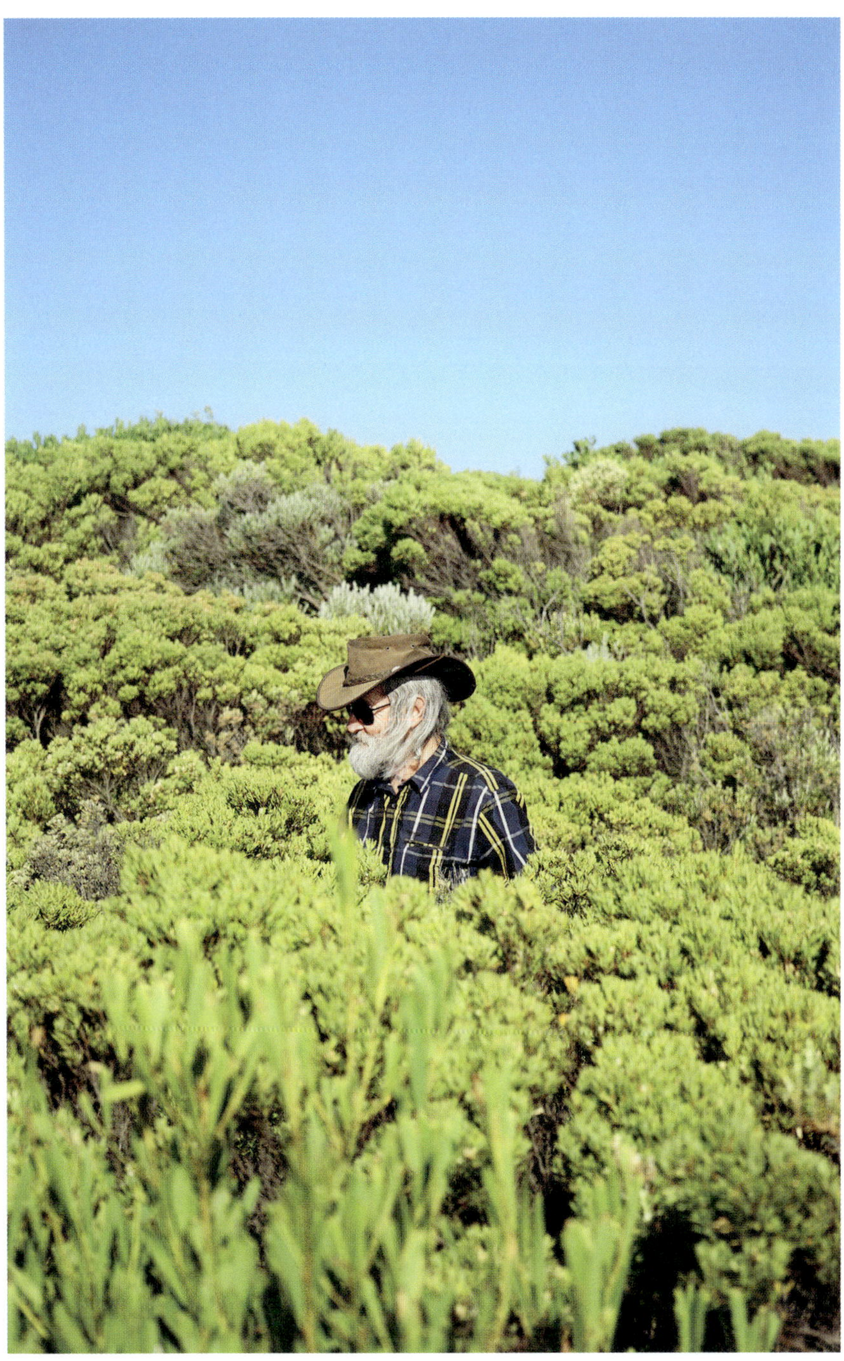

Maherttar Ram Tandon

by Brian Cassey
Churela, Chhattisgarh, India

Maherttar Ram Tandon is one of the last surviving
members of the Ramnami Samaj, a small Hindu
sect whose members were historically tattooed from
a young age with the name of their god, Lord Rama.
The practice was an act of rebellion in response
to discrimination by privileged castes.

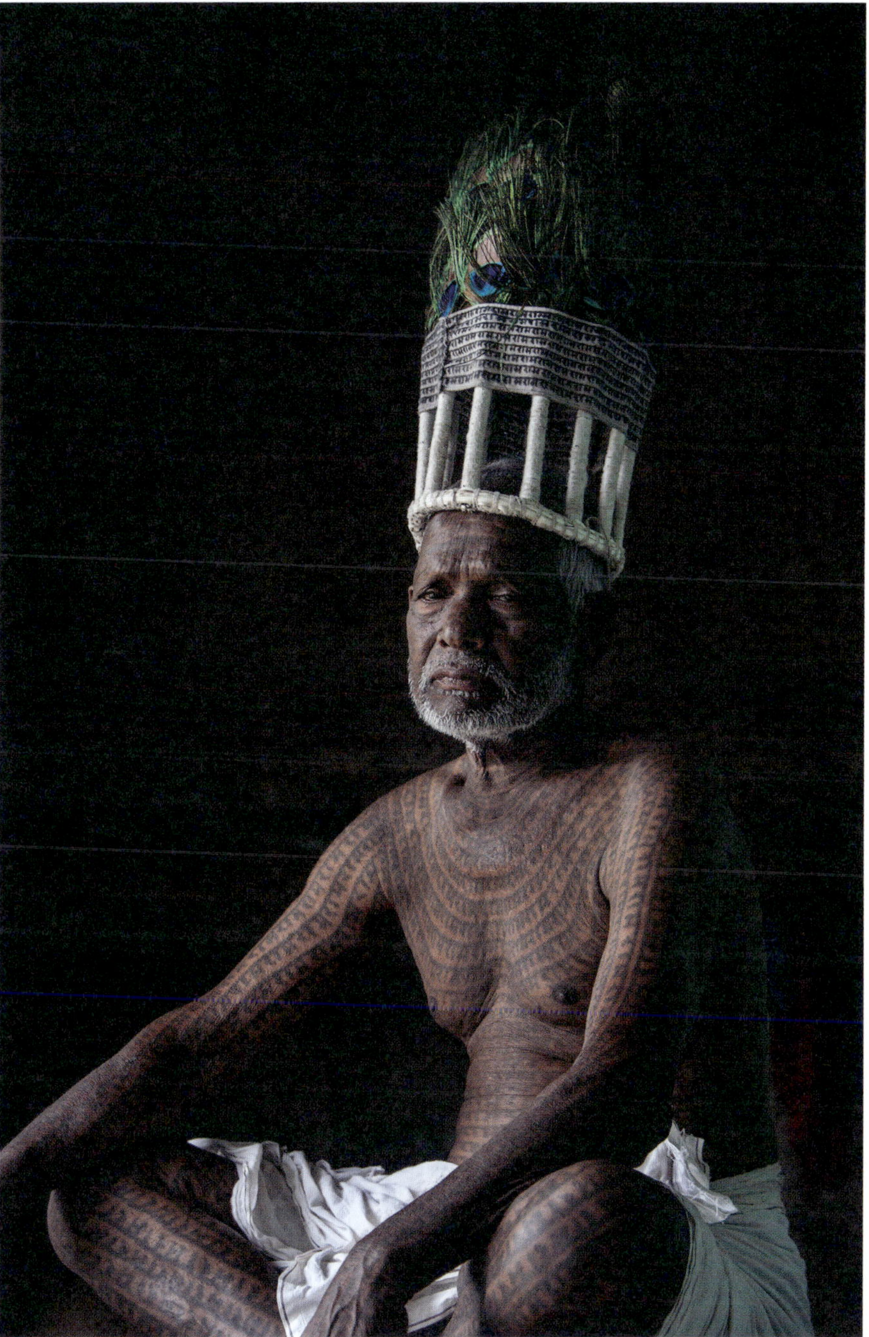

Between Walks at Paris Fashion Week
by Rory Langdon-Down
Paris, France

Mame Anta Wade is a model who was walking
at Paris Fashion Week for a show I was filming. I asked
Mame if we could shoot some stills before the
show, which was due to take place in an ornate ballroom
in a hotel. I focused on her reflection in the large
mirrors of the vast golden room.

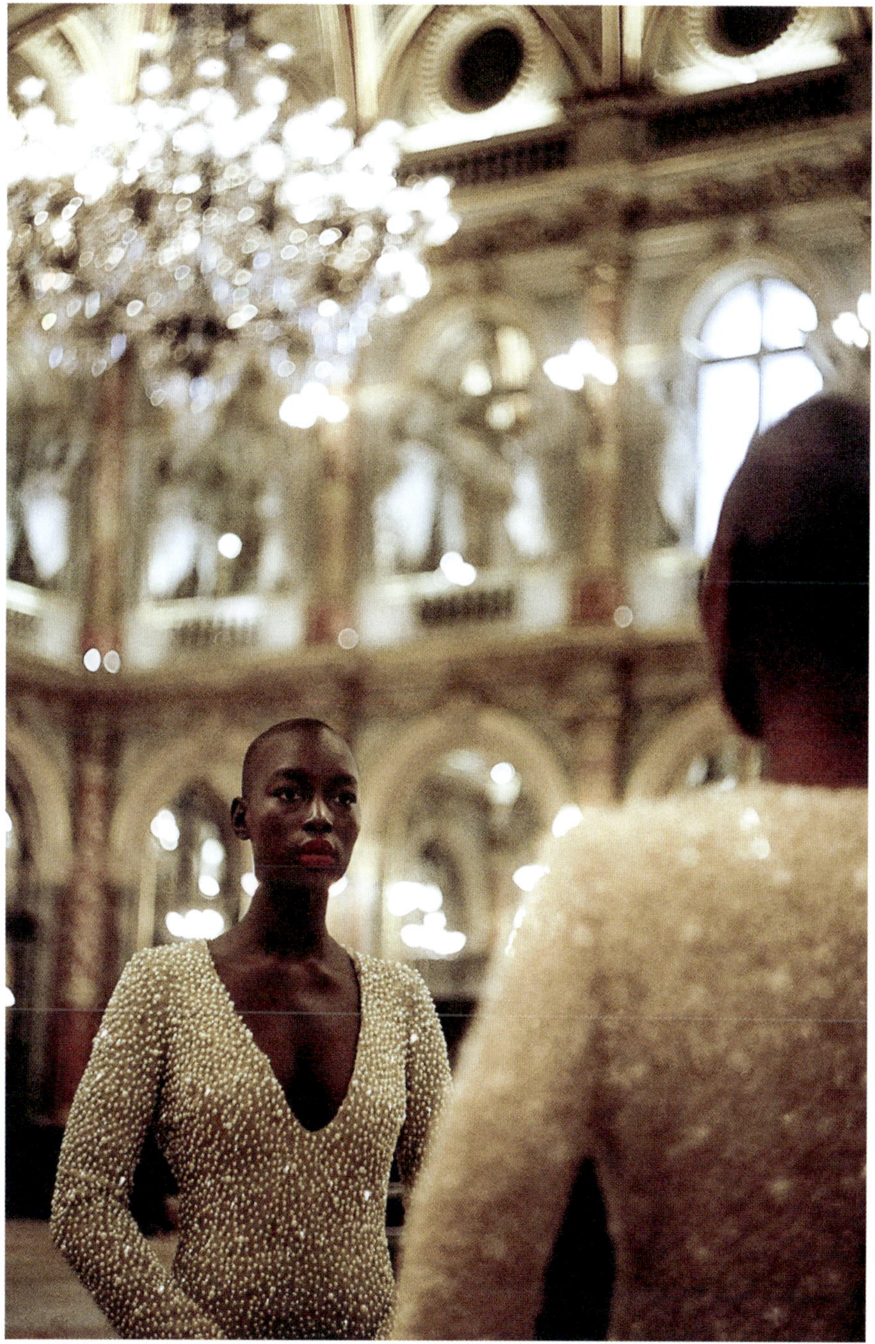

Rocío
by Jesus Rubio
Seville, Spain

I met Rocío at Feria de Abril, one of
the most popular events in the Andalusian capital,
where locals meet to celebrate friendship and family
with wine, food and traditional dancing.

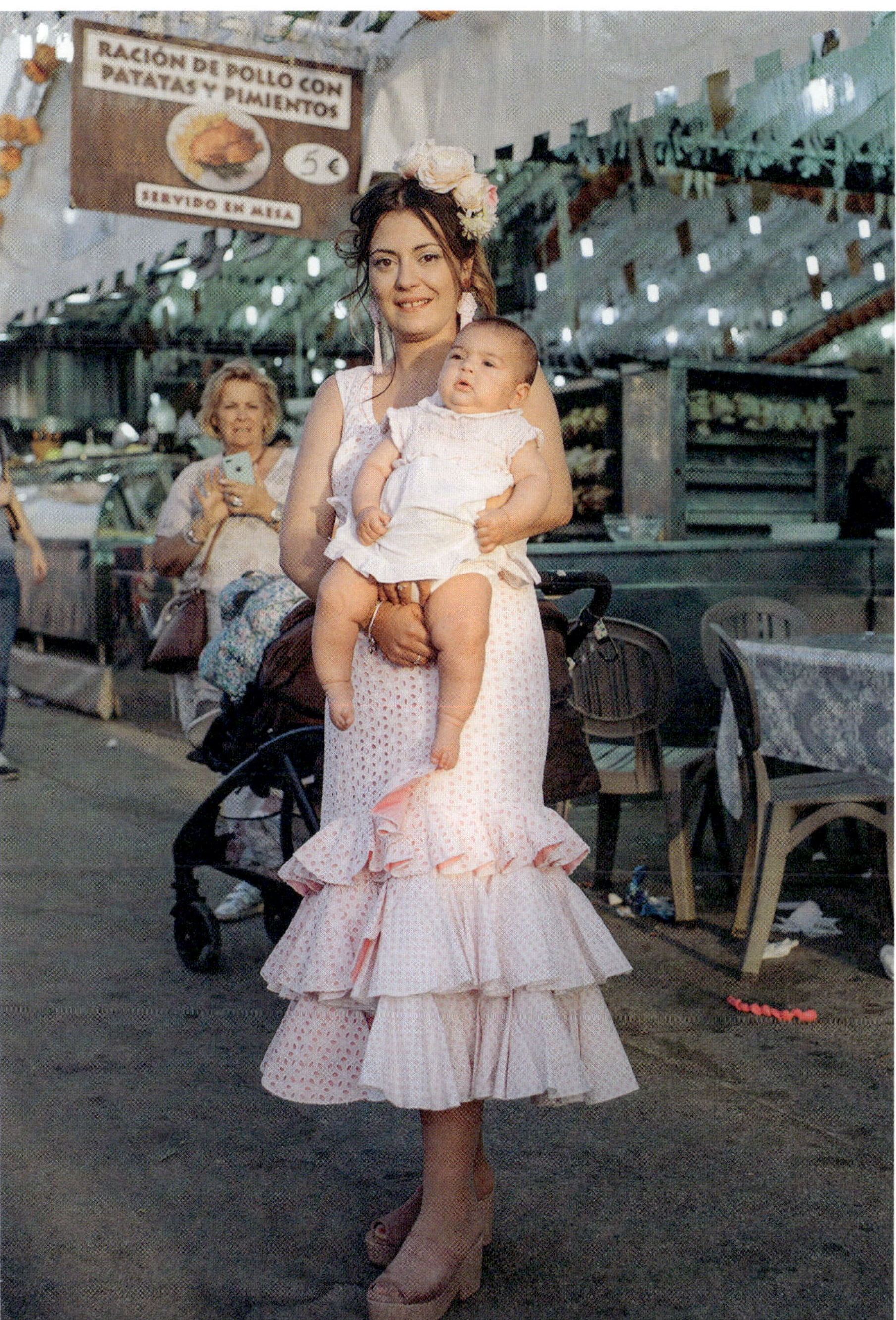

RACIÓN DE POLLO CON
PATATAS Y PIMIENTOS
5 €
SERVIDO EN MESA

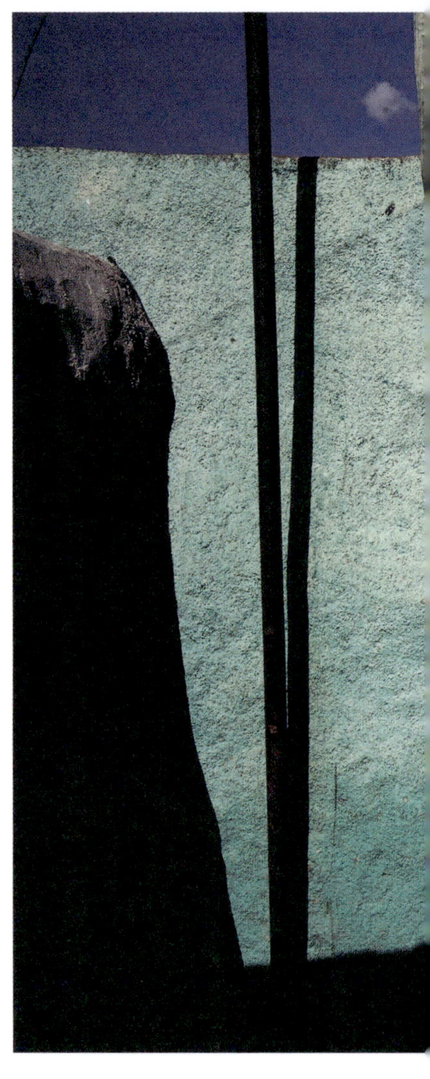

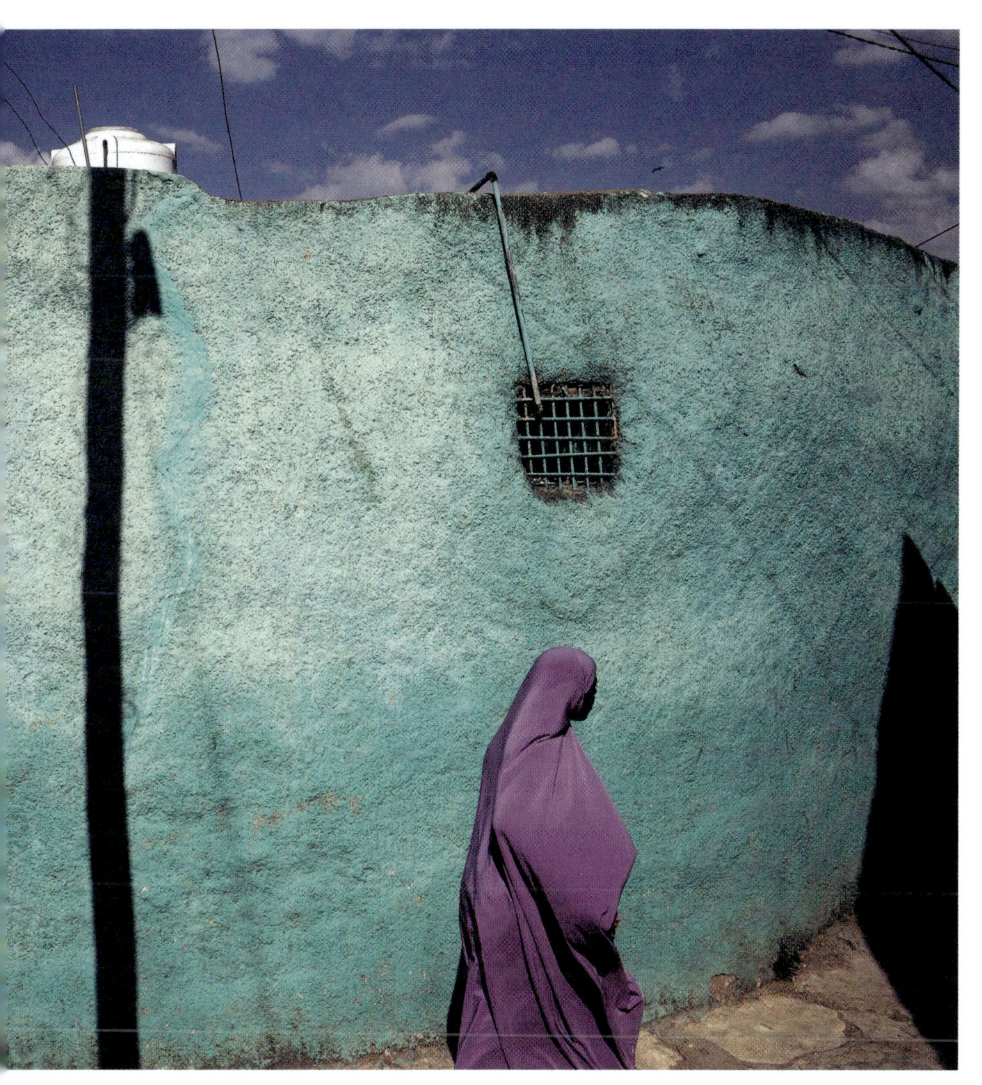

Colours of Harar
by Marika Poquet Morgat
Harar, Ethiopia

International Albinism Day
by Denisse Ariana Pérez
Dodoma, Tanzania

This beautiful little girl was walking hand
in hand with her grandfather, her main caregiver,
and her little brother, who also has albinism.
The grandfather had come to Dodoma to learn more
about the condition and to gain access to the
community and special healthcare, which is difficult
to access elsewhere. He wanted to ensure his precious
grandchildren had a dignified future.

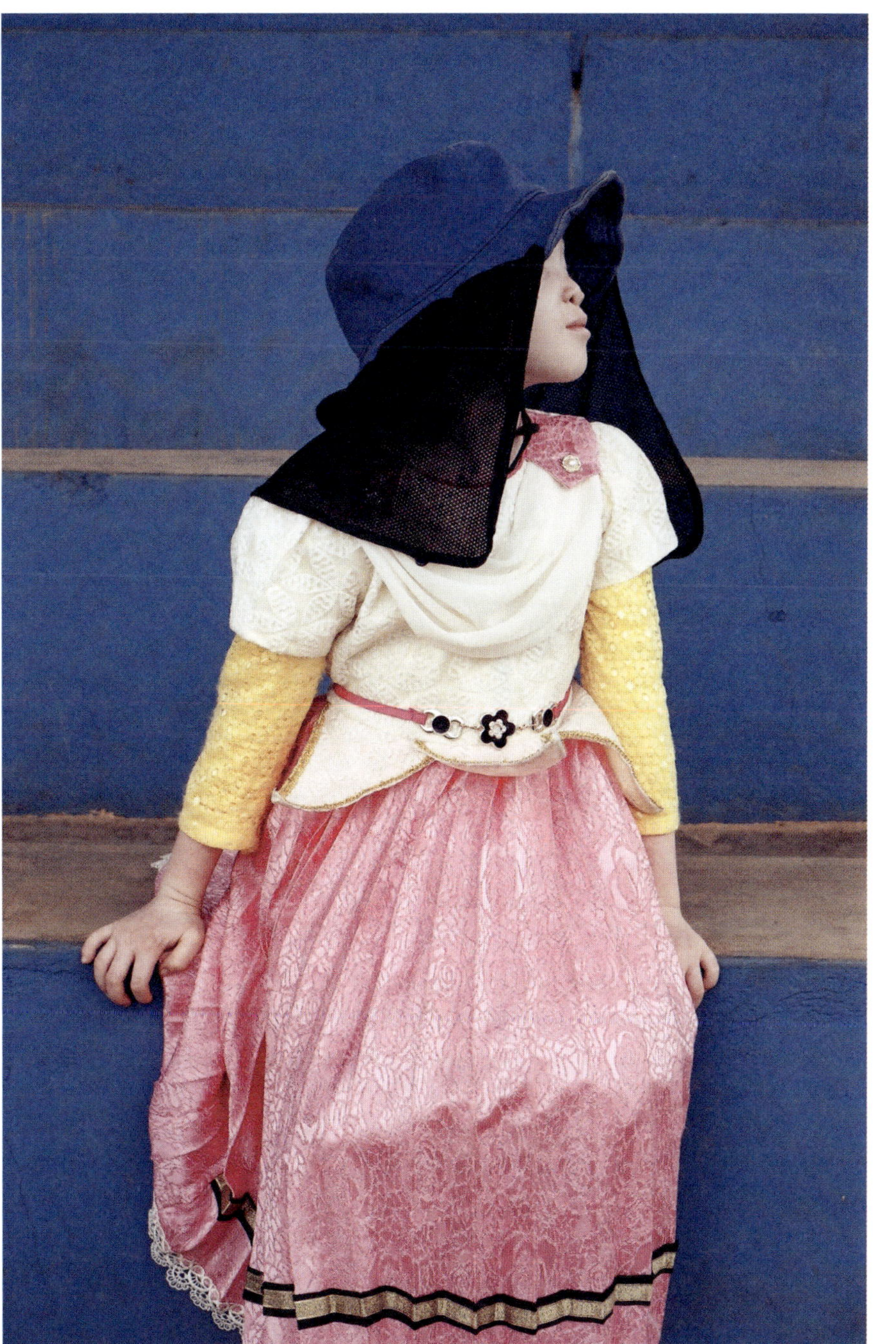

Ma Weisheng
by Hui Choi
Guangzhou, China

I took this picture for Ma Weisheng who
was happy to tell me that he was about to undergo
gender reassignment surgery and would
become 'a perfect woman'.

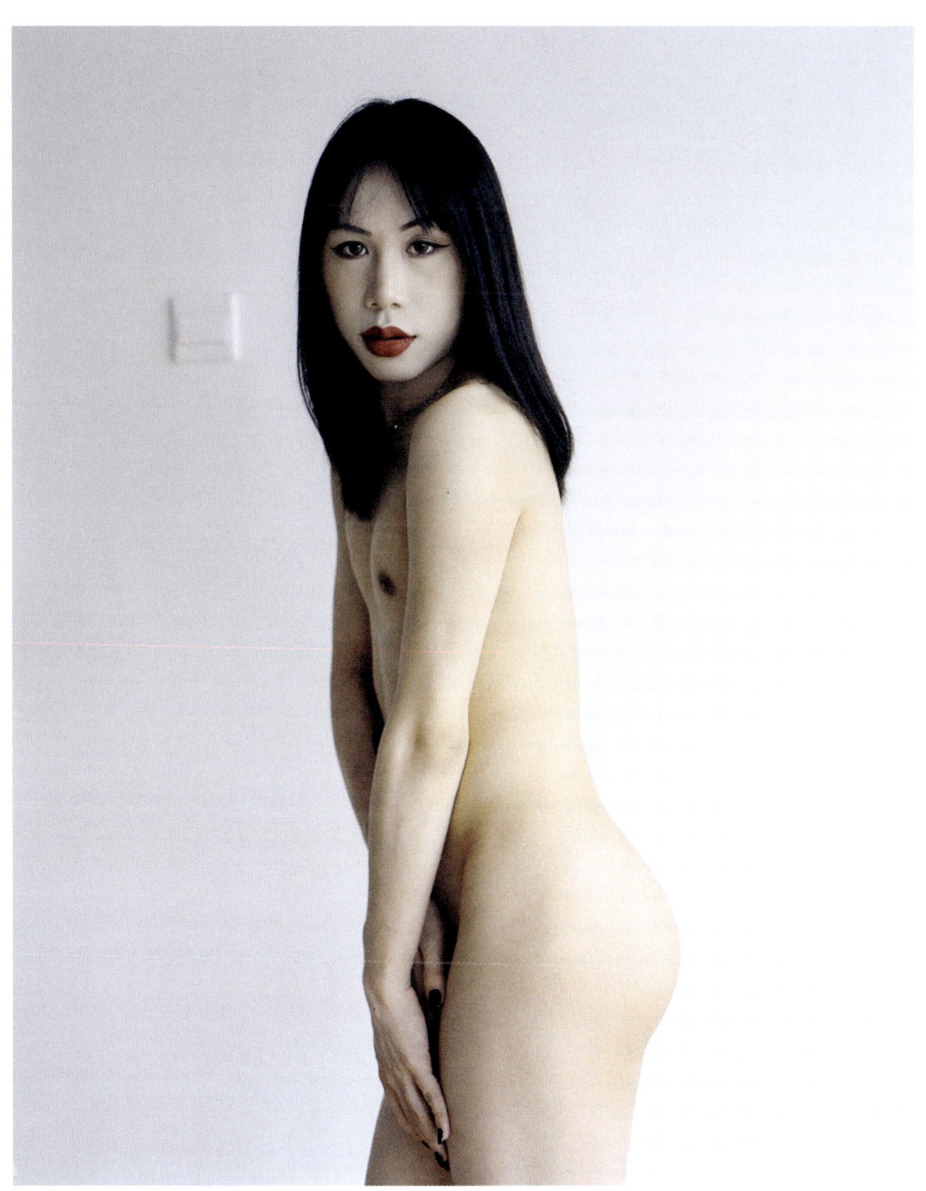

Rolando Martínez
by Katinka Herbert
Havana, Cuba

Rolando is a classical ballet dancer who lives
in Cuba. The country's Communist regime retains
a certain level of popularity among older generations
but many younger Cubans dream of a way out.

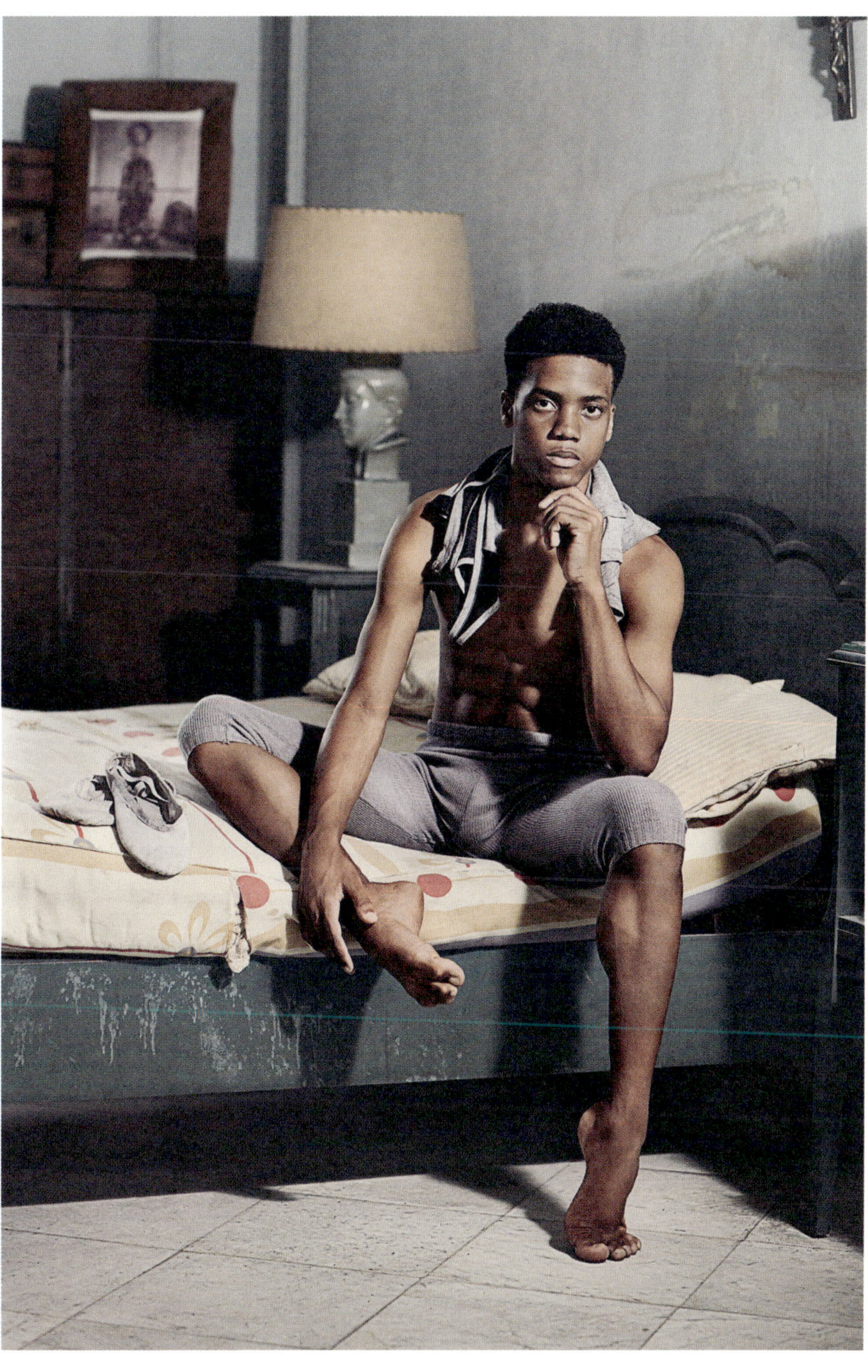

The Inuit Man
by Michael Novotny
Ittoqqortoormiit, Northeast Greenland

Mike (Inuits have Western names nowadays)
is a seal hunter in a small, remote village above
the Polar Circle in Greenland. His shotgun is for defence
against polar bears, which roam free in this frozen
land. Here he takes a break during a long dog-sledding
trip. The world needs more places like
this magical land.

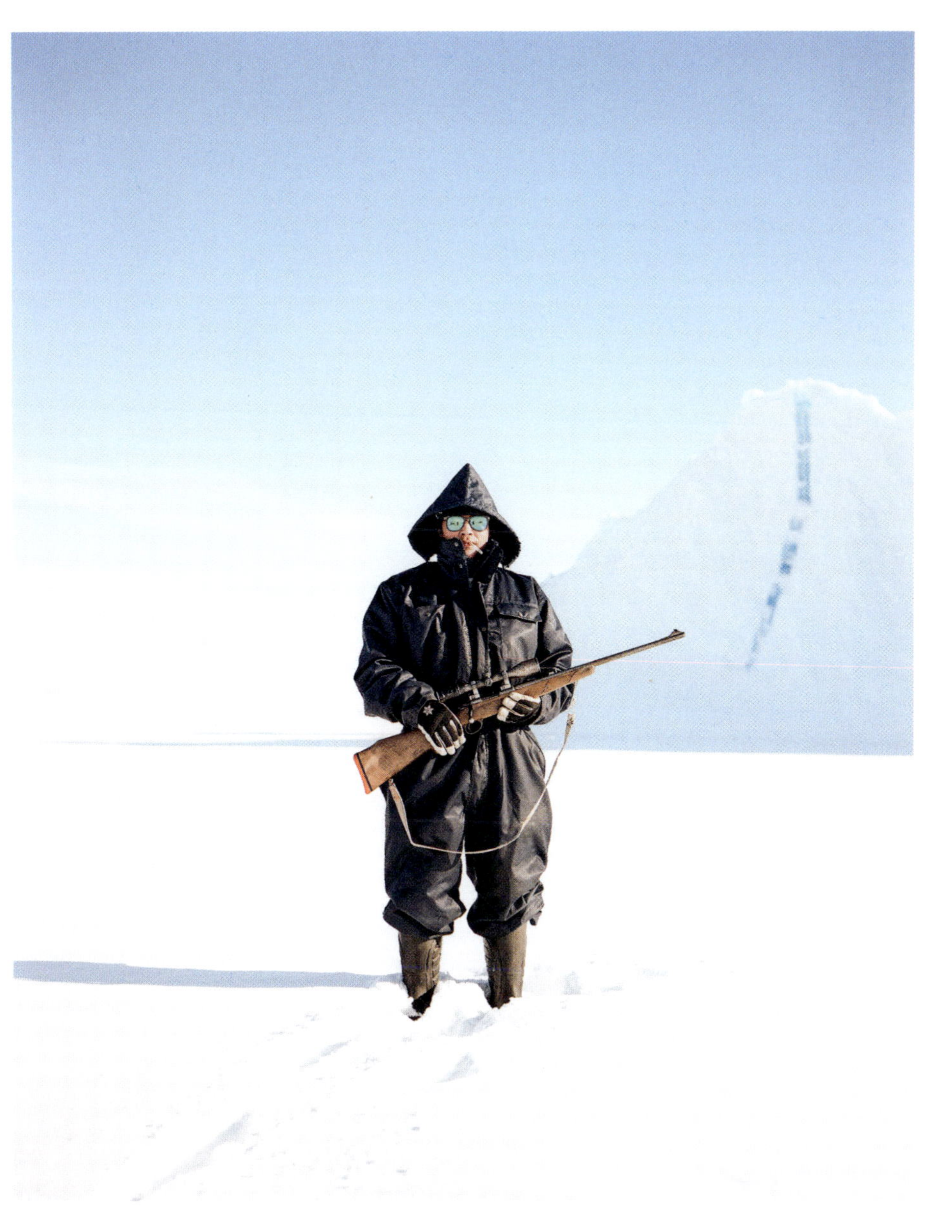

Abuti
by Obakeng Molepe
Sebokeng, South Africa

I came across this brother and sister one Good Friday
morning after they had been to church. They and many
others were walking long distances in the name
of their faith. I wanted to celebrate a day that means
so much to people of faith and to try and
understand why they are willing to sacrifice so
much for a god who might not exist.

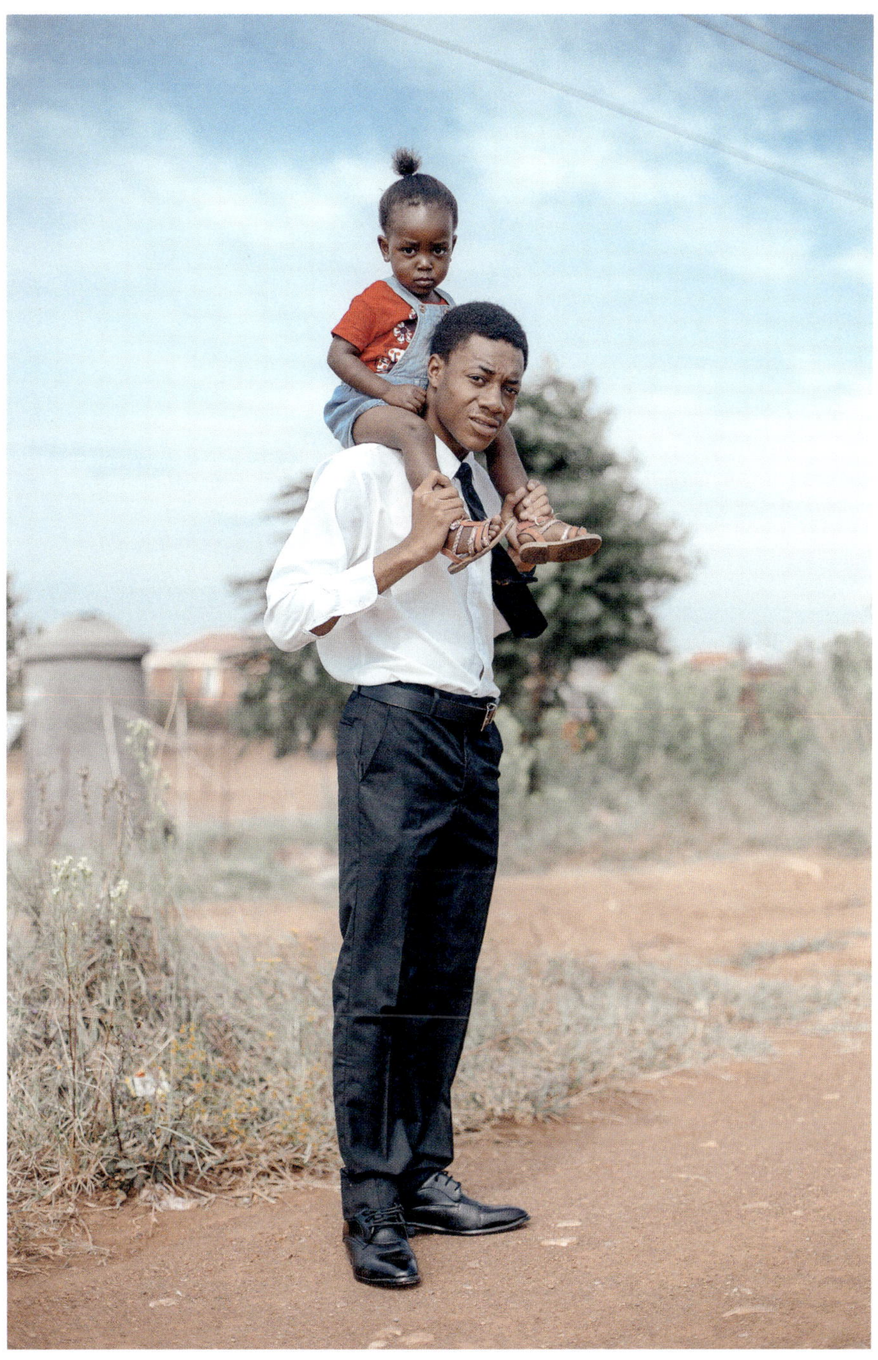

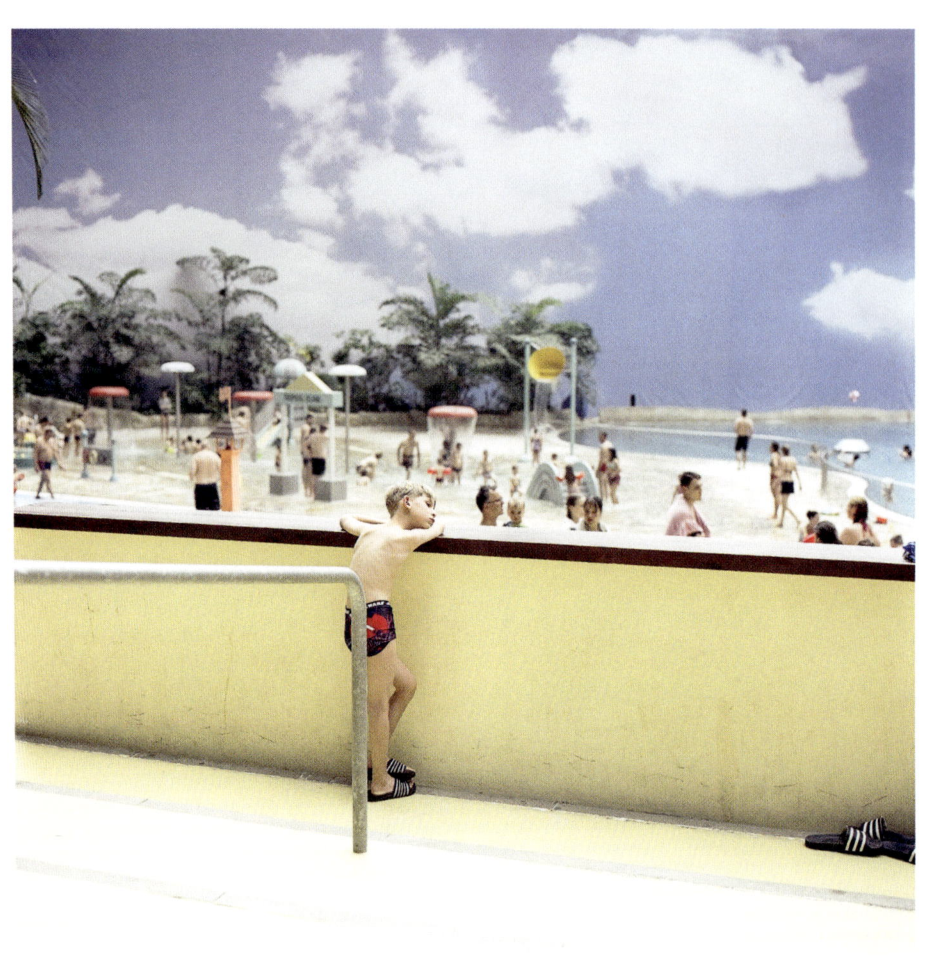

Untitled
by Milena Villalon
Brandenburg, Germany

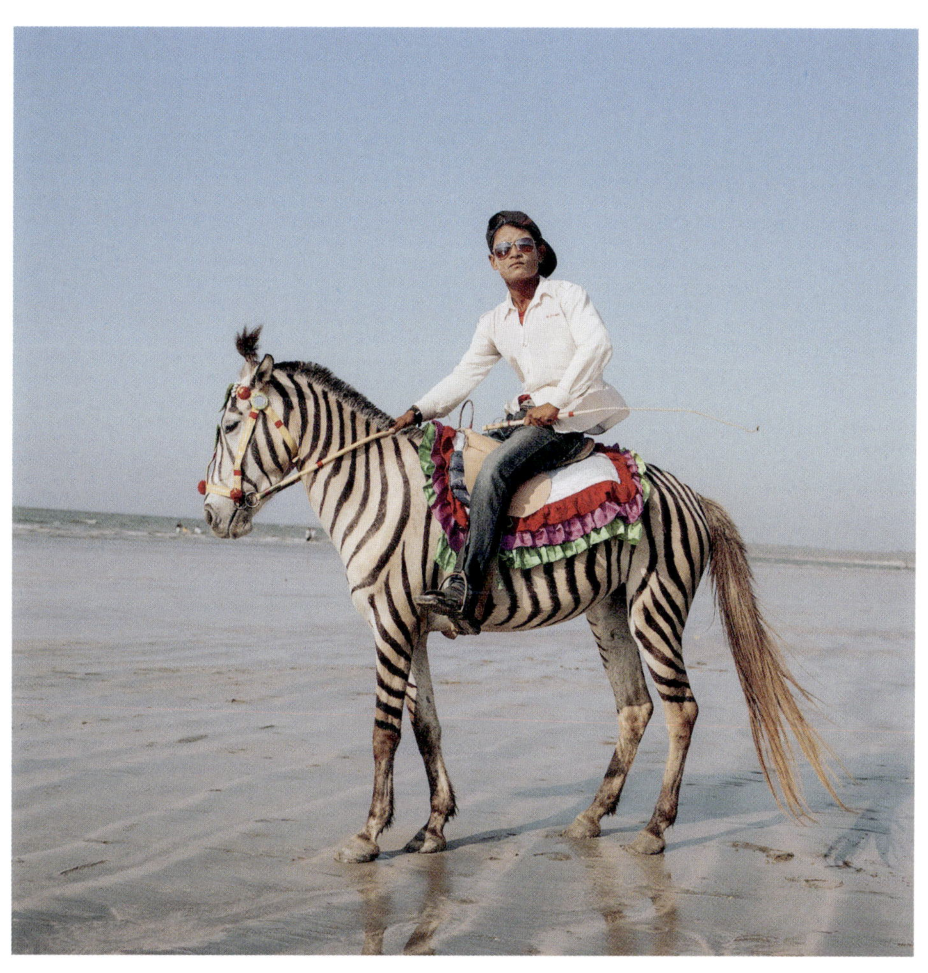

A Zebra in Myanmar
by Bruce Collier
Chaung Thar, Myanmar

While travelling in Myanmar I came across this
entrepreneurial local who had painted his horse to resemble
a zebra. He was charging visitors for rides and this was
his way of making his service stand out.

Bikes of Hanoi – Ball Man
by Jon Enoch
Hanoi, Vietnam

A local delivery rider distributes goods around
the stalls and shops in central Hanoi. I shot a series of
images depicting the bikes of Hanoi and their
unusual loads. The city is looking to restrict motorbikes
from the centre and rapid economic growth means
vans are increasingly replacing the two-wheeled
delivery riders.

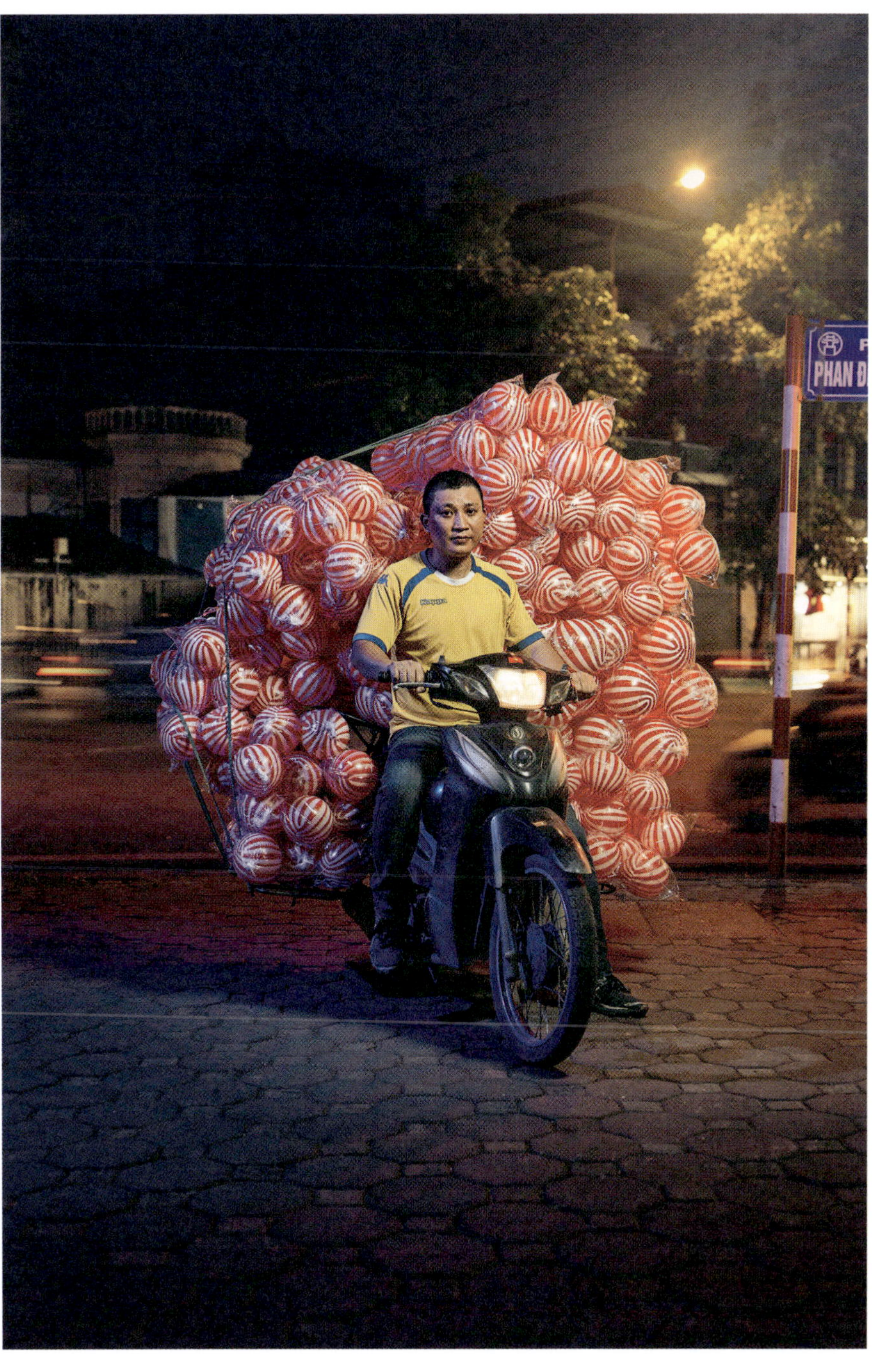

PHAN Đ

Homeless in North America
by Jan van Dasler
New York City, New York, USA

Ronnie lost his job, his wife and his house and
has since become homeless. He told me I was the first
person to talk to him in about three months.
He has been diagnosed with terminal liver cancer
and is trying to make the best of things.

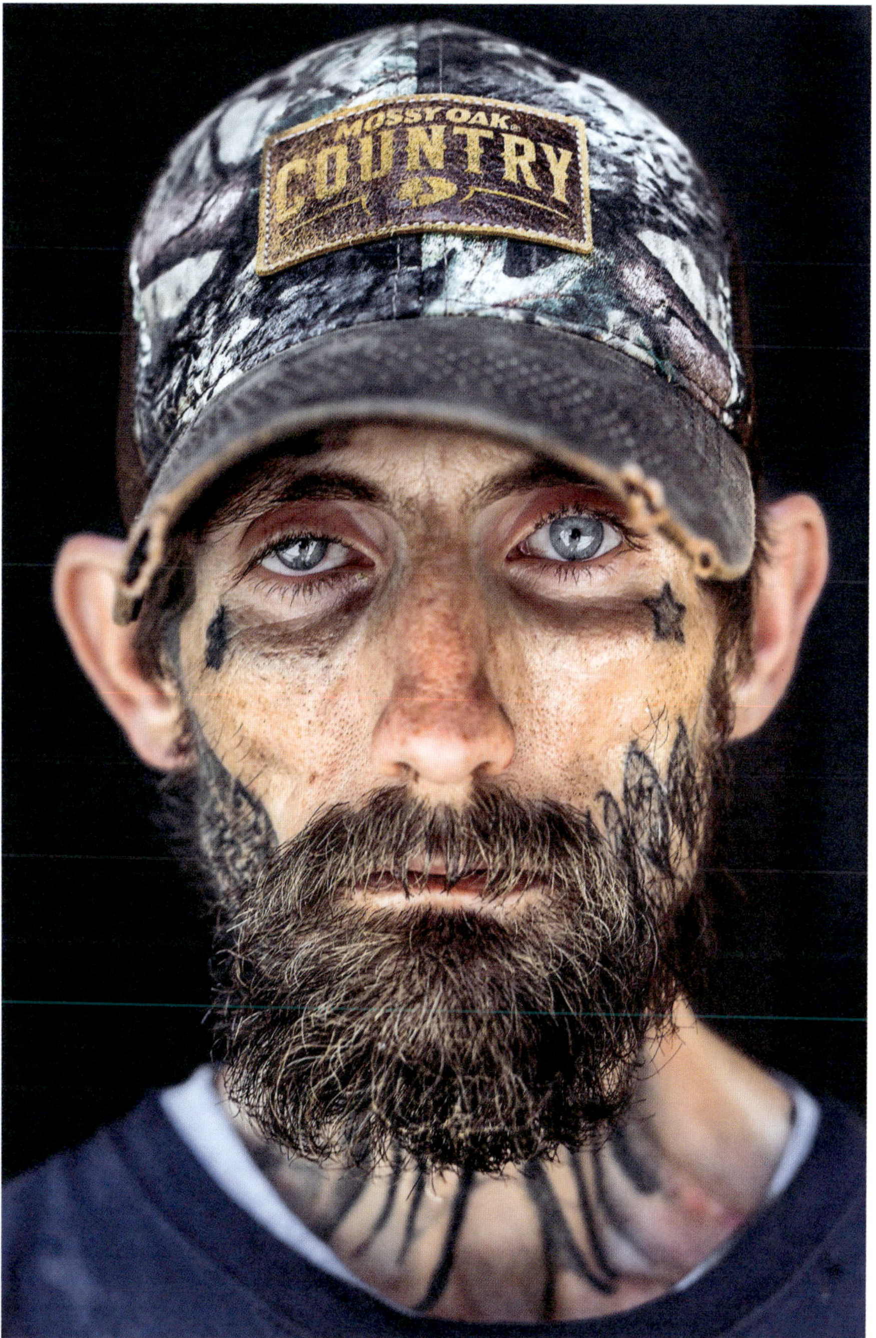
MOSSY OAK
COUNTRY

Arctic Convoy Veteran
by Jamie Williamson
Kilmarnock, Scotland

David Craig, 94, was 18 when he served on
the SS Dover Hill. Part of the 'Forgotten Convoy JW53'
that set out from Loch Ewe on 15th February 1943
for Murmansk in Russia, the ship was attacked
by German bombers on 4th April that year. A bomb tore
through the decks a few yards from where David
was standing, blowing him off his feet. David and two
officers helped to disarm the bomb for which
he received the King's Commendation.

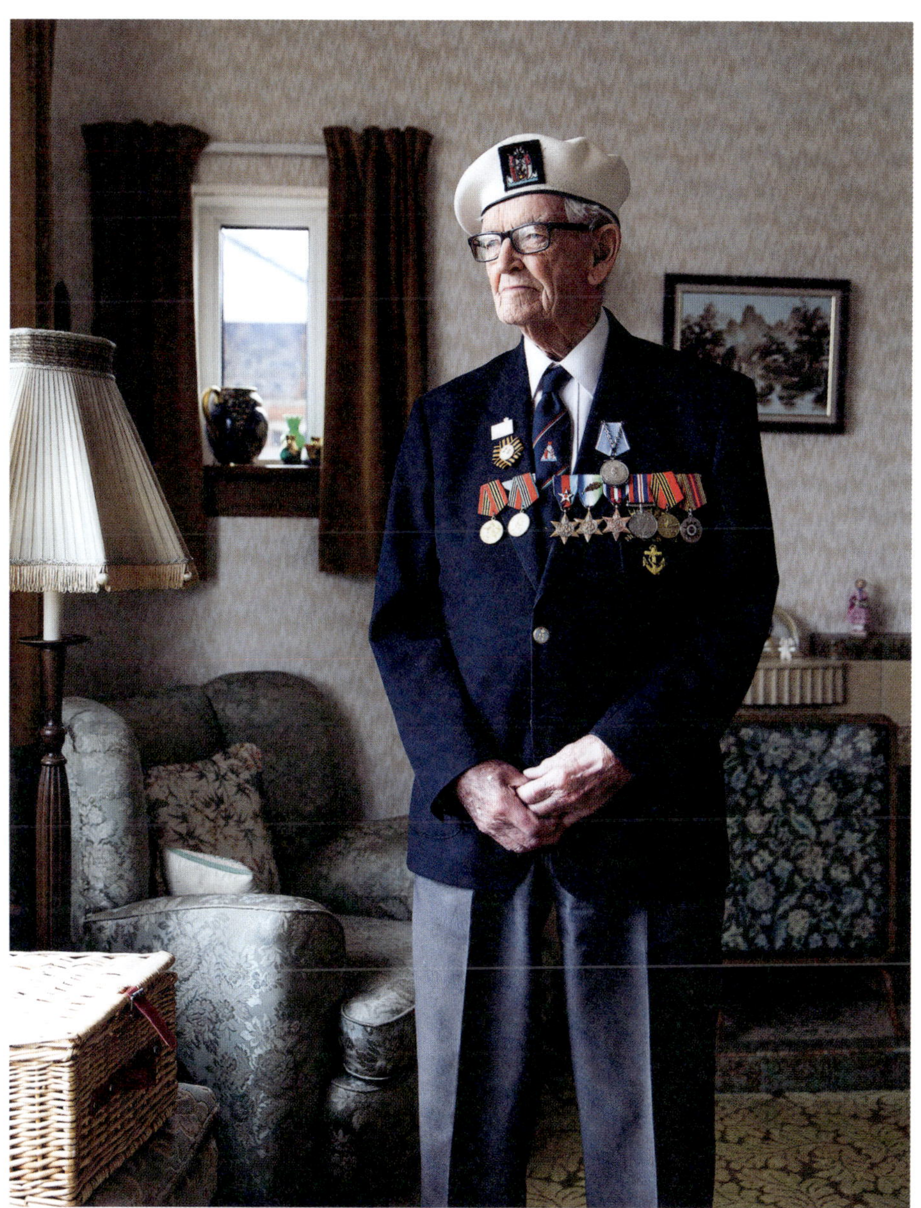

Beau
by Brock Elbank
London, UK

'On 15 April 2016 my life changed forever.
I slept at a friend's, expecting to go to work in the
morning, but I woke up from a coma three
months later. I'd received third degree burns to 65
percent of my body and fourth degree burns to
my left hand. I've been told I wrapped my friend in
blankets and helped her out the third storey
window and I went back into the fire to get my friend's
roommate. I've been told I'm a hero, but I wrestle
with that idea because I don't remember anything
of the accident.' – Beau

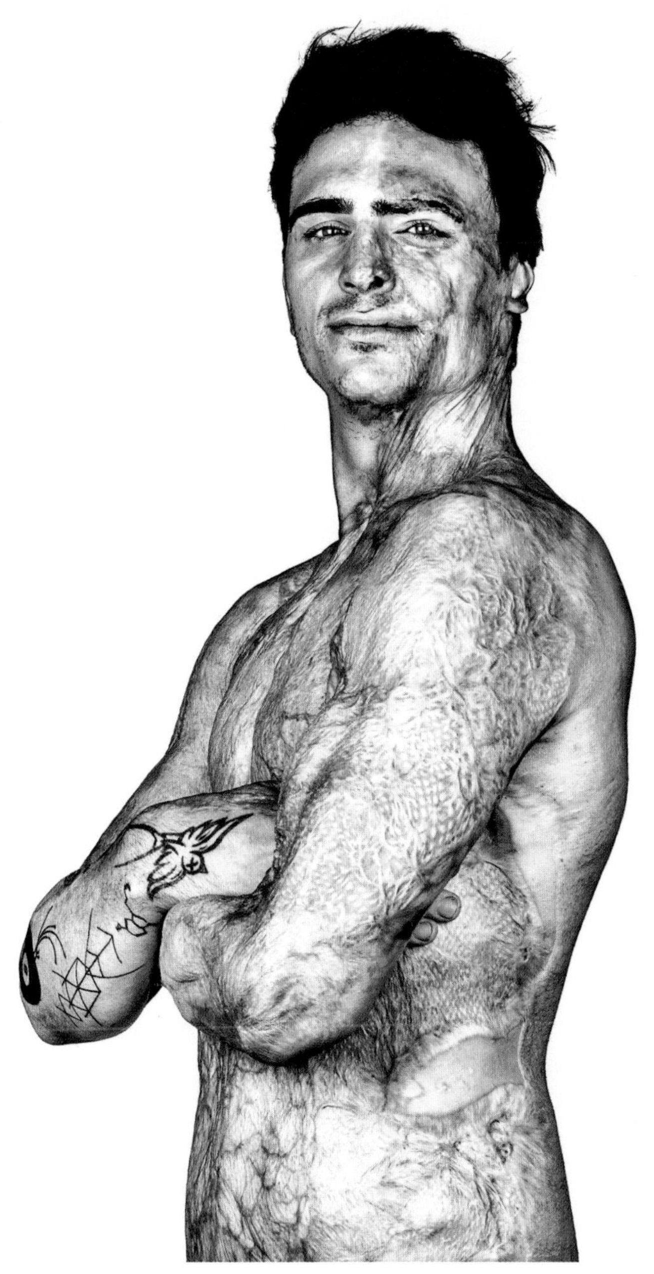

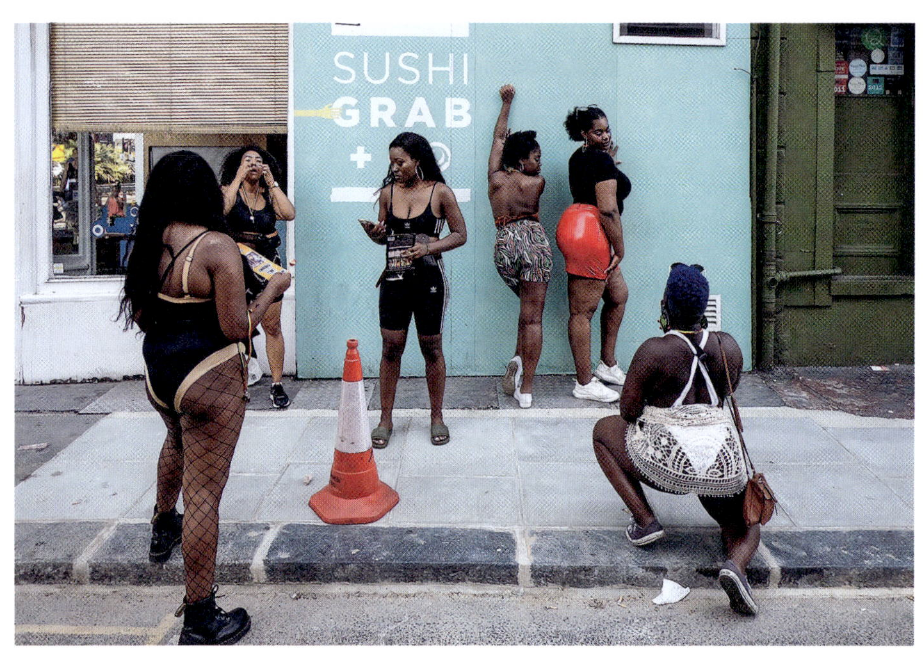

Notting Hill Carnival
by Matthew Roberts
London, UK

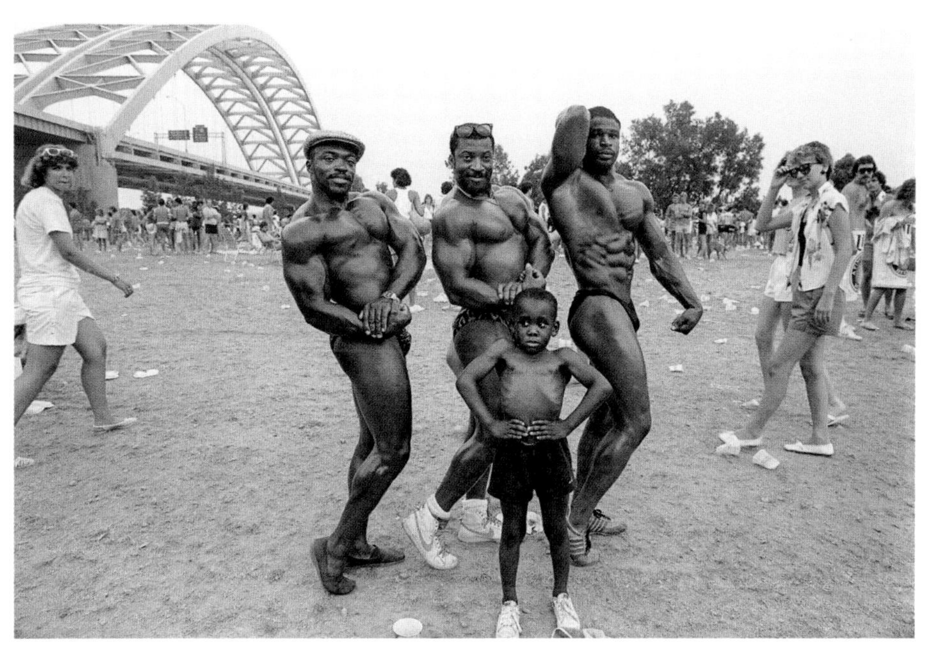

Muscle Men

by Maureen France
Cincinnati, Ohio, USA

I took this photo at a summer festival on
the banks of the Ohio River. Organisers created a
'beach' from tons of sand. It was a warm day.
I noticed a group of bodybuilders and a child walking
past me. I asked to take their photograph and they
struck this pose. The young boy did the same.
It was completely unrehearsed.

Alphonso Pollock
by Miles Kiernan
London, UK

Alphonso Pollock is a kind, friendly octogenarian
who has witnessed, and continues to witness,
an important era in Tottenham's history. He has lived
in Kenley, one of the tallest tower blocks in
the Broadwater Farm area, long enough to have seen
the flashpoints that placed the estate at the
forefront of British cultural and political history since
its completion in 1973. In the 1980s, the estate
acquired a reputation as one of the worst places
to live in the UK.

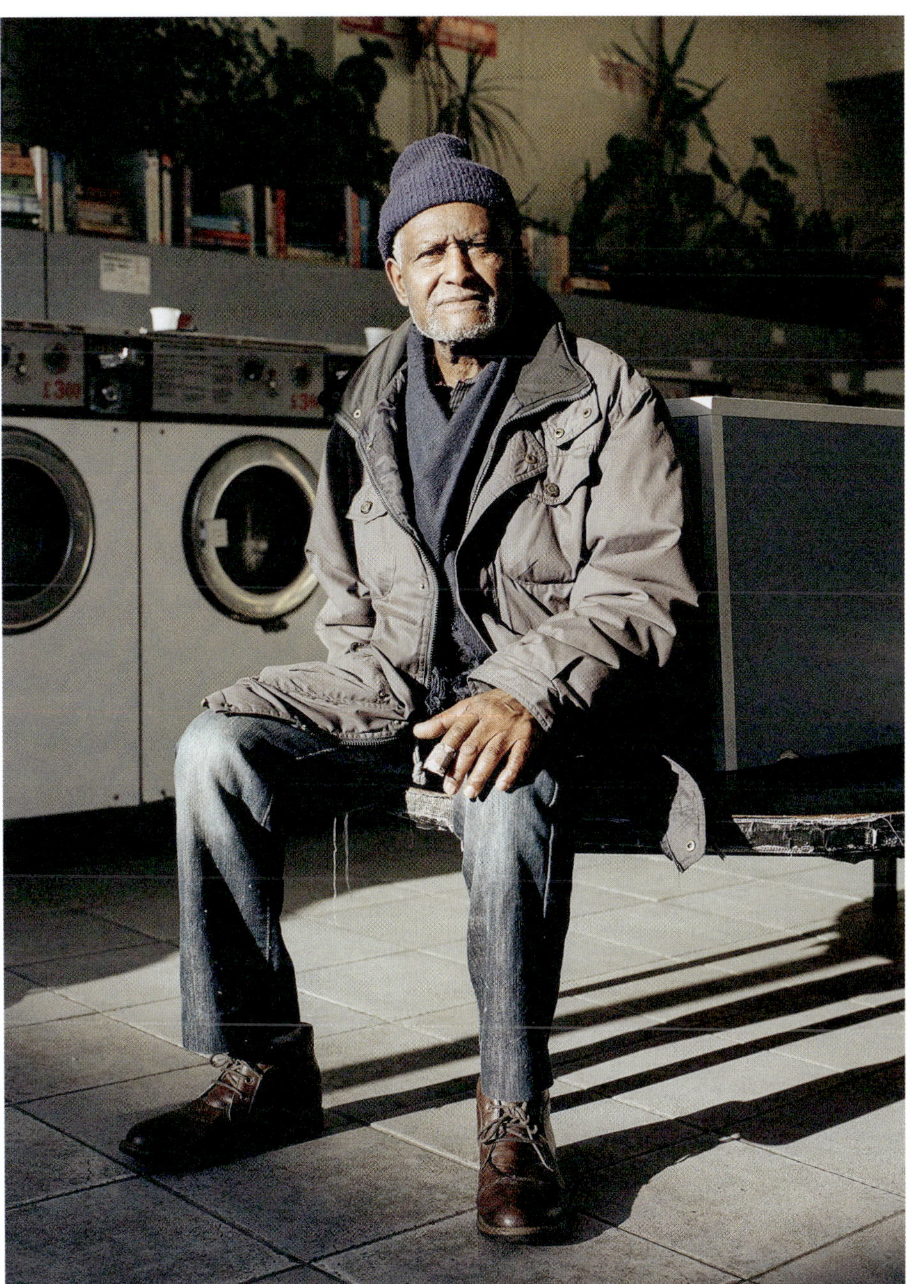

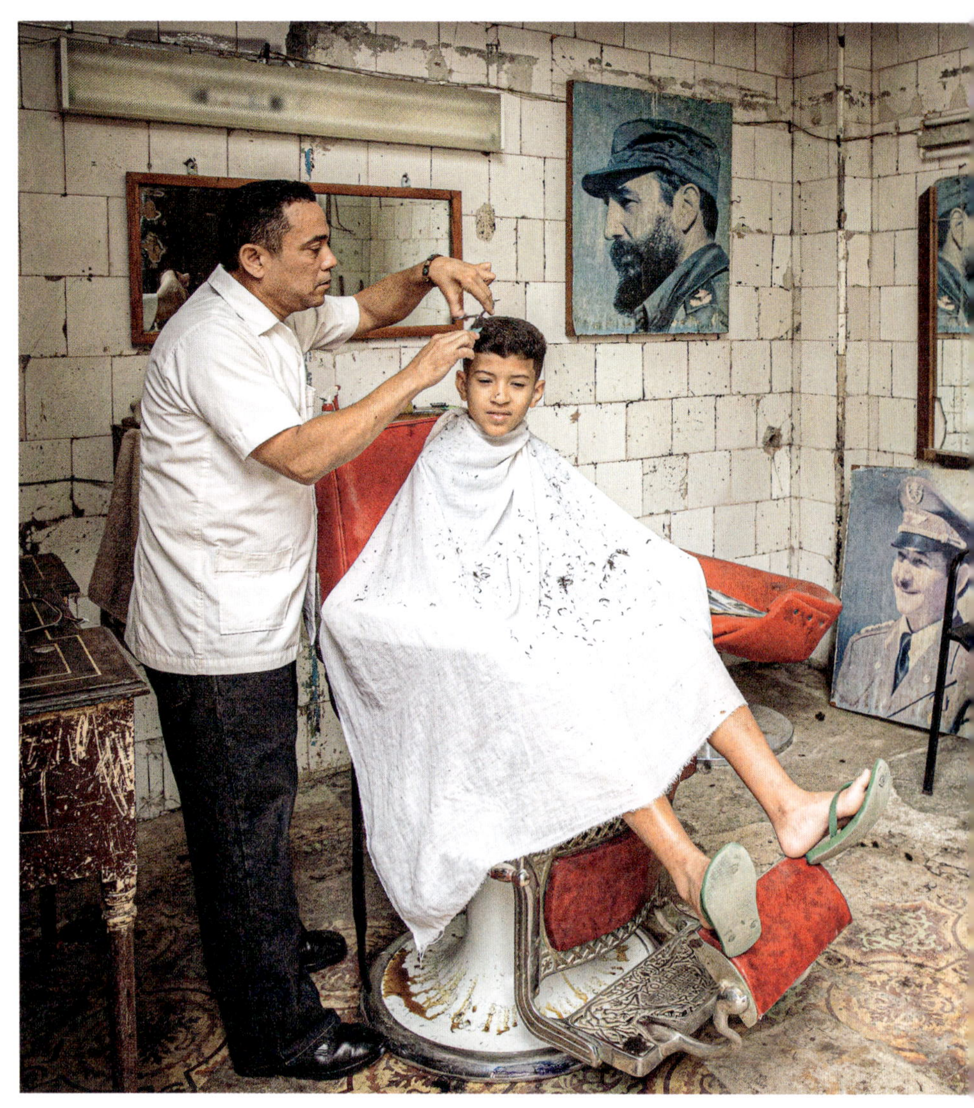

The Barber's Shop
by Roy Morris
Havana, Cuba

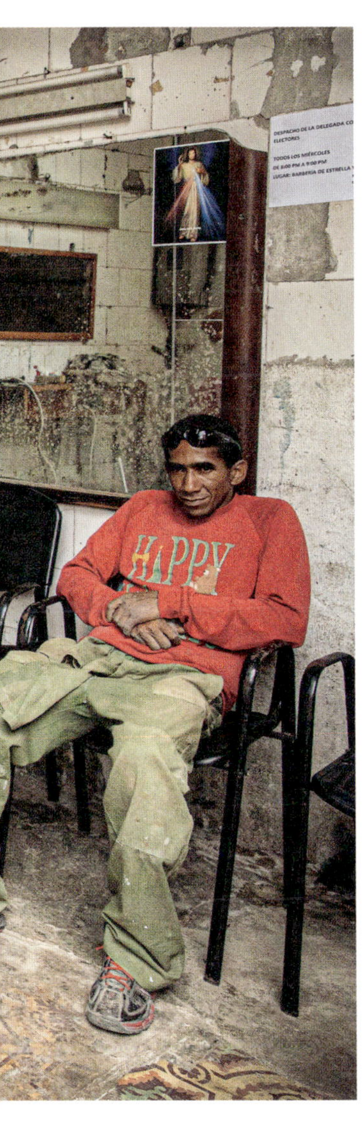
DESPACHO DE LA DELEGADA CO
ELECTORES

TODOS LOS MIÉRCOLES
DE 6:00 PM A 9:00 PM
LUGAR: BARBERÍA DE ESTRELLA Y
HAPPY

Father and Son
by Isiah Babilonia
Norfolk, Virginia, USA

I often photograph the residents in the communities
around my university. I had previously taken a portrait of
this man's son and when I returned to give him
a print he pulled me aside and asked if I could take
a picture of him with his son.

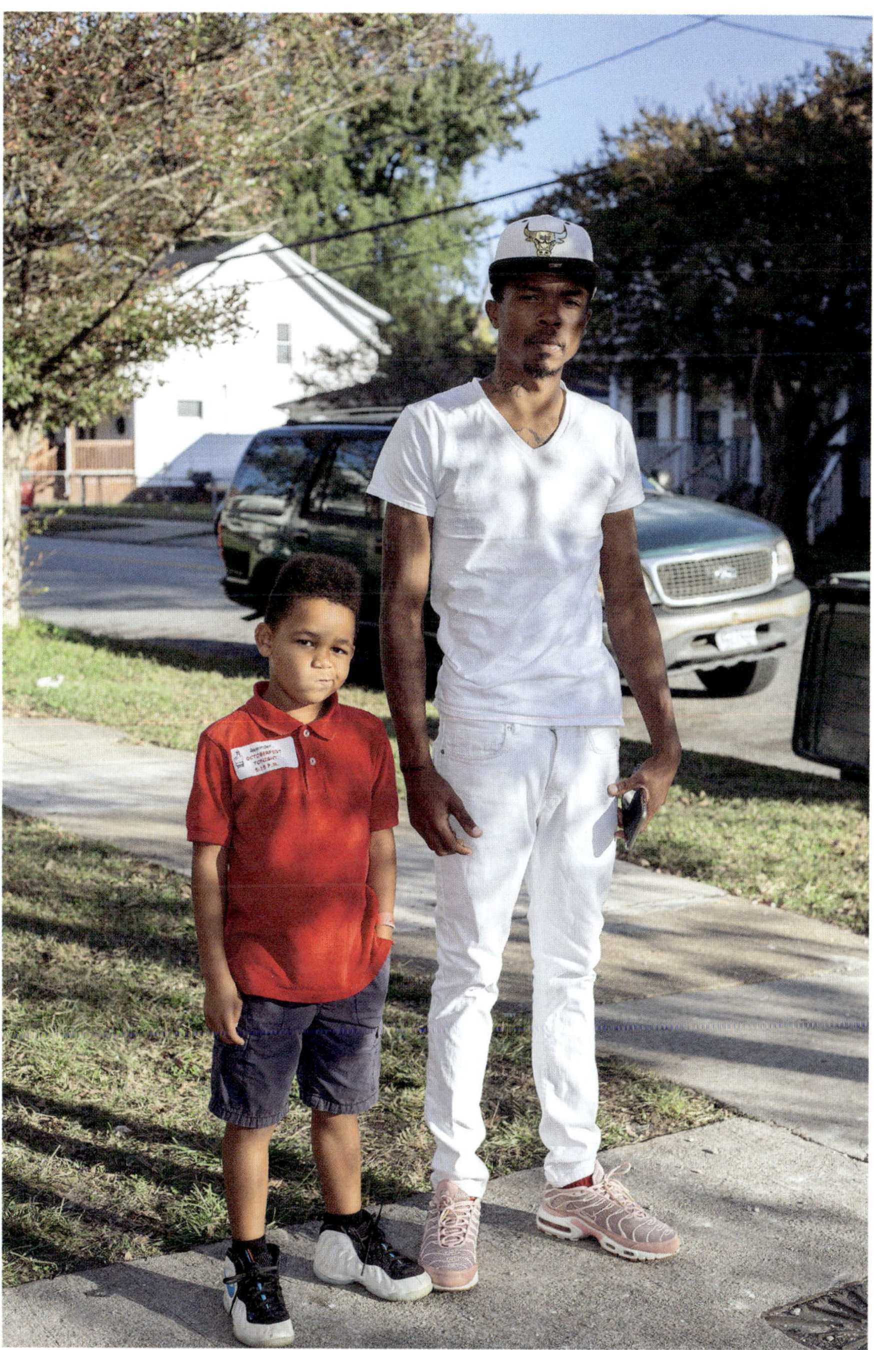

Jason (They/Them)
by Ross Landenberger
New York City, New York, USA

I met Jason in an internet skateboarding forum
in 2006. We were both closeted and had gone online
because we felt isolated by sexism and homophobia
in the sport. We're working to make skateboarding more
welcoming to queer people.

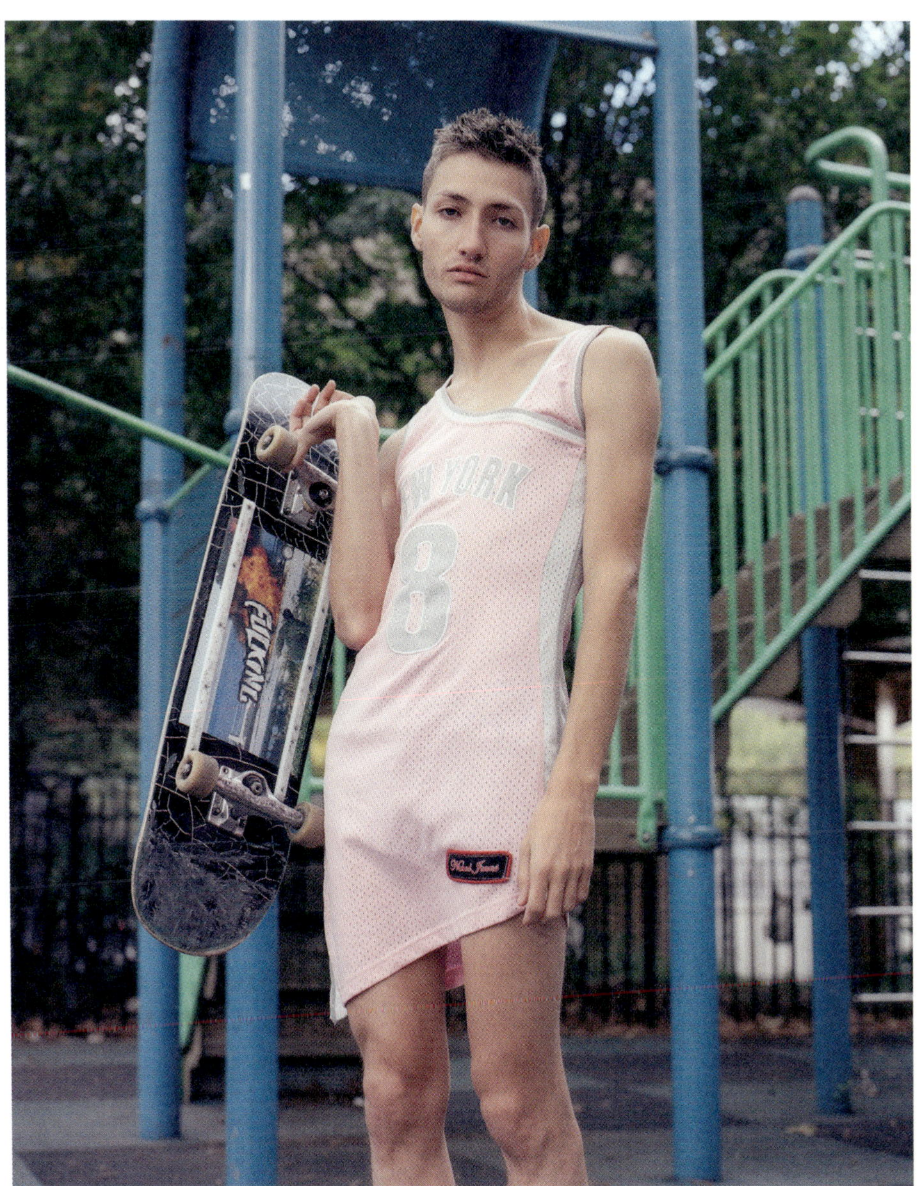

Borya
by Michal Solarski
Odessa, Ukraine

I met Borya on the beach in Prymorsk. I was
attracted to his slim figure, posture and overall look.
I only managed to ask his name before he
disappeared in the dark waters of the Black Sea.

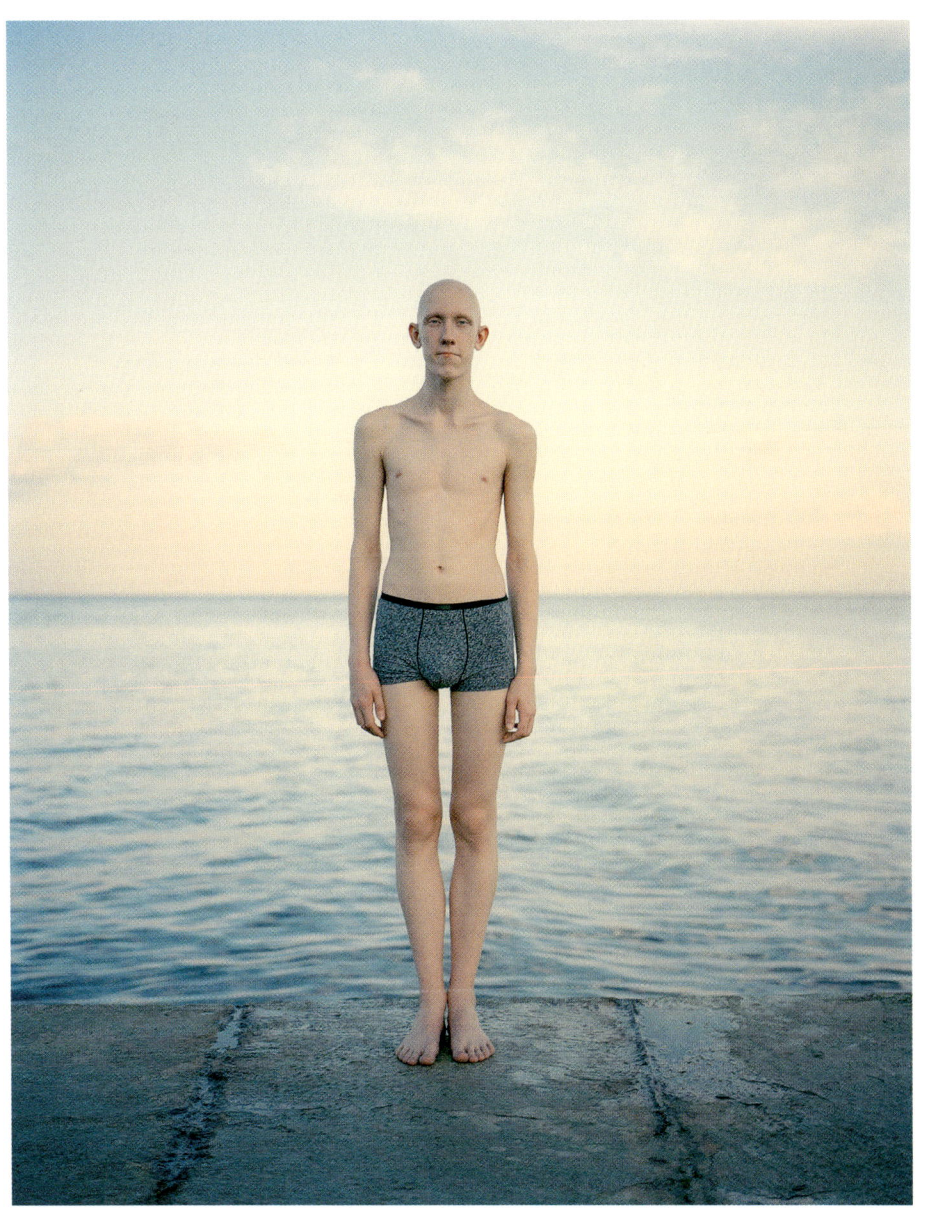

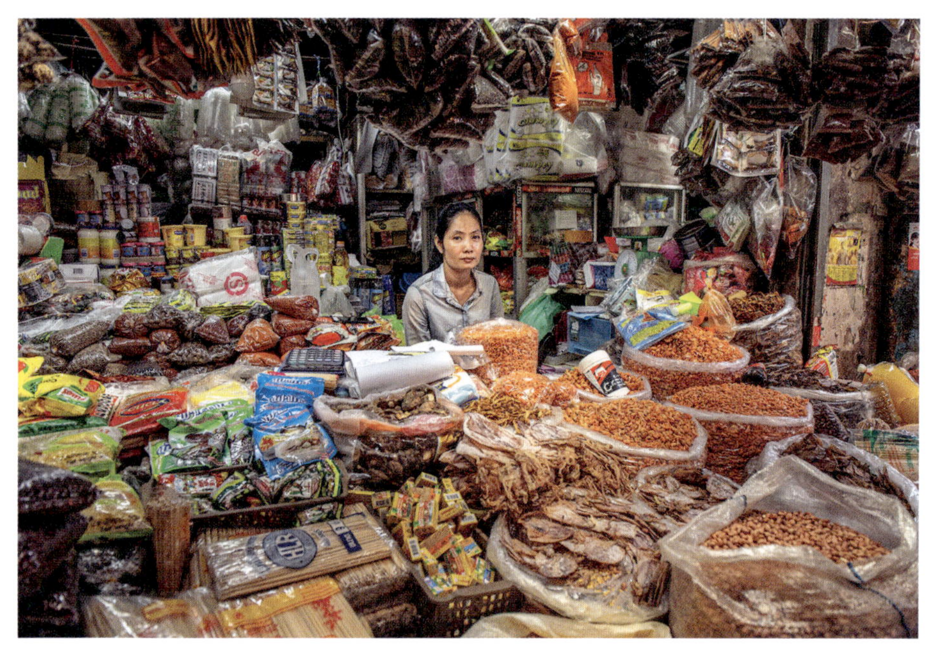

Saleswoman
by Miriam Ramalho
Siem Reap, Cambodia

I saw this woman while visiting a market. She was
selling so many items, which made it difficult to get in
close to talk to her. She looked frozen in position.

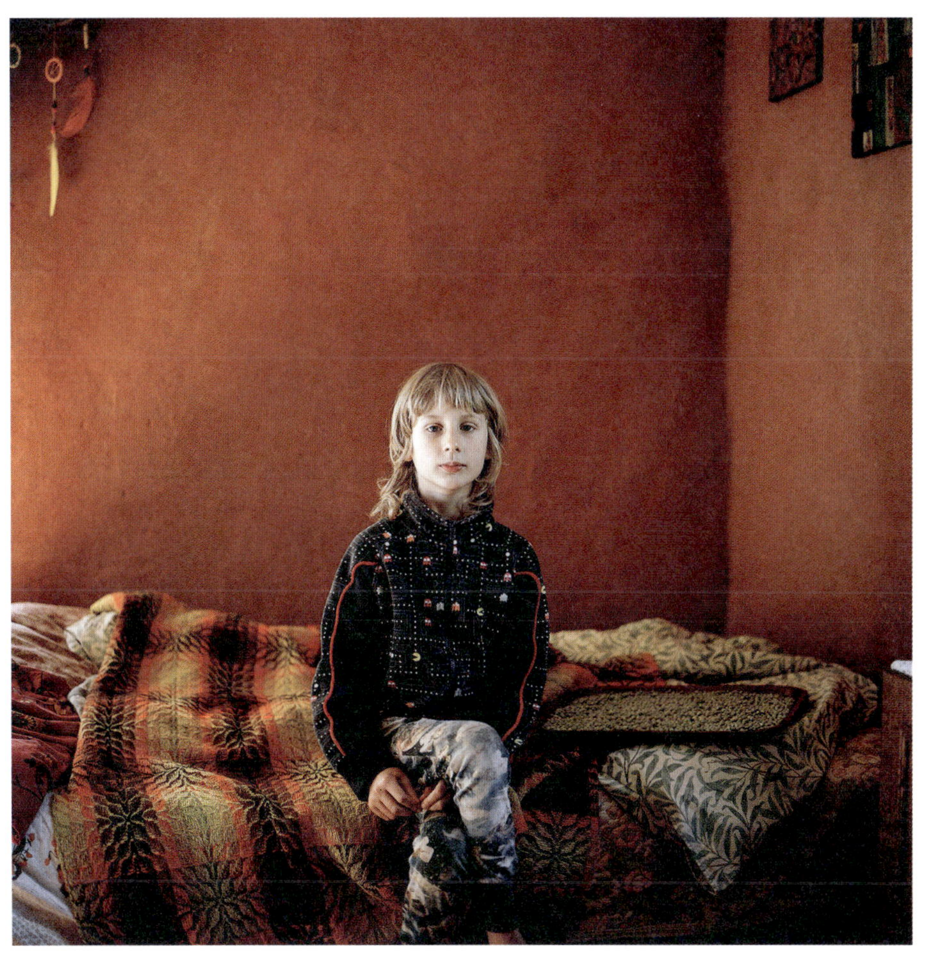

Boy with Pea Seeds
by Kadri Otsiver
Külaoru, Estonia

This is Louie, the son of Triinu who runs Estonia's
biggest permaculture garden. The permaculture community
believes that small-scale community-based agriculture
is the future of food.

Mangrove Oysters
by Vincent Karcher
Casamance, Senegal

A woman who harvests oysters for a living
poses in front of her canoe. She had been waiting for
the low-tide so she could harvest the oysters that
grow on the roots of the mangrove.

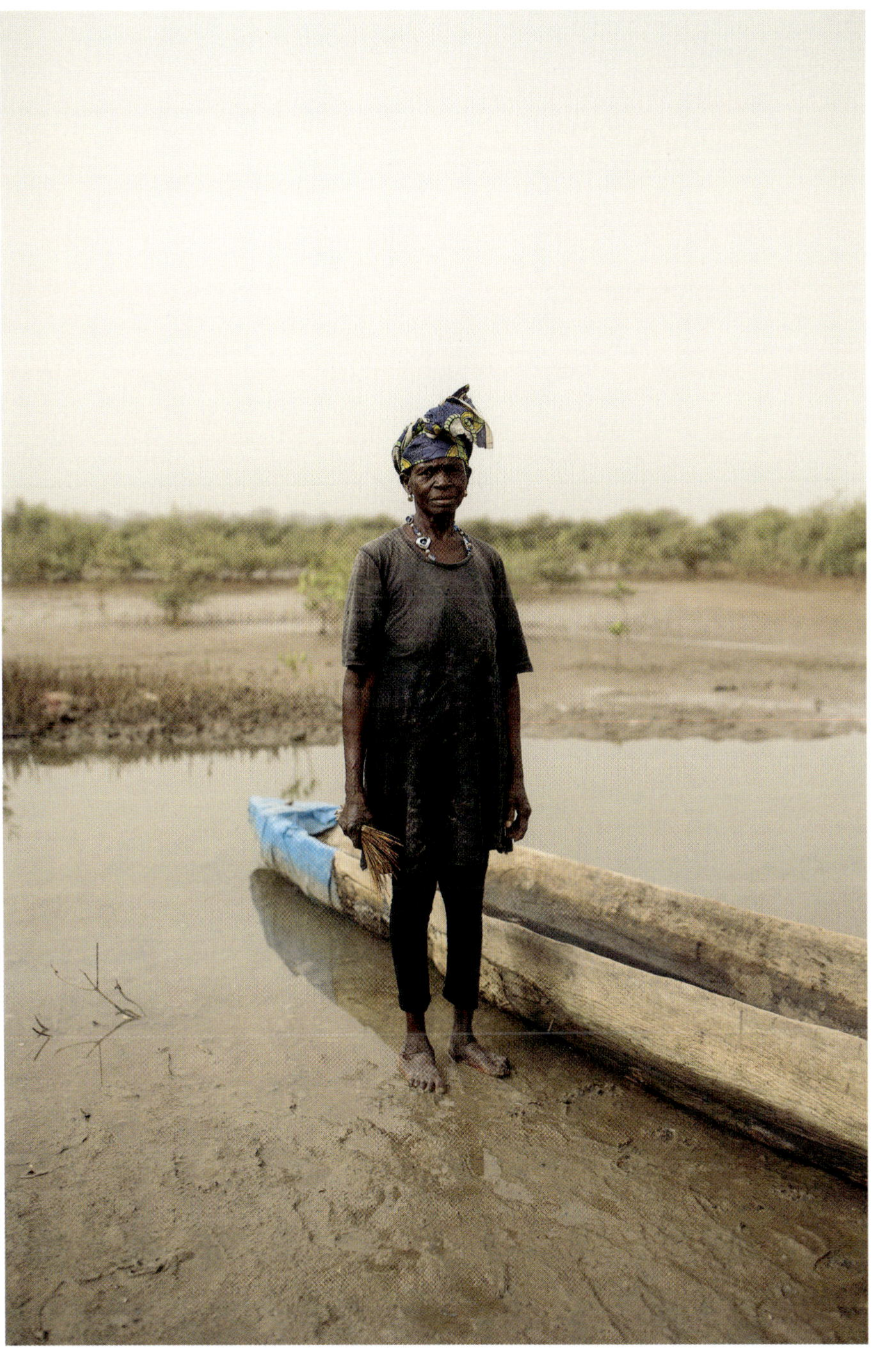

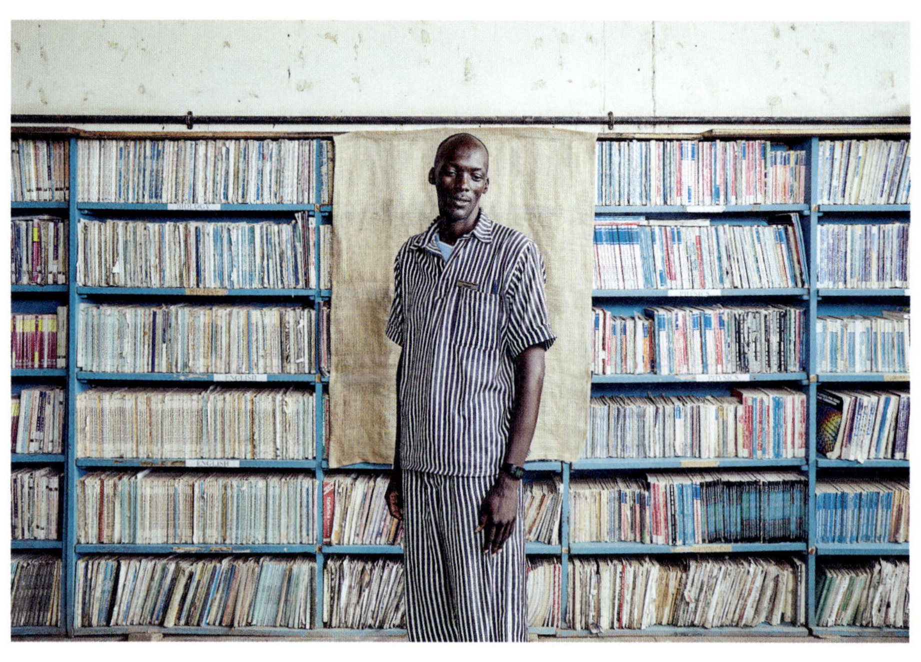

Mbola in the Library
by Jack Lawson
Naivasha, Kenya

Mbola is serving time in Naivasha Maximum
Prison, a couple of hours drive from Nairobi.
He is working with the African Prisons Project as
a paralegal, helping other inmates with legal
matters such as appeals.

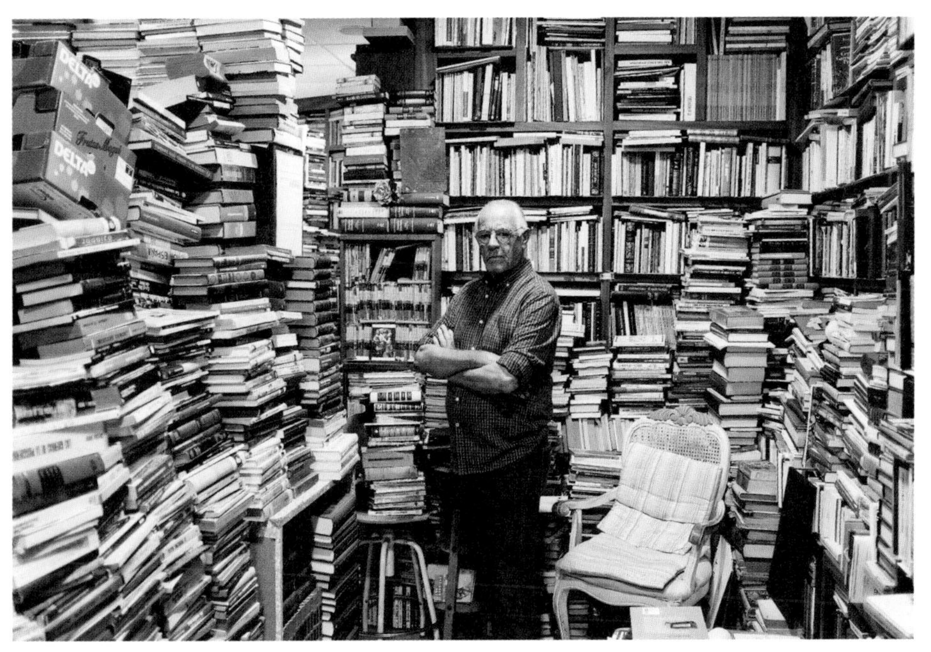

The Literary Passage
by Matteo Delred
Andalusia, Spain

With his folded arms and stern look, this man,
pictured here in secondhand bookshop Planeta ZOCAr,
looks like some kind of literary gatekeeper.
The shop has more than 30,000 books from floor to
ceiling. It is a place that believes in community
art and supports local artists by giving them
somewhere to collaborate and exhibit.

Darren
by Aiyush Pachnanda
London, UK

Darren is a barber and a former musician.
I met him through a project I made about tattoo
culture, which has become an ongoing body
of work. People often judge Darren because he is
heavily covered with tattoos. The more
I spend time with him, the more I care for him.

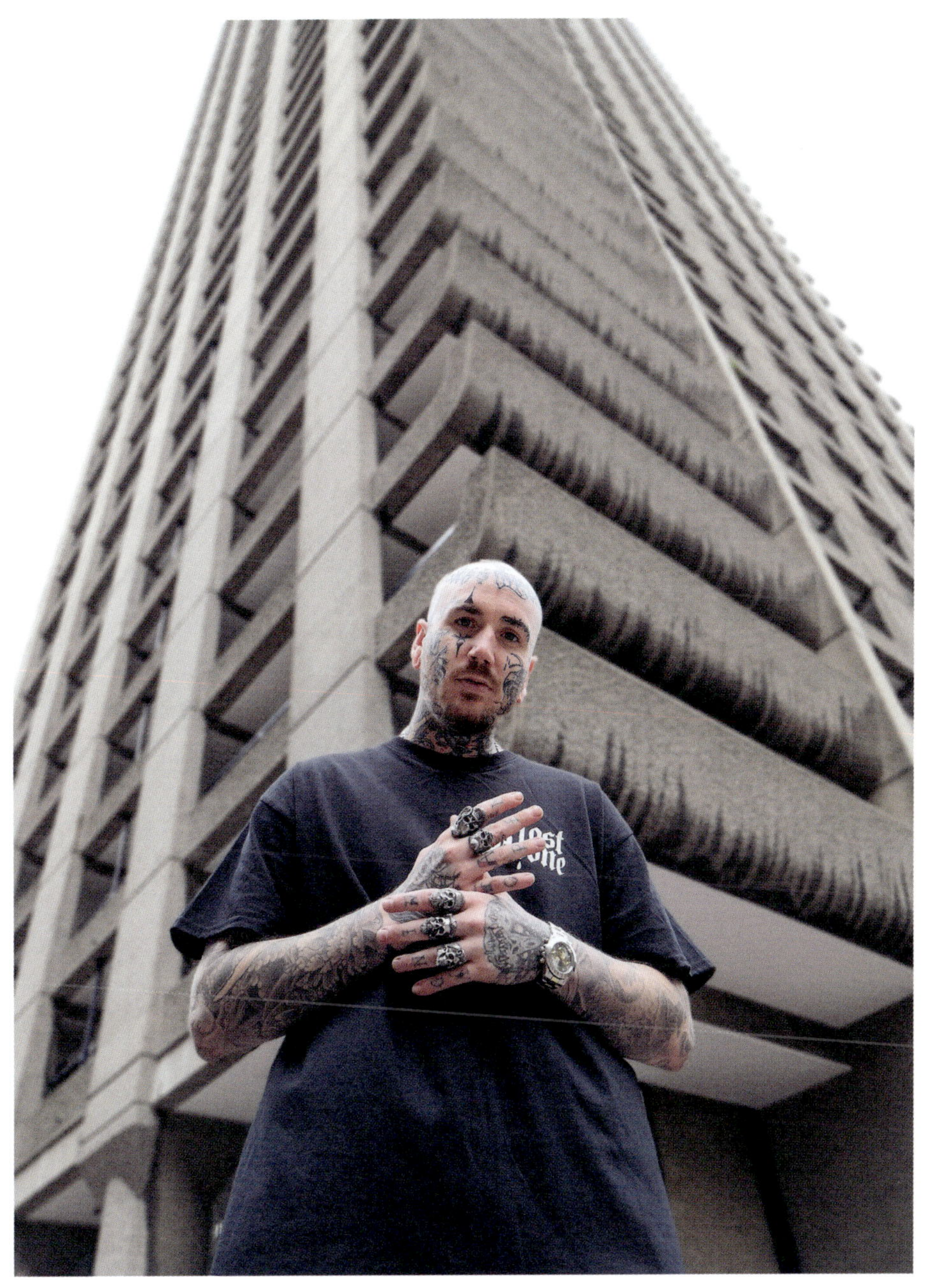

Marieke Polderdijk
by Wouter le Duc
Arnhem, The Netherlands

Marieke is a performance artist who creates art
with her body and voice. She is also one of my best friends.
A burnout triggered a deeper awareness of her
body and soul. I took this portrait when she was only
able to be active for a couple of hours each day.
In the months that followed, Marieke started to get better
and has since graduated from art school and continues
to write and create performances.

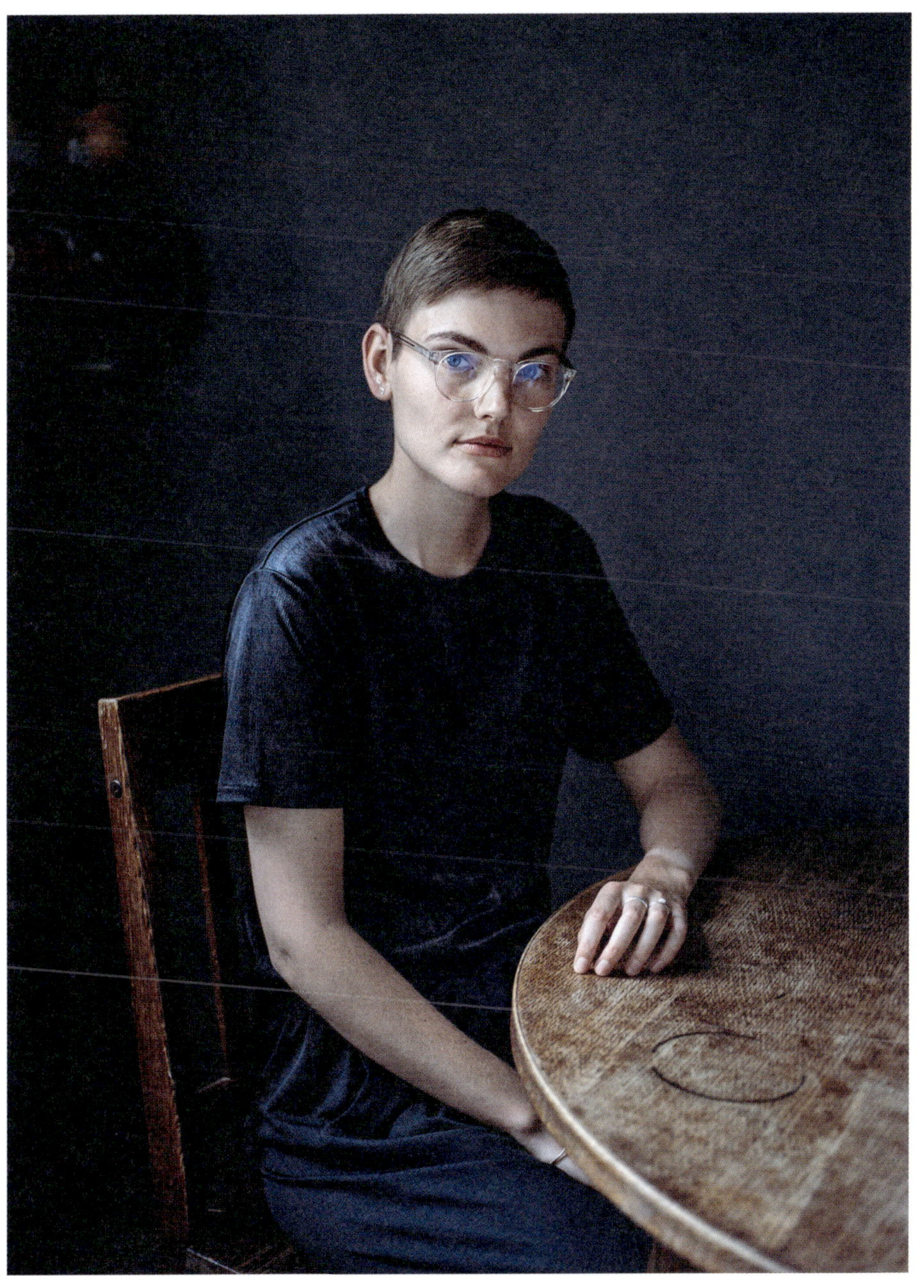

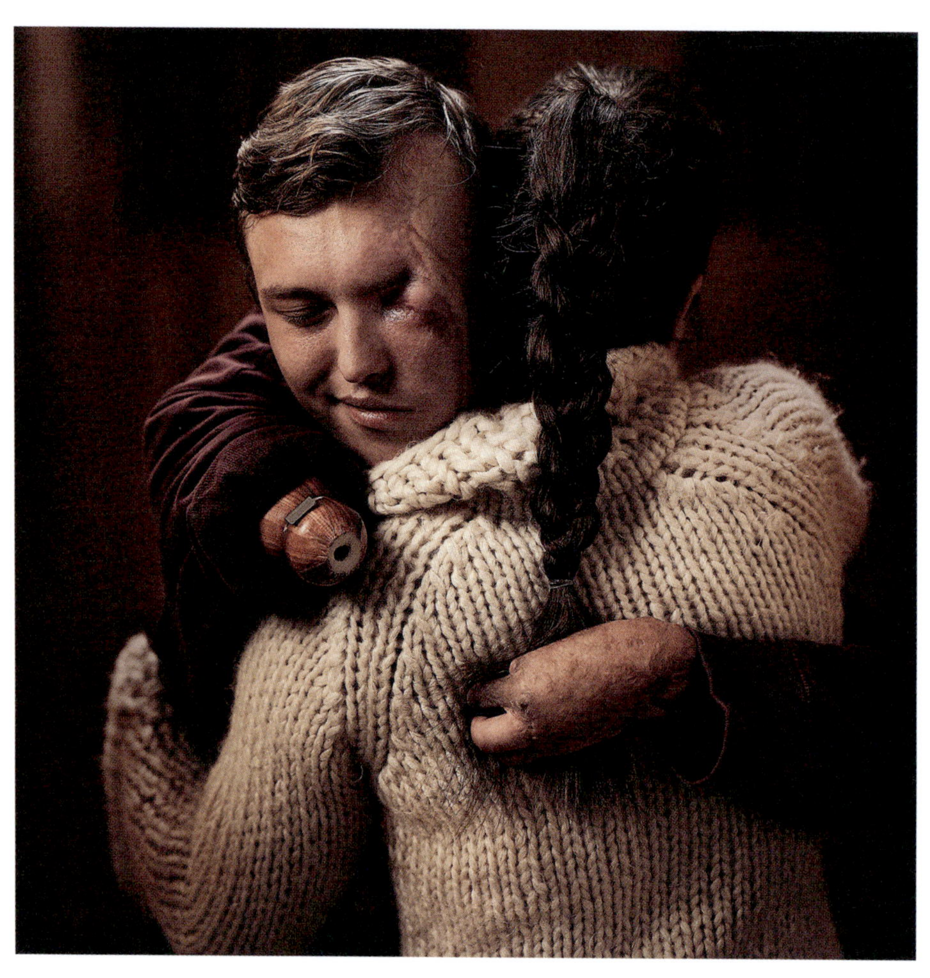

Joeri

by Kurt Stallaert
Brussels, Belgium

Joeri, 15, was seriously injured after a car accident.
He hugs his mentor who is helping him to rebuild his life.
Joeri wants to help others who have also been
involved in car accidents.

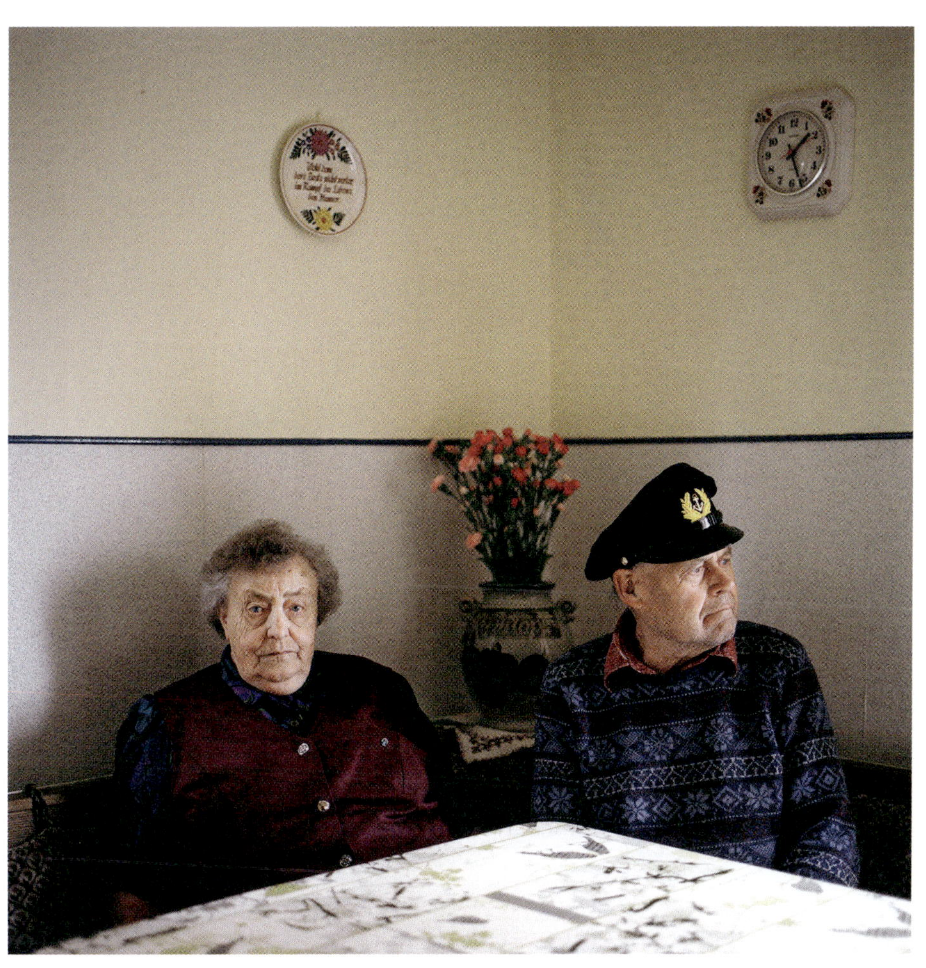

Anke and Bernhard Diedrichsen
by Antony Sojka-Metcalfe
Hooge, Germany

Anke and Bernhard have been married for 60 years.
I took this portrait in the couple's kitchen while Bernhard,
a former ship builder, looked out of the window, thinking
about where his favourite ship used to be docked.

Whitaker Malem
by Frederic Aranda
London, UK

British design duo Whitaker Malem
(Paddy Whitaker and Keir Malem) pose for a
portrait. 'Having been together professionally and
personally for 34 years we know it's our differences
as individuals combined with our shared interests
that have continued to stimulate our shared life.
Somehow we have grown more physically
alike.' – Whitaker Malem

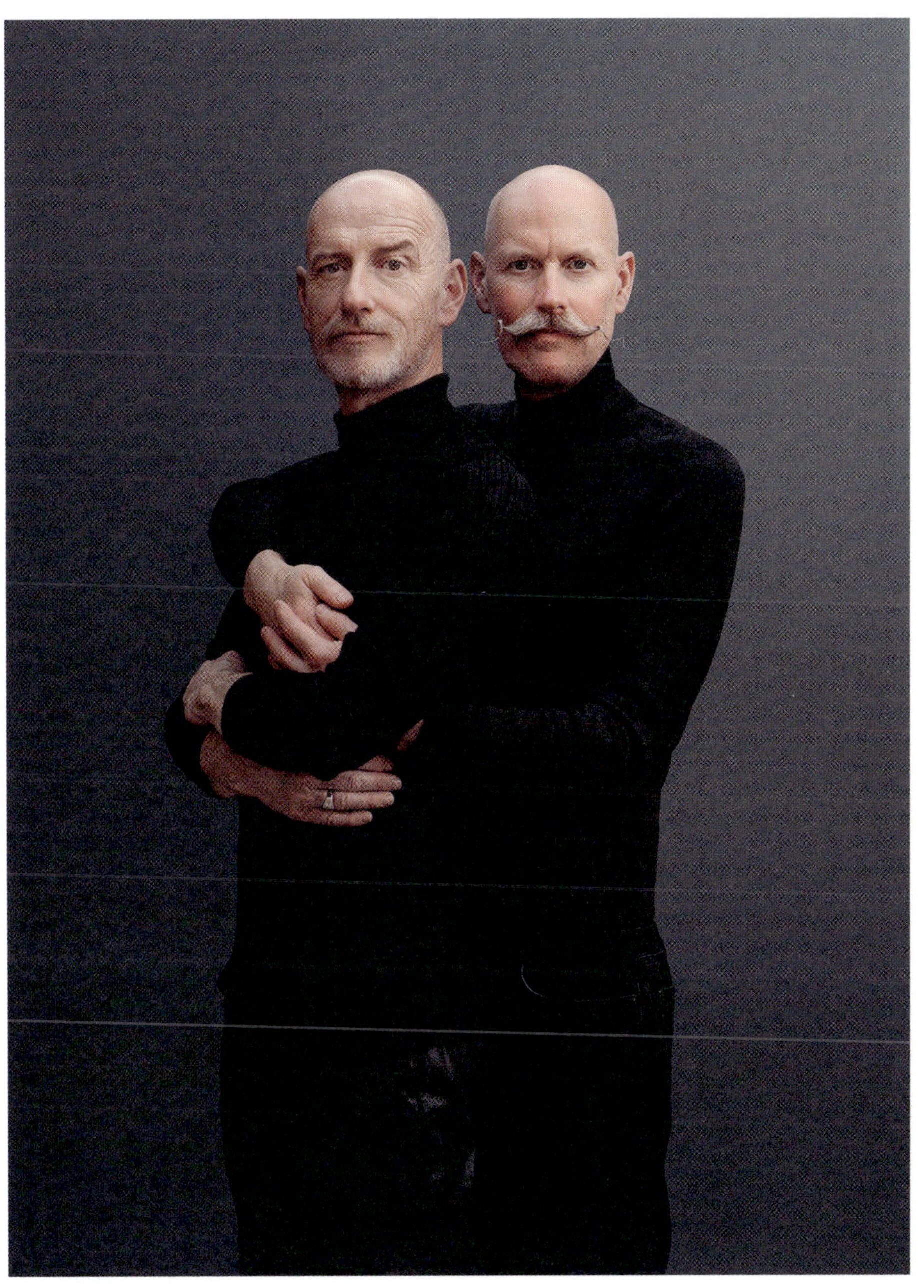

Marte, Fat Activist
by Marie Hald
Oslo, Norway

'All my life I've been trying to lose weight,
to get smaller, to take up less space. Body activism
and fat positivity was a big eye-opener. Suddenly,
I had permission to just be me, to not try to
change, and I began to enjoy life.' – Marte

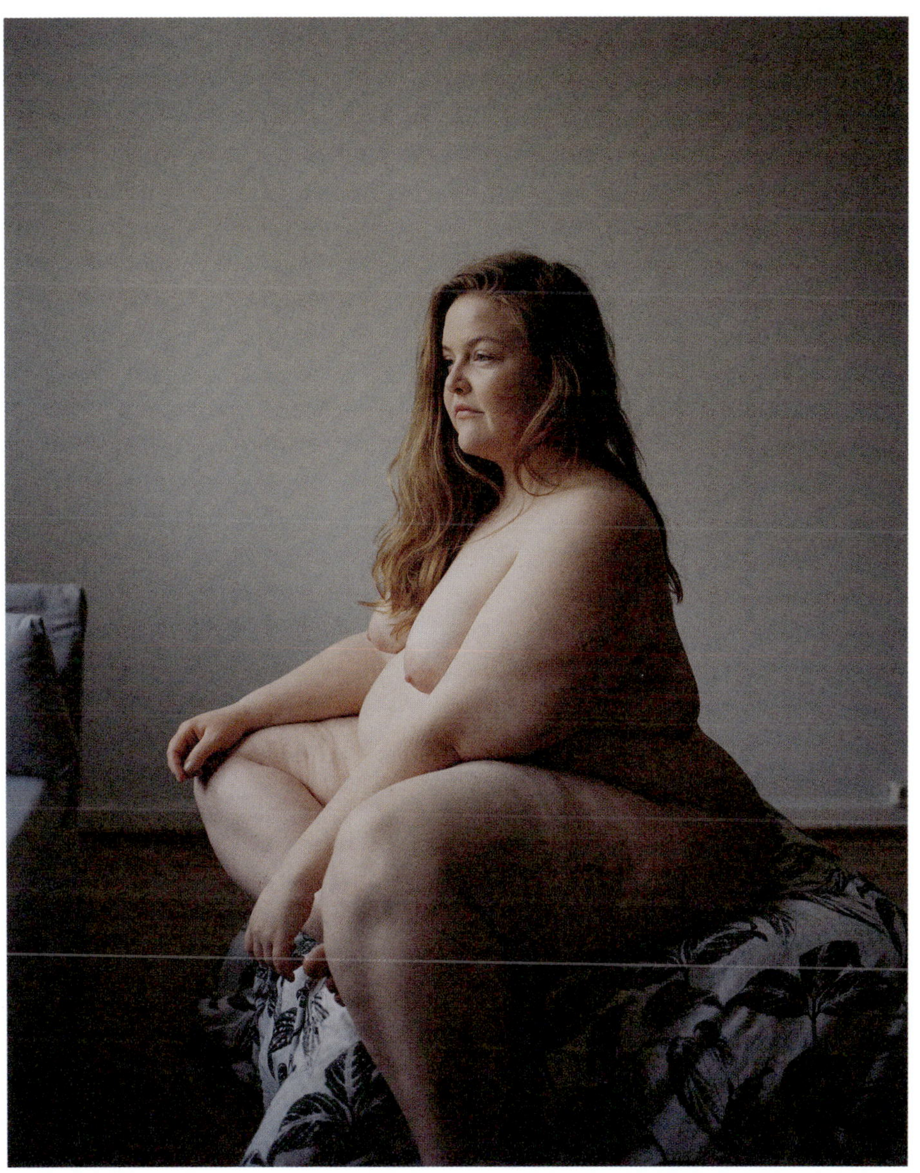

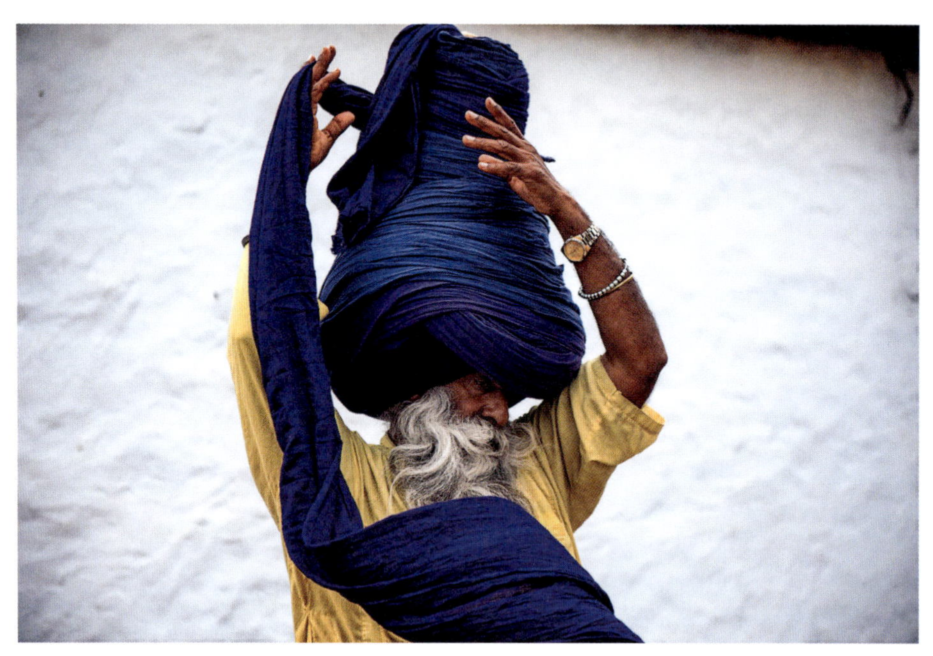

Easy Lies the Head
by Sankar Sridhar
Anandpur Sahib, India

A member of the martial Nihang sect at the Hola Mohalla
festival where people show off their strength and
display their prowess through horse riding, swordsman-
ship and forms of self-defence. This elder gave
me permission to photograph him while he tied his turban
comprising 900 metres of cloth. He told me his turban
would weigh 16 kilograms once complete.

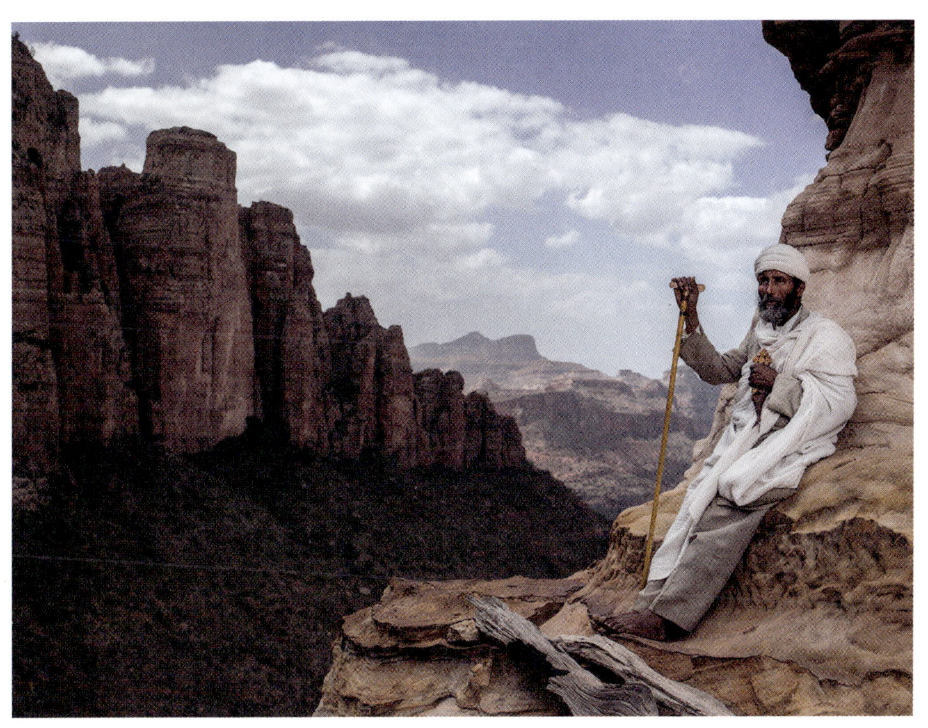

Closer to Heaven
by Mauro De Bettio
Tigray, Ethiopia

Keshi Assefa Hagos is a priest at Abuna Yemata
Guh church, arguably the most inaccessible place of
worship on earth. The monolithic church,
perched high atop a vertical rock with steep drops
on all sides, is only accessible by foot.

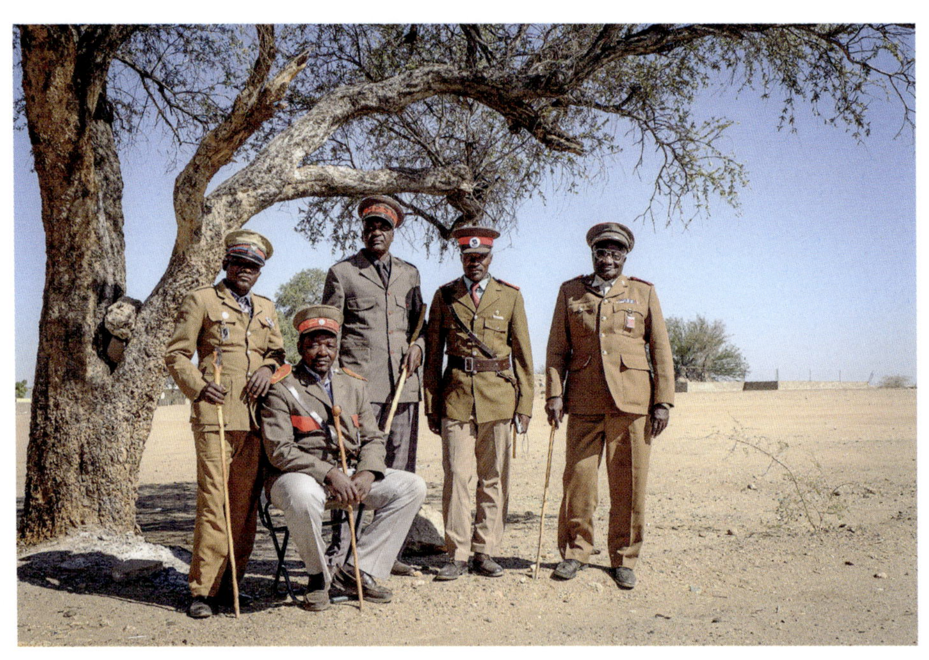

Herero Commemoration
by Laurent Nilles
Okahandja, Namibia

Every year in August, Herero people from
all over Namibia gather in the town of Okahandja
to commemorate their former leaders.

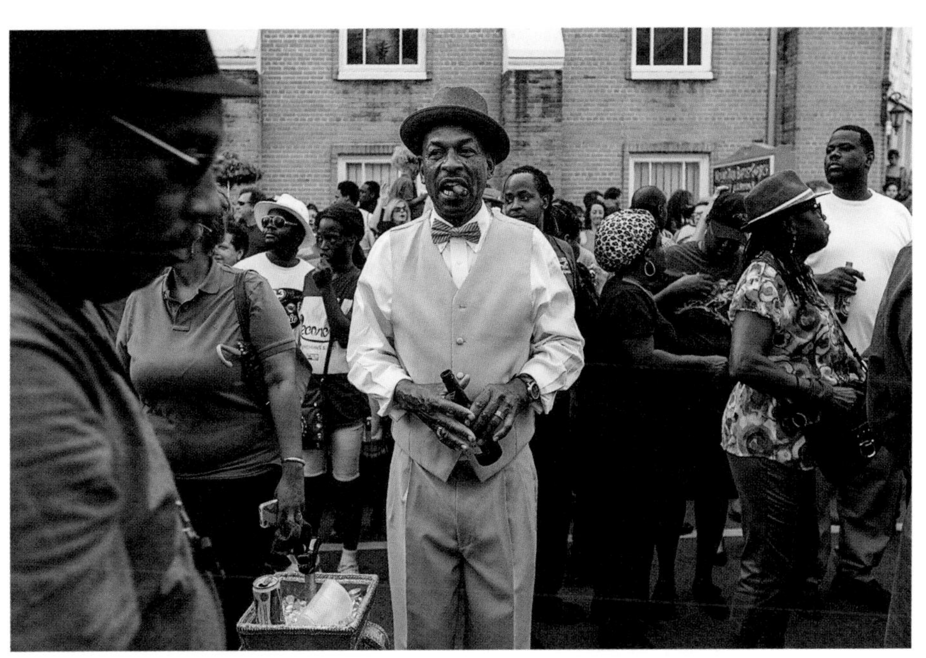

Man with Cigar
by Jon Wollenhaupt
New Orleans, Louisiana, USA

I happened to be in New Orleans the day the artist
Prince died. Two days after his death, a parade
was held in the Tremé neighbourhood to honour and
celebrate his life. The parade featured a flatbed
carriage drawn by white horses that transported a coffin
draped in purple through the streets accompanied by
a large brass band and around 8,000 marchers.

Majorettes
by Meredith Andrews
Hamilton, Bermuda

Members of the Pembroke Hamilton Club
Majorettes & Drum Corps at a Bermuda Day parade.
Majorettes are a big part of my memories of
Bermuda Day celebrations growing up. I fondly
recall watching the floats make their way
down Hamilton's Front Street from the balcony
of my grandfather's liquor store. I remember the sounds
of the drummers, the spectators sat curbside and
the flash of sparkles as the majorettes' glittering
batons flew through the air.

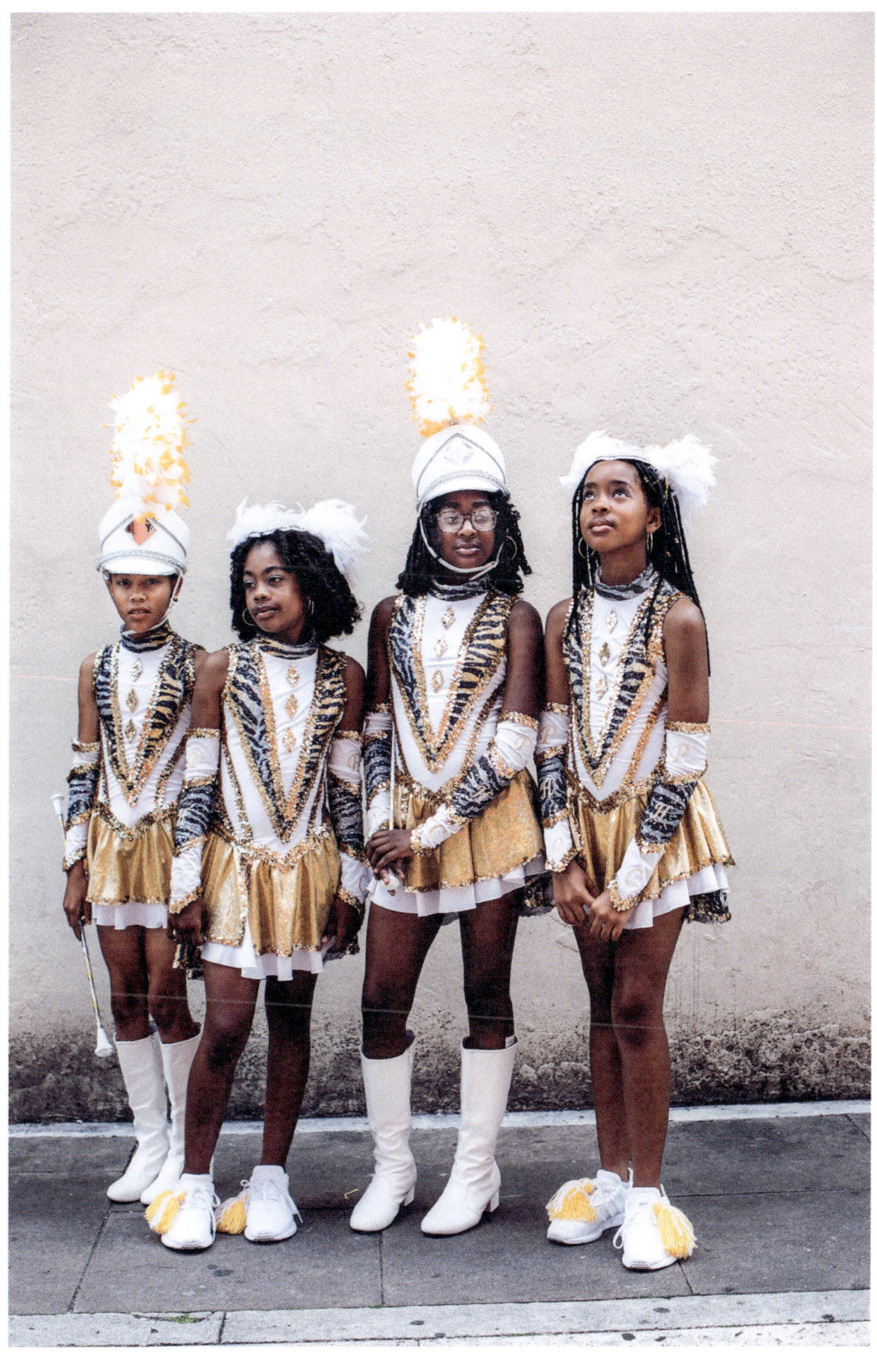

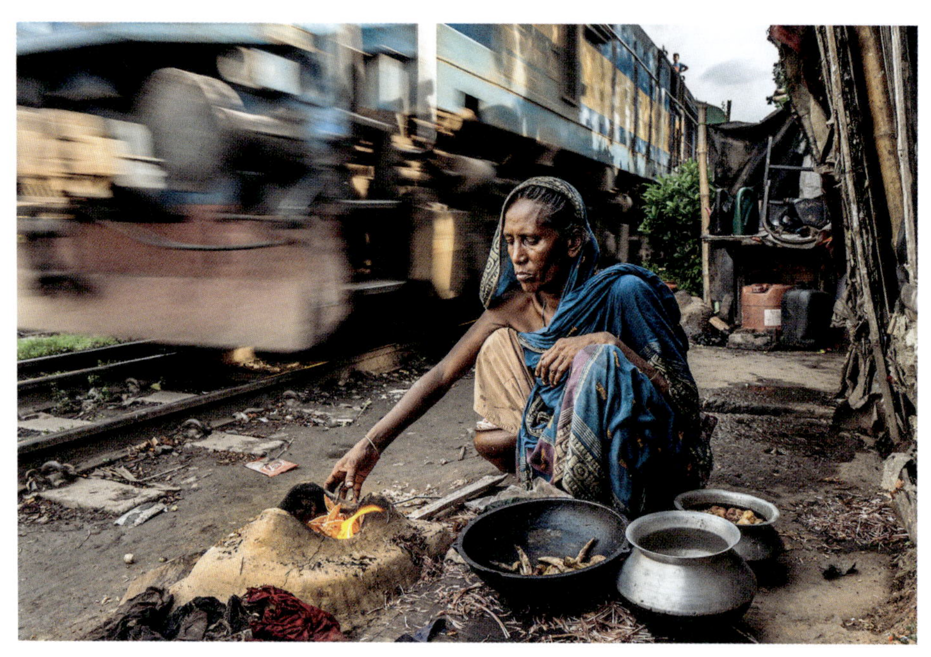

Woman of Steel
by Kathryn MacPhee
Dhaka, Bangladesh

This woman is among the millions of people
who have been forced to leave their rural surroundings
and move to Bangladesh's capital in search of work.
Her home is next to the railway track.

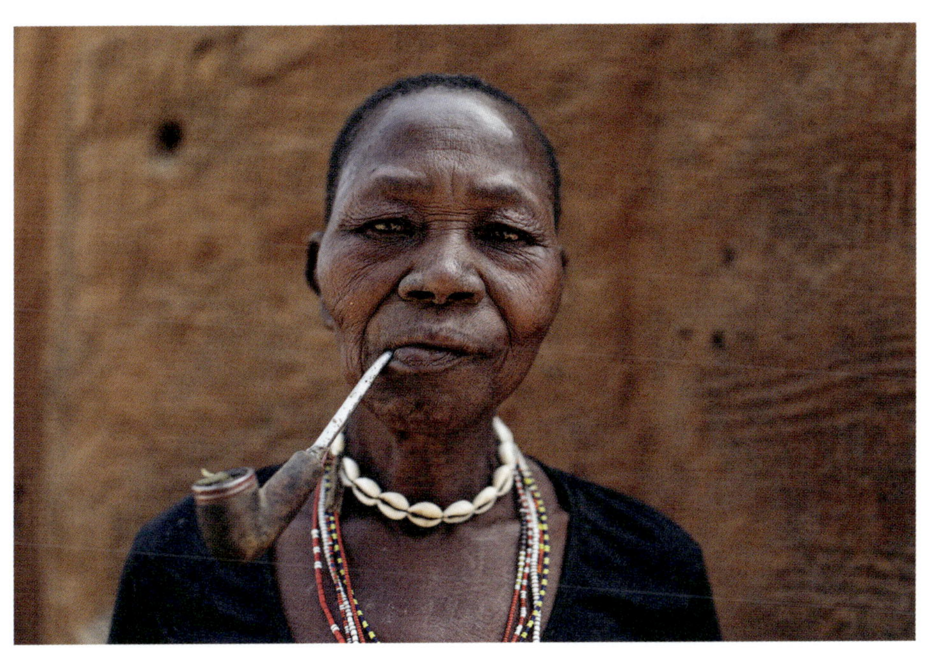

Women Smoke Pipes Too
by Ingetje Tadros
Koutammakou, Togo

Koutammakou, the land of the Batammariba,
was listed as a World Heritage Site by Unesco in 2004.
The village where this lady lives is made of
traditional mud tower-houses, which are seen as
a symbol of the country. It is not unusual for
a woman to smoke a pipe here.

Ifugao Elder
by Morgan Silk
Banaue, Luzon, Philippines

Marcos, the high priest of the Ifugao tribe
in his ancestral home, the rice terraces of Banaue.
Marcos's father was famous for sacrificing the buffalo
in Francis Ford Coppola's classic, *Apocalypse Now.*
Hundreds of Ifugao villagers were transported
to and lived on the set to create Coppola's vision
of Colonel Kurtz's compound.

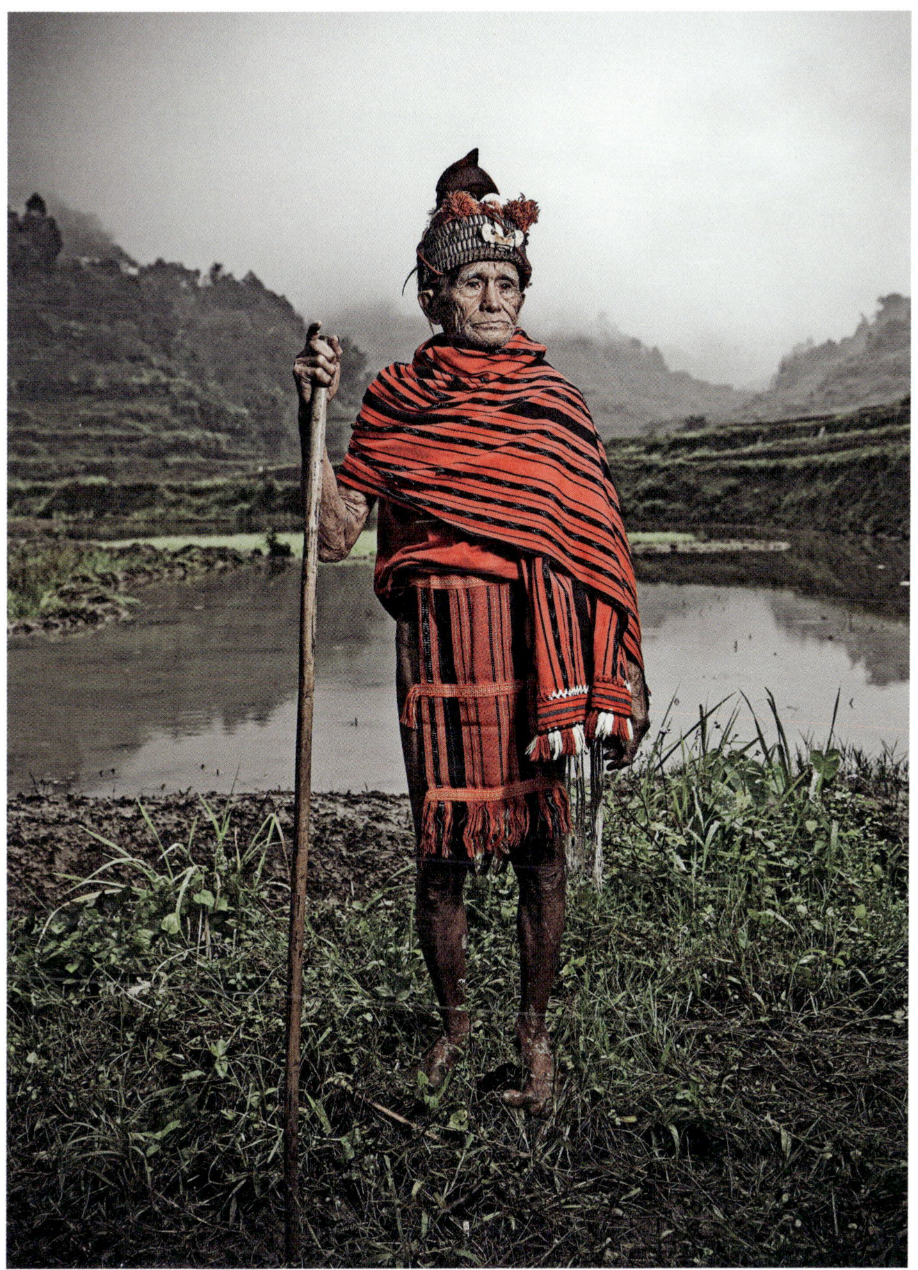

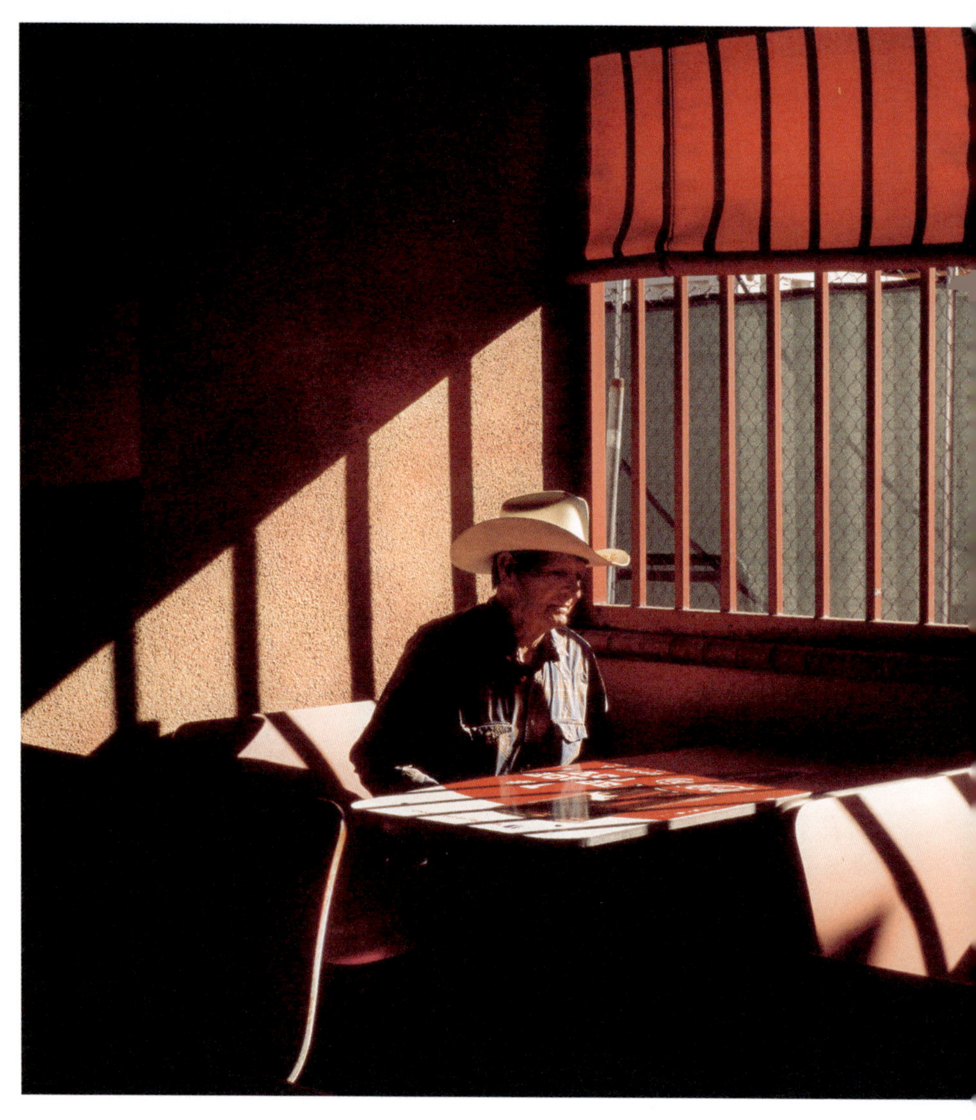

By Myself
by Seung Jong Lee
Los Angeles, California, USA

190

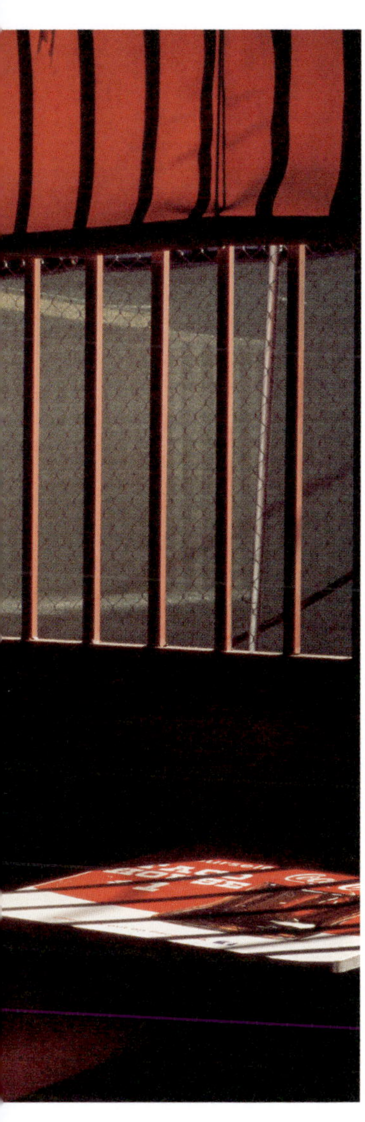

Tyrese at a Chinese Restaurant
by Mauricio Murillo
Orlando, Florida, USA

I was waiting in line at my local Chinese restaurant
when I noticed Tyrese sitting at the table next to me.
He told me this is how he normally dresses.

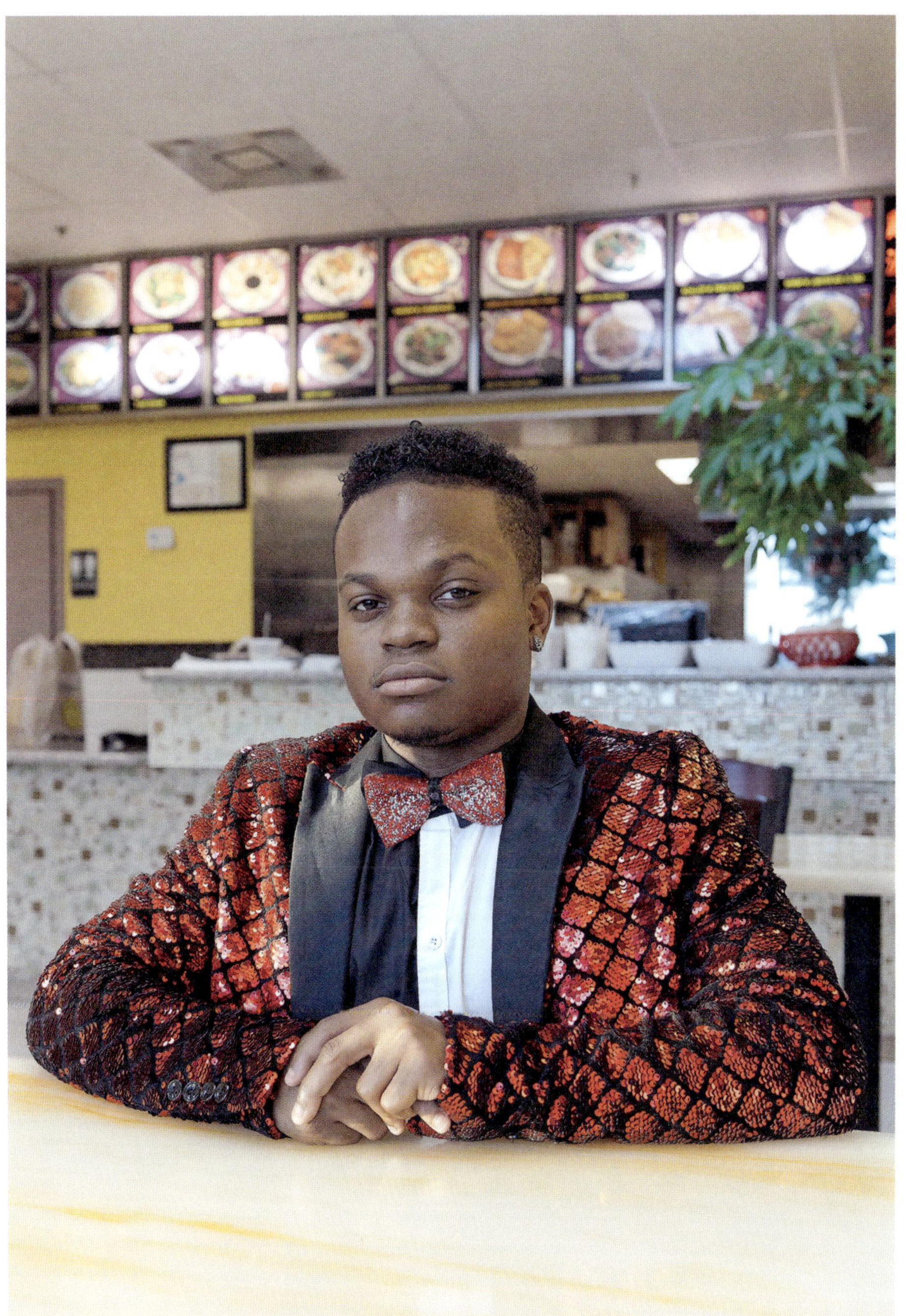

Freedom
by Ngadi Smart
Grand-Bassam, Côte d'Ivoire

Models Saadia and Frédéric Ablé stand outside
a dilapidated building in the old French-colonial seaside
town of Grand-Bassam, once Côte d'Ivoire's capital.
The town, a World Heritage site, is filled with
arresting 19th and 20th-century architectural ruins.
From September to November 2019, coastal
floods damaged streets and homes. Coastal erosion
is a growing problem for West African nations.
I wanted to capture the atmosphere of traditional
and modern culture at risk of being lost.

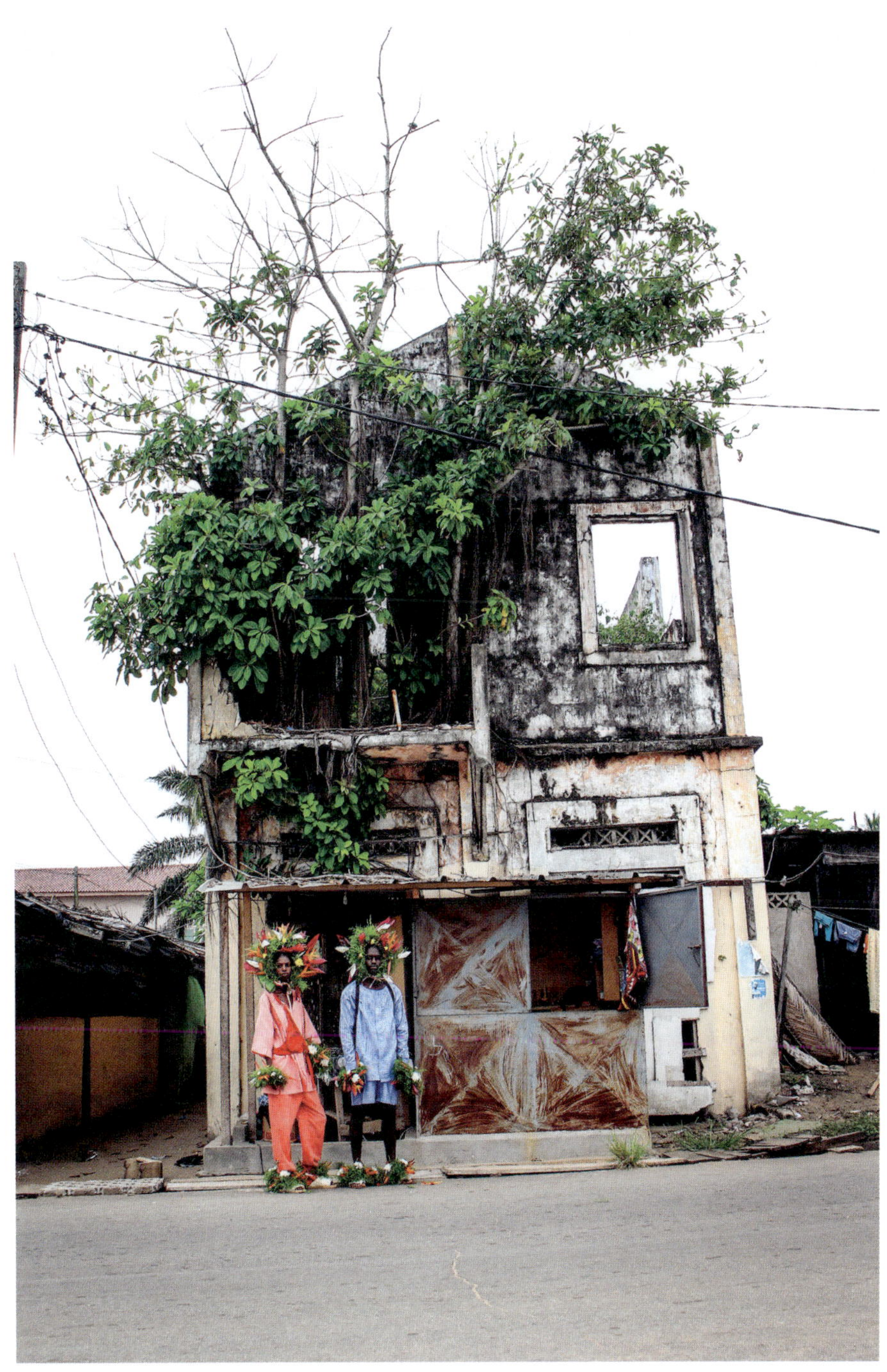

Eha #4
by Sirli Raitma
London, UK

My mother Eha, originally from Estonia, lives with
me and my son in London. In 2015, she began to suffer
from depression so I came up with a plan to give her
something to focus on. I began to take her portrait and
the 'Eha' project was born. My mother revealed
herself to be a natural model, happy to play along
with my visual fantasies.

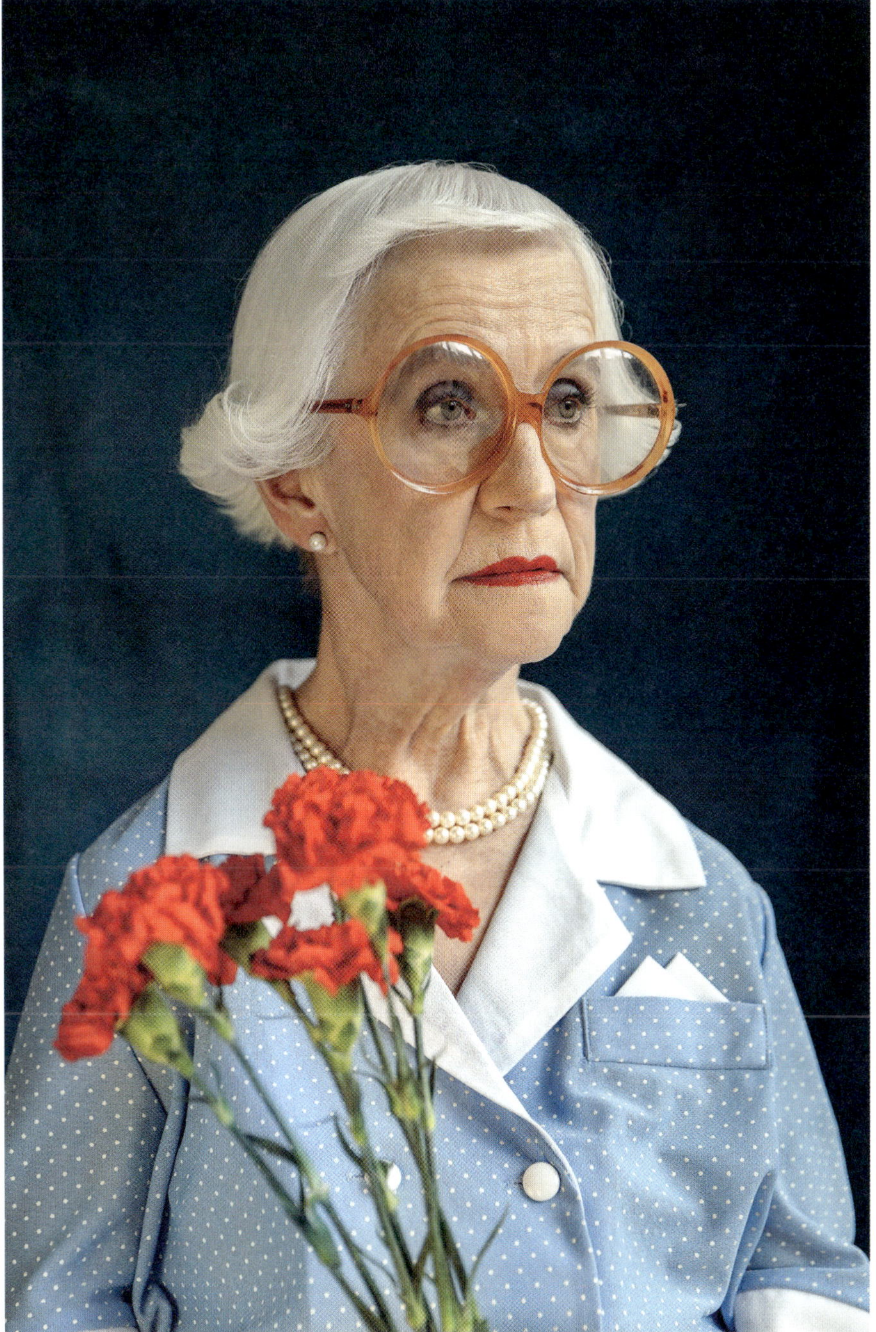

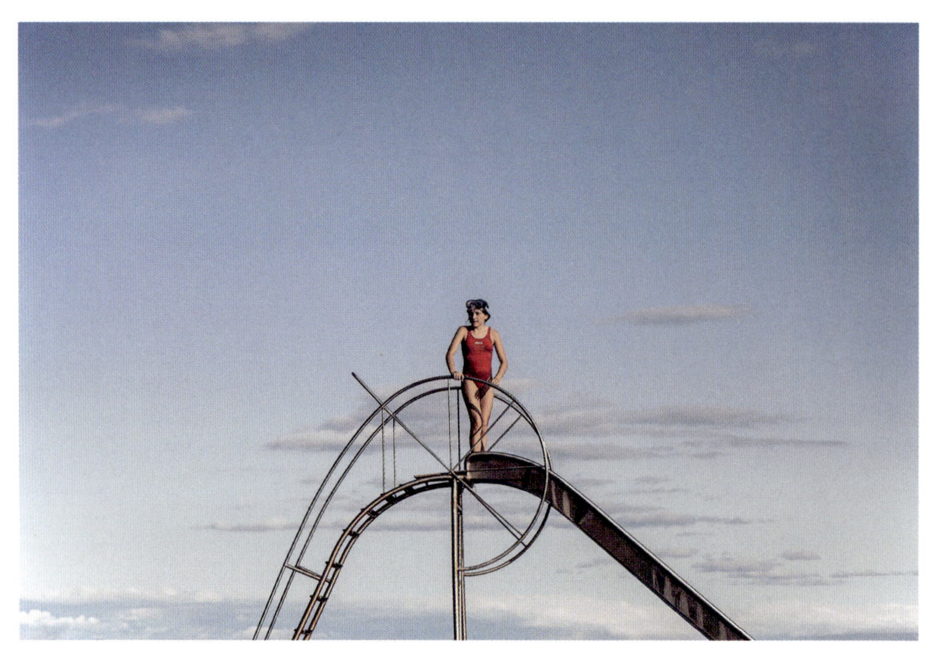

Unknown Girl

by Orsolya Boncser
Opatija, Croatia

A girl stands at the top of a slide on the
beautiful promenade of Lungomare in Opatija
where we were on a family holiday. This little
girl in her red swimming costume came up the steps
and stood silently, immersed in what she saw
from above. Everything was so peaceful and perfect
for a moment so I took a picture.

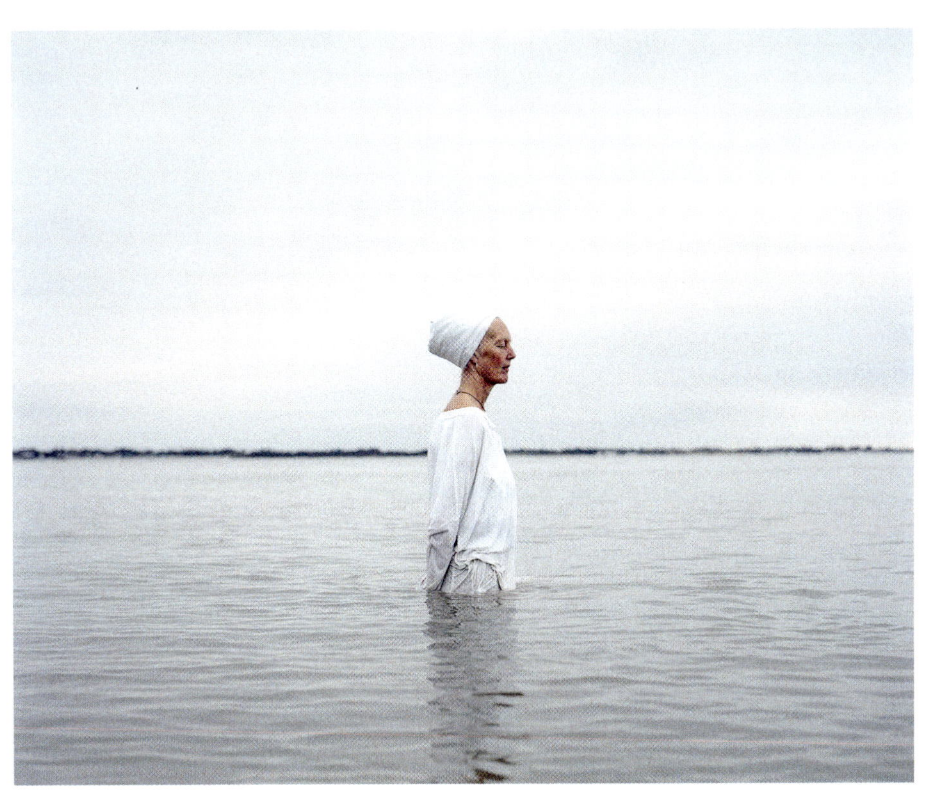

Grace
by Tom McGahan
Blackwater Estuary, Essex, UK

Grace is a friend who I met at our local Buddhist centre.
She was diagnosed with breast cancer and decided
not to receive conventional treatment. Grace is using
alternative therapies, including cold water therapy,
to treat the tumour.

Mother and Daughter

by Lena Bushart
Berlin, Germany

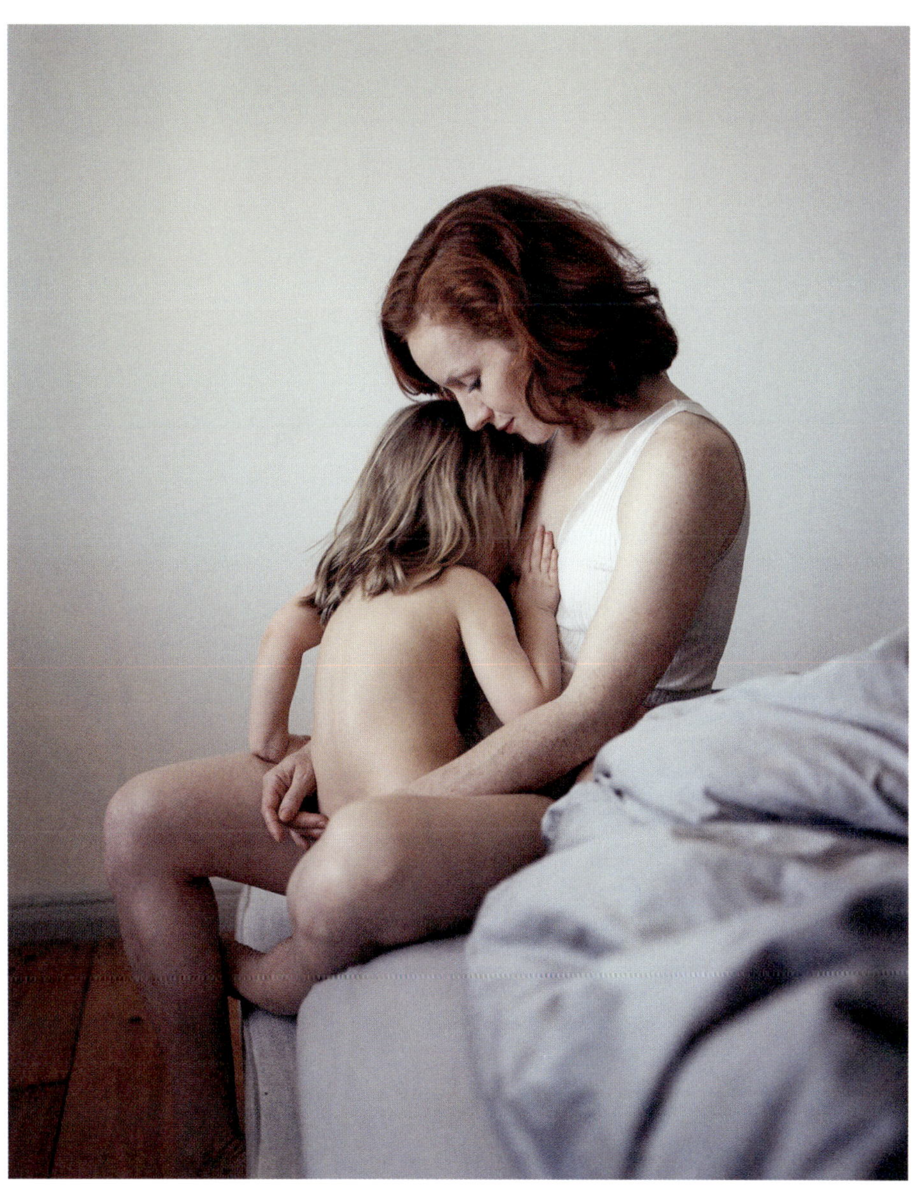

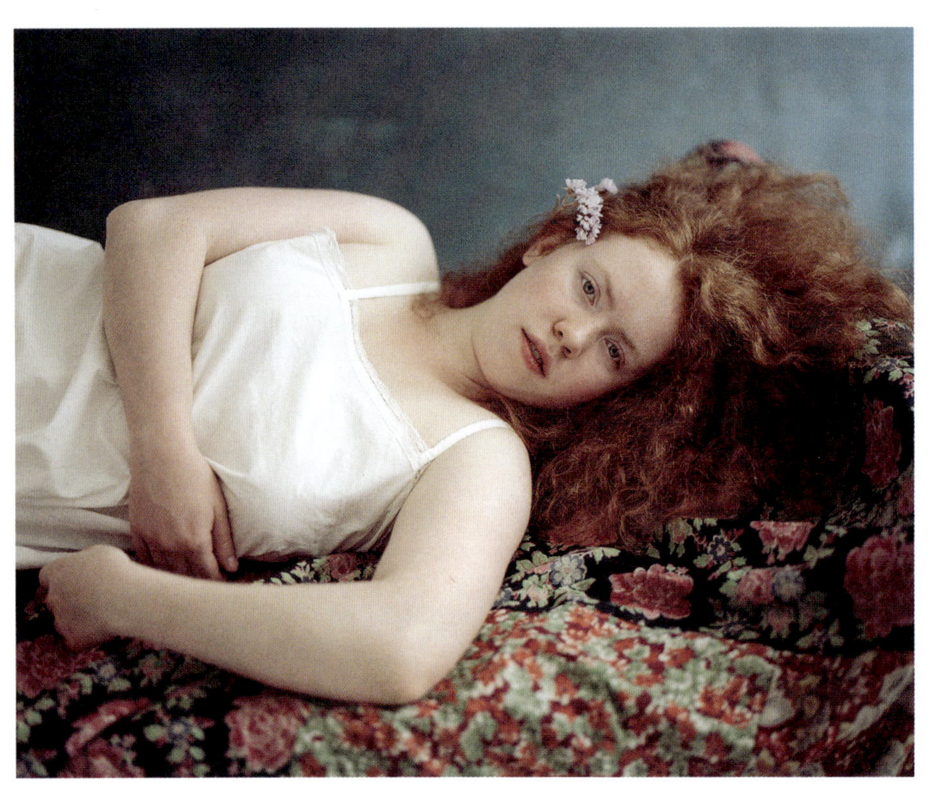

Mascha
by Lena Bushart
Berlin, Germany

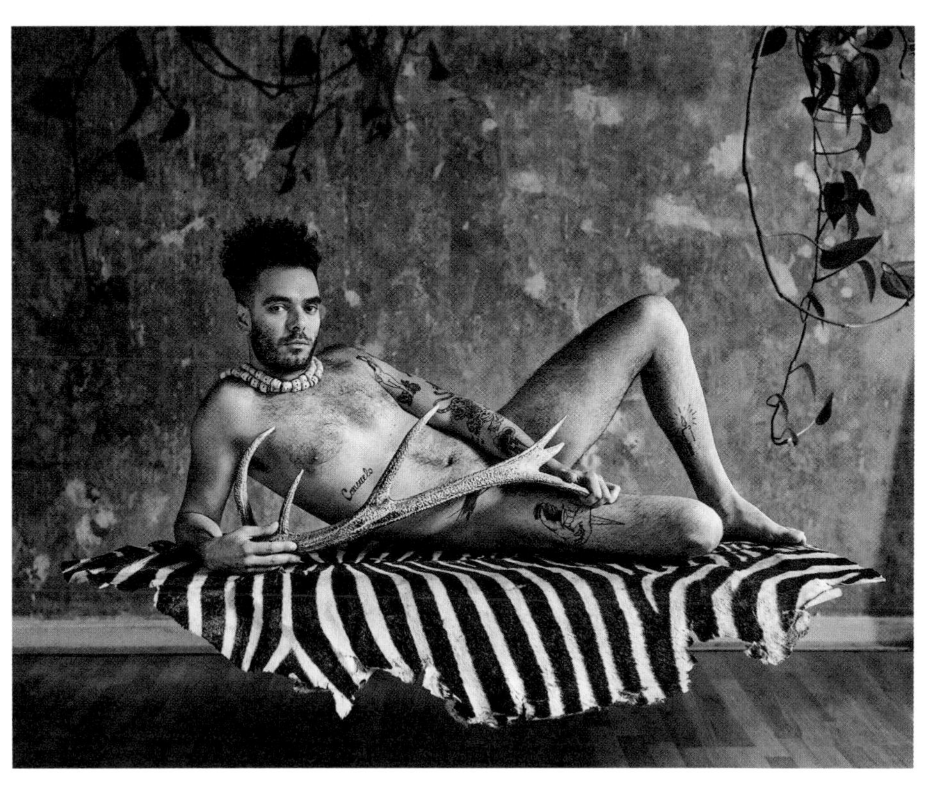

Jackie Smith
by Adrian Lach
Berlin, Germany

I was doing a fashion shoot in Jackie's apartment
and asked if I could photograph him. Originally from
El Salvador, Jackie says it was his destiny to move
to Berlin, a place he loves for its freedom.

Kristin
by Diana Feil
Los Angeles, California, USA

Kristin has breast cancer. Our goal was to
capture and commemorate Kristin's boobs before
the mastectomy. The shoot ended up being
a celebration of femininity and we went through
all kinds of emotions. It was the beginning
of a friendship.

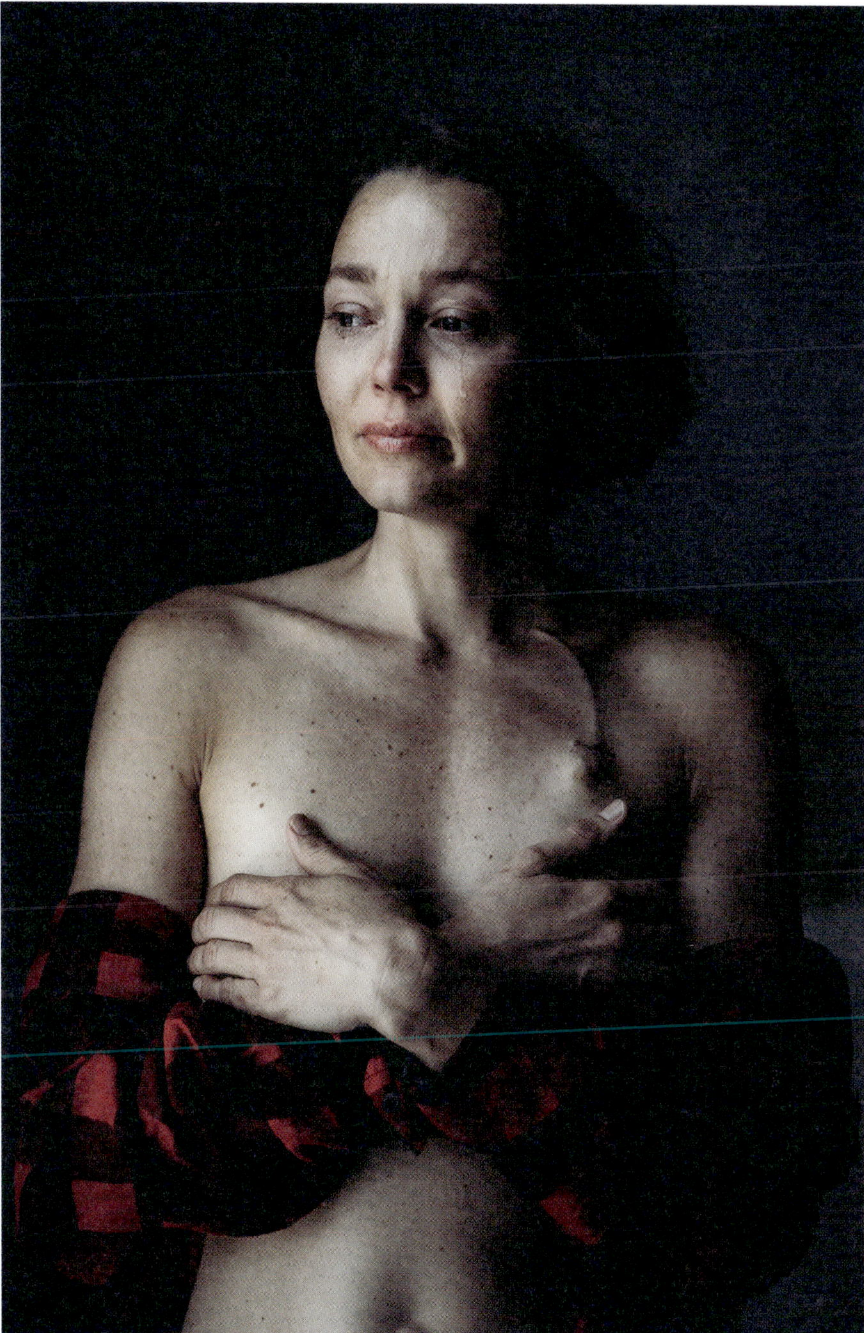

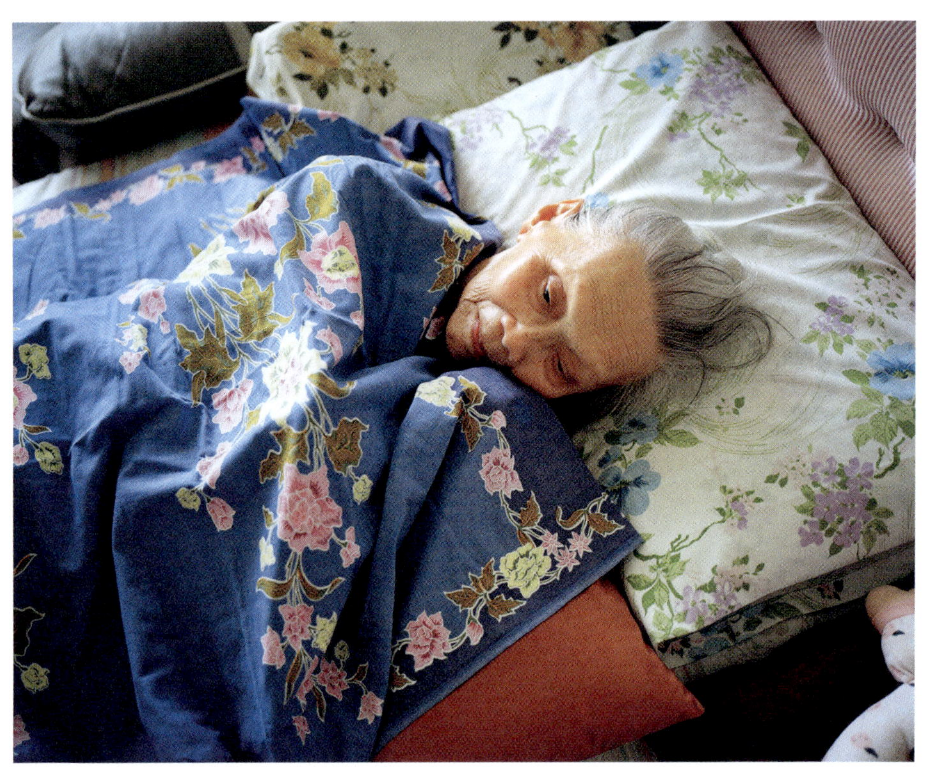

Kong Fung Tsze
by Anne Moffat
Sandakan, Malaysia

Photographing my 90-year-old grandmother over
several years was a process of trying to understand more
of who I am and who she was while watching her
lose her independence and sense of self to Alzheimer's.
She passed away in August 2019.

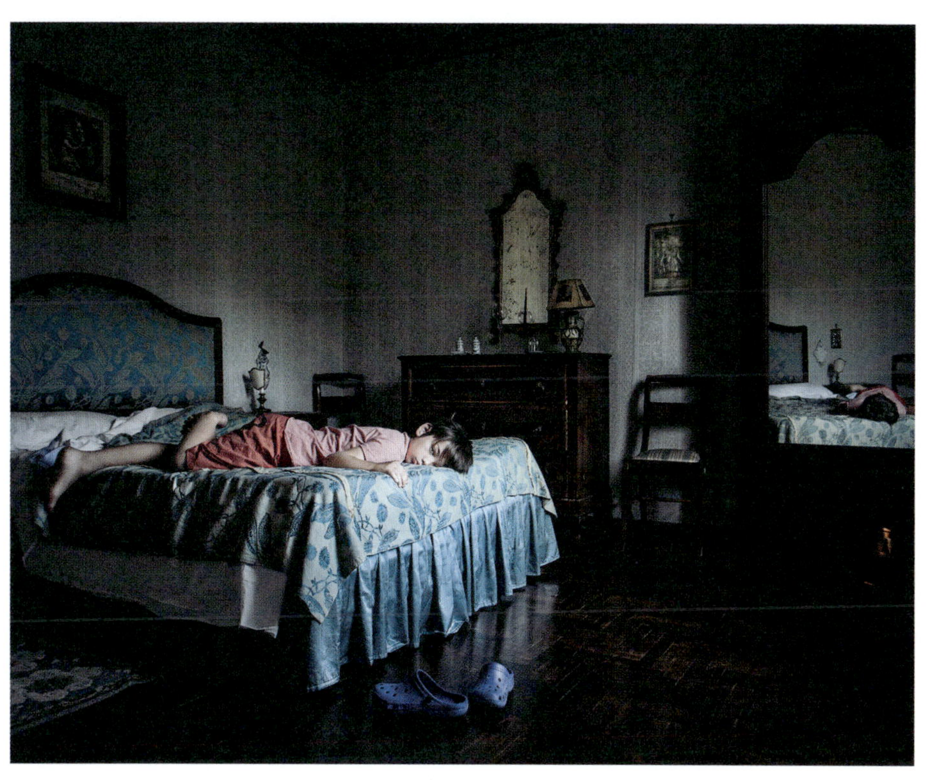

Iliya

by Marina Kazakova
Tuscany, Italy

My grandson is the most important person in
my life. The way he lives, what he feels and thinks,
and the way he fills my days gave rise to a series
of photographs about the poetics of childhood,
adolescence and youth.

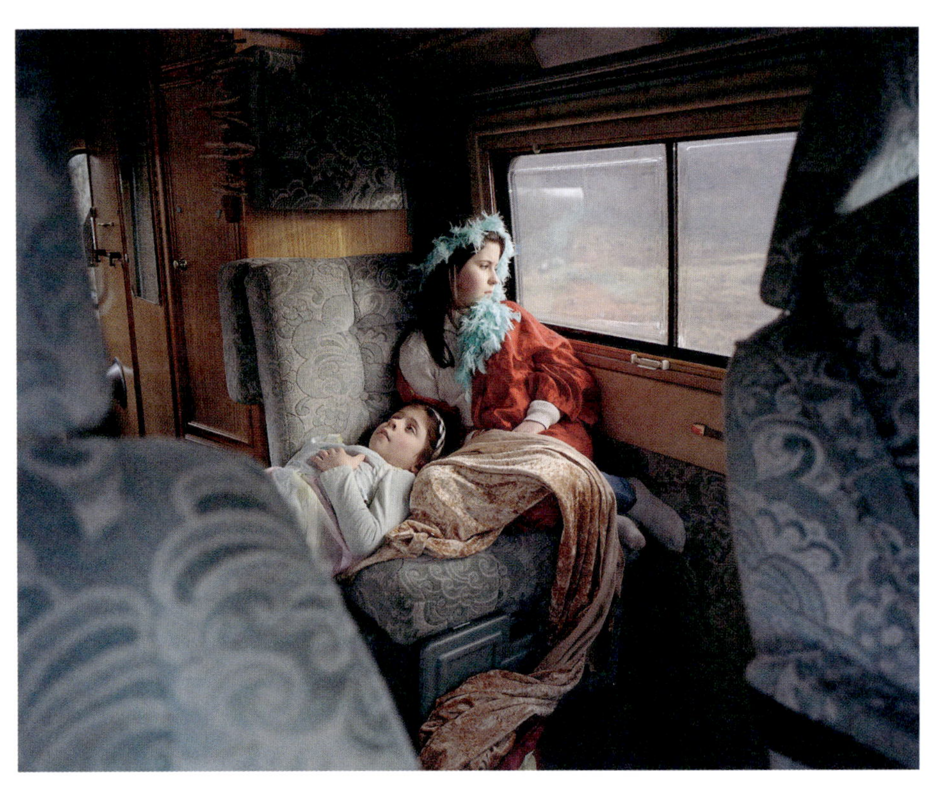

Alice and Sarah
by Mat Hay
Central Highlands, UK

Alice and Sarah live with their parents in Glen Lyon,
Perthshire. Here they are in the family's campervan
on their small domestic farm. 'Living in the glen is great
because we have so much space around us.
Many people can't believe we have no mobile phone
reception but it doesn't impact us at all.' – Alice

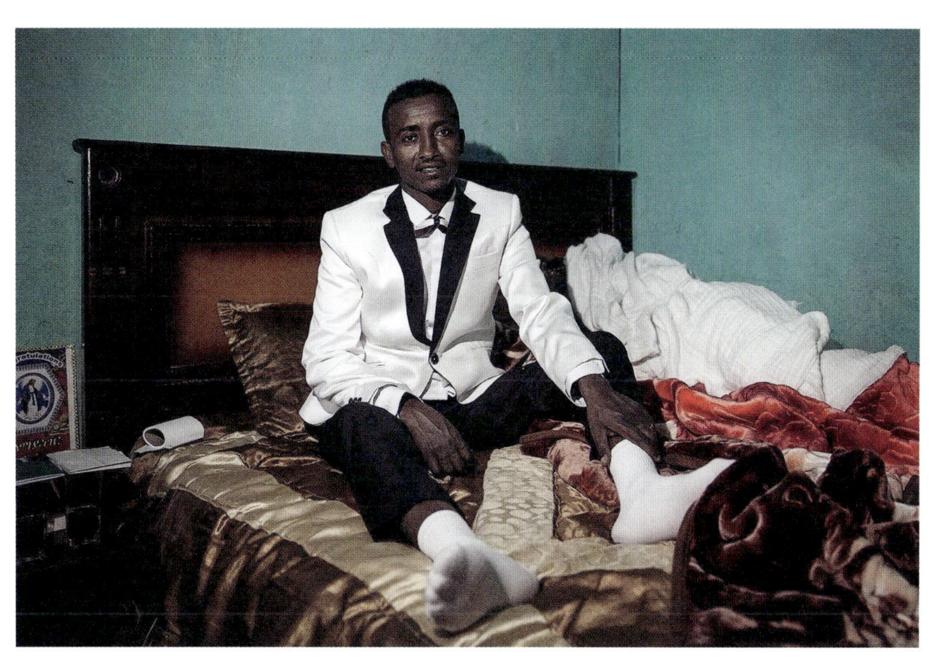

The Groom
by Coralie Maneri
Adigrat, Ethiopia

In this remote village in the Tigray region, not
far from the border with Eritrea, a traditional wedding
is always a very special event. The celebrations can
sometimes last a few days. The whole community shares
music, dancing and local food. My Ethiopian friend
invited me to celebrate his wedding. He was exhausted
after the festivities but was bursting with pride.

Ariana
by Matt Burgess
Havana, Cuba

Ariana is an Italian dancer at the Cuban
National Ballet School. She was meant to graduate
in March 2020 but this was delayed due
to the Covid-19 pandemic.

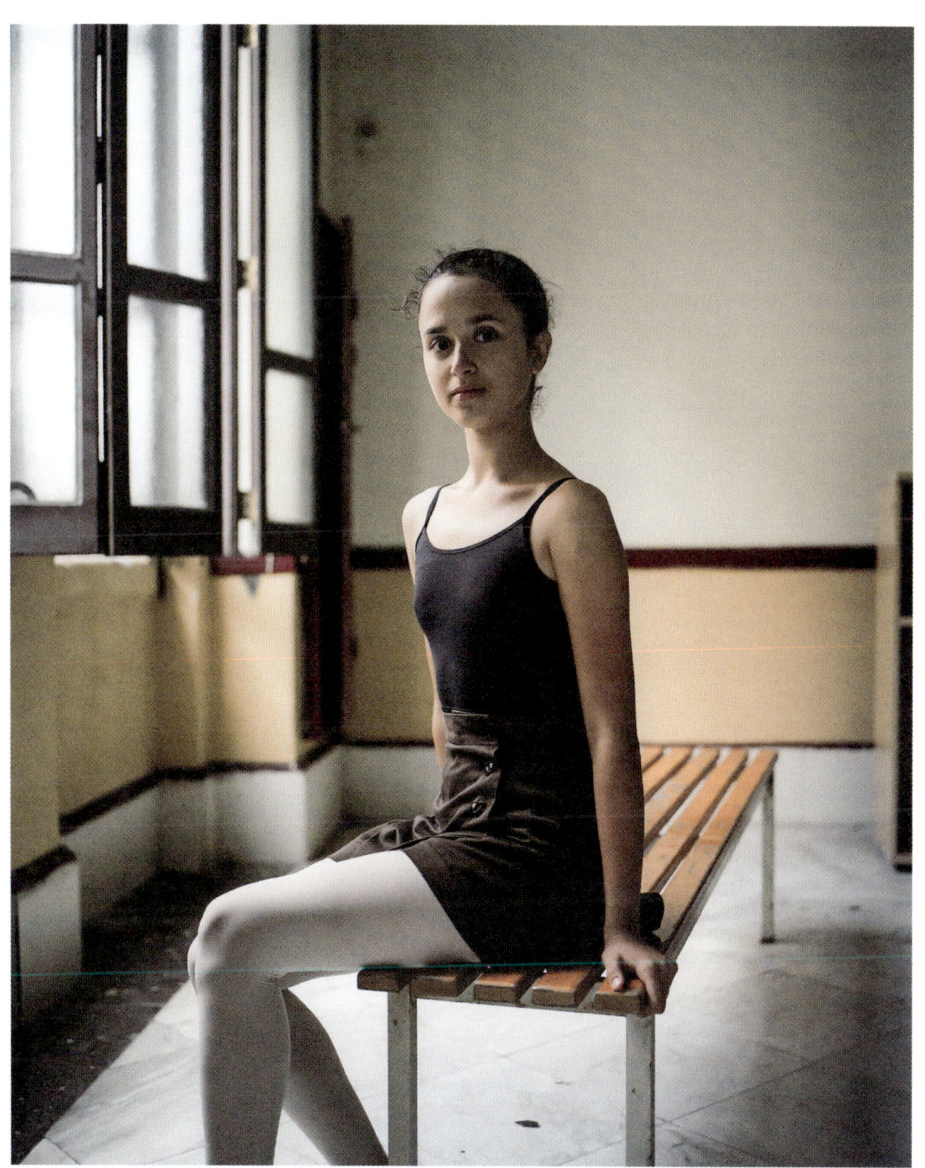

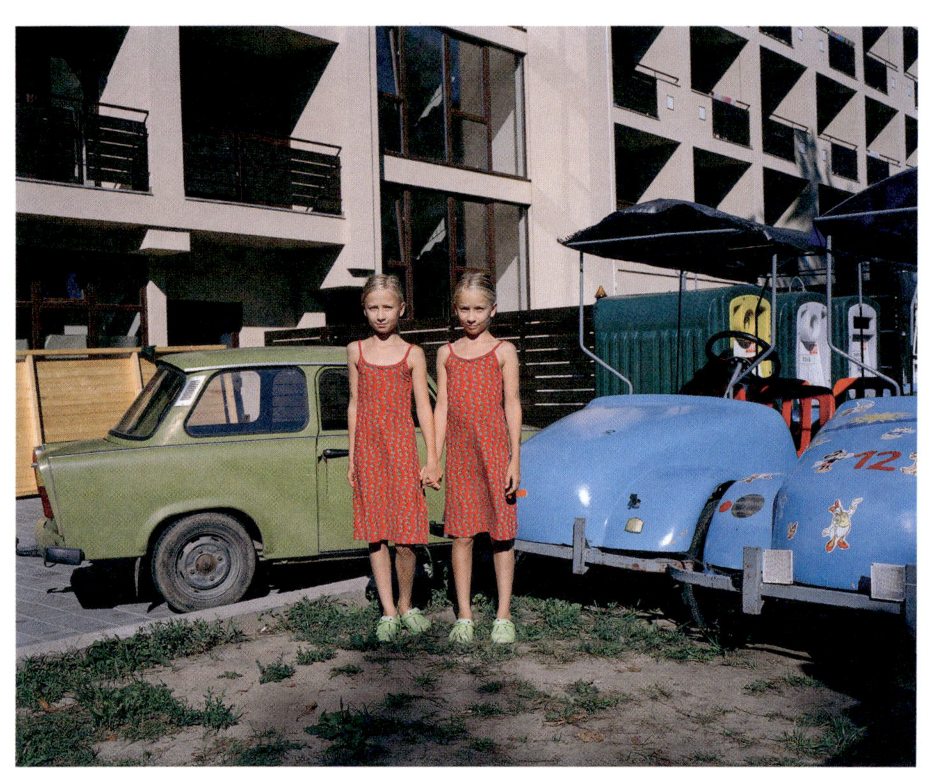

Austrian Twins

by Michal Solarski
Siófok, Hungary

These twins were on a family holiday in Siófok,
a popular summer destination on the southern bank of
Lake Balaton, famous for its beaches and nightlife.
Tourists from across Eastern Europe, Germany
and Austria flock there.

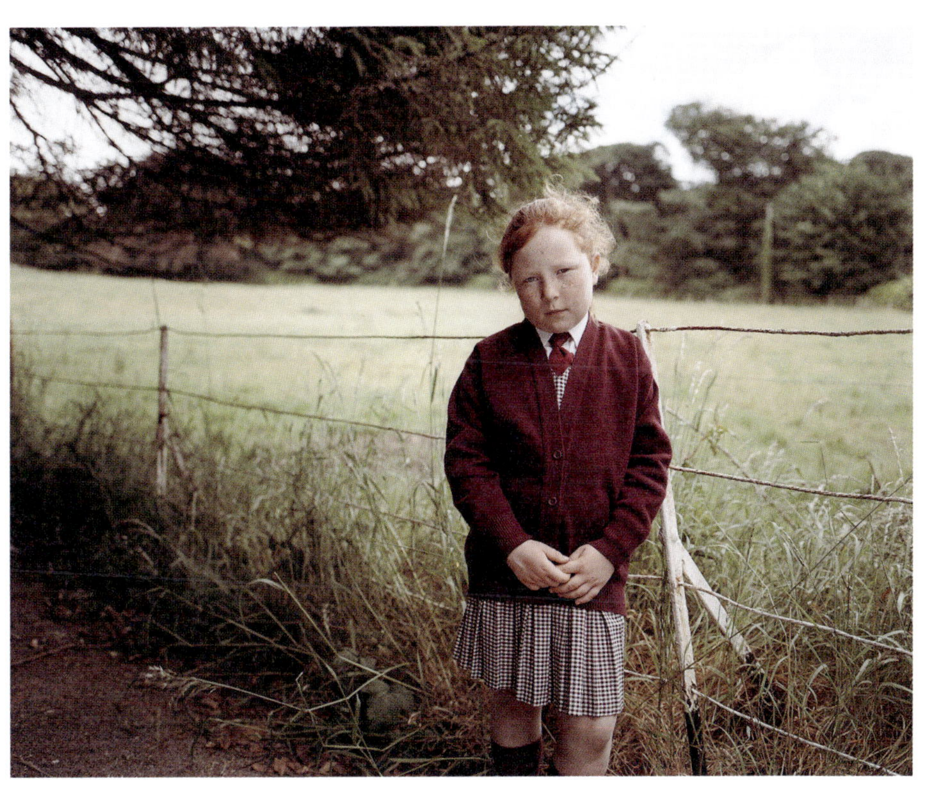

Girl in School Uniform
by Lena Bushart
Clonakilty, Ireland

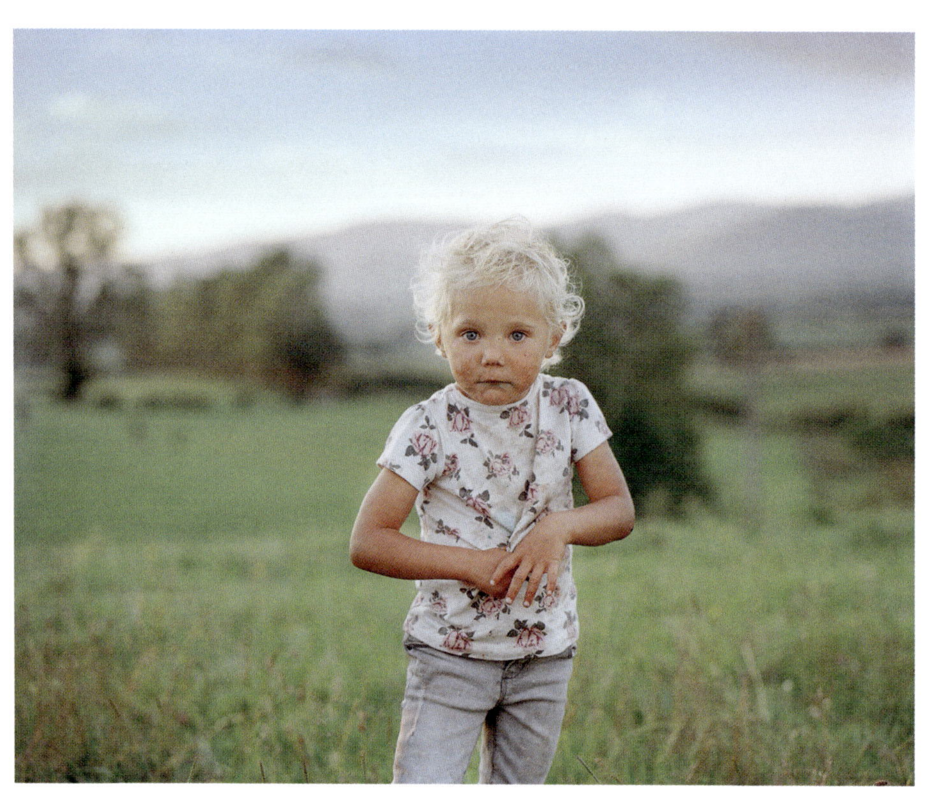

Indie
by Chris O'Donovan
Cumbria, UK

I have been visiting Appleby Horse Fair for
five years and always bump into Indie and her siblings.
What drew me to Indie is how wild she is at a time when
childhood seems to be increasingly sanitised.

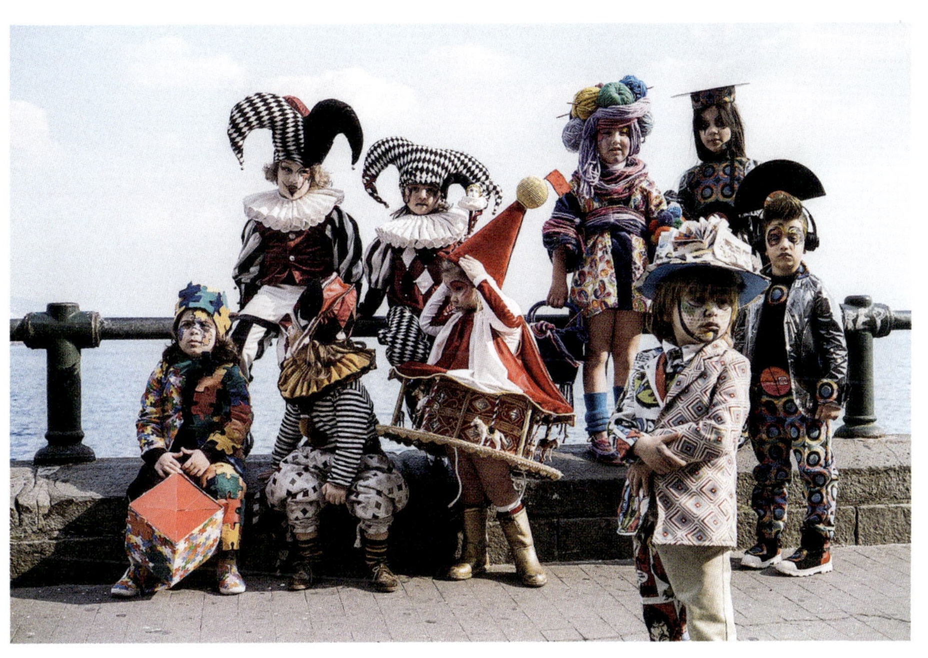

Carnival
by Tiberio Sorvillo
Napoli, Italy

A group of kids dressed up for carnival poses on the
promenade. I have fond memories of carnival
from when I was a child. We carry childhood memories
with us our entire life. To me this photograph looks
like a memory because of its grainy, washed-out
look and the unique costumes.

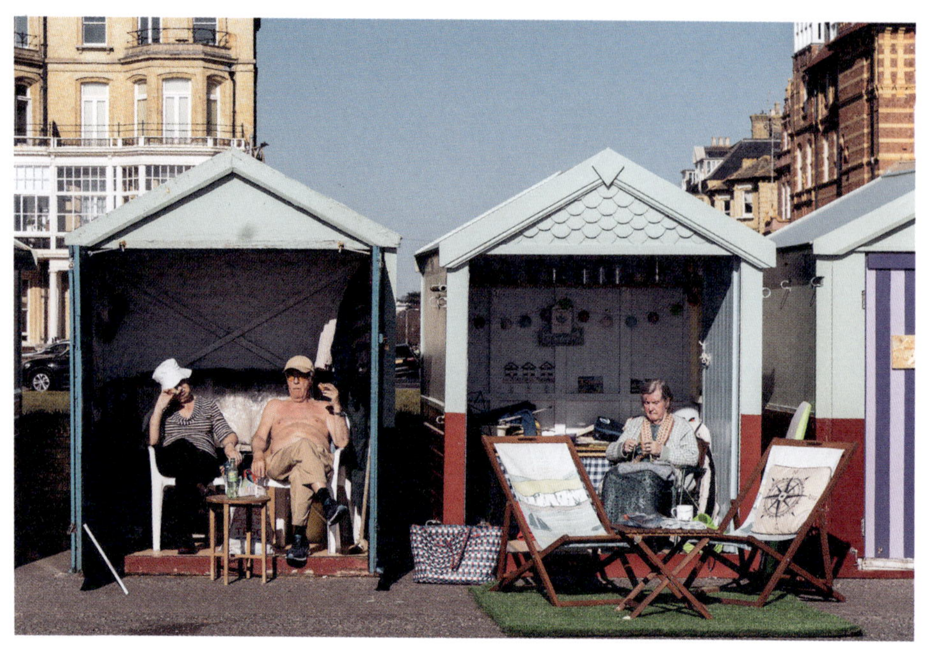

British Summer
by Bernard Galewski
Brighton, UK

On the first warm day of the year in February, Brits
use every opportunity they can to get some sun.

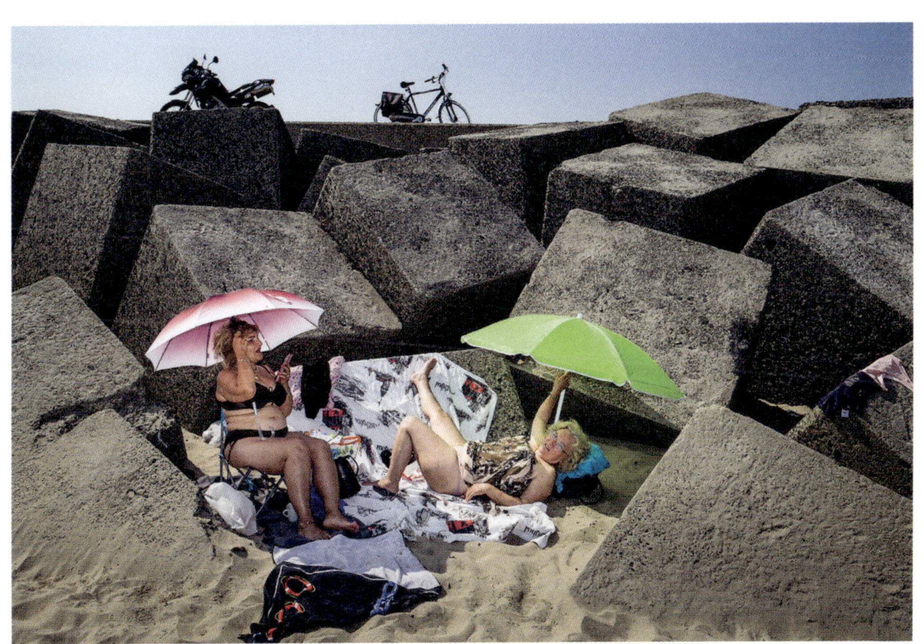

Untitled

by Giedo van der Zwan
Scheveningen, The Netherlands

Who are these two ladies? Friends or family?
The colourful umbrellas, bicycle and
motorbike, concrete blocks and clothes on the right
look like they could belong to a staged scene
but this is from real life. I like people to create
their own stories from my images.

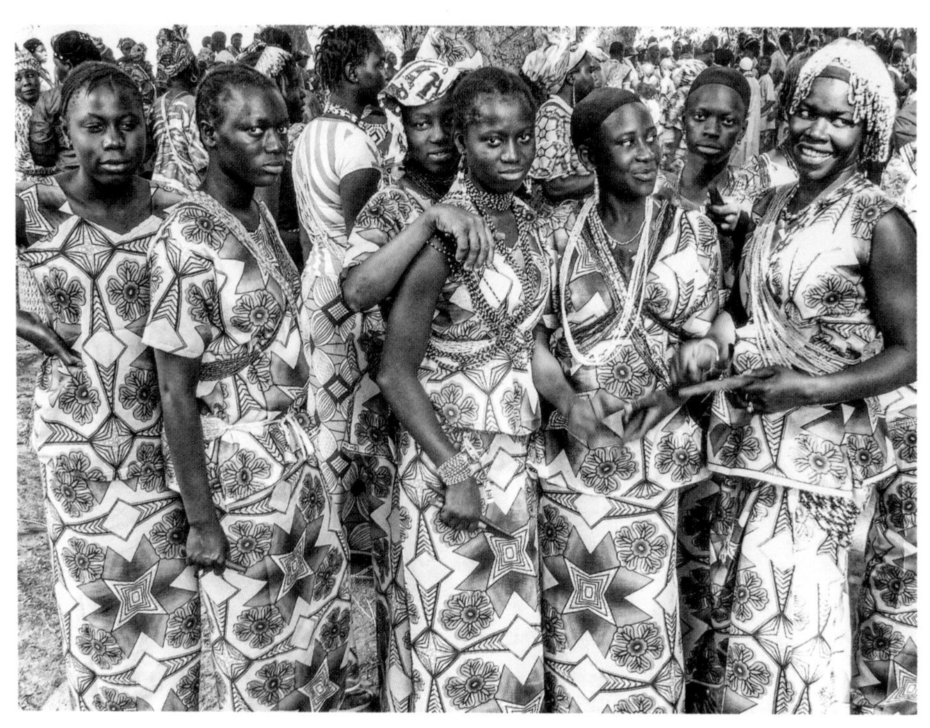

Diola Girls
by Trevor Pollard
Dombondir, Senegal

My friend Moussa invited me to his ancestral
village to take part in a traditional celebration of
the ethnic group Diola. The celebrations are
huge affairs. The young girls clubbed together to
buy metres of fabric to make their outfits.

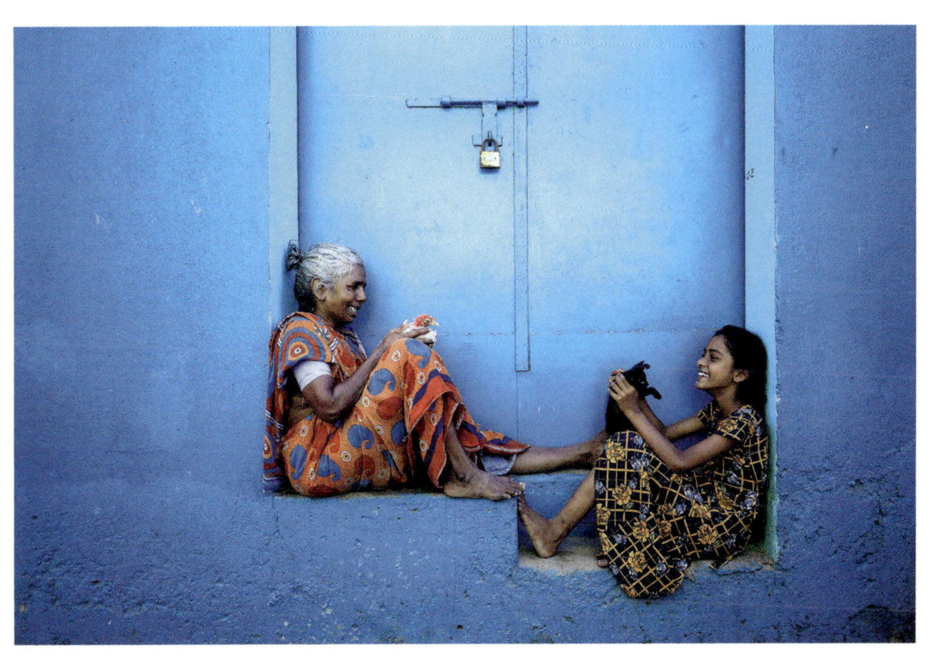

A Moment Shared

by Udayan Sankar Pal

Chennai, India

Dancing Halmonis
by An Rong Xu
New York City, New York, USA

These women belong to a senior dance troupe
that performs for the Korean American community
in Queens, New York City. In their 60s, 70s and 80s
these Halmonis ('grandmothers') dance, jive and
are having the time of their lives.

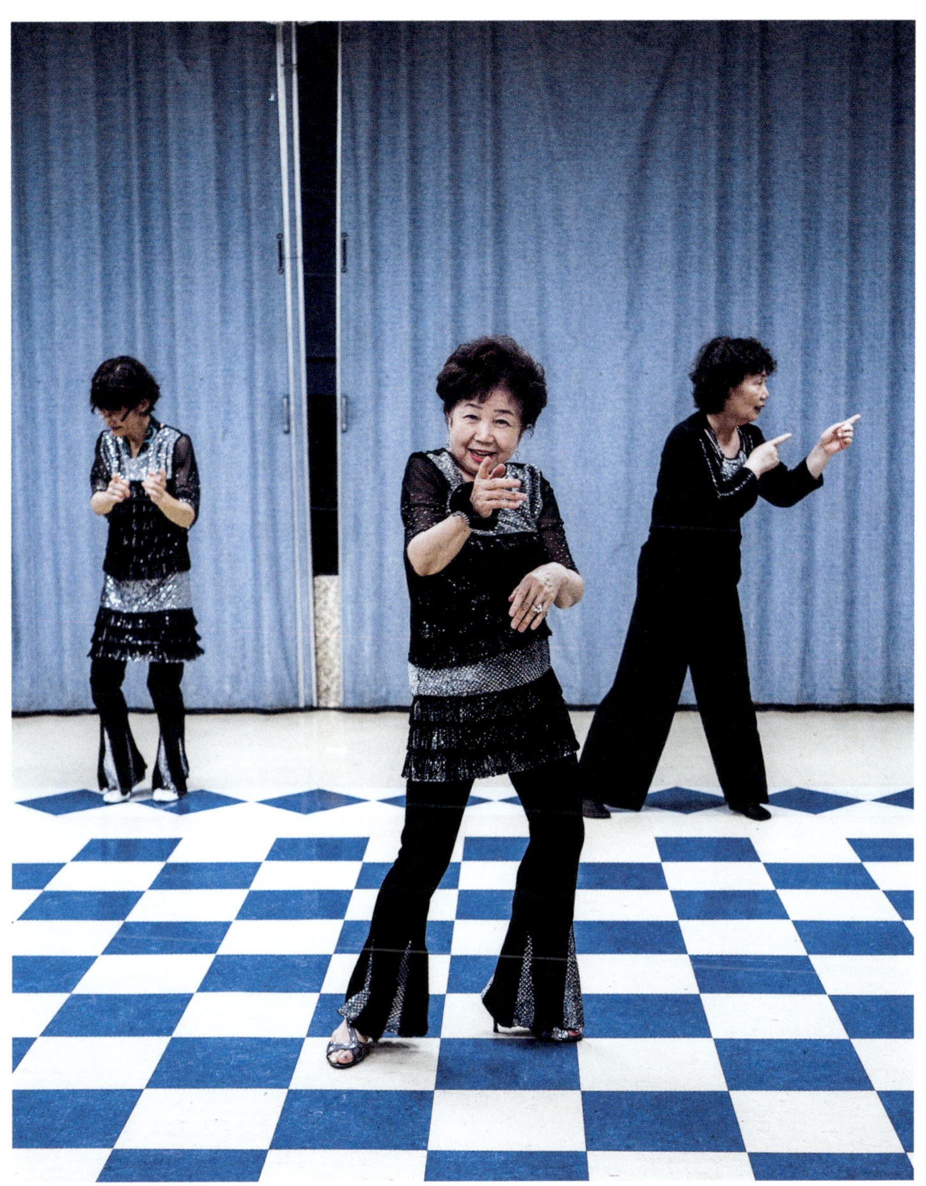

Sierra After a Chance Encounter
by Wesley Verhoeve
New York City, New York, USA

Sierra Odessa is a Harlem-based photographer.
I met her by chance one morning in Brooklyn. We were
both at a talk by renowned relationship therapist
Esther Perel. I walked past Sierra and noticed
her enigmatic and magnetic presence. About a week
later she sat for a portrait.

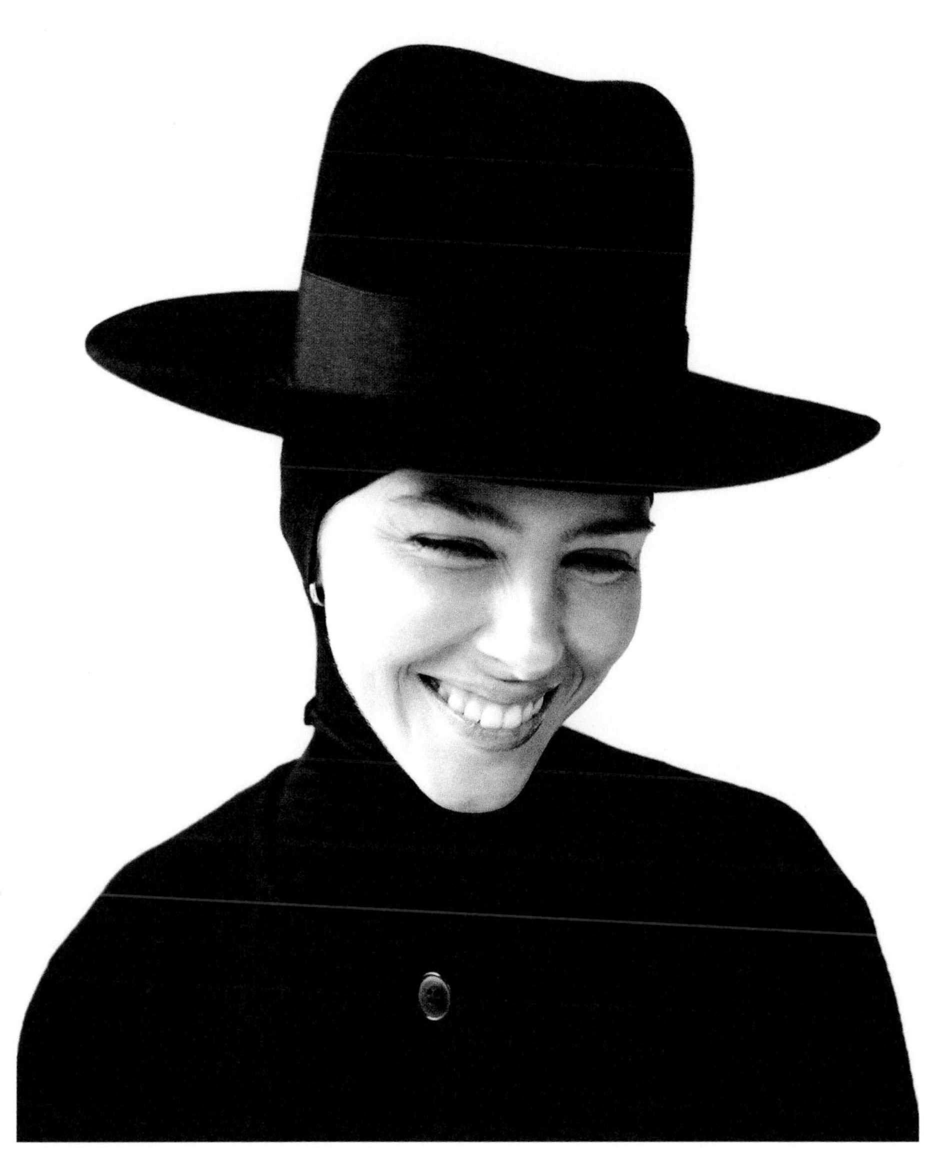

Equality's Girl
by Michał Szymończyk
Warsaw, Poland

This person cuts a consciously provocative and
confident figure at Warsaw's annual Equality Parade.
Some 50,000 attendees may be not enough
to change Polish mindsets towards LGBT communities
once and for all, but it is enough to temporarily
take over the city enabling people to express themselves
in the way they want without judgement.

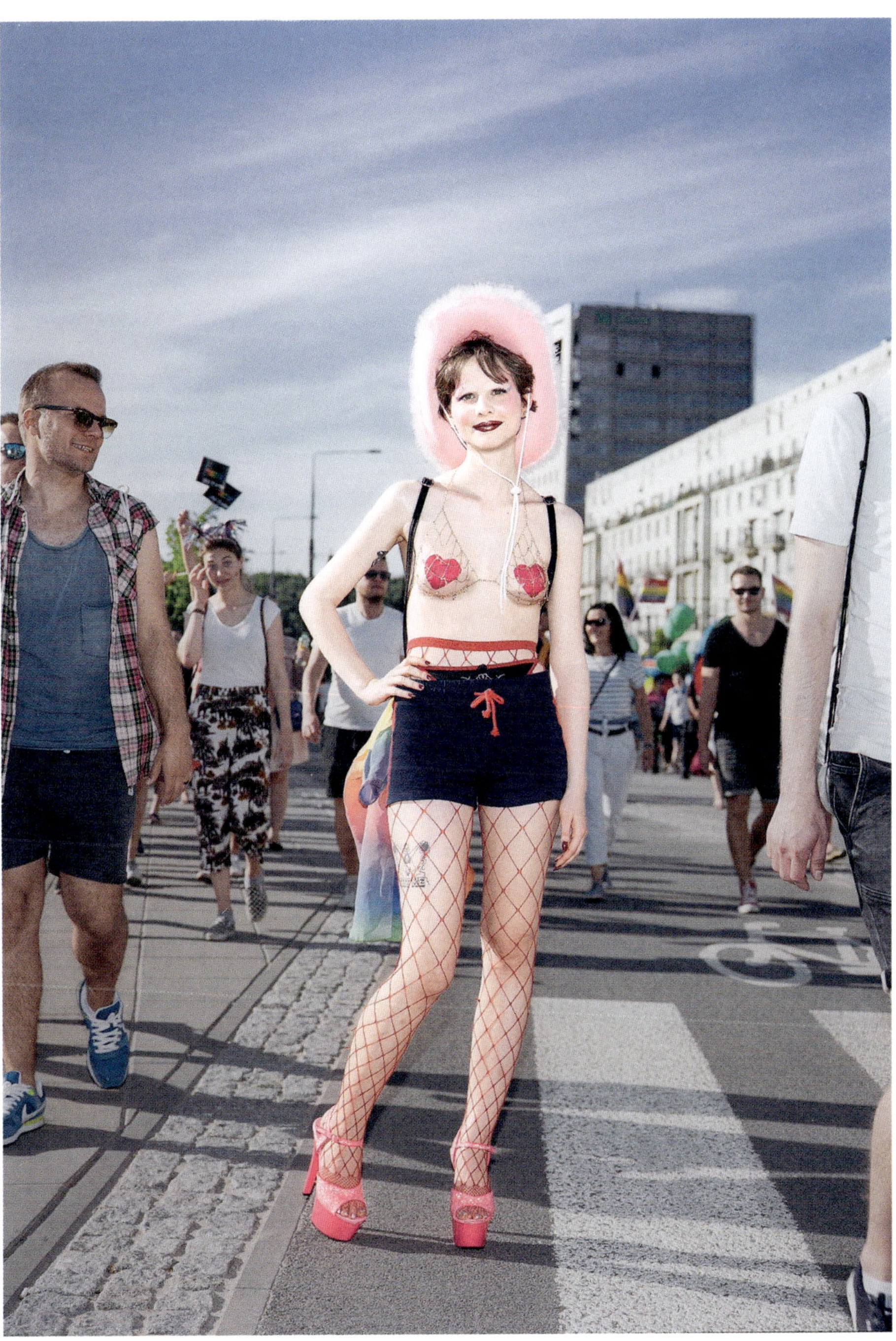

Marked as Possession
by Jonas Palm
Chin Village, Myanmar

The tattoos on this woman's face were made
with thorns and ink from pig fat, cow bile, plants
and soot. She has had them since the age of seven.
The procedure was extremely painful and she got very ill
afterwards. The tradition of tattooing women's
faces was to ensure they were not taken by men from
other villages. The practice was banned
in the 1960s. Today, only a handful women
with these markings remain.

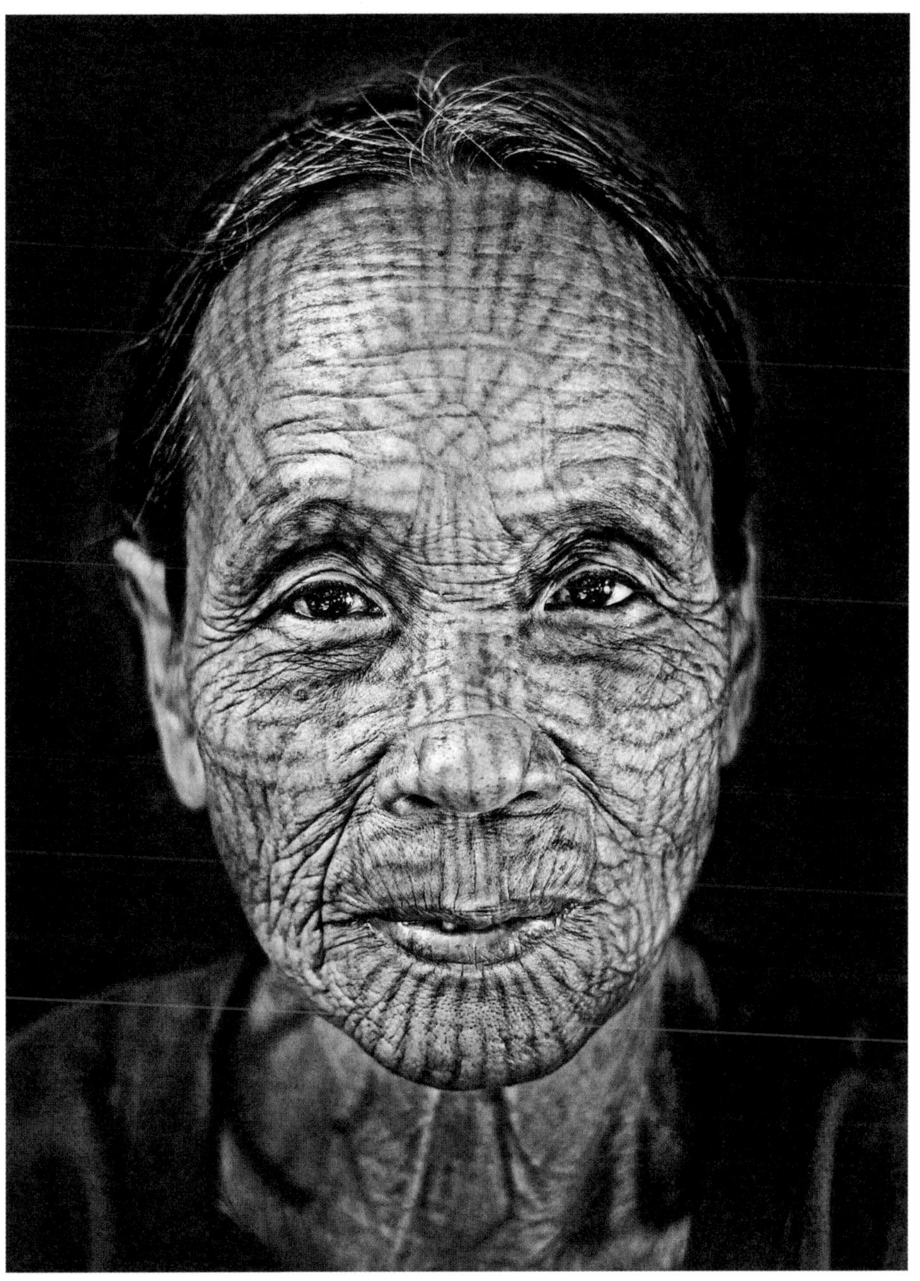

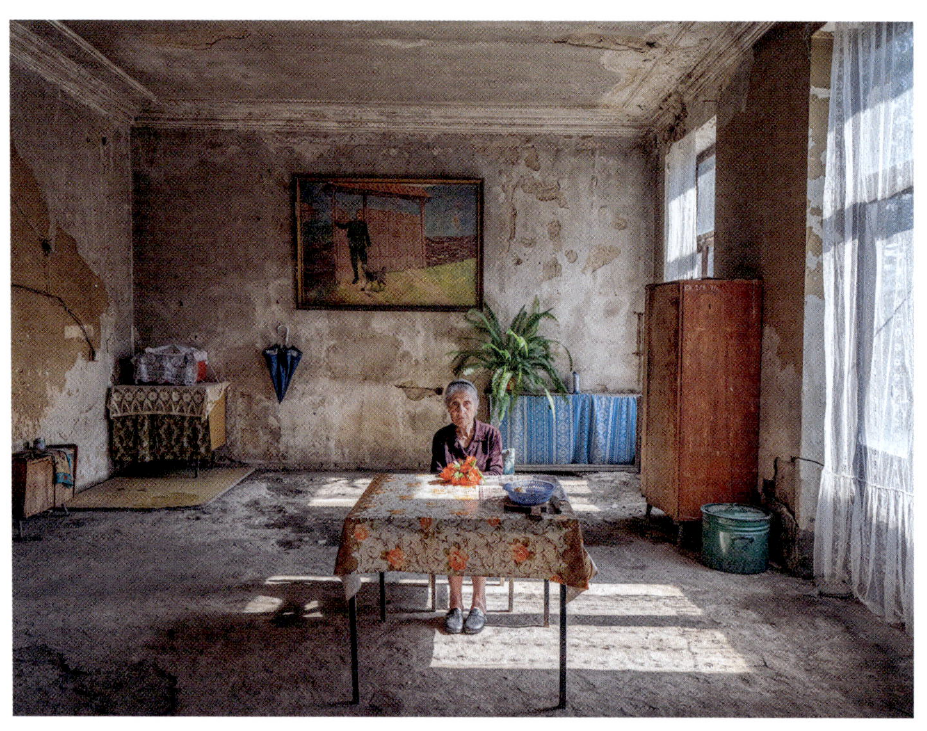

Blackout
by Hossein Fardinfard
Tskaltubo, Georgia

Merry is one of the victims of the war in Abkhazia
that broke out in 1992. Her brother and husband were
murdered in the conflict. With a wounded leg,
Merry escaped and hid in a forest for two weeks.

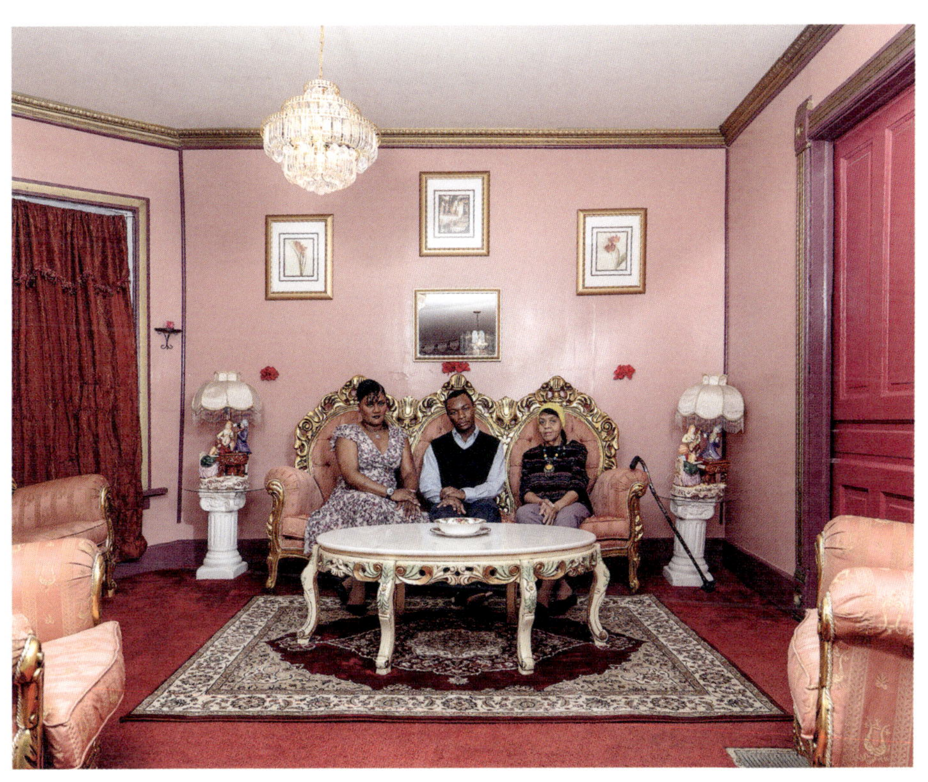

The Anderson Family
by Vivian Wan
Chicago, Illinois, USA

The Andersons live in one of the most famous homes
on Chicago's West Side. The pink and white
house was built in 1894 and stands tall as a
symbol of strength and resilience.

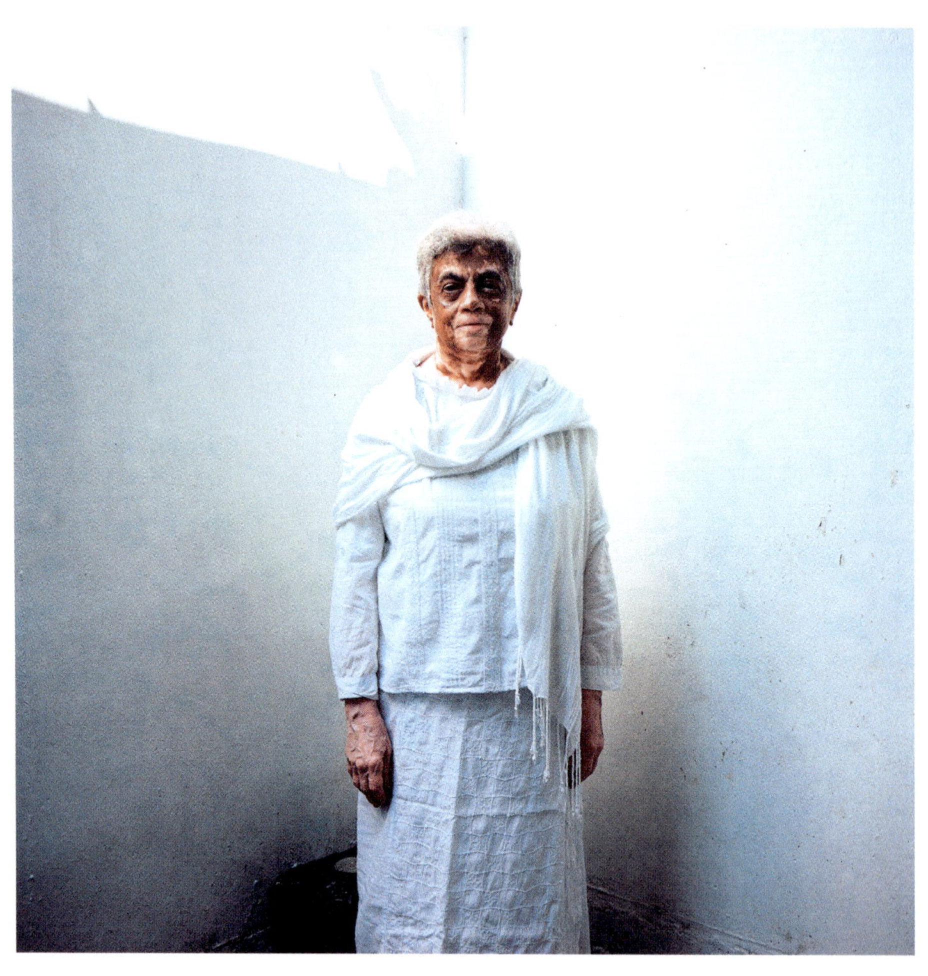

Neetha in Her Kitchen
by Charlotte Javelot Ward
Colombo, Sri Lanka

Neetha, a friend I made during my travels in Sri Lanka,
is a fervent Buddhist. She very generously welcomed
me into her home for a week before I undertook a Buddhist
pilgrimage around the island country.

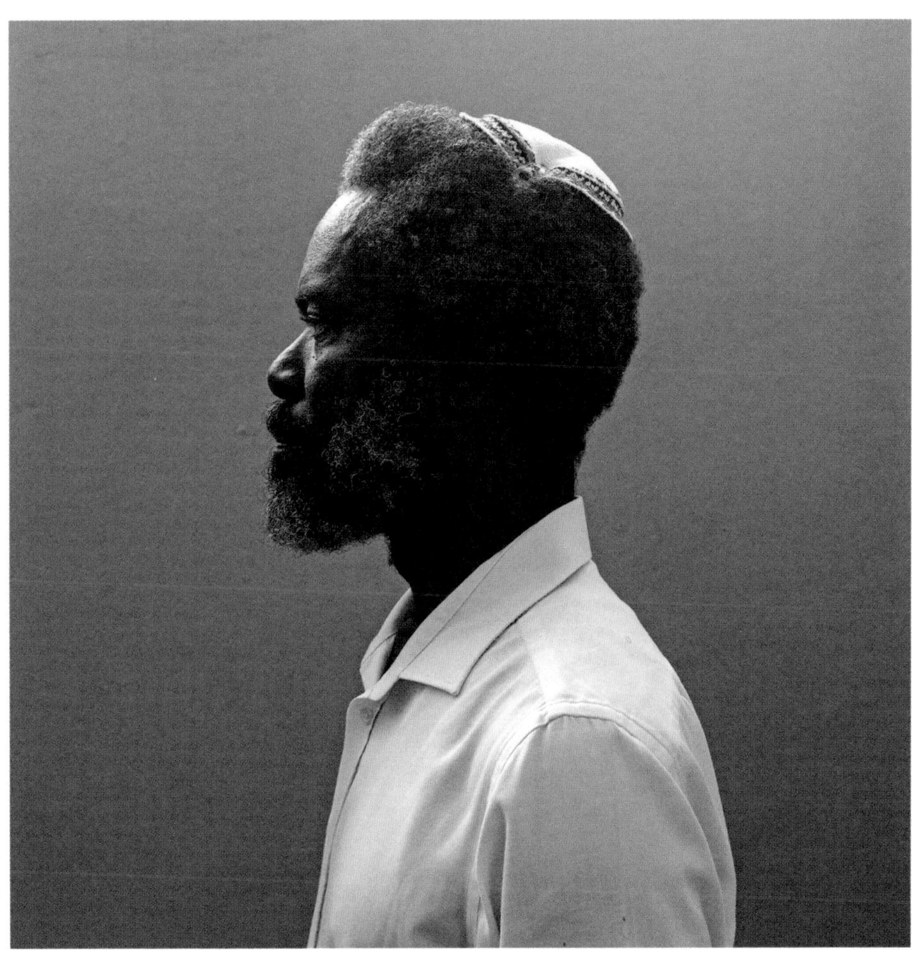

Trinidadian Jewish Man
by Robert Huggins
Port of Spain, Trinidad and Tobago

I met this man in my home town. We had a long
chat about his conversion to Judaism.
He told me he was a recent convert and quietly but
diligently practises his faith with his family.

Pastor Seburikoko Alberta
by Hannah Maule-ffinch
The Border of the DRC and Uganda

Pastor Seburikoko Alberta and his family
were abducted in January 2018 by Mai-Mai rebels
in the Democratic Republic of Congo who demanded
a ransom for their release. The pastor escaped
and walked for days to reach the Ugandan border.
He was immaculately dressed and such a
calming soul who was so happy to talk to me.
I felt blessed to have met him. His empathy
for those around him despite all he had been
through was mind-blowing.

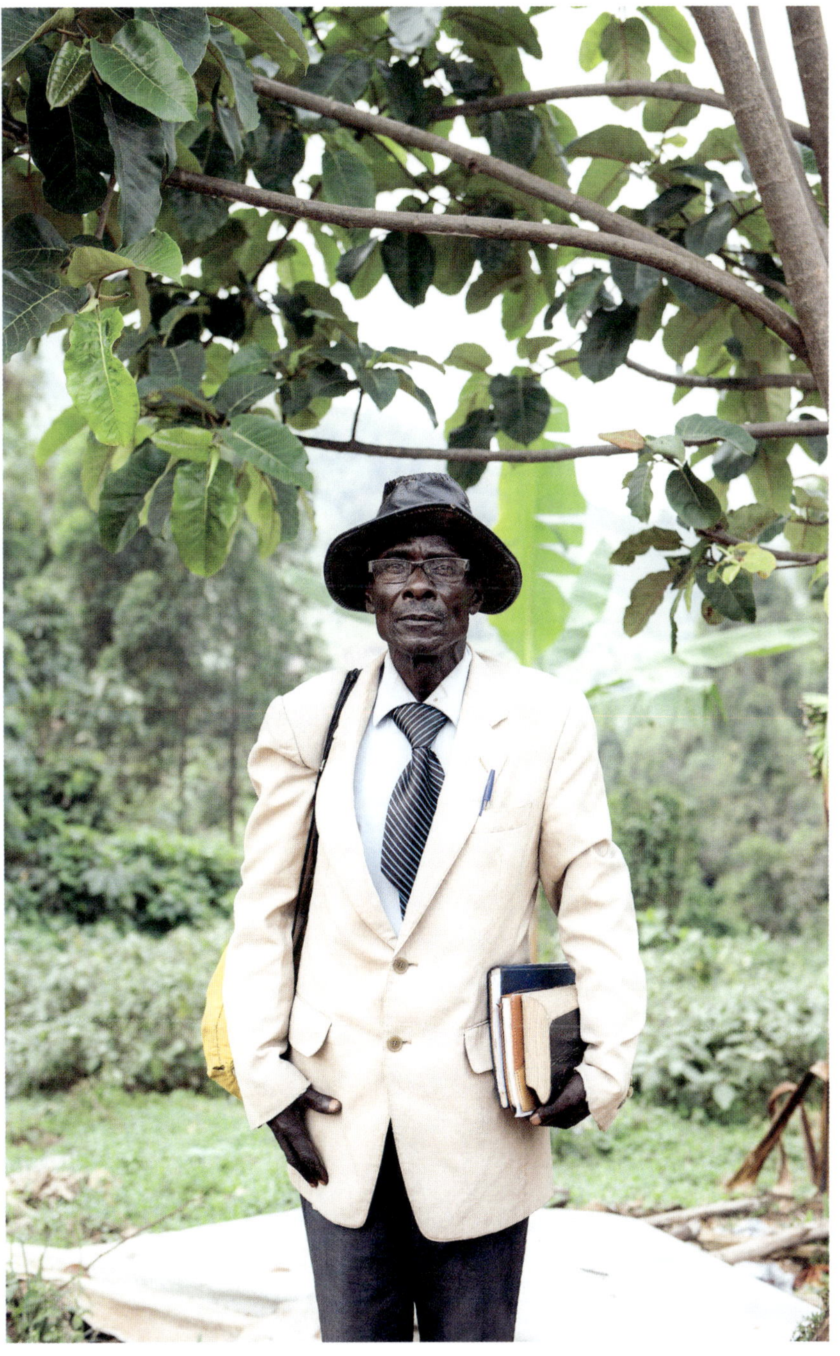

Henry

by Severien Vits
Tonbridge, Kent

Henry, 7, is the youngest of my children.
He does not like having his picture taken at all.
I needed a portrait of him for his passport
and after a few failures he unwittingly posed.
I started to enjoy the grumpiness and didn't wait
for a smile or even a neutral expression.

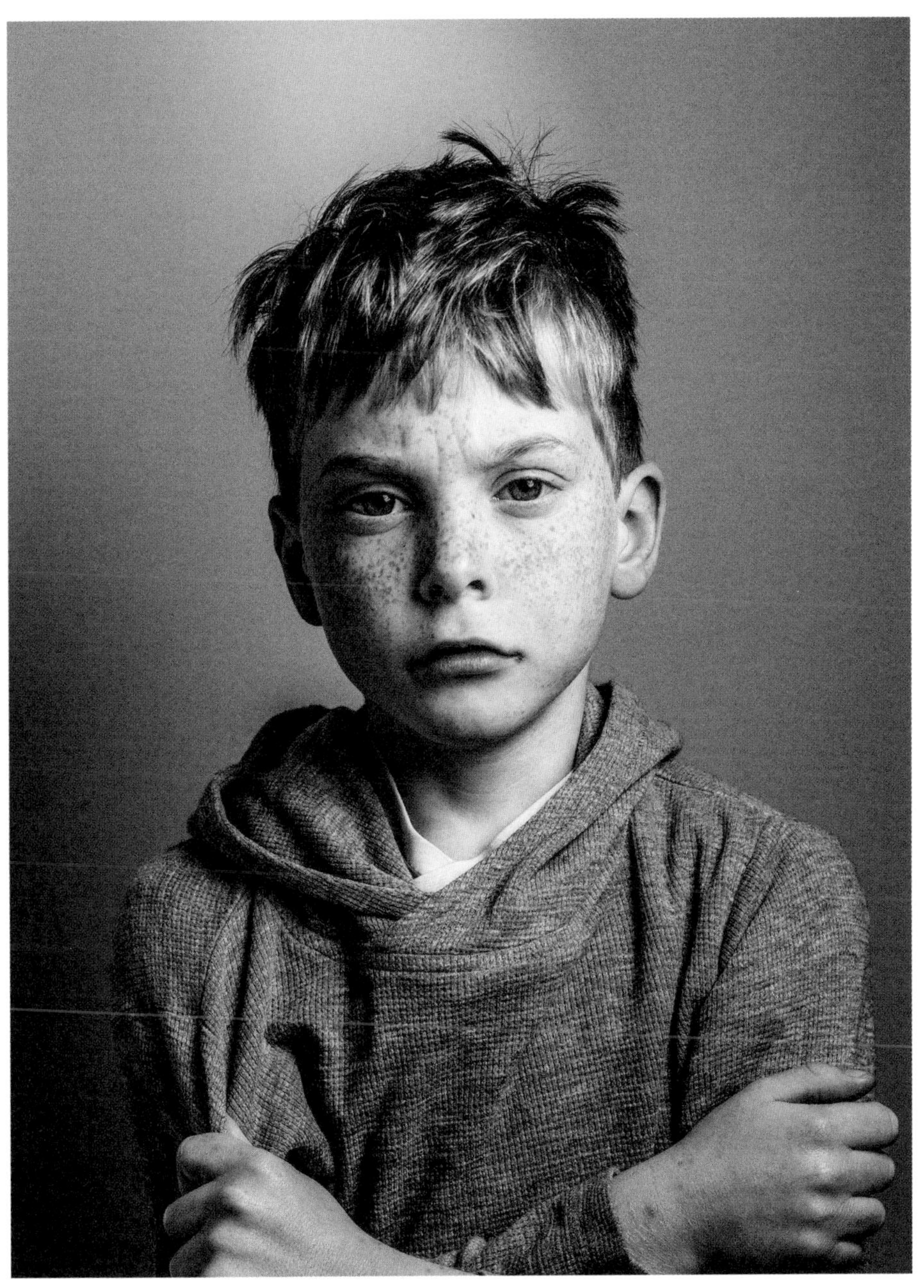

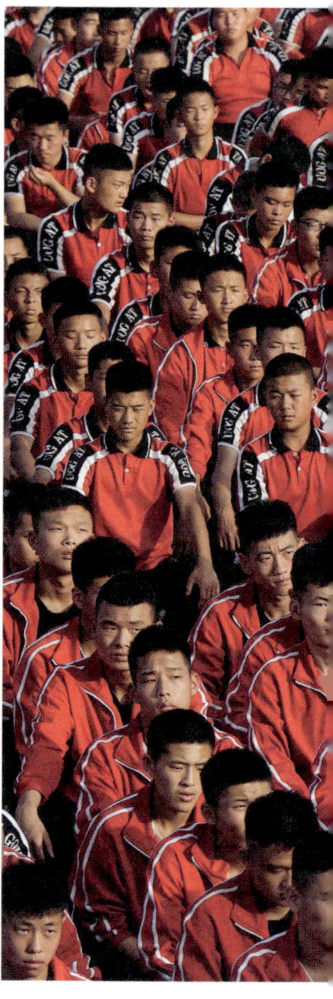

236

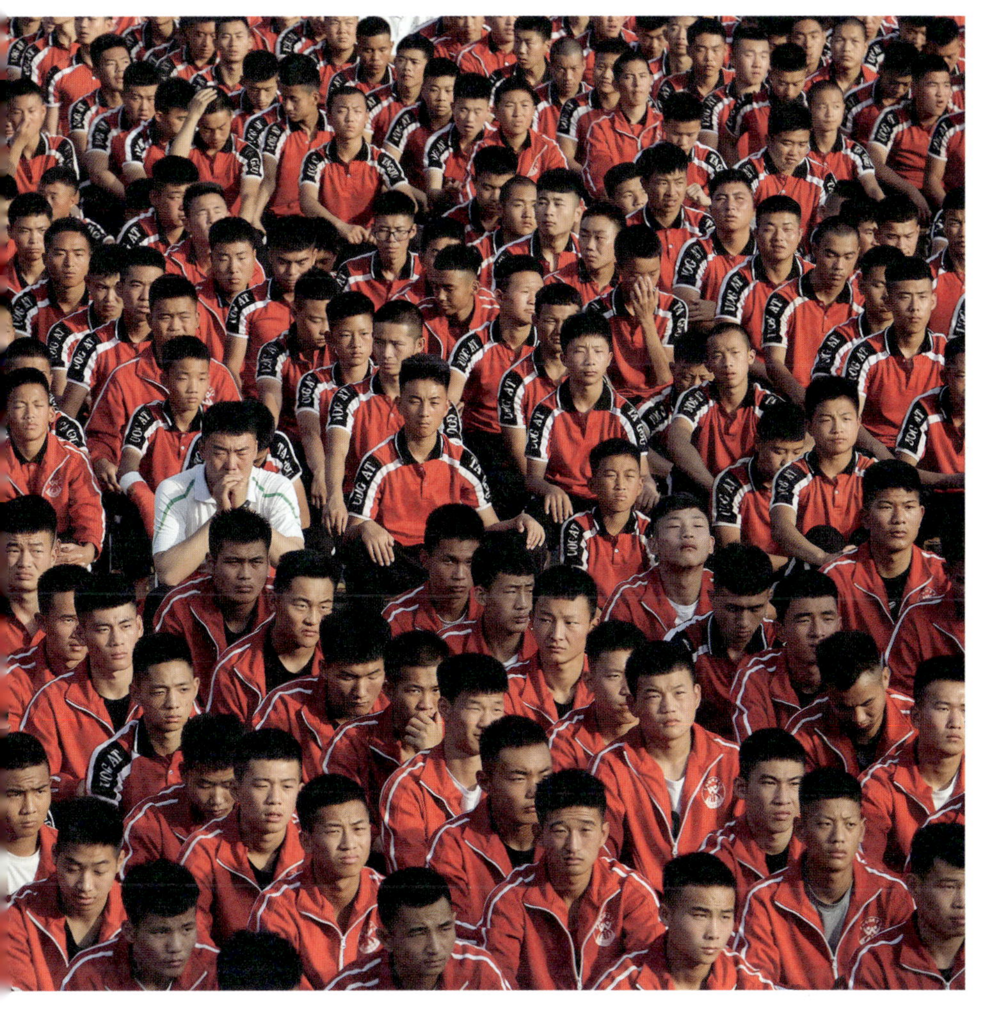

Concentrating

by Zeev Parush

Hunan, China

During a visit to the Shaolin Temple I witnessed a huge gathering
of kung fu students. It was interesting to see the way the
instructors were set apart from their students by their uniforms.

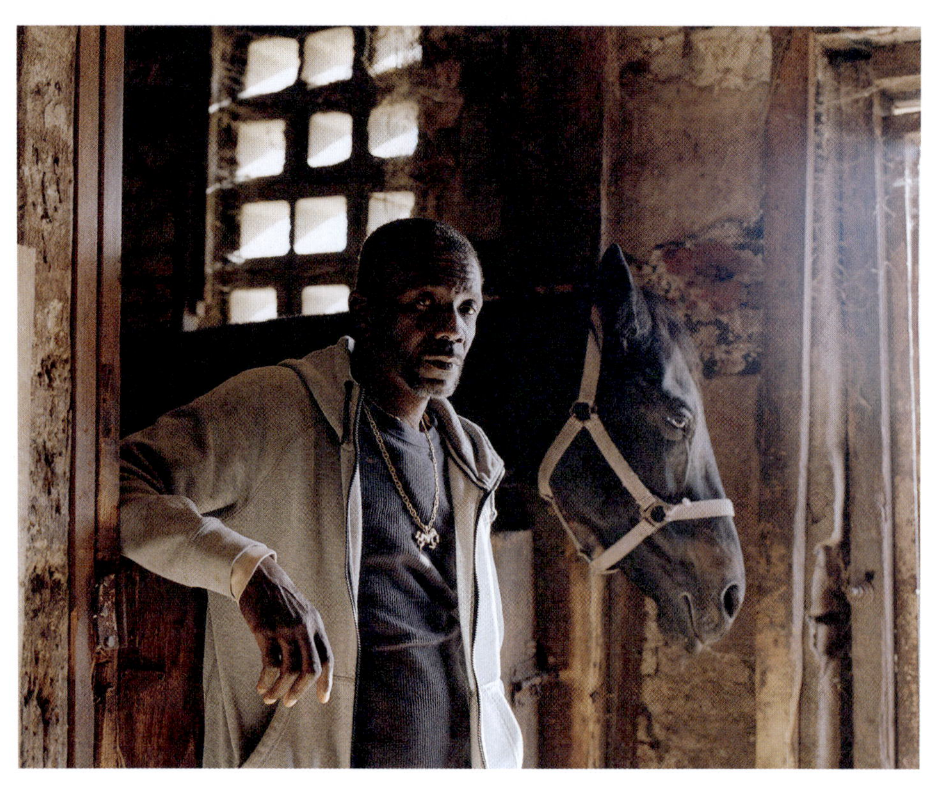

Stevie

by Cian Oba-Smith
Philadelphia, Pennsylvania, USA

Stevie is one of the older riders at Fletcher Street
Urban Riding Club who spends time looking after
and riding horses at the stables.

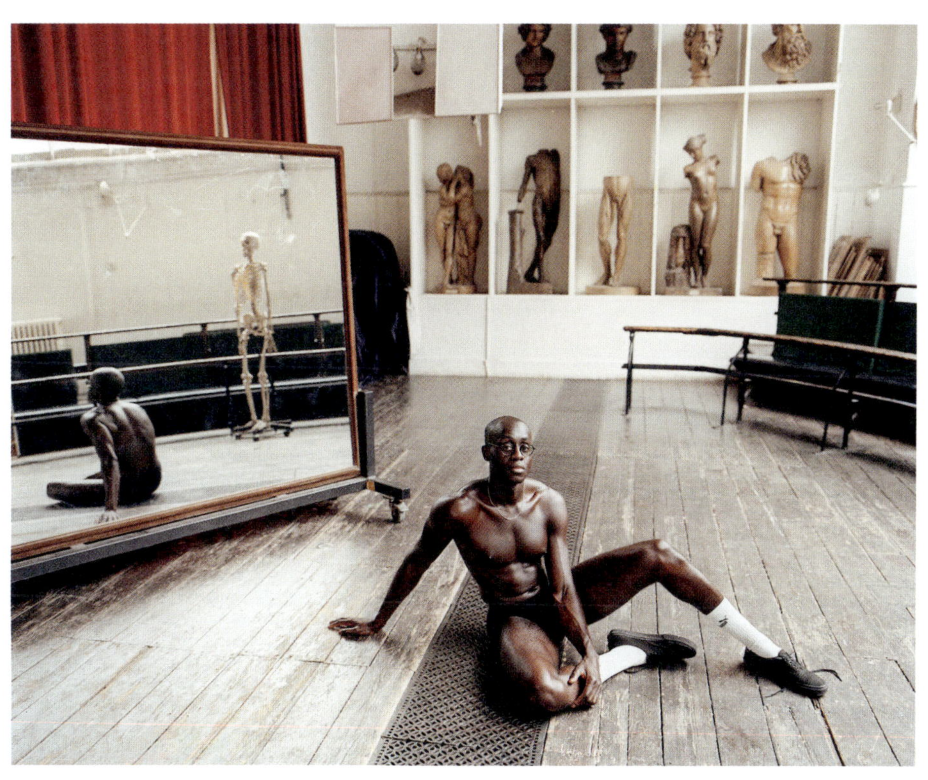

Joe
by Jooney Woodward
London, UK

Joe is a pharmacist who agreed to let me
take his portrait. Here he is in the Life Room at
the Royal Academy Schools, which is steeped
in history and tradition.

White Rooster, Blue Wall
by Alex Franco
Dimeka, Ethiopia

I saw this boy on market day. It was my first
time in Ethiopia and we had been driving for three days
from Addis Ababa to Turmi in the Omo Valley
when we made a stop at Dimeka. I was struck by how
the boy from the Hamar tribe and rooster
looked against the blue wall.

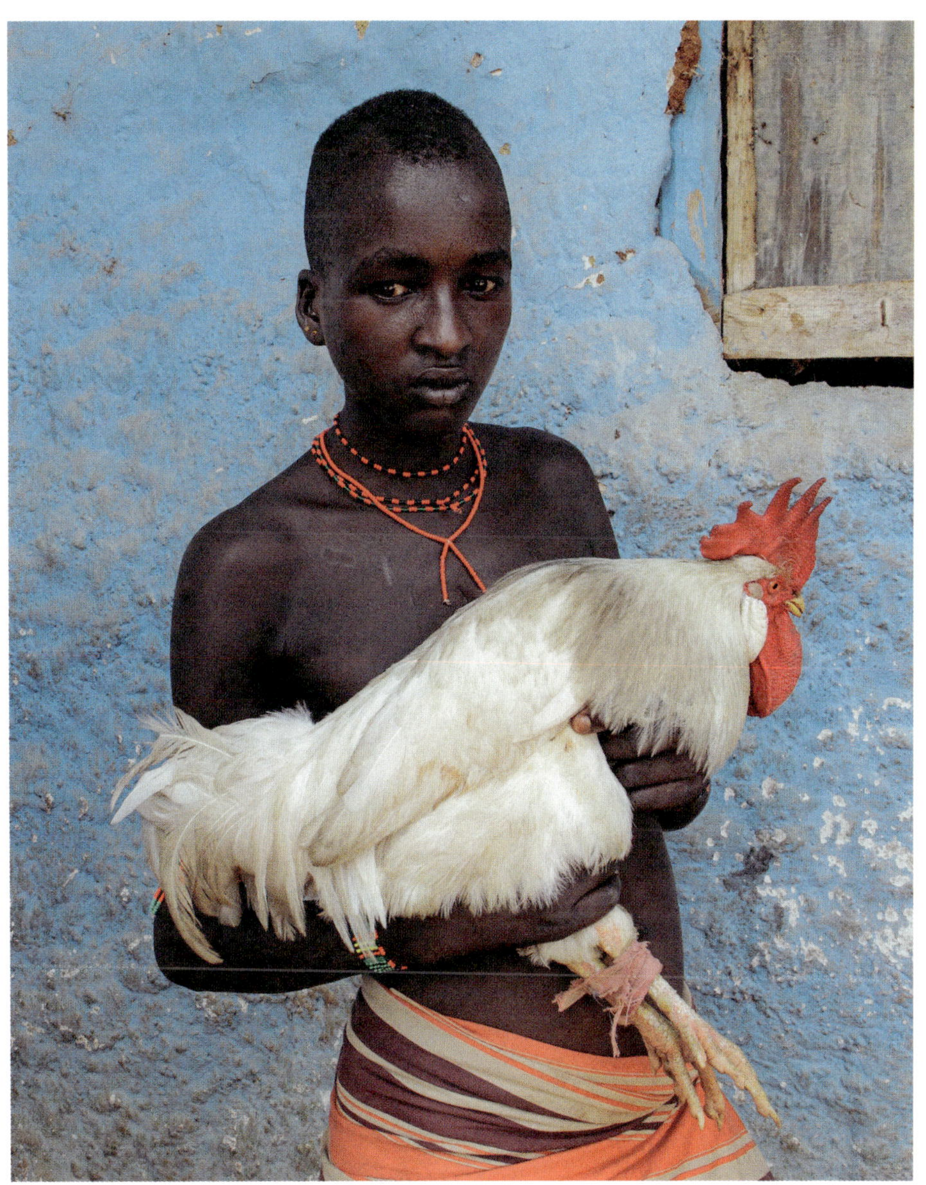

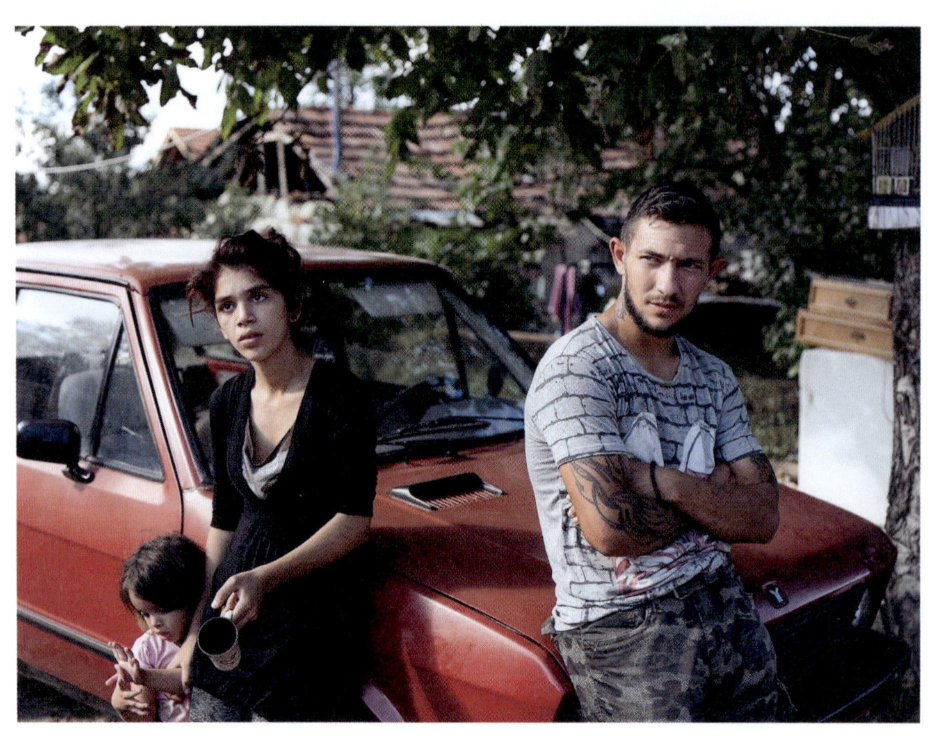

Marija and Nino
by Claudia Leisinger
Merošina, Serbia

Marija and Nino listen to a mutual friend
talk about his life abroad and employment. Finding
work is one of the biggest problems for
Serbian Roma families.

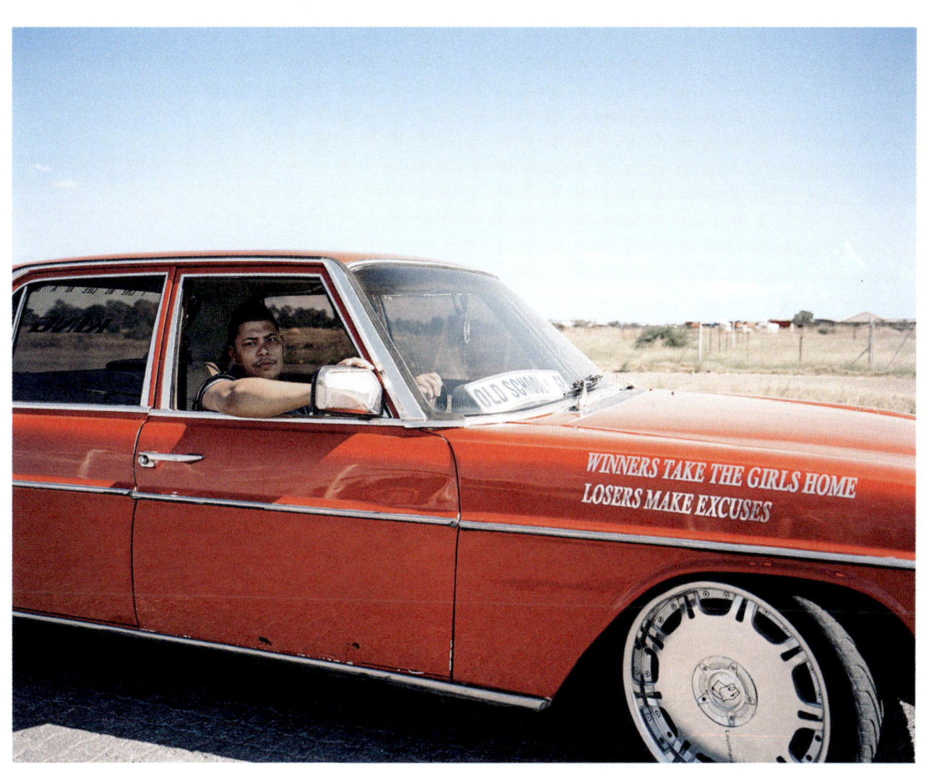

King G

by Ilan Godfrey

Kimberley, Northern Cape Province, South Africa

There was a time when 'King G' made a living
buying and selling diamonds from informal diamond
diggers in the area. He now entertains crowds
by spinning and drifting his classic Mercedes-Benz
at the Monstermob Raceway.

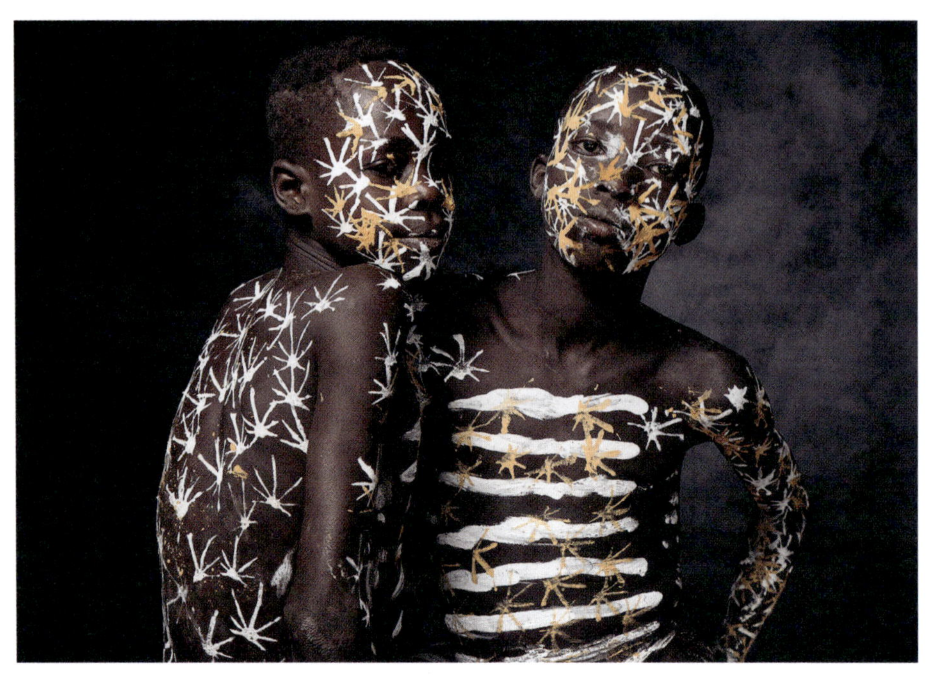

In the Name of Tribe

by Biljana Jurukovski
Kibish, Ethiopia

These young boys are from the Surma tribe and
live on the border between Ethiopia and South Sudan.
The region, with its ancient and mystical civilisation,
is the avant-garde of the tribal world, where nature
inspires creativity and self-expression.

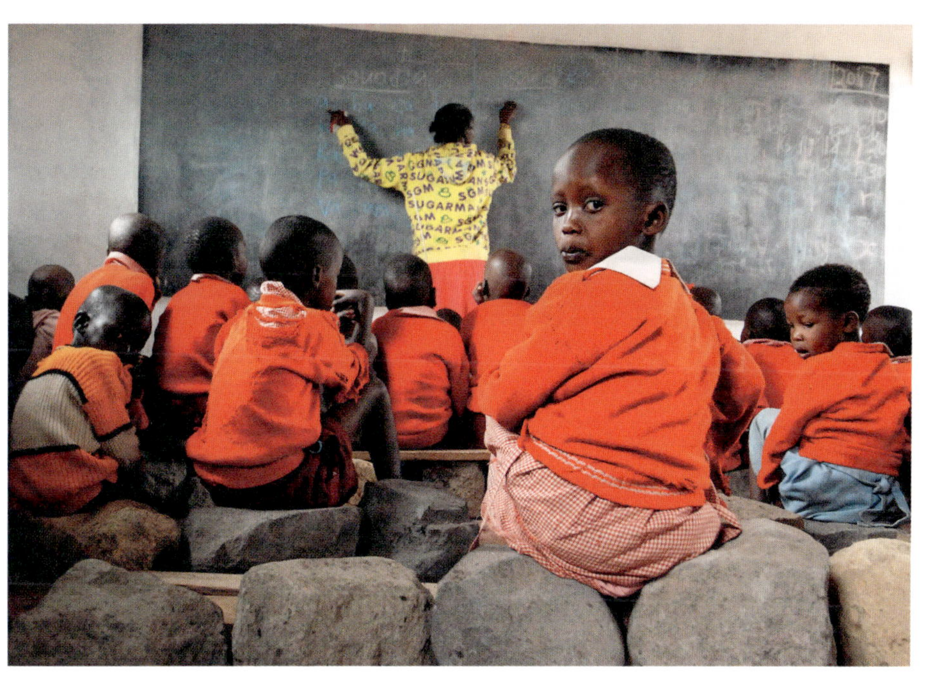

The Gaze

by Mercedeh Mirshamsi
Maasai Village, Narok, Kenya

I was on a volunteer mission in Kenya and travelled
to a Maasai village on the border with Tanzania. I helped to
make tables and chairs for the schoolchildren who usually
sit on rocks during lessons. The children were always
in high spirits, interactive and curious.

Window to the World
by Felipe Aguilar
Camagüey, Cuba

These young people are members of Ballet de Camagüey,
the city's classical ballet ensemble. To me they
embody a dynamic energy in an otherwise static city.
This moment of camaraderie shows the closeness
of the group. That the dancers are looking at a mobile
phone is significant: Cuba has been expanding
access to the internet in recent years and they can now
keep up to date on the current state of ballet
and everything else around the globe.

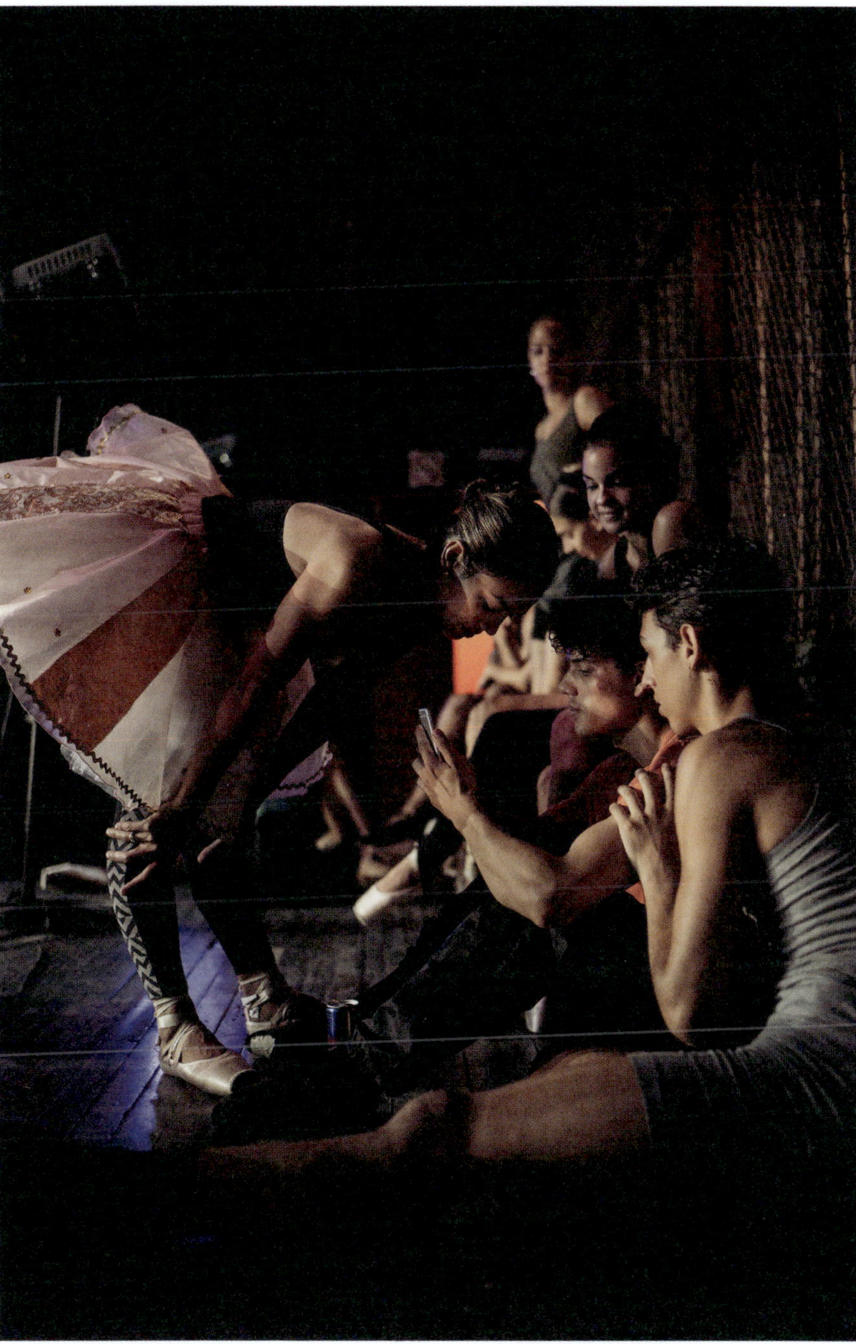

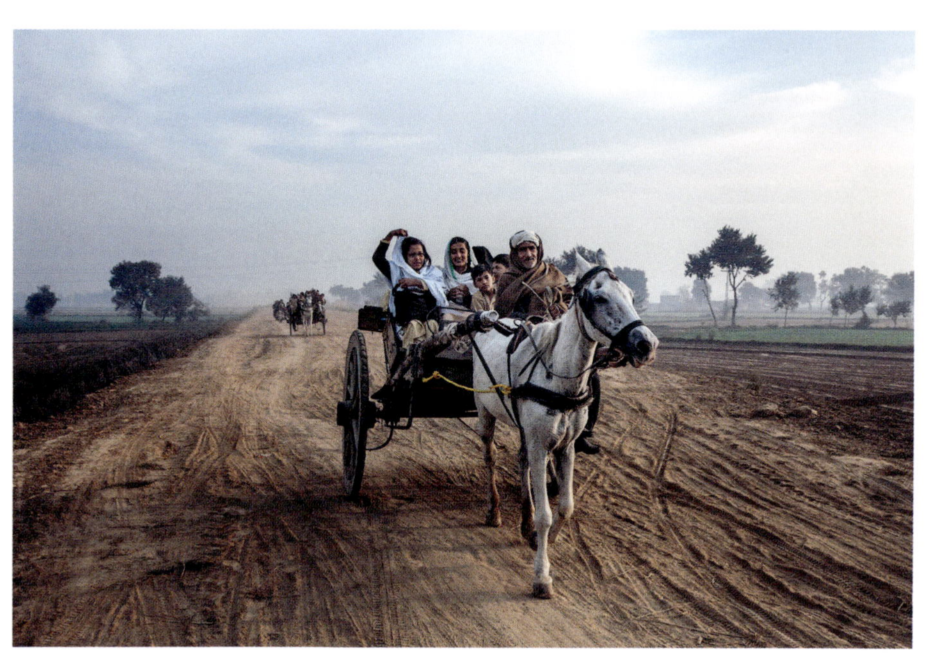

Education for All

by Albertina d'Urso
Between Nathoki and Minhala, Pakistan

Children leave their homes early in the morning
to reach schools run by non-profit organisation
The Citizens Foundation (TCF). Founded in 1995,
the TCF provides high-quality education
for the most unprivileged through purpose-built
schools embedded in the heart of Pakistan's
urban slums and rural communities.

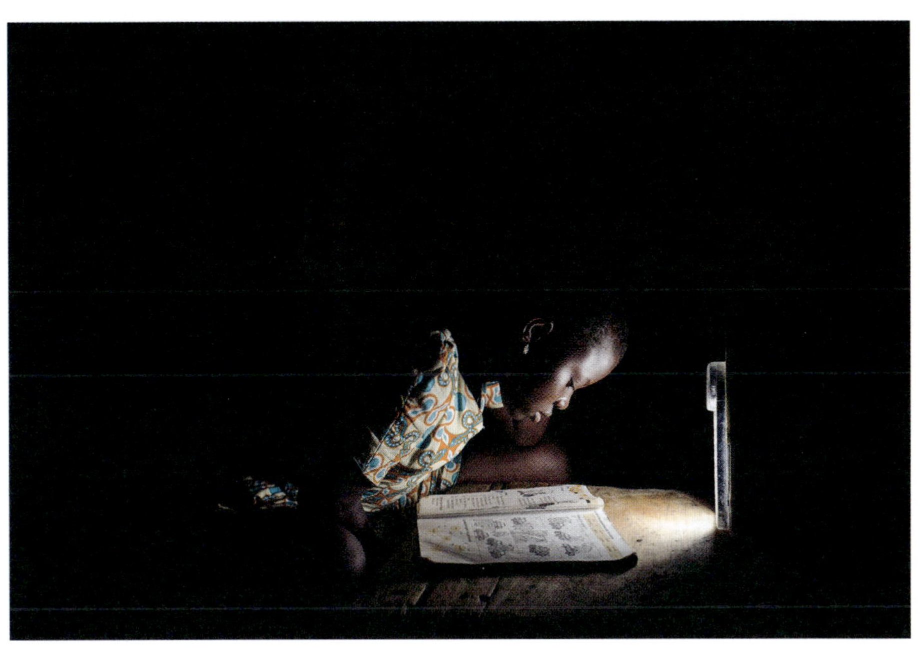

Rita Reading

by Nyani Quarmyne
Volta Region, Ghana

Seventeen-year-old Rita reads aloud from
an English textbook. She is the picture of tenacity.
Her father said she had been living with relatives
who made her work in the marketplace rather than go
to school. Rita started classes after moving to
her father's home in early 2014. Her determination
to make up for lost time was palpable.

Empty Mirror
by Roger S. Echegoyén
New York City, New York, USA

A scene from Gay Pride in West Village. The man
in the centre dressed in old fashioned clothes and holding
old camera gear appears to be trying to recapture
the past, yet, like the person next to him, he is unable
to escape the technology of the present; ironically
he kept looking at his phone.

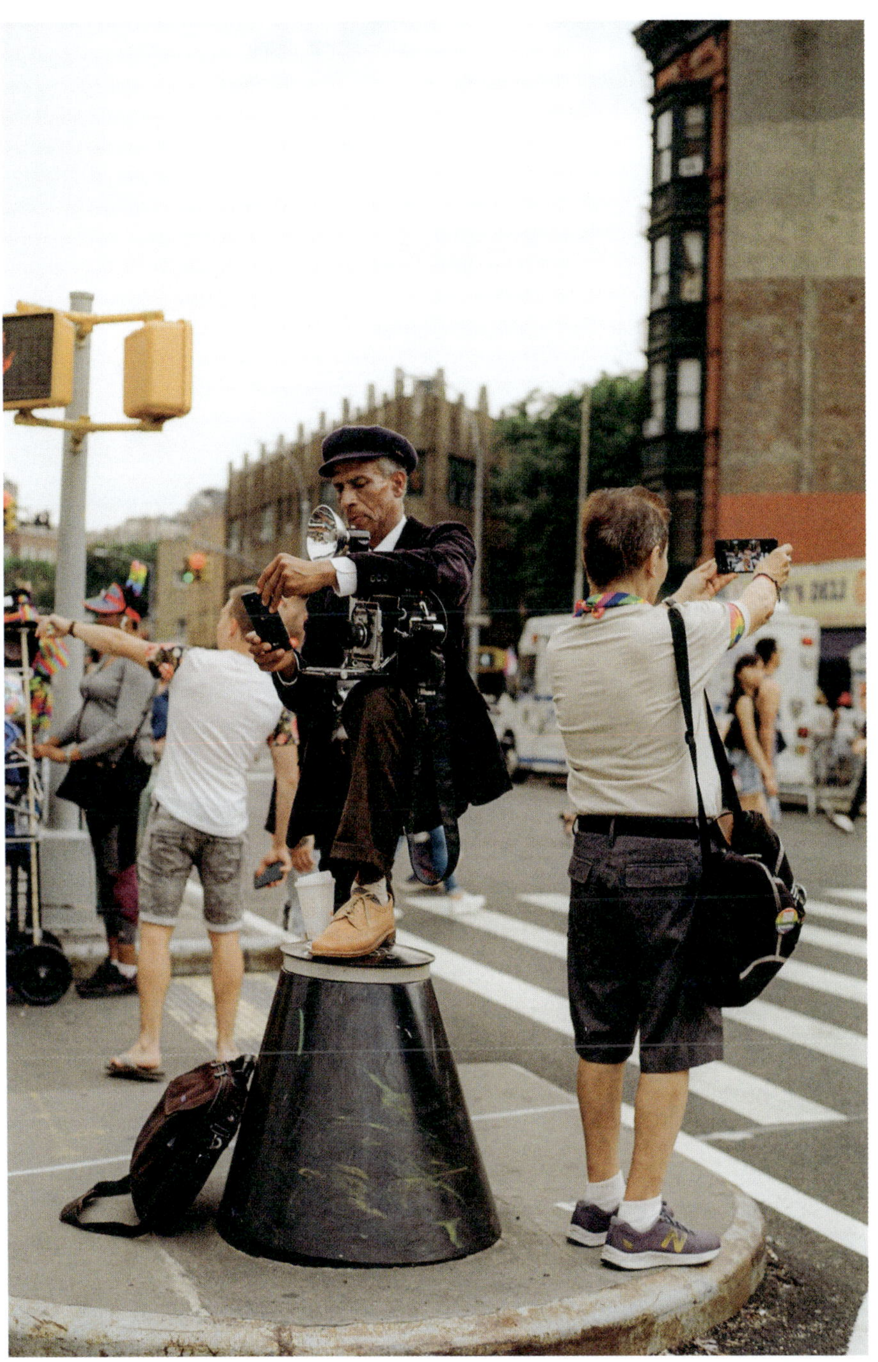

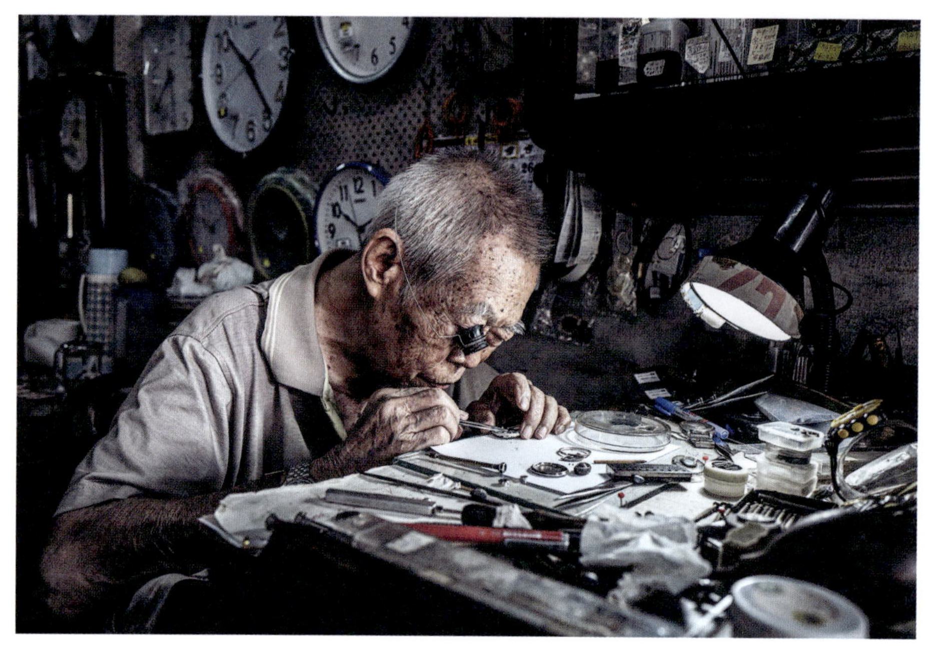

The Old Time Keeper

by Toh Ee Siew
Klang, Malaysia

This hardworking elderly man repairs watches,
clocks and other timepieces. He is 83 years old and his
eyesight has not yet failed him. 'I will grow older
and weaker if I stop fixing time,' he said.

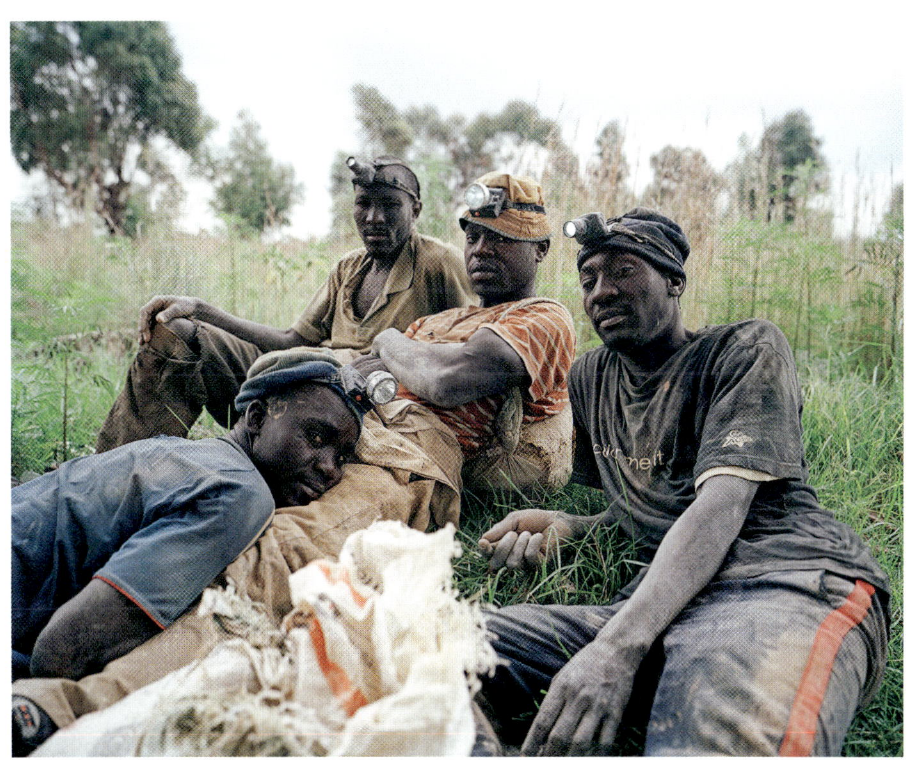

Legacy of the Mine
by Ilan Godfrey
Johannesburg, South Africa

A group of 'informal' gold diggers rests
after a night's work. They are highly skilled and
have many years' experience. To the local
community they are brave men who are respected
for their ability to find gold.

Mr Lee
by Zico O'Neill
Auckland, New Zealand

Mr Lee on his lunch break along Auckland's
Dominion Road, a go-to place for Asian cuisine. But
it is more than that. The restaurants provide
a livelihood for a whole community. I was interested
in the people behind the facades and bright lights
of this strip of restaurants.

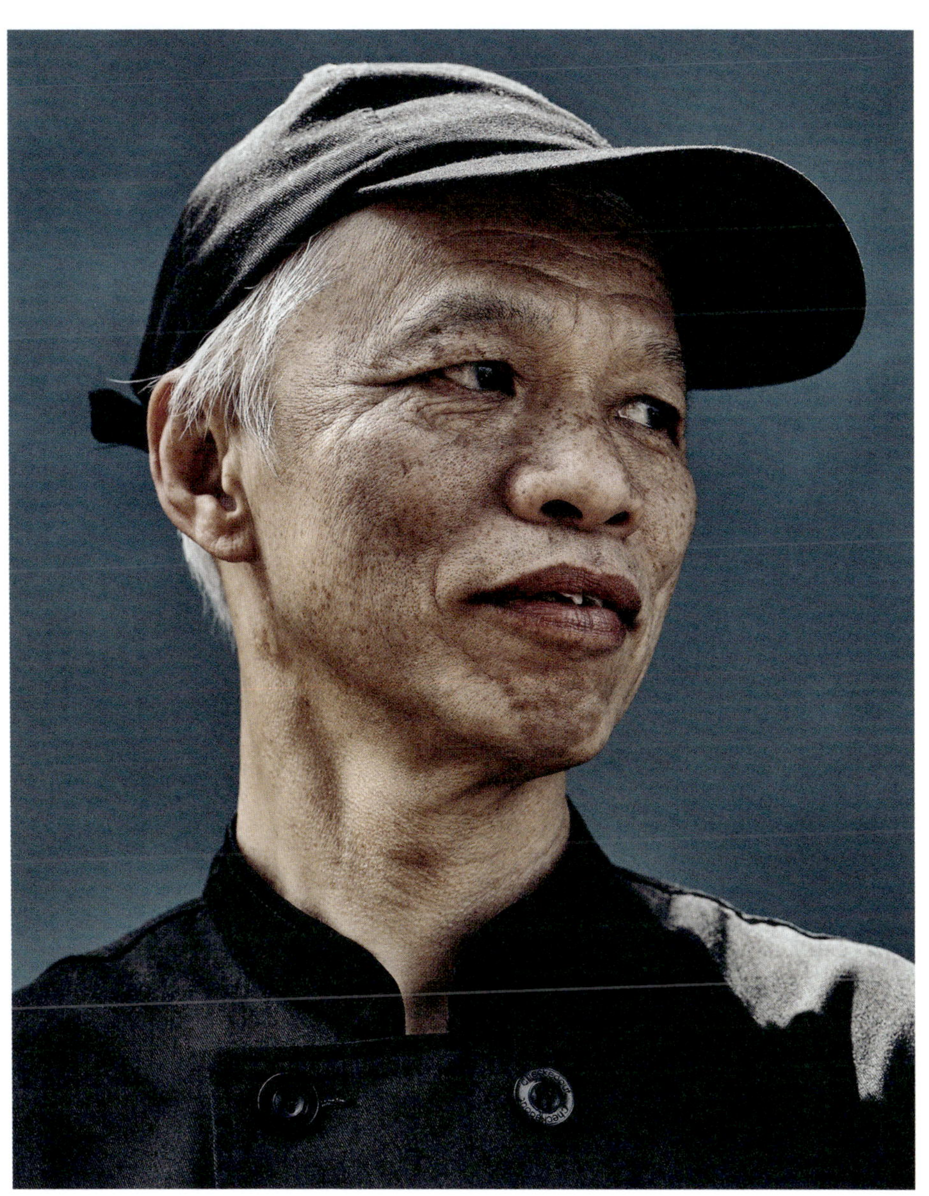

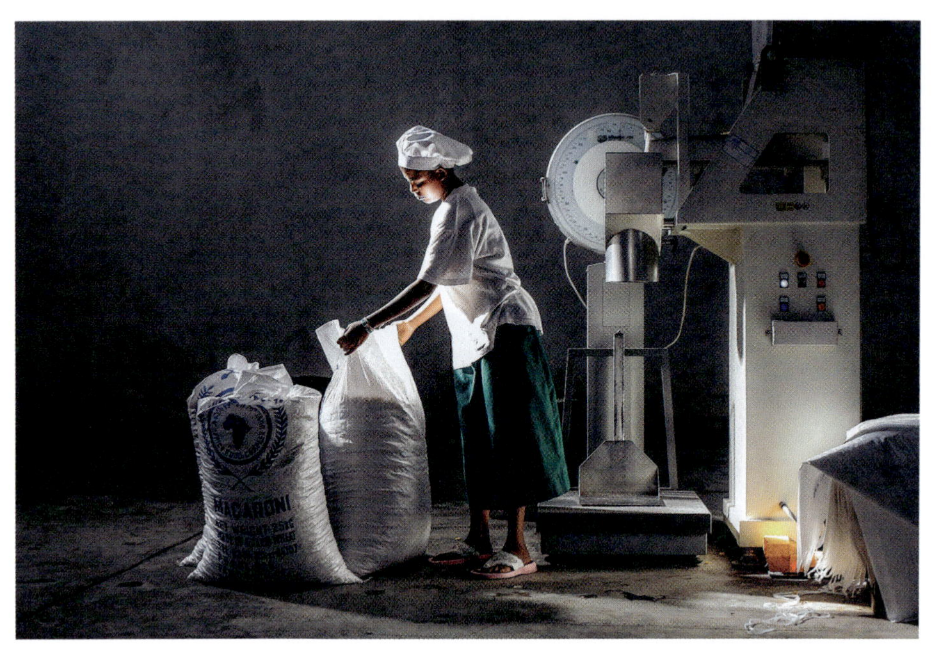

Leke

by David Levene
Nazret, Ethiopia

Leke is a former street child who had recently been
rescued. The Forum on Sustainable Child
Empowerment (FSCE) helped Leke find a safe place to
live and a job in the local pasta factory. Now 17,
Leke provides inspiration to younger girls
being cared for by the FSCE who hope to live
and work in a safe environment.

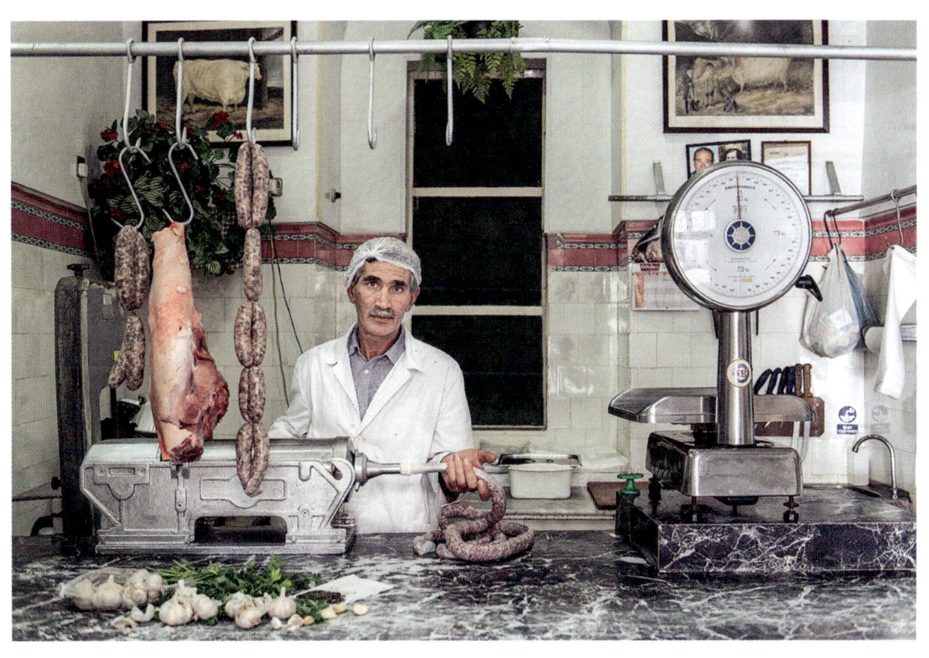

Village Butcher
by Joseph Smith
Żurrieq, Malta

Anthony Vella, the village butcher,
produces traditional local delicacies, particularly
Maltese sausage. He is a third generation butcher
and this type of sausage is his speciality.
I love the environment and his deadpan demeanour.
'This is the life I know and I have been taught
to give my clients only the best,' he said.

Tchiloli Man
by Rui Camilo
São Tomé, São Tomé and Príncipe

This is Metaba, an actor from one of the oldest
Tchiloli theatre ensembles in the country. Tchiloli is
a type of traditional performance that combines drama,
dance and music. Metaba is very passionate about
Tchiloli. I liked his determination and pride.

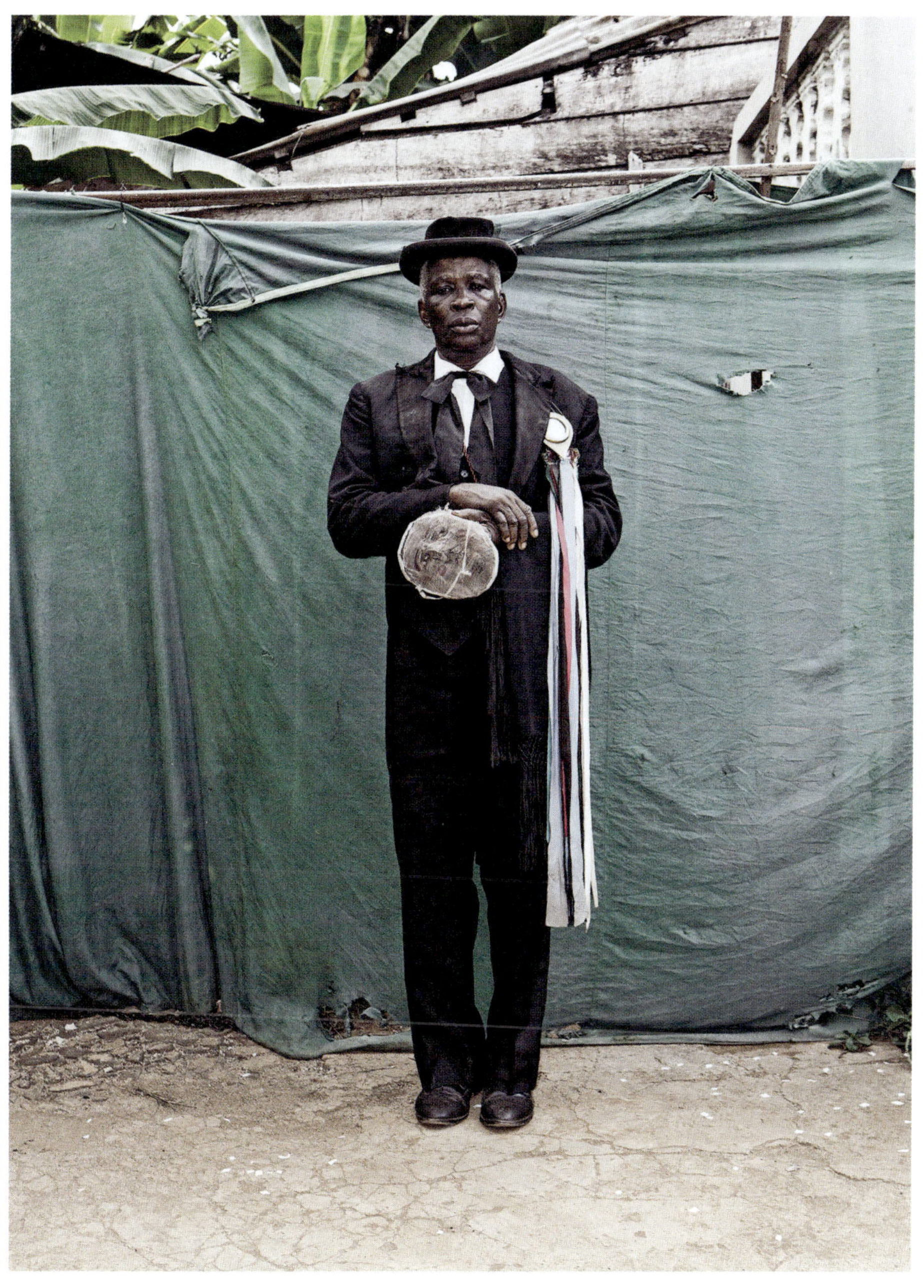

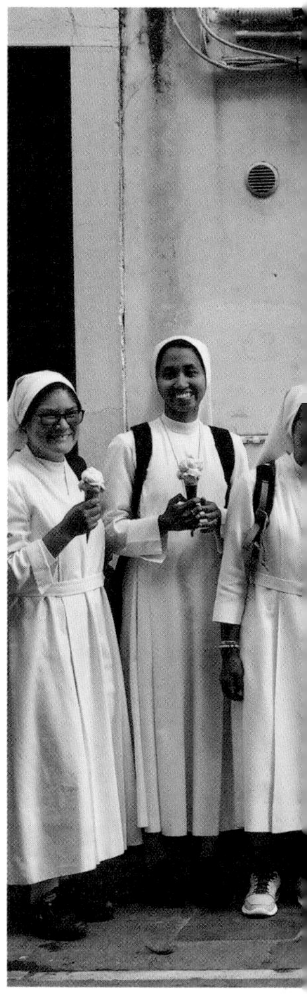

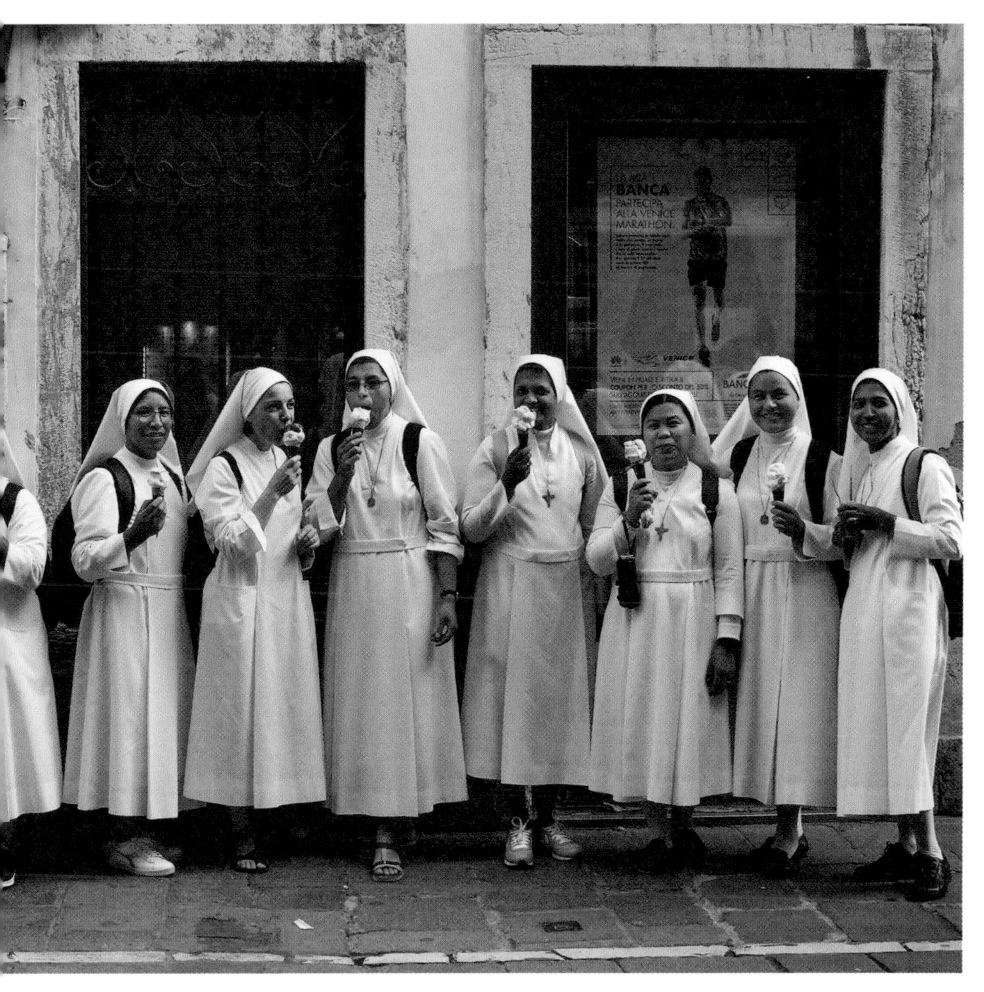

Rio Terà Lista di Spagna
by Richard Morgan
Venice, Italy

I came across a group of nuns ordering ice cream
in Venice. They were talking excitedly and laughing together
as they queued, and gladly agreed to a portrait.

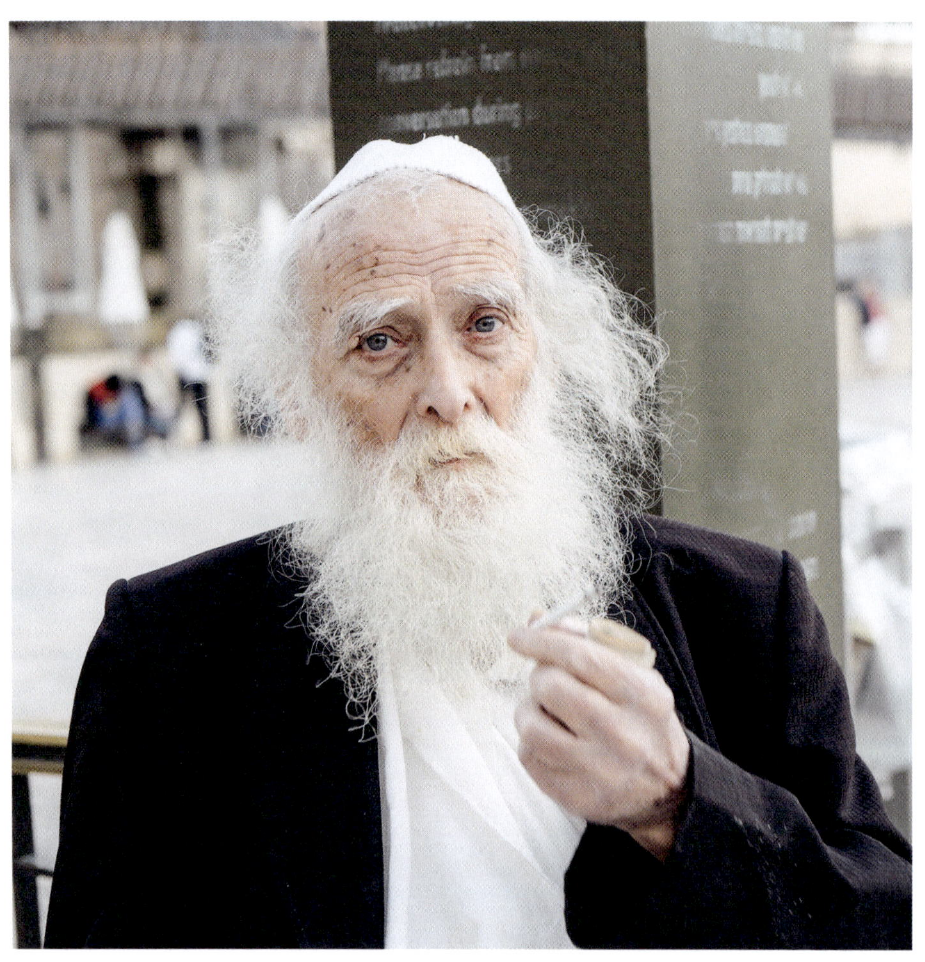

Old and Wise
by Noah Shahar
Jerusalem, Israel

I noticed this gentleman by the entrance to
the plaza in front of the Western Wall in the Old City
of Jerusalem. His peaceful yet solemn demeanour
made him stand out from the crowd.

262

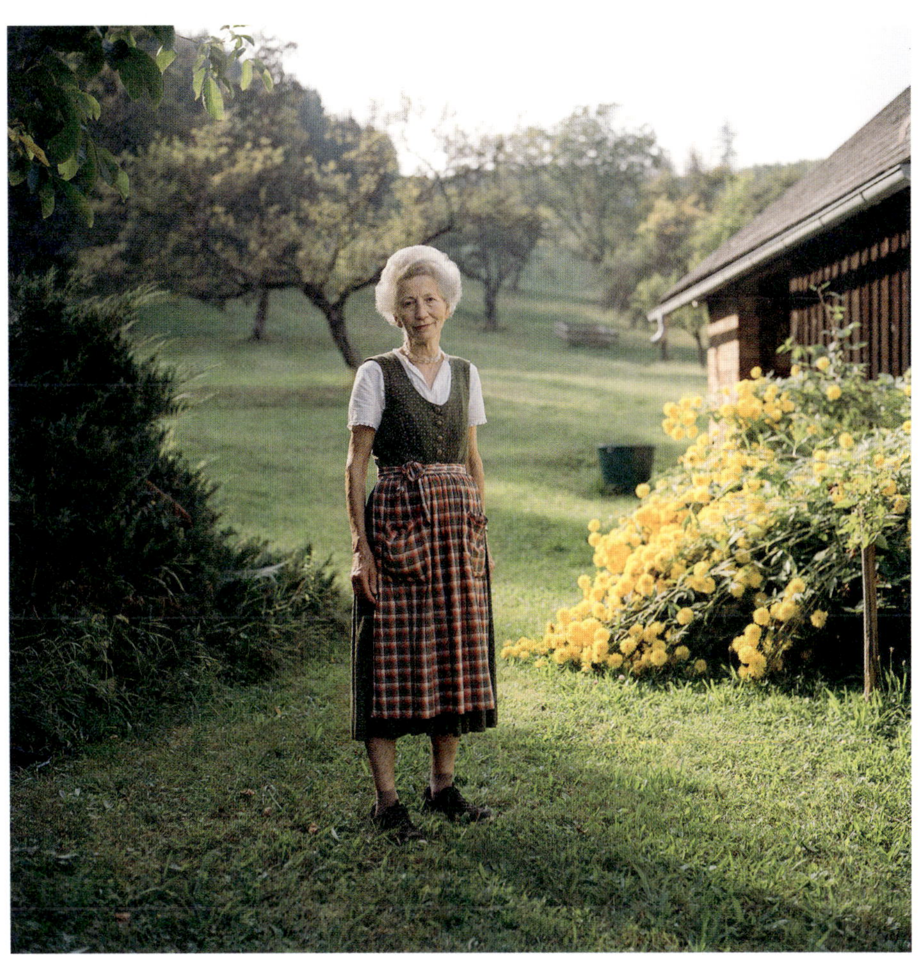

Maria
by Peter Pflügler
Kaumberg, Austria

Maria is from a small farming family. Her thyroid gland
stopped functioning properly one day and she began
to lose a lot of weight. Maria has refused medical treatment.
She told me: 'If God wants me to shrink like an old
plum, that's fine with me.'

Painter
by Alexander Rhind
Mbale, Uganda

This man works at Child of Hope school in
the Namatala slum. The school educates children
who otherwise wouldn't be able to afford
to go to school.

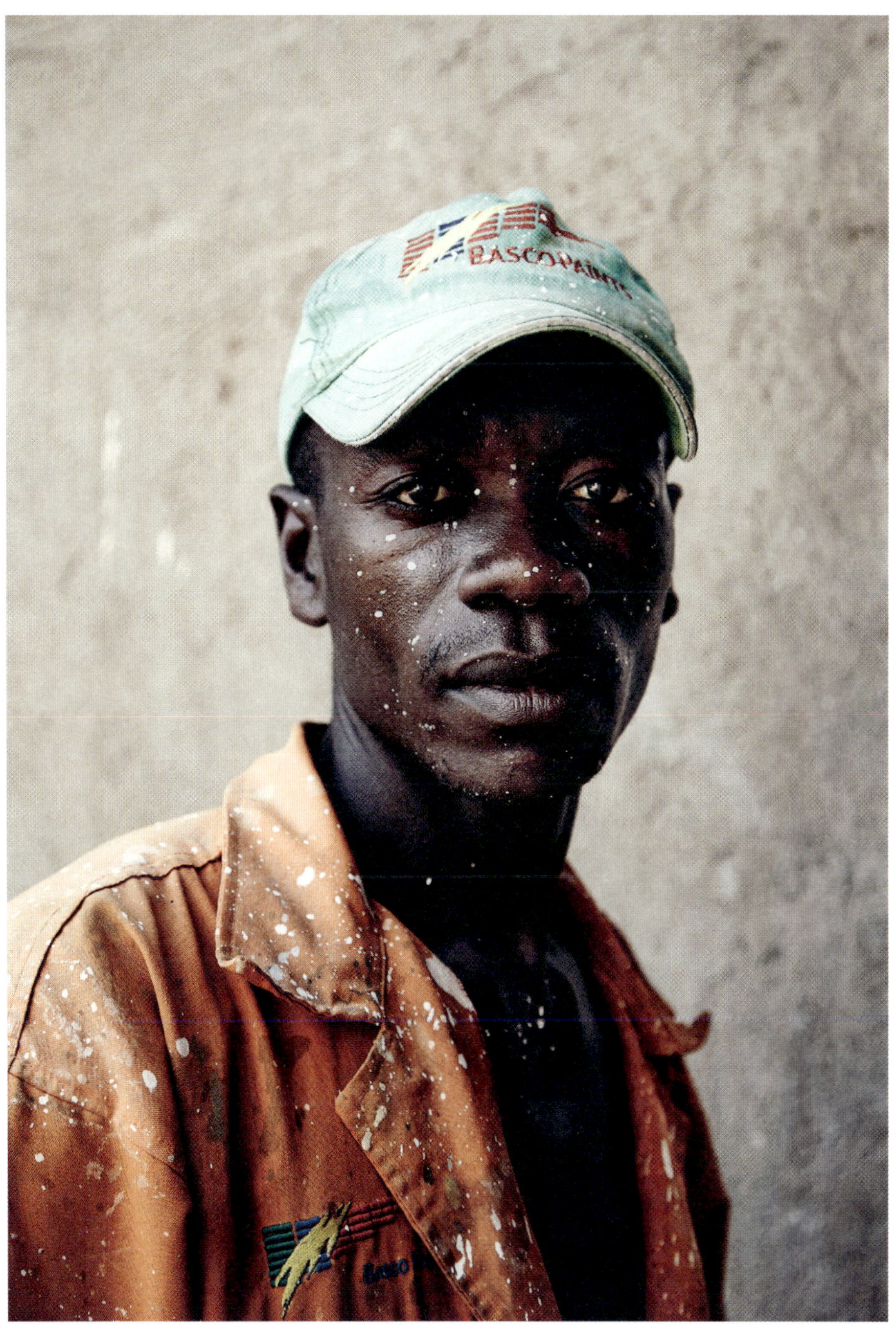
BASCO PAINTS

On the Road to Appleby Horse Fair
by Juliet Klottrup
A65, North Yorkshire, UK

Nineteen-year-old Paddy and his family
were parked up on the side of the road with their
impressive bowtop horse-drawn wagons.
It was the beginning of summer and they were on
their way to Appleby Horse Fair in Cumbria.
Explaining why they had stopped off here, Paddy told
me: 'The water's fresh around here. It's good for the
horses… and I just had a wash in the stream.'

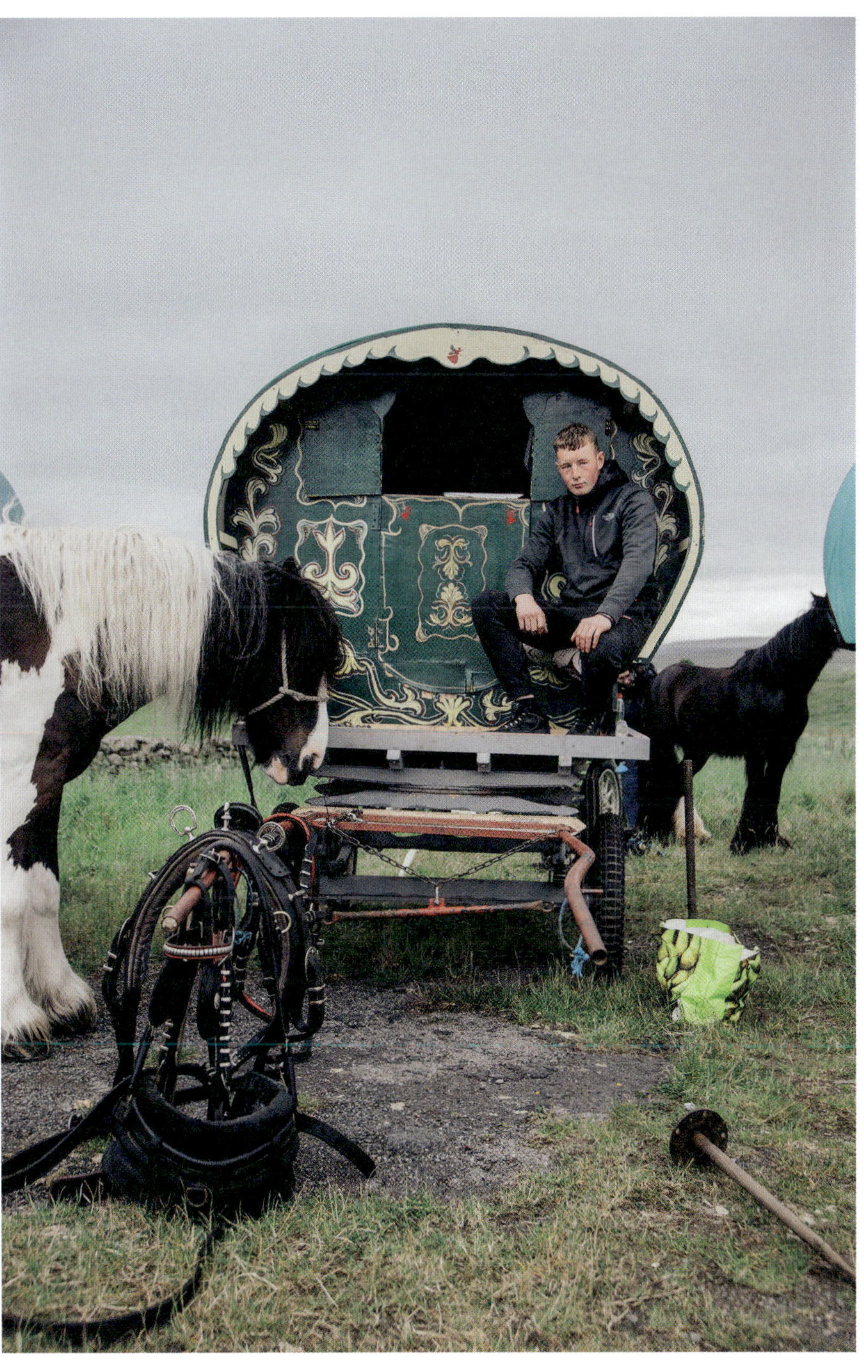

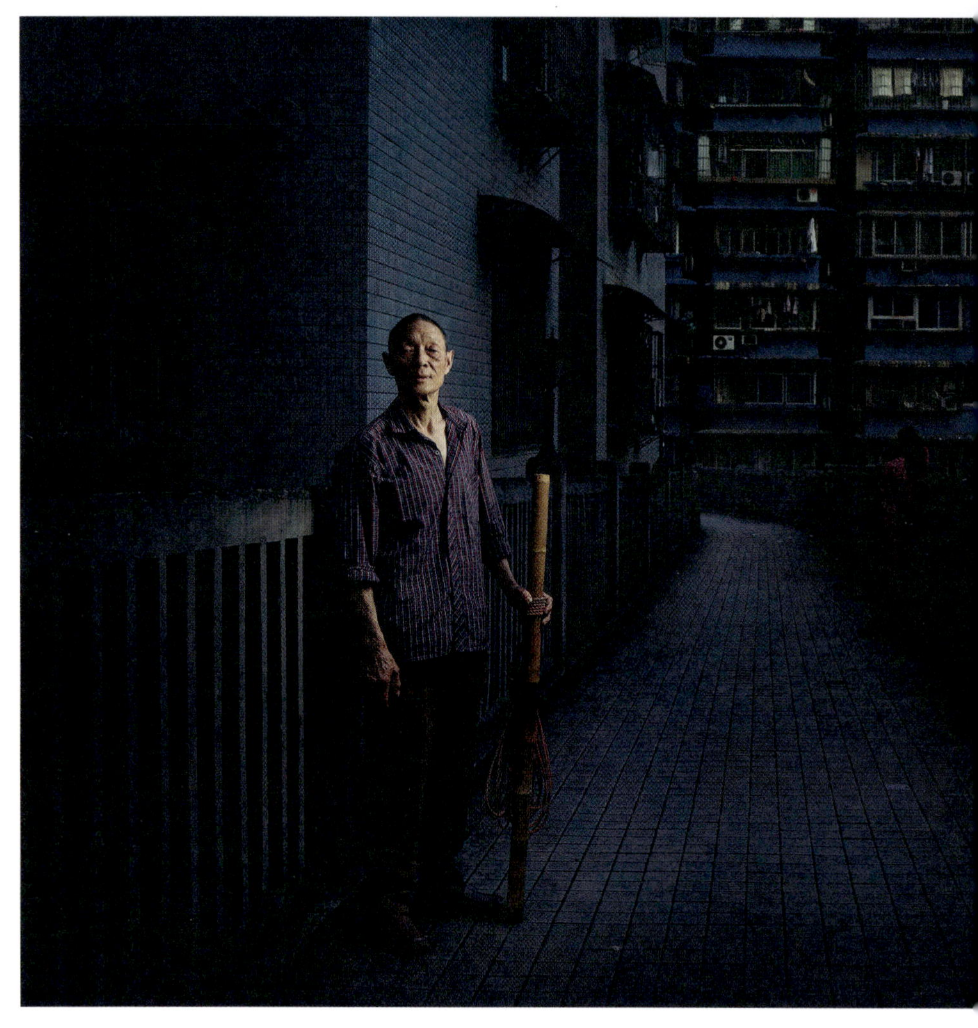

The Last Bang Bang Man
by Ken Hermann
Chongqing, China

Rao Gang has been a 'bang bang man' (labourer) for more than
30 years. Bang bang men have existed for hundreds of years but due
to societal change their work is vanishing and so are they.

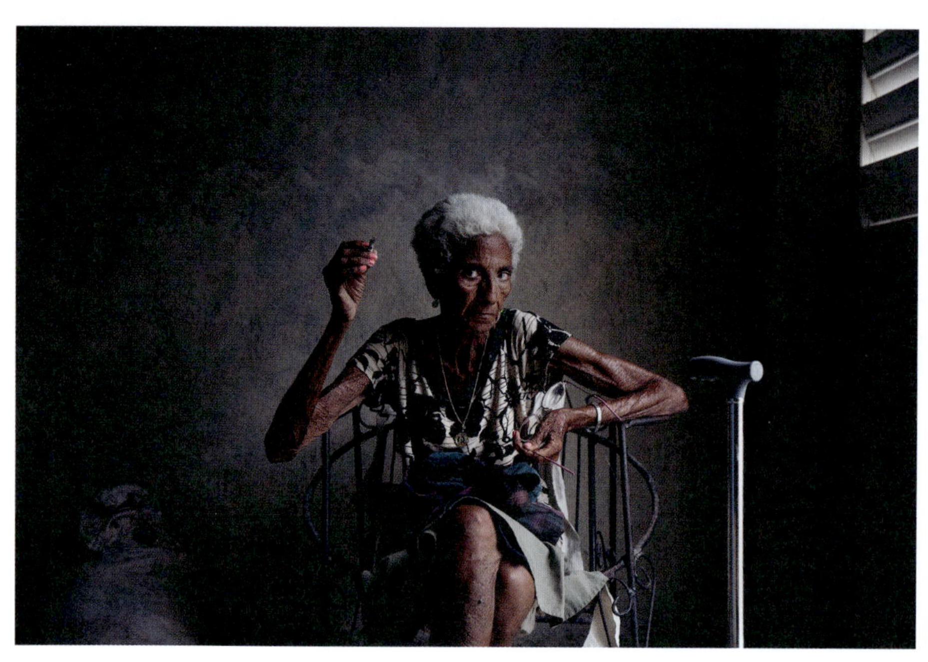

Leonada
by Oded Wagenstein
Cienfuegos, Cuba

Over the last six years I have met elders in different
communities around the world. I have listened
to their stories, their longings, their fears. Too often our
society is focused on younger generations and we miss
the opportunity to learn from our elders. Leonada's
calmness, power and beauty amazed me.

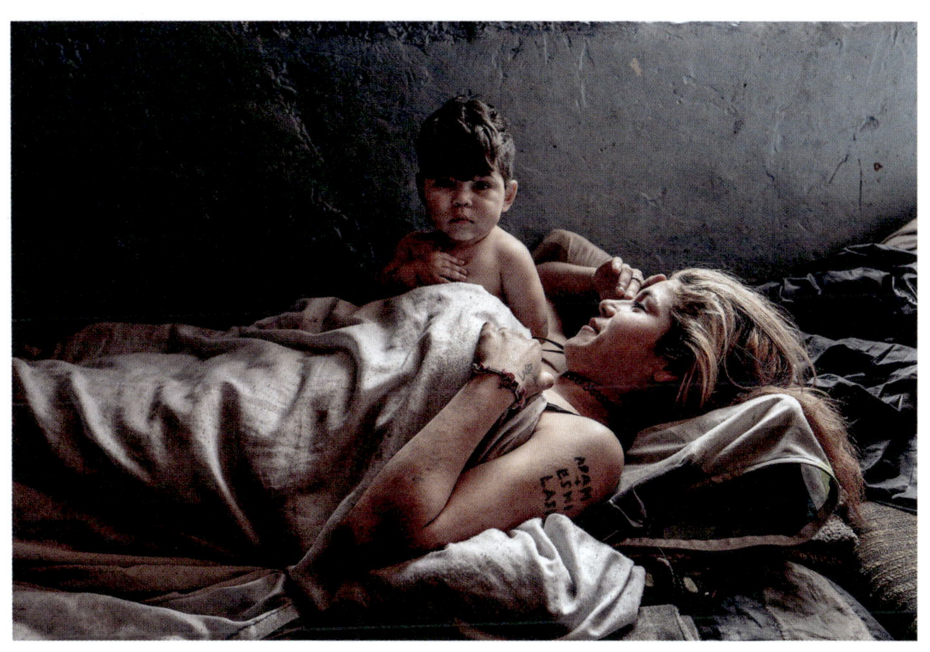

Roma Girl with Her Son
by Kristof Huf
Svinia, Slovakia

Svinia consists of two settlements of a similar size.
One is inhabited by Slovaks and the other by Roma who
live in appalling conditions. Unemployment
is almost one hundred percent.

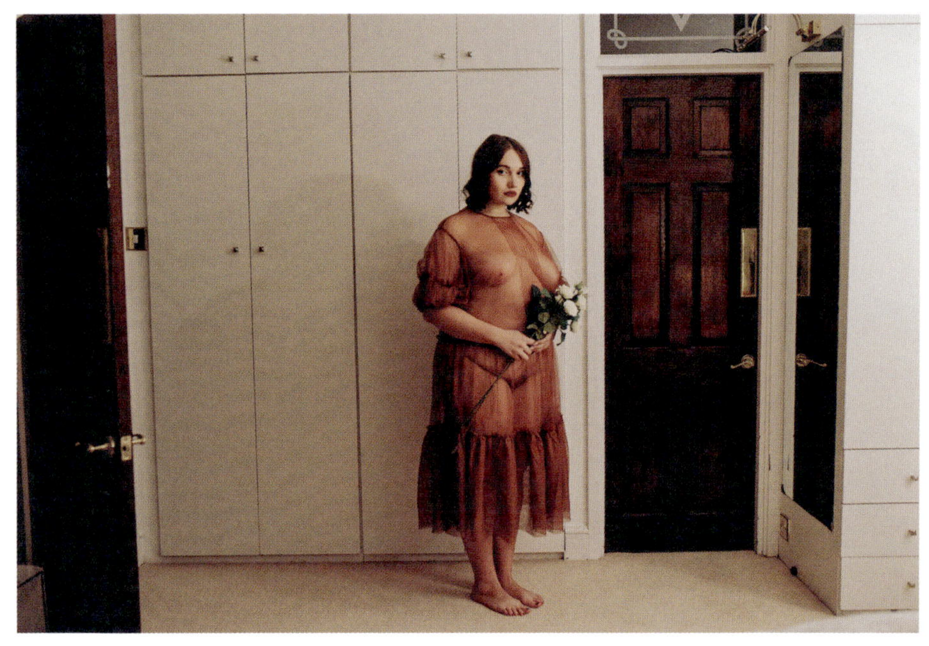

Aphrodite

by Natalia Kamenetskaya
London, UK

Stasi is my close friend who taught me how
to love and accept myself the way I am. We initially
wanted to take photos outside but due to rain
we stayed indoors. Stasi changed into a dress and decided
to wear nothing underneath. To me she looks
very fragile and precious.

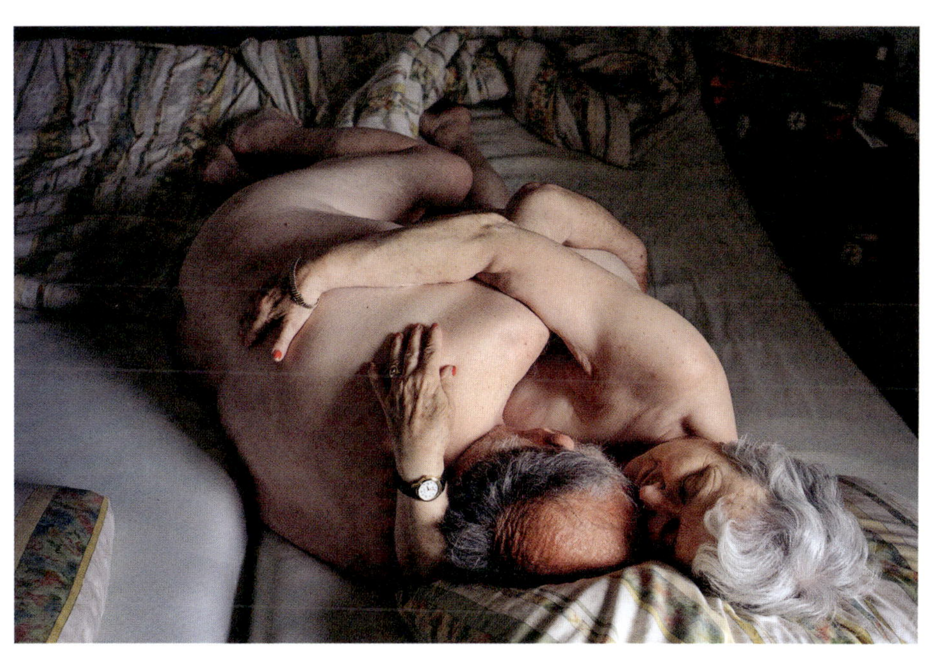

Irene and Günter
by Mirja Maria Thiel
Diepholz, Germany

Irene, 80, and Günter, 79, have been married
for 60 years. I got to know them for my series about love
and sex in old age. They are both art enthusiasts
and painters who have a very loving connection
to their own bodies and each other's.

Meri

by Sergei Pavlov
Unknown location, central Italy

Meri is a very dear friend who has taught
me much about the art of being yourself. Three days
before this photo she sent me a message saying:
'I'm in Italy with my lover and we have a van. Join!'
So I did. The following weeks were blissful.
We buried our burdens and washed away our
regrets and shame in Italy's deep lakes.

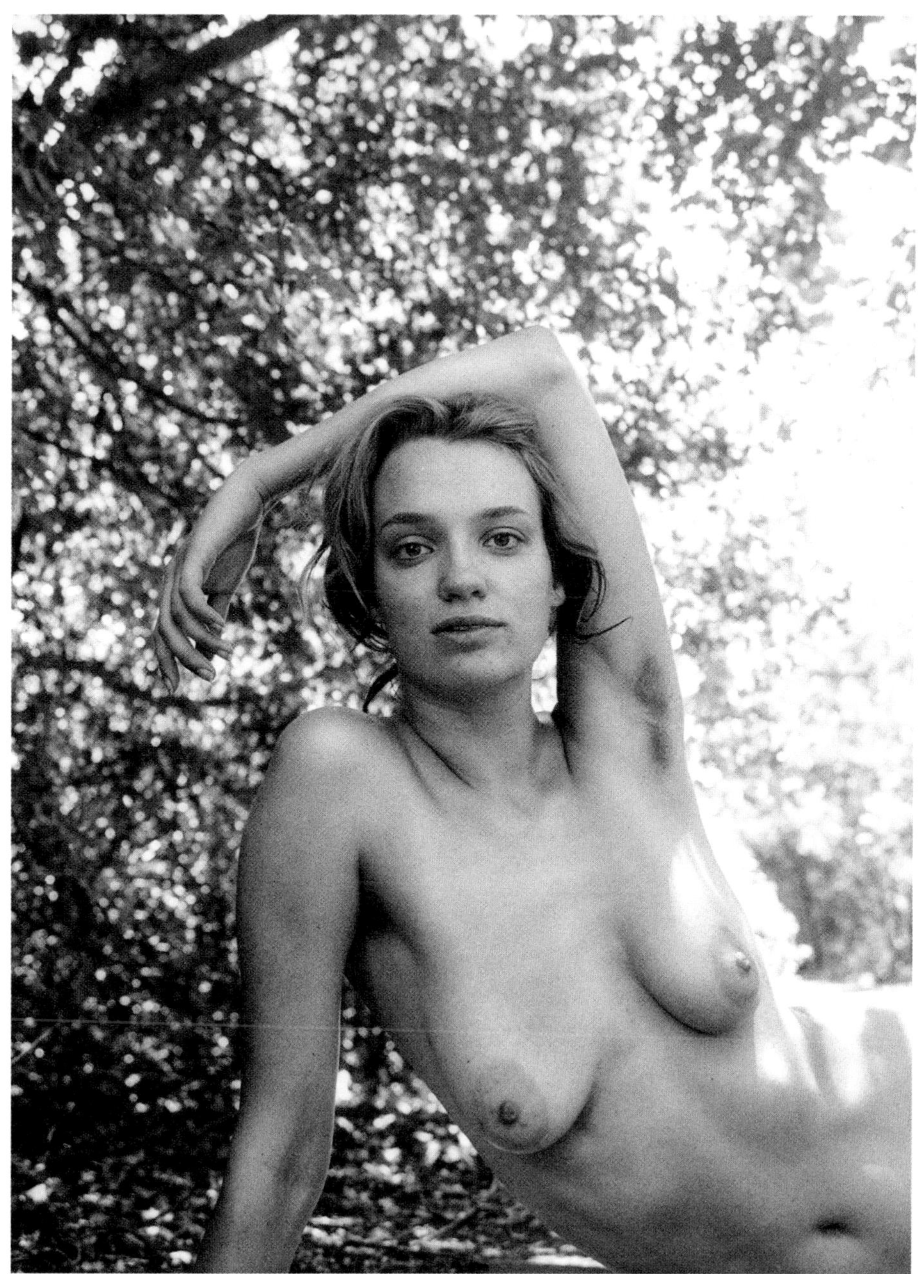

Sisters
by Naomi Ngoo Richmond
Cumbria, UK

It was the final day of Appleby Horse Fair
and gloomy weather and the knowledge that the
festivities were coming to an end hung in the air.
These two girls in matching Victorian-esque
dresses were walking along with their mother
and stood out in the surroundings.

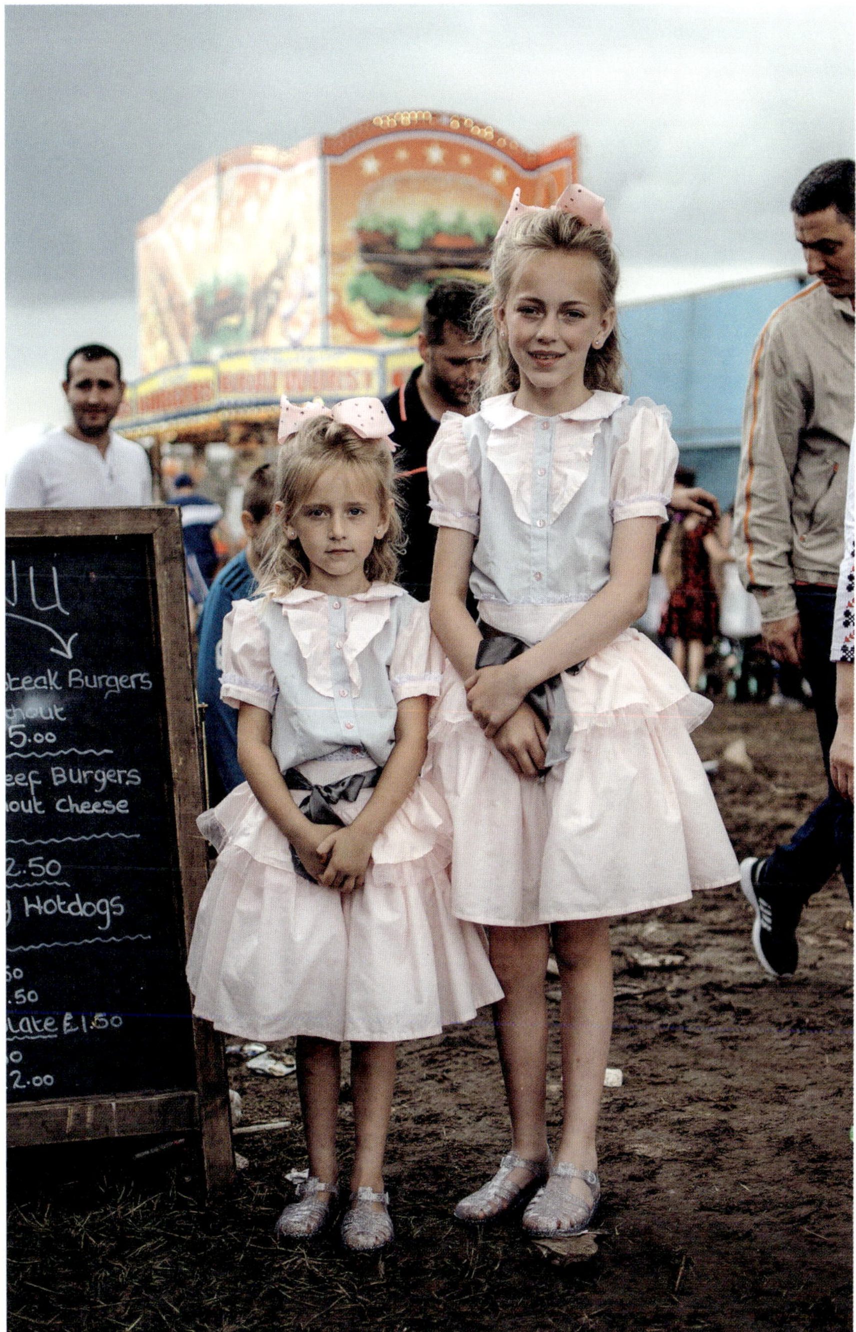

NU
Steak Burgers
thout
5.00
eef Burgers
hout cheese
2.50
Hotdogs
50
.50
late £1.50
50
2.00

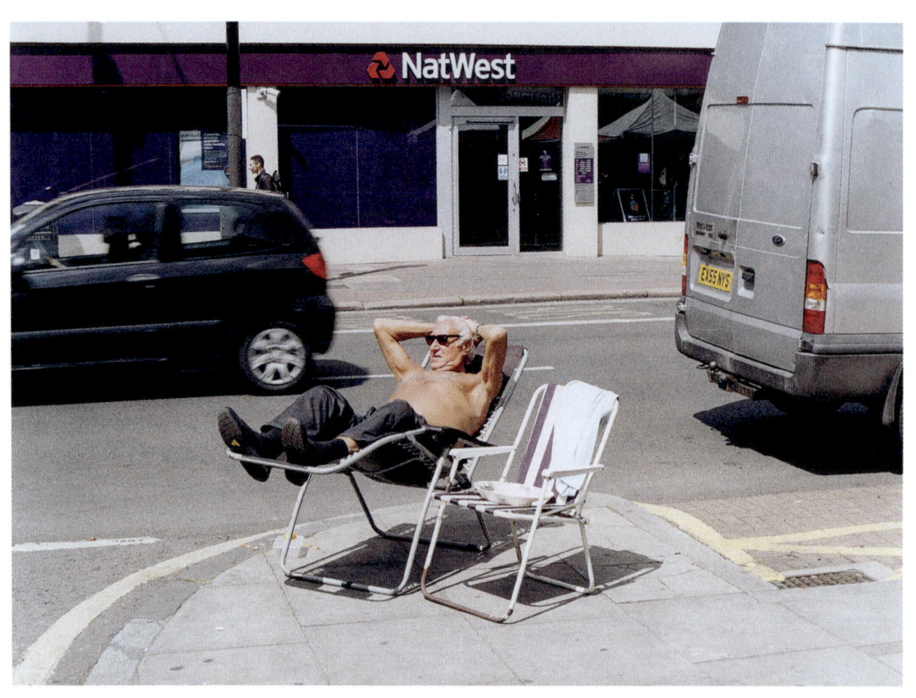

Not a Worry in the World
by Alexandru Micu
London, UK

A local legend in Bethnal Green takes his
sunlounger and places it in the middle of the pavement.
Apparently he does this a lot.

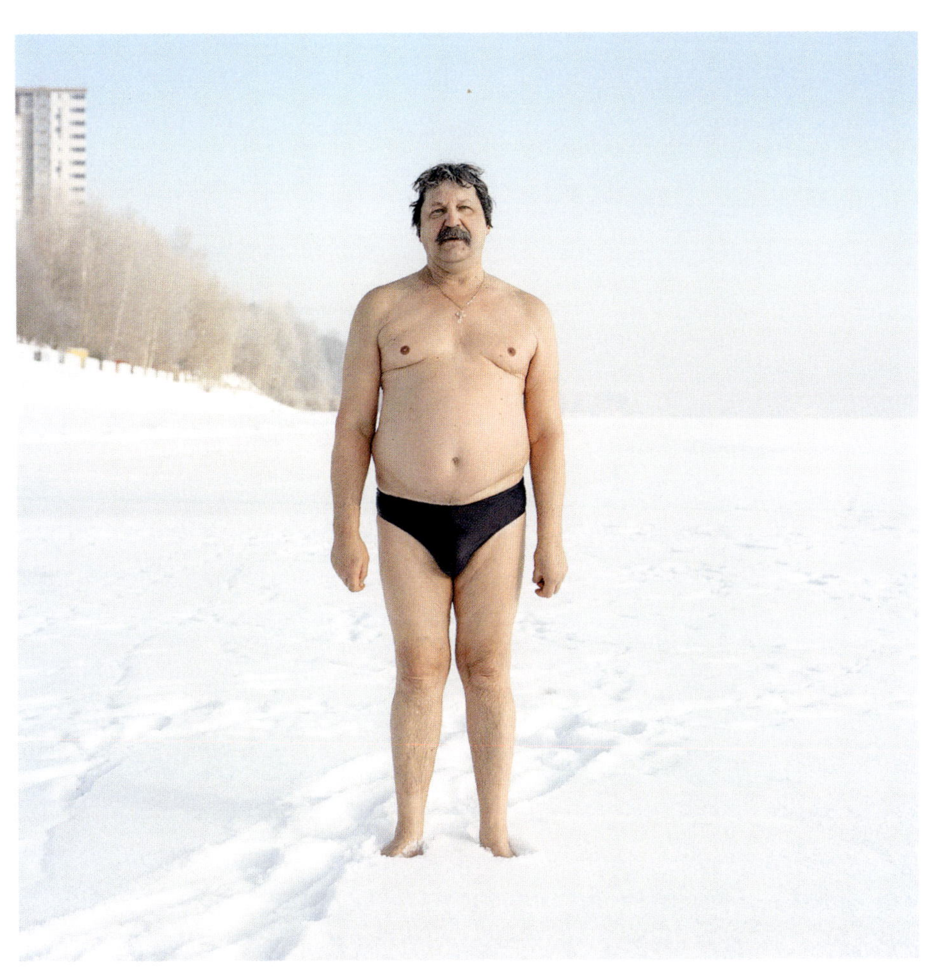

Ice Swimmer
by Snezhana von Buedingen
Perm, Russia

During winter in Perm the temperature drops to -30°C.
Ice swimming is an old tradition in Russia. It is
a kind of religion, almost, a belief in the purification of
the soul and healing of the body through icy water.

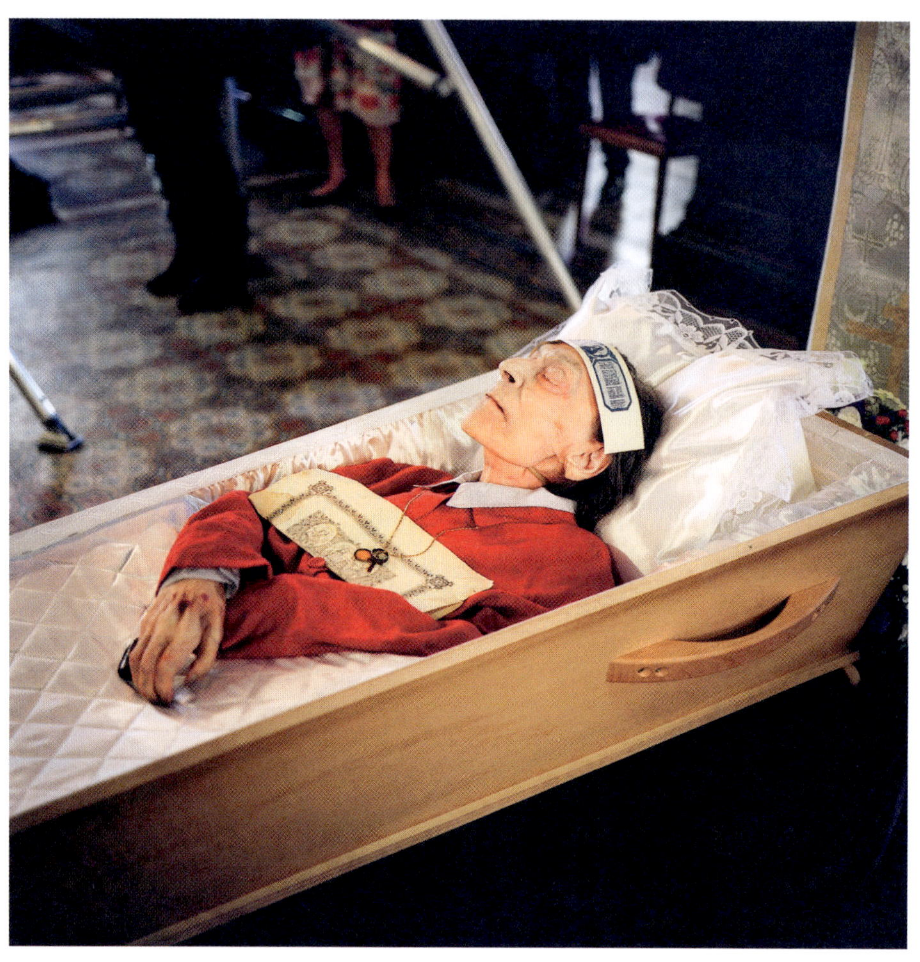

Her Serene Highness Princess Natalia Galitzine Heseltine
by Charlotte Javelot Ward
Geneva, Switzerland

Natalia was my great grandmother. My family
and I stood around her coffin as the priest conducted
the funeral ceremony. My grandmother gave me
permission to take the picture.

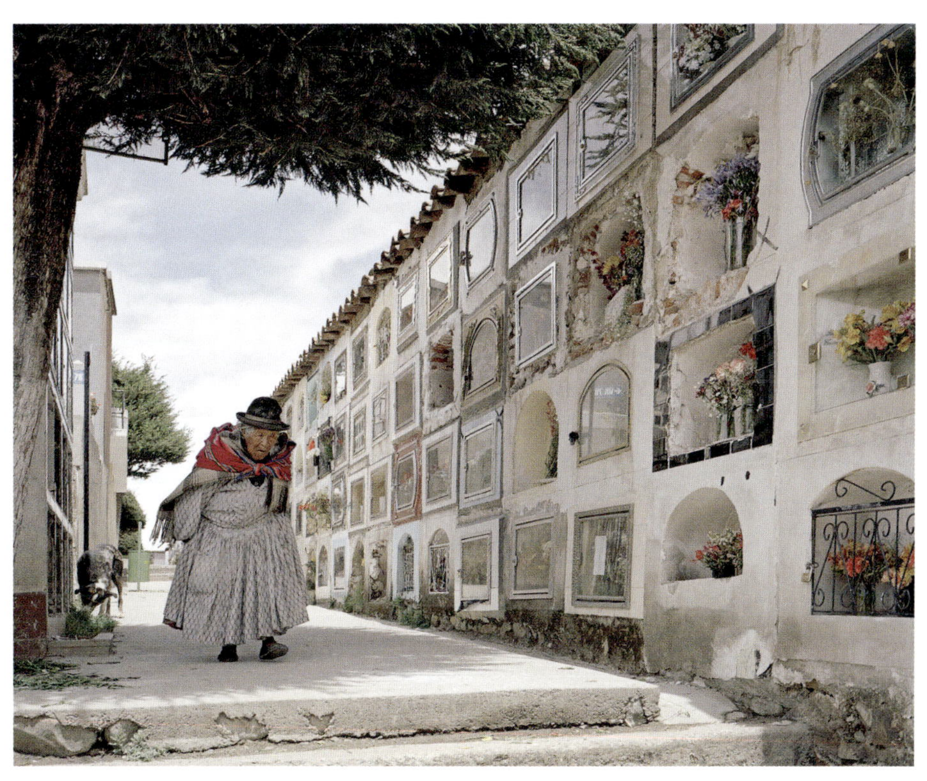

A Restless Soul on All Saints' Day
by Silke Kirchhoff
La Paz, Bolivia

An old lady walks between the graves in a cemetery
on Día de Todos los Santos (All Saints' Day). Bolivians
believe that at midday on this day the souls of the
dead come back to earth for 24 hours.

Xueli

by Brock Elbank
London, UK

Xueli's adopted mother contacted me to produce
a portrait series of her incredible daughter who has
albinism. Xueli lives in the Netherlands and is
originally from China. She has extremely limited vision
and her eyes suffer in bright light. This almost
14-year-old was fun to collaborate with. The way the
light worked with Xueli's hair and skin was
amazing. She has the finest hair I've ever seen.

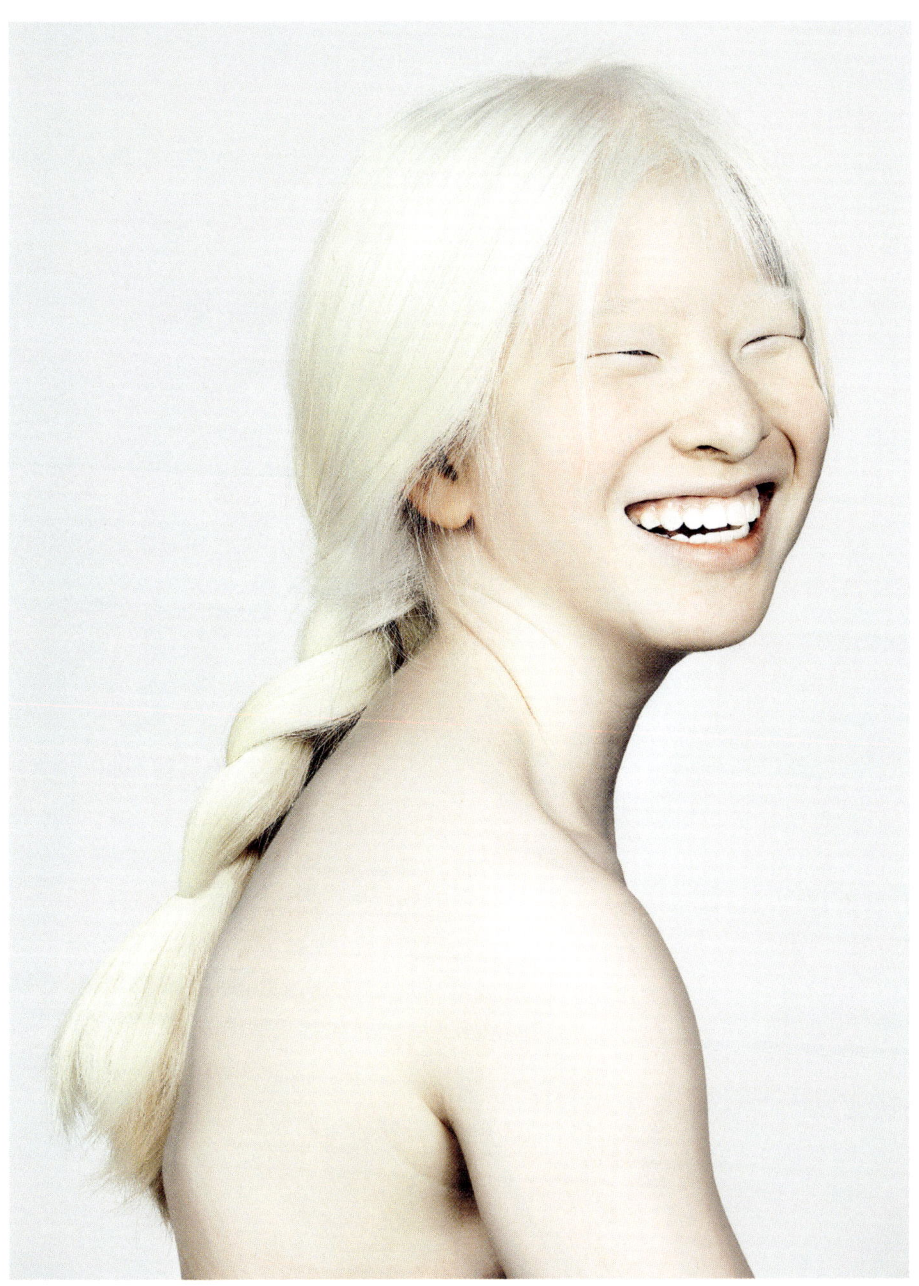

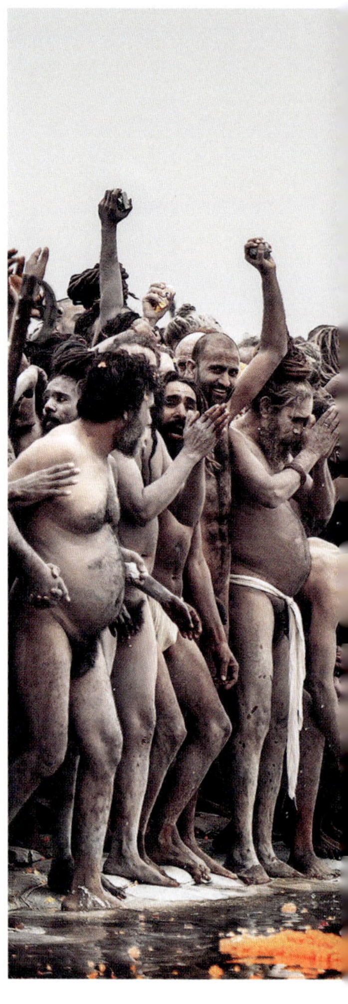

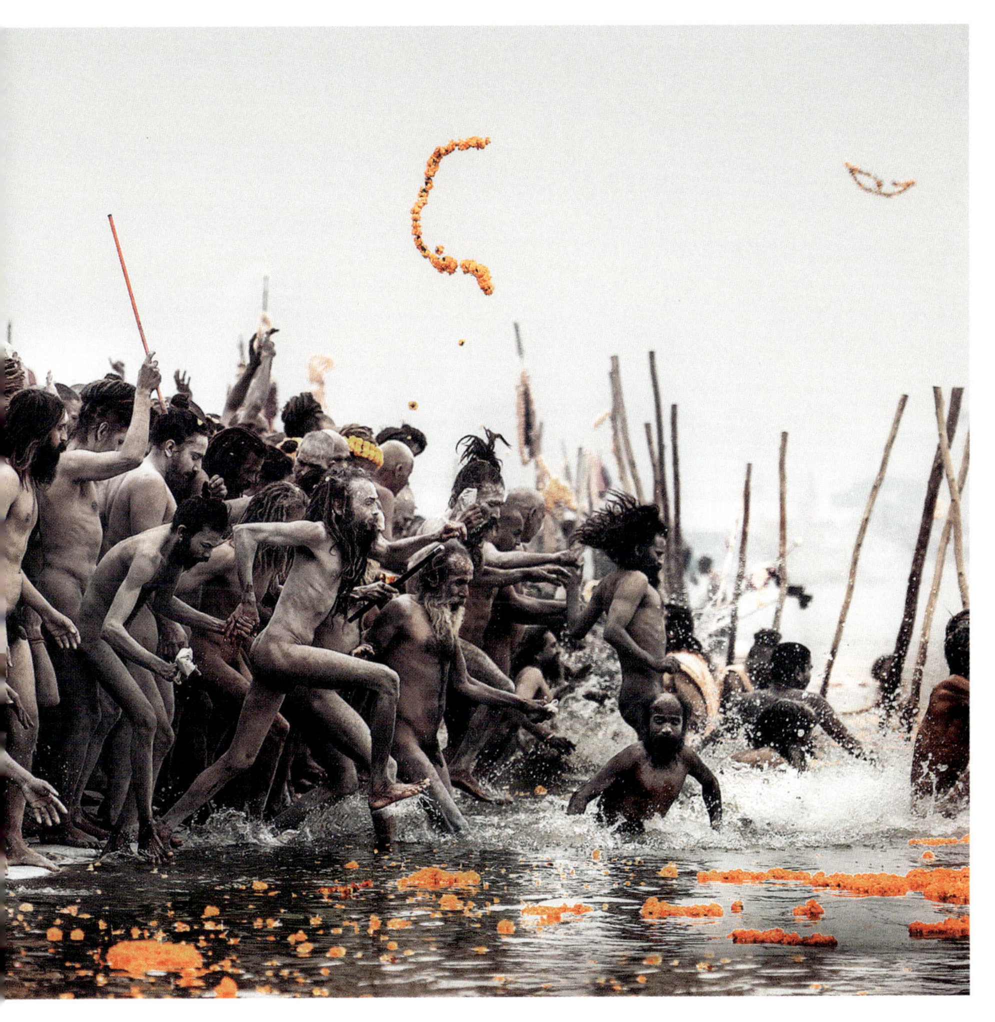

Naga Sadhu Ritual
by Roberto Nistri
Allahabad, India

Naked and covered in ash, Naga Sadhus of
Juna Akhada take a dip in the Ganges at sunrise during
the Hindu festival, Prayag Kumbh Mela.

Leopold at 101
by Karsten Thormaehlen
Berlin, Germany

Leopold is one of several centenarians I cast
for a fashion shoot to celebrate the 100th anniversary
of the shirt maker Seidensticker. He's something of
a celebrity in Germany and has been featured
in newspapers as Berlin's, and maybe even the world's,
oldest swimming trainer. Leopold visits his local
pool twice a week to teach children to swim. He was
married to Hildegard for more than 70 years
and since her passing draws strength from his
beautiful memories.

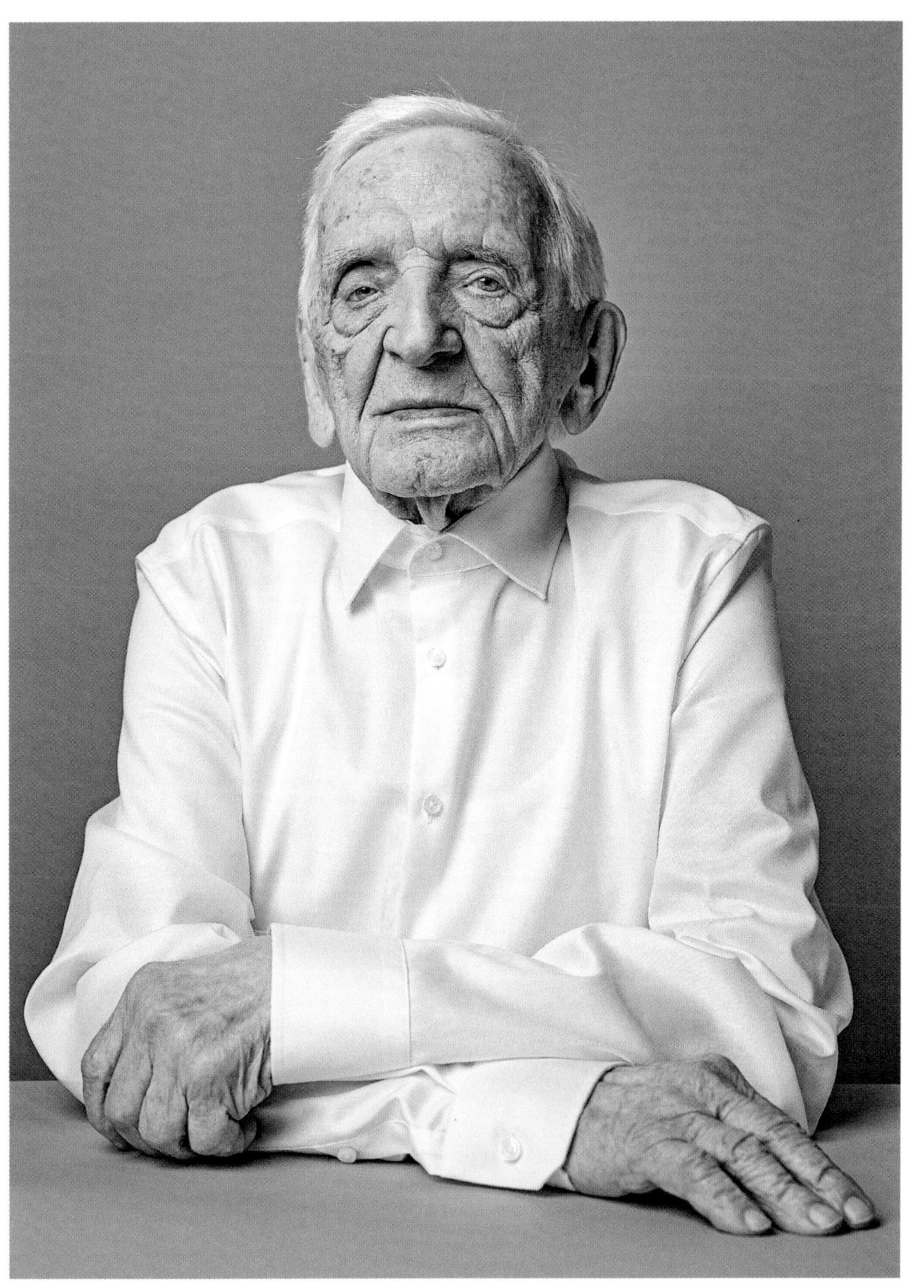

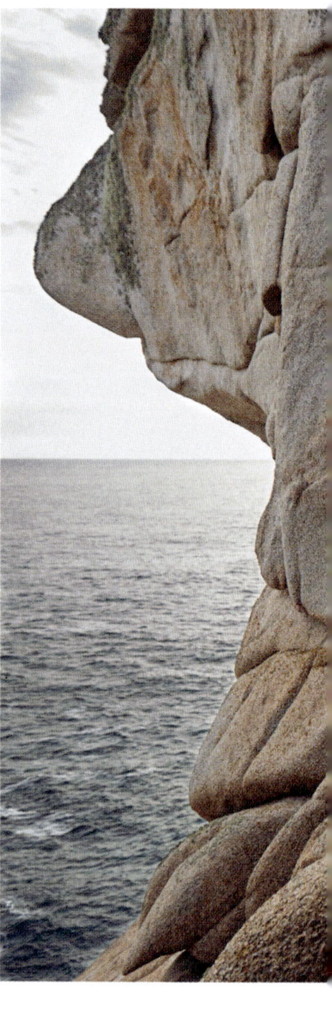

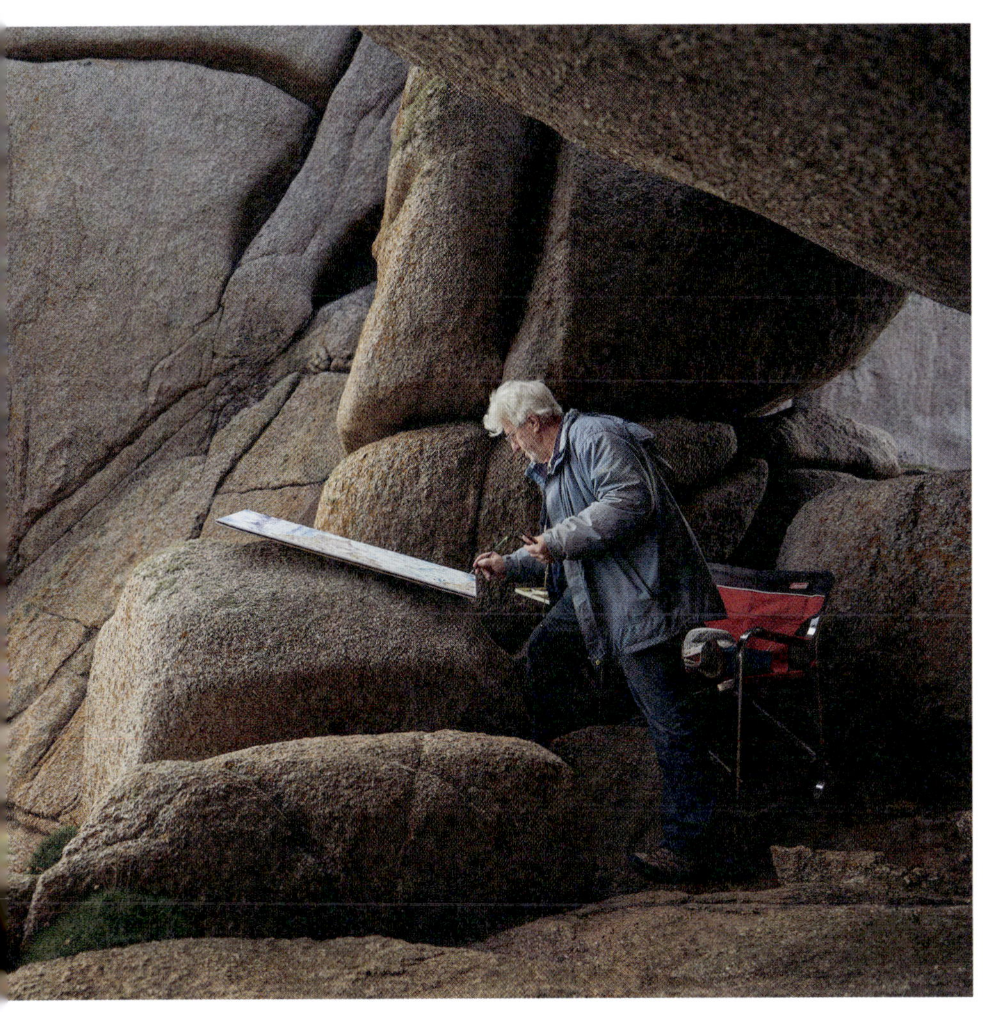

Best Office in the World

by Gary Morrisroe
Isles of Scilly, UK

I was shooting a job and headed out to the
headland where I spotted artist Stephen Morris hidden
away. I sat with him for a while as he painted.

Abdullah

by Marko Risovic
Bihać, Bosnia and Herzegovina

Abdullah, who is from Afghanistan, poses for
a portrait in an abandoned factory where thousands
of refugees have settled in a makeshift refugee camp.
He lost two sons in a tribal clash in his home country
after which he left for the sake of his family.
Abdullah dreams about having his family gathered
together again in a safe country and lives
for the day when he will be able to hug his
three daughters and remaining son.

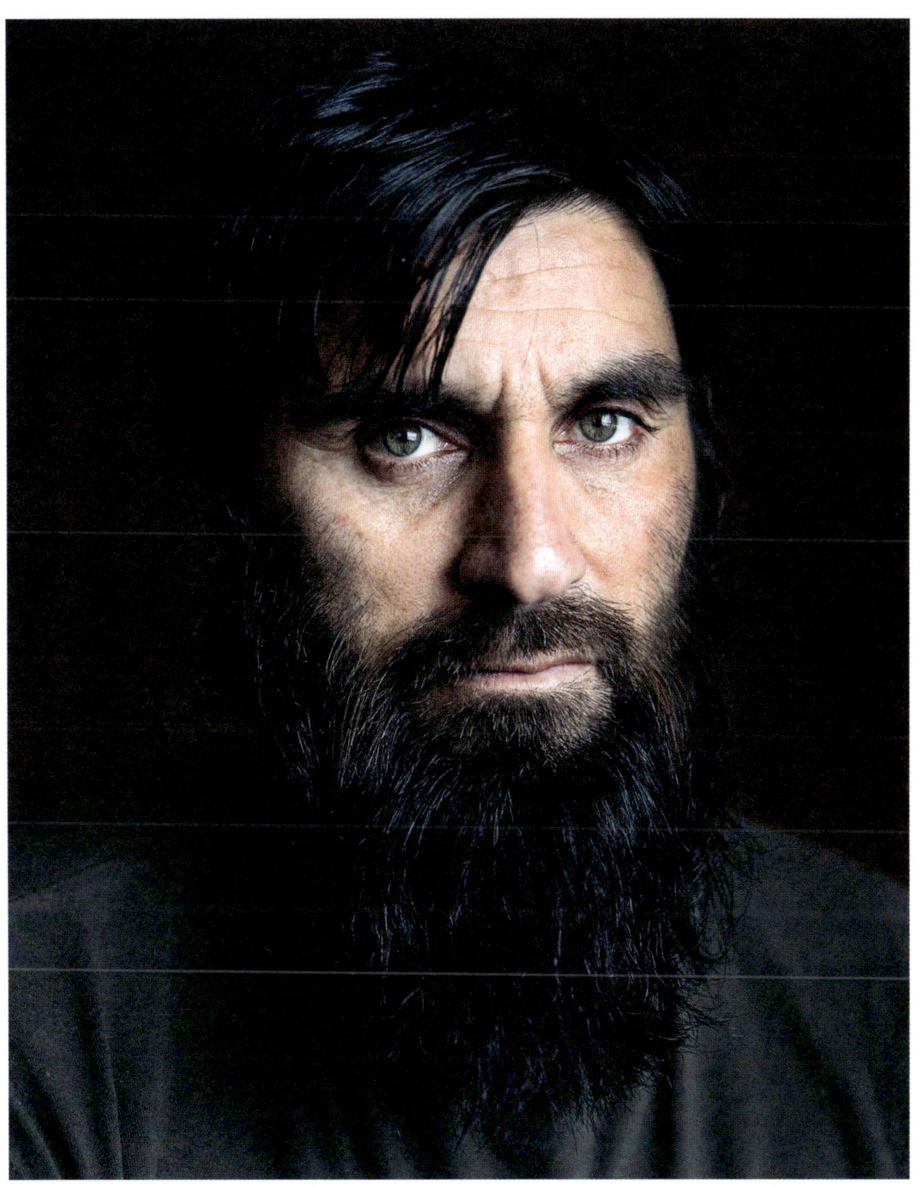

Swimmers

by Attilio Fiumarella
Birmingham, UK

More than 100 swimmers gather in the empty
gala pool to stand against the closure of local icon
Moseley Road Baths, which first opened its doors
in 1907. Birmingham City Council intended to
close the swimming pool permanently in 2015 but the
World Monuments Fund recently included the historic
site on its watch list, giving new hope.

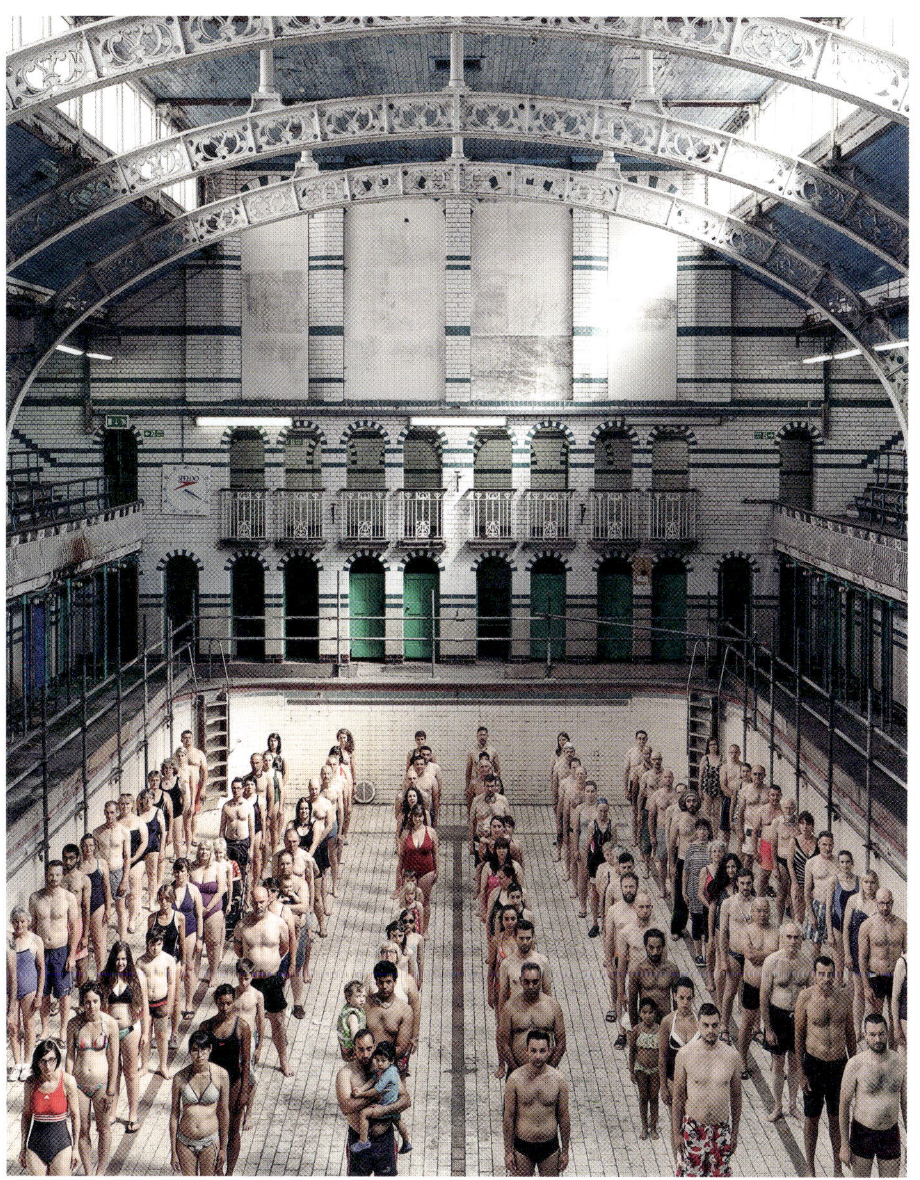

The Last Jockey
by Marko Risovic
Belgrade, Serbia

Covered in mud, a jockey who was among
the last to finish in a race at Belgrade's hippodrome
poses for a portrait. I started going regularly
to the hippodrome with my camera some years ago.
It's a fun place with so many emotions, so
much excitement, beautiful animals and interesting
people. This was one of my favourite days there.
The rain contributed so much to the scene.

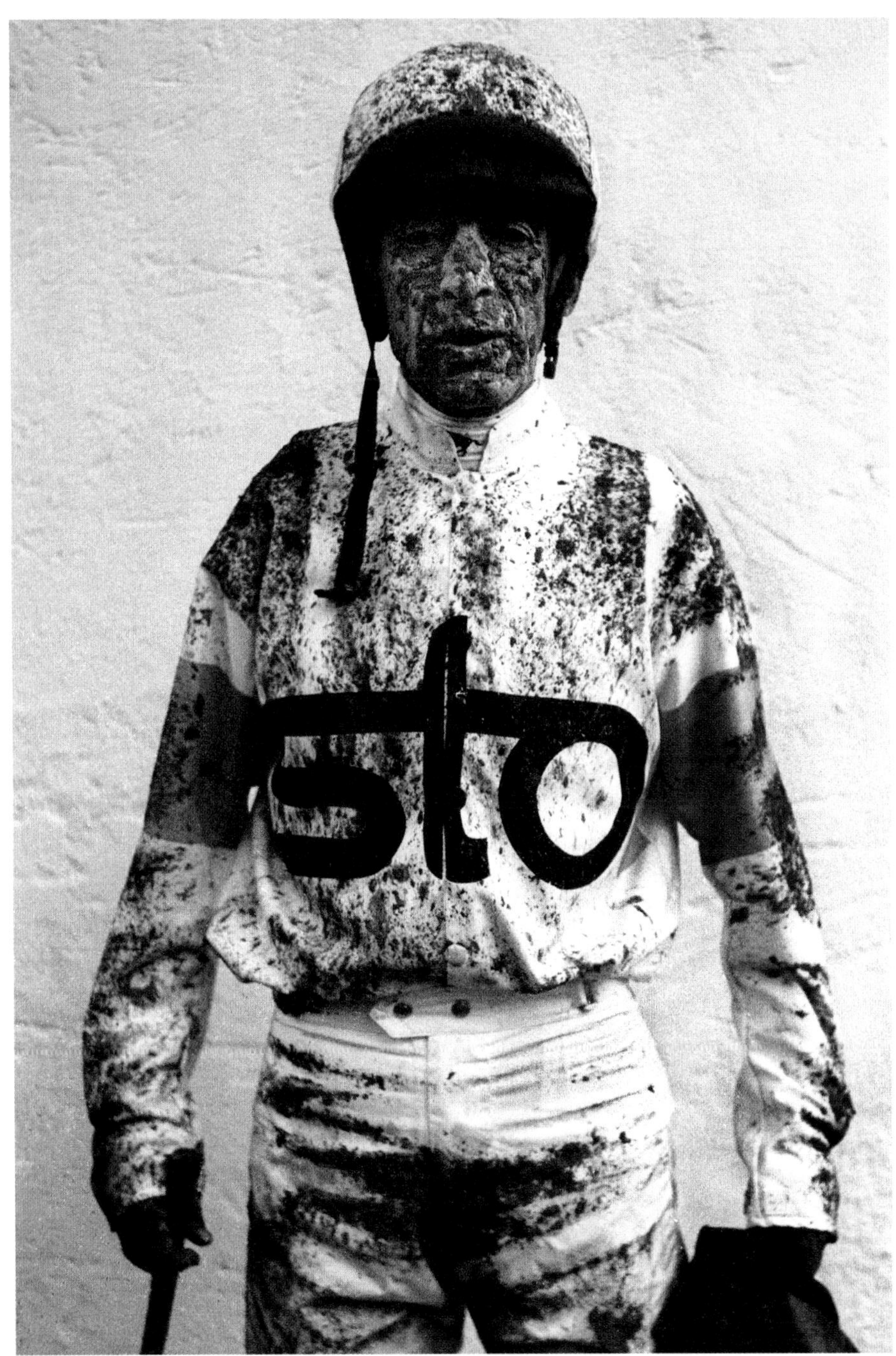

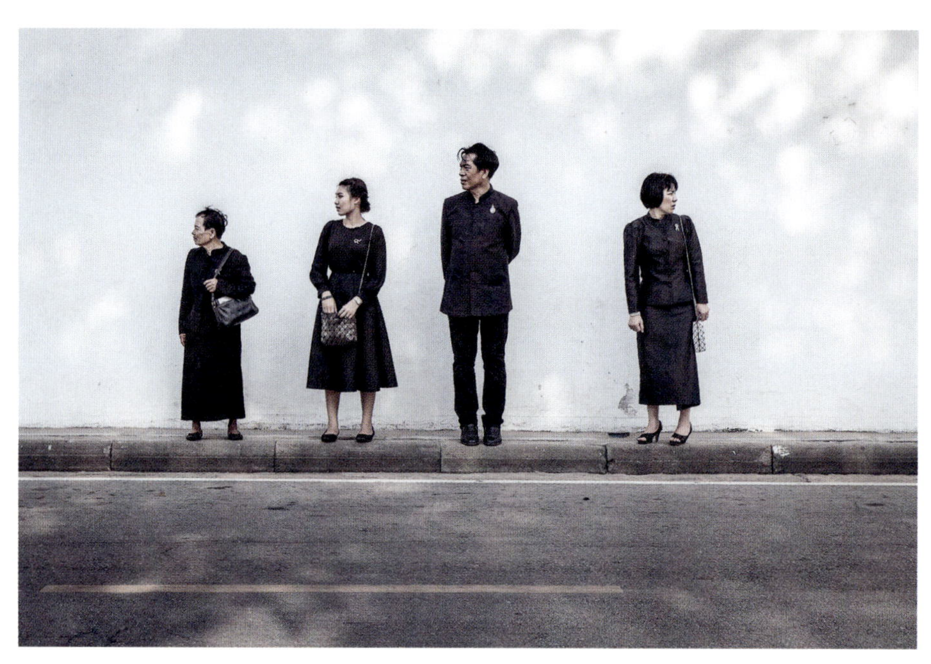

The Beloved King
by Coralie Maneri
Bangkok, Thailand

Thousands of people in Thailand remember
the late King Bhumibol Adulyadej on the anniversary
of his death. Each year since his death in 2016
various religious ceremonies, events and military
parades are held throughout the country and
everyone dresses in black.

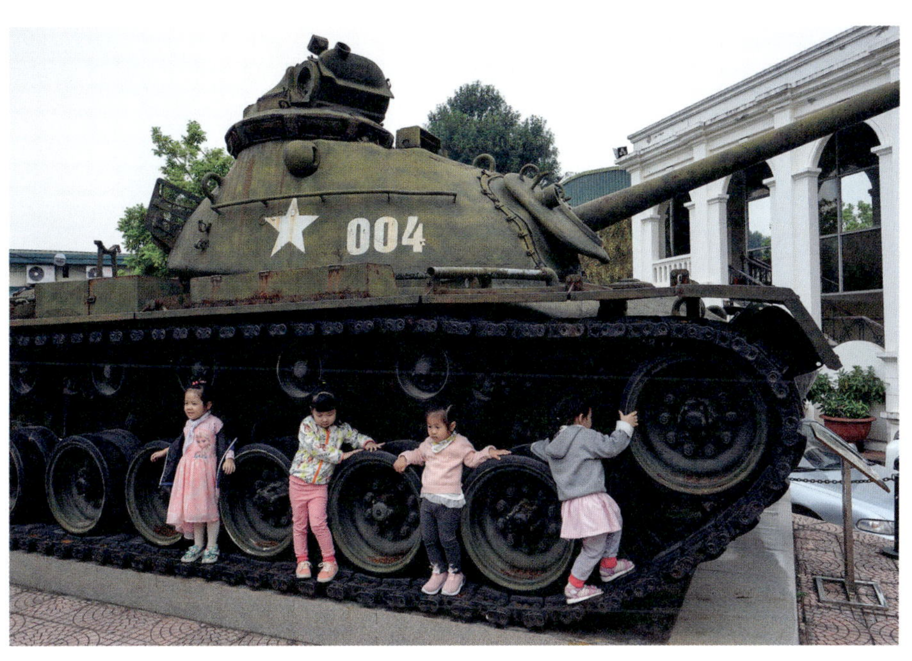

War Games
by Roberto Macagnino
Hanoi, Vietnam

Vietnamese children play on a tank that
was used in the Vietnam war.

Le Petit Prince
by Alex Franco
Orkhon Valley, Mongolia

Part of the new generation of horse keepers
in the valley, this boy stands tall on top of a rock at
sunrise. He is observing where the herd of
horses has spent the night as it is time to bring
them back to the camp.

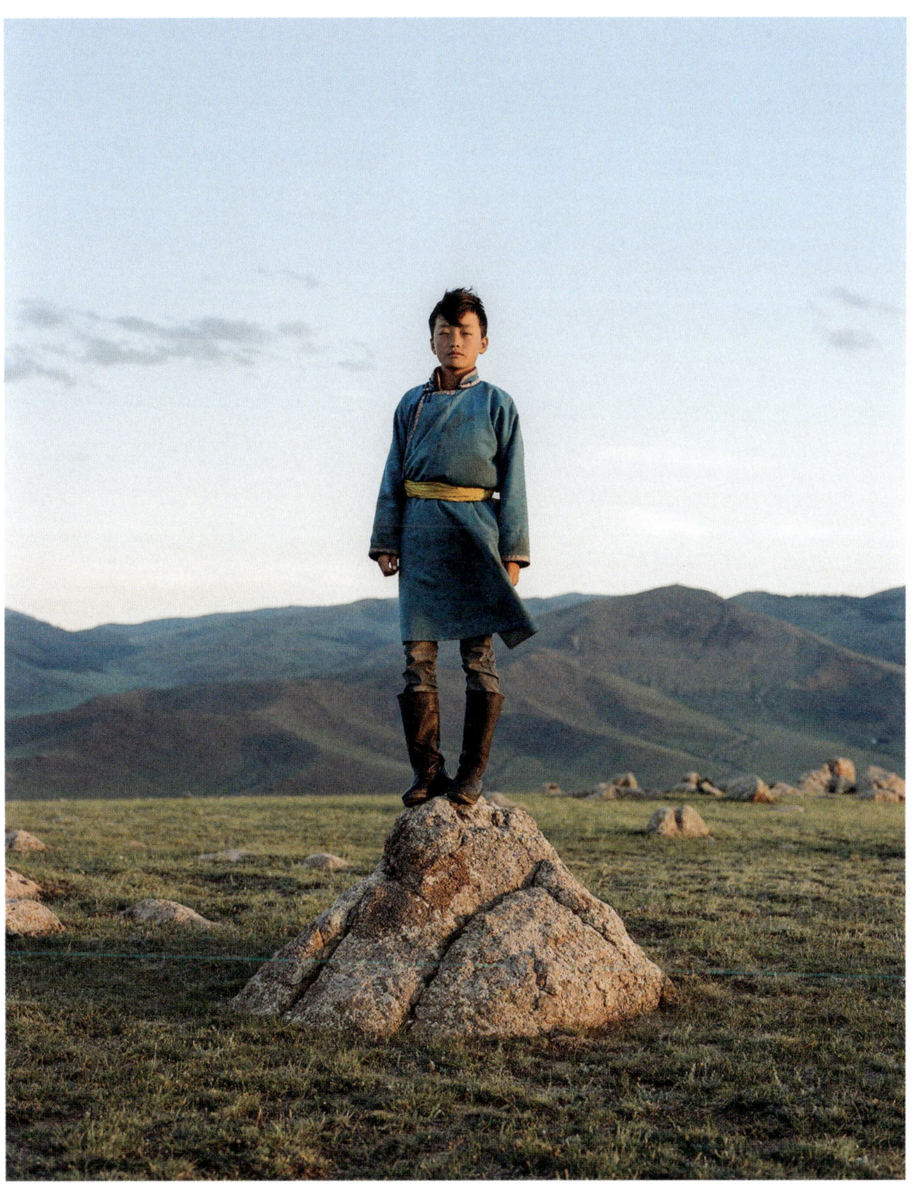

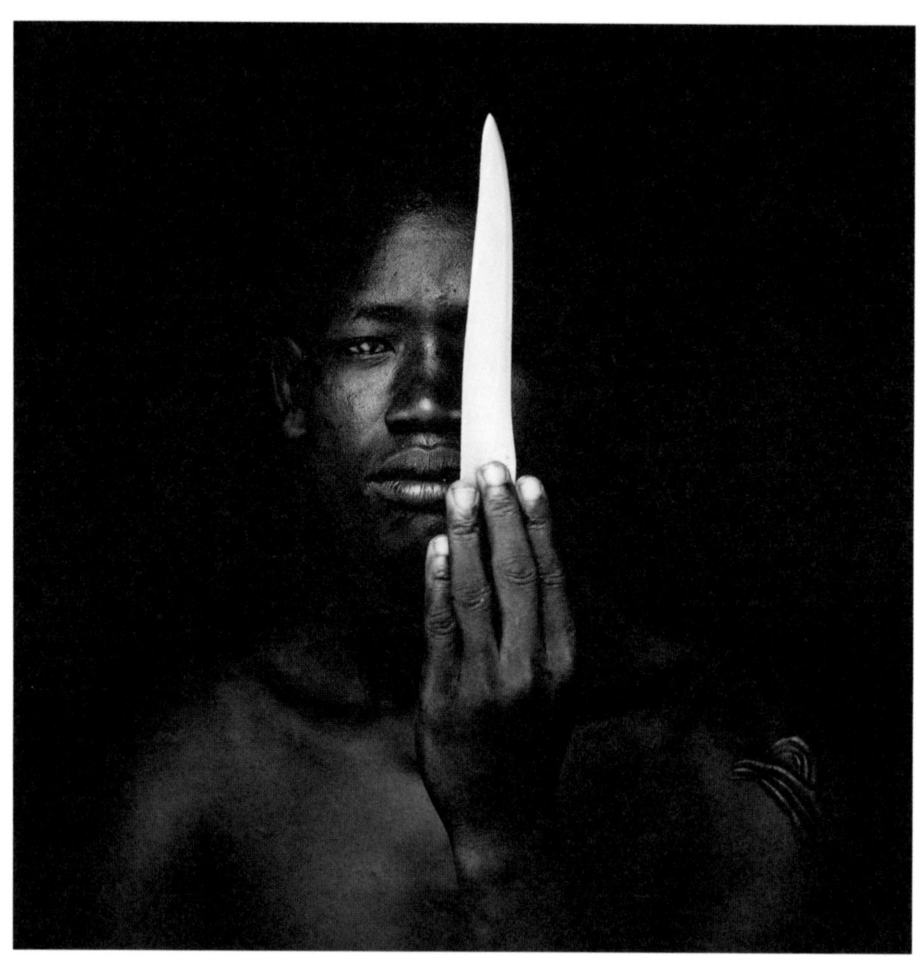

Barduri
by Alberto del Hoyo Mora
Omo Valley, Ethiopia

Barduri is a young Suri tribe warrior. He lost the sight
in his right eye during an ancestral ceremony that involved
fighting members of neighbouring tribes with sticks.
Barduri is proud he has shown his family that he is a brave man.

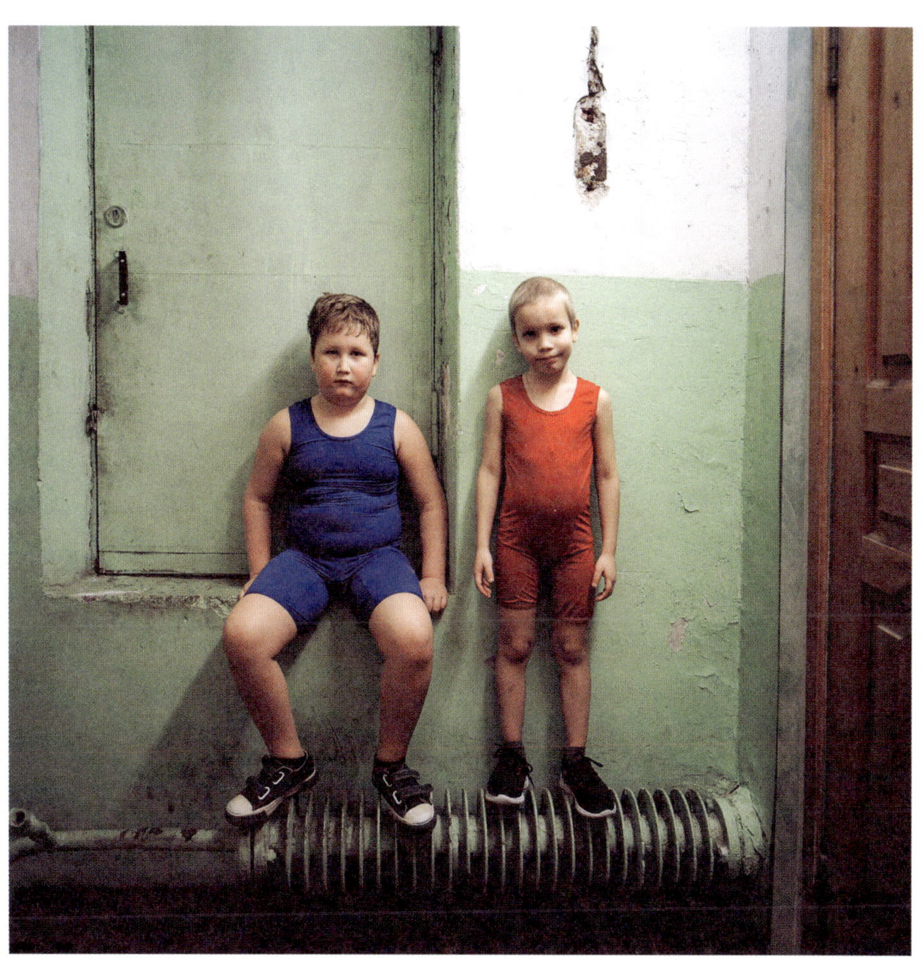

Two Young Wrestlers
by Snezhana von Buedingen
Perm, Russia

It is not just physical strength but mental fortitude that
wrestling gives those who participate in this sport, whatever
their age. I photographed young wrestlers between the ages
of seven and 18 to bring their personalities to light.

Paldi in the Basement Gym
by Tero Puha
Budapest, Hungary

Paldi is a junior bodybuilder. 'I've always
done bodybuilding for myself, not to impress other
people. I was always the skinny kid. I started
lifting weights when I was 15 years old and fell in
love with it immediately. Being strong is
not a masculine thing in itself; I think it's more
about one's behaviour.' – Paldi

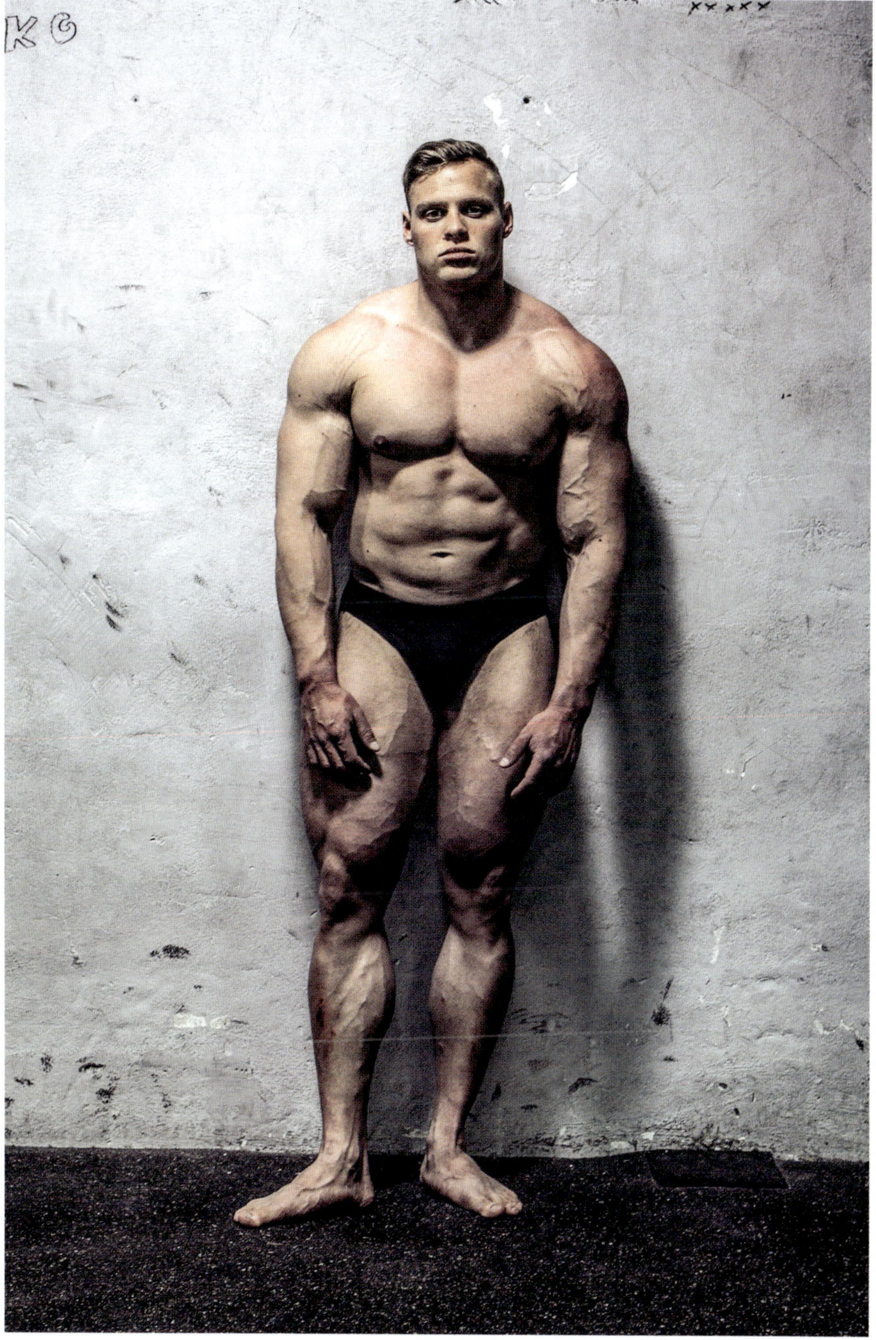

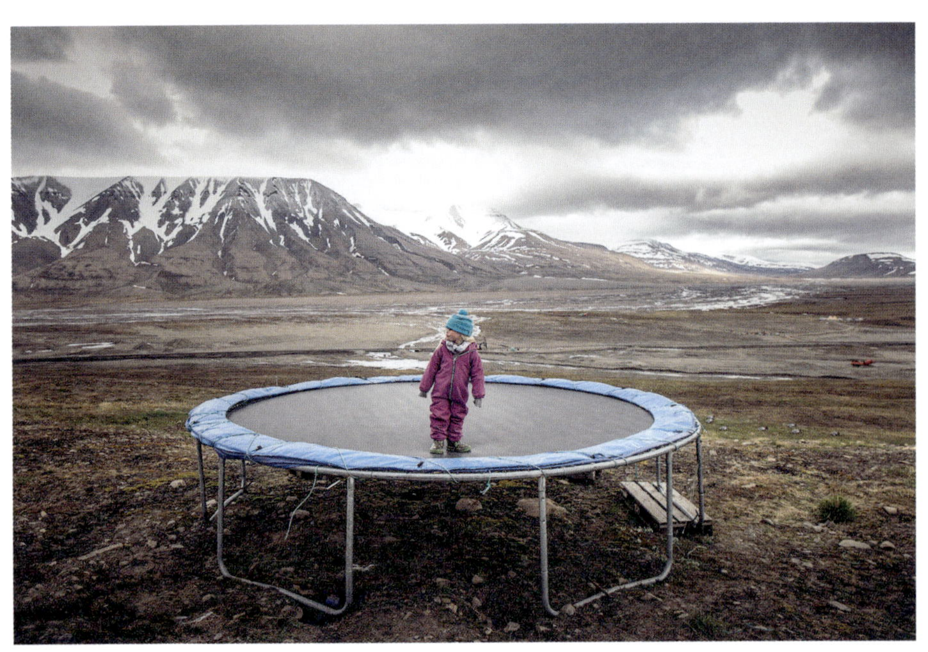

The Family at the End of the World
by Michael O. Snyder
Svalbard, Norway

This is Saga Bernlow behind her house on
the remote Arctic archipelago of Svalbard. Longyearbyen,
where the family lives, is the world's fastest warming
town. Her parents moved there to take advantage
of the growing tourist trade and are raising their family
on a rapidly changing frontier.

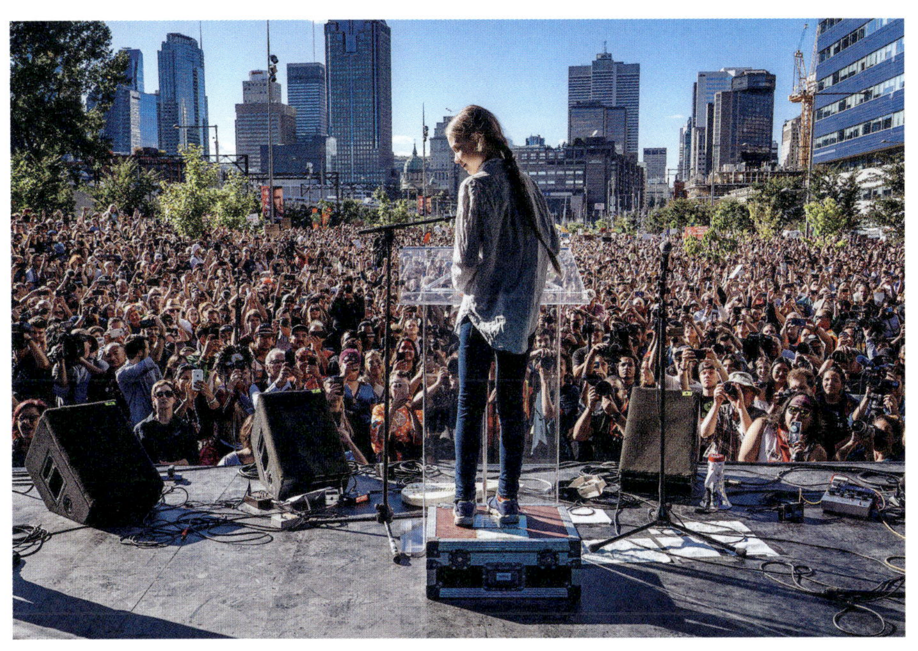

Greta Thunberg on Stage
by Eric Demers
Montreal, Canada

When Greta Thunberg announced she was going
to be in Montreal for a march, everyone knew it was
going to be huge. With 500,000 protesters, it was the biggest
demonstration in Canadian history. She turned towards
the sun and cracked a little smile. I did too.

David
by Joey Carrapichano
Reinbek, Germany

David is the brother of an artist friend of mine.
'I never let myself be photographed. I don't remember
why I made an exception, but I learned that
sometimes it can be great to do something that you
wouldn't do.' – David Tschaikowski

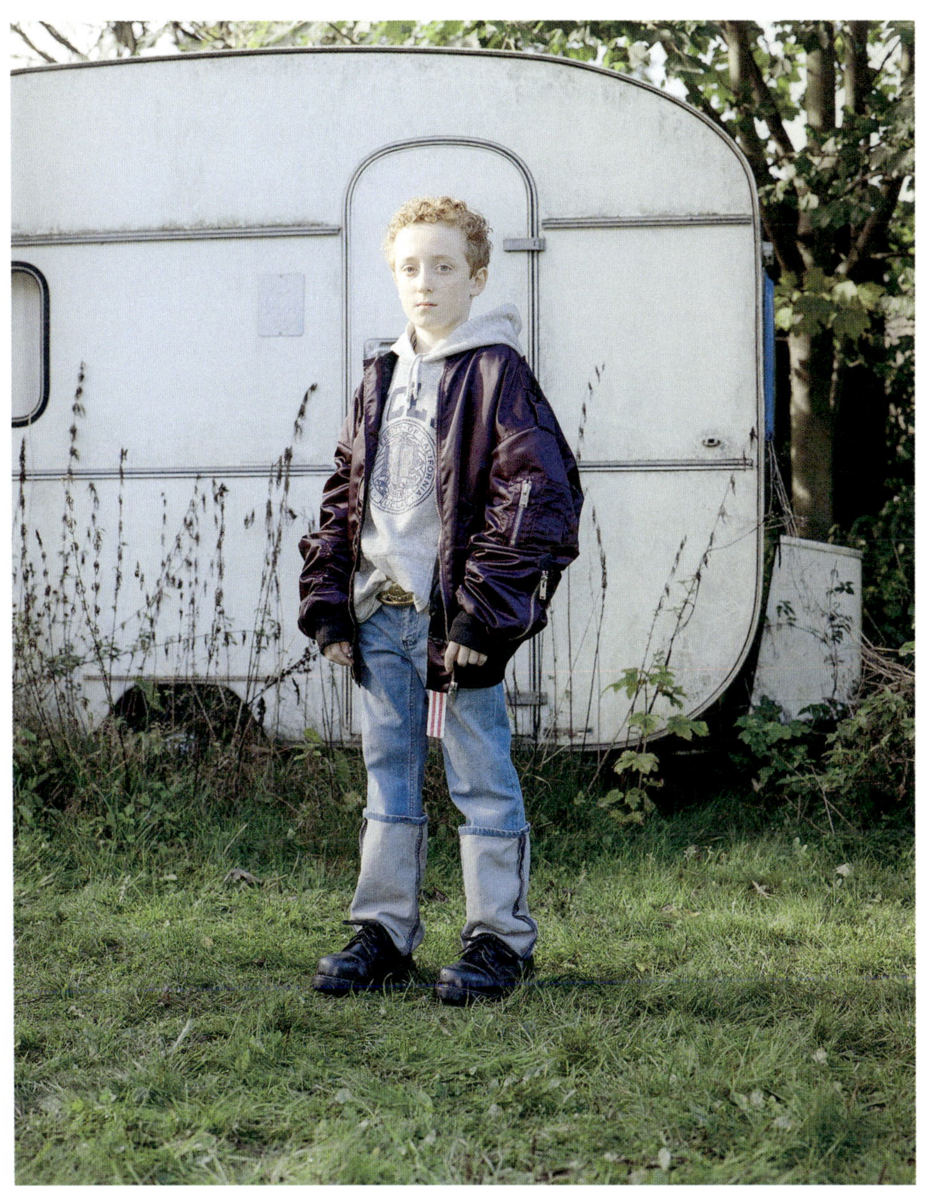

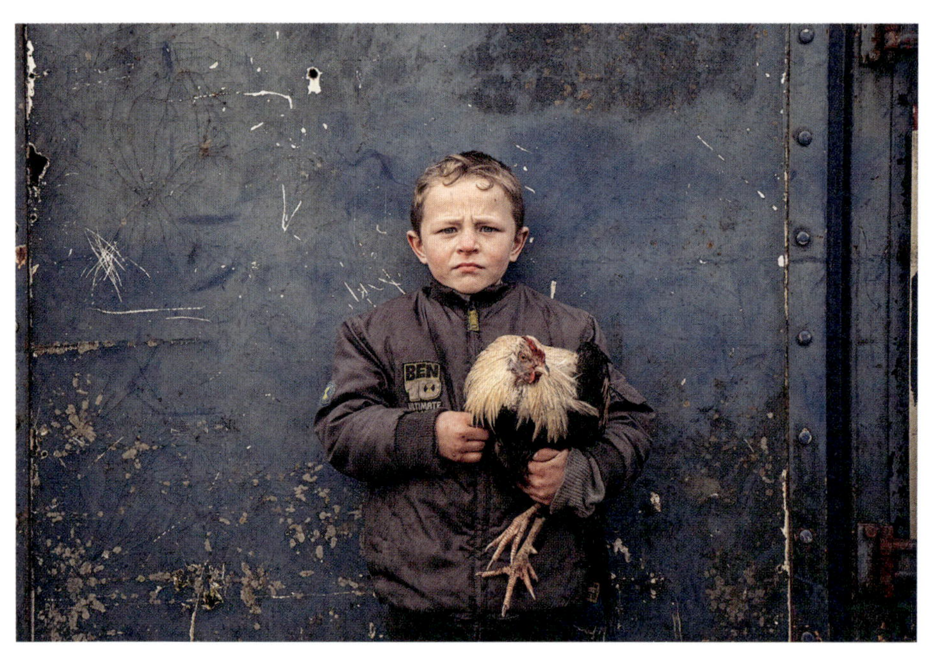

Pa and His Rooster
by Bob Newman
Cashel, Ireland

Pa is one of eight children from an Irish Traveller
family. It was February and it was cold and
windy. Pa was outside the family trailer playing
with his pet rooster. A few minutes later
he was off playing with his brothers and sisters.

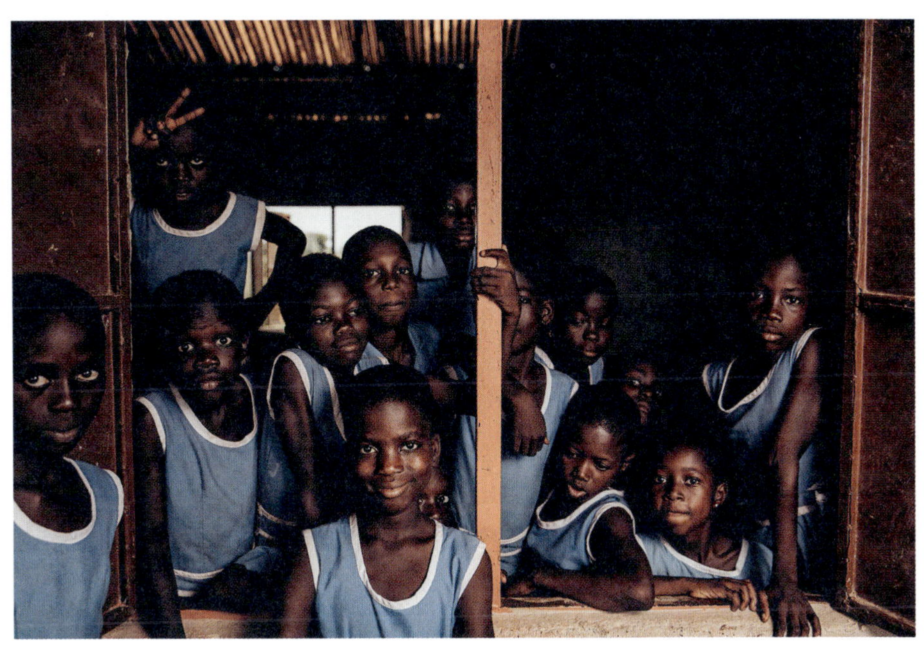

The Next Generation
by George Baxter
Lingbunga, Ghana

This group of Ghanaian children attends a
rural school run by the organisation The King's Village
in Ghana. The kindness, love and joy that these
children give despite their difficult living situation amazed
me. I wanted to challenge the kind of images that
typically come out of developing countries by focusing
on the people's characters rather than on the hardship.

Kurdistan Mon Amour

by José Farinha
Uraman Takht, Iran

I met these boys while walking through
Uraman Takht in the Kurdish area of Iran,
near the border with Iraq. In very basic English
they proudly explained to me that they
were wearing traditional trousers and hats,
symbols of their Kurdish heritage.

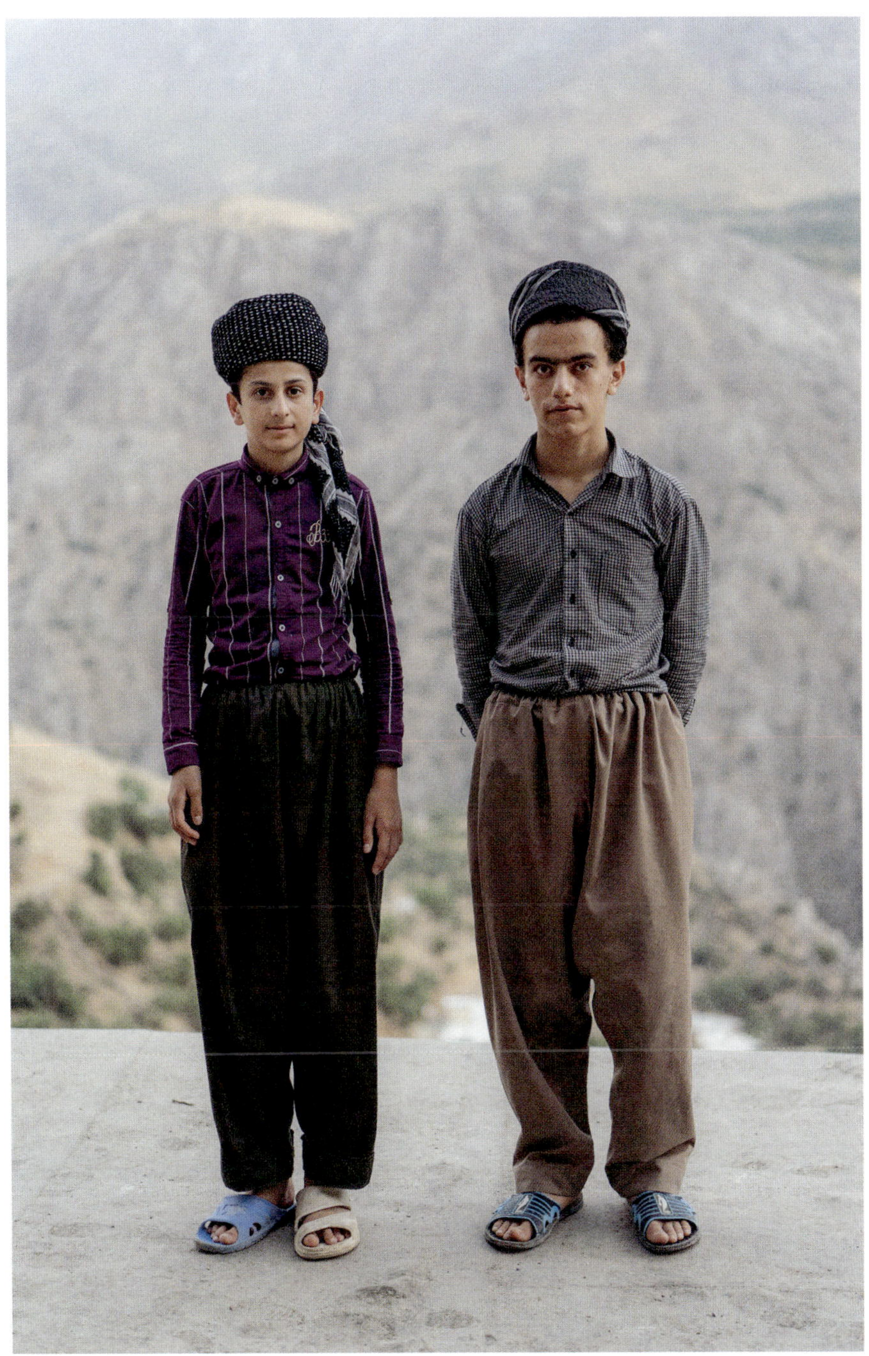

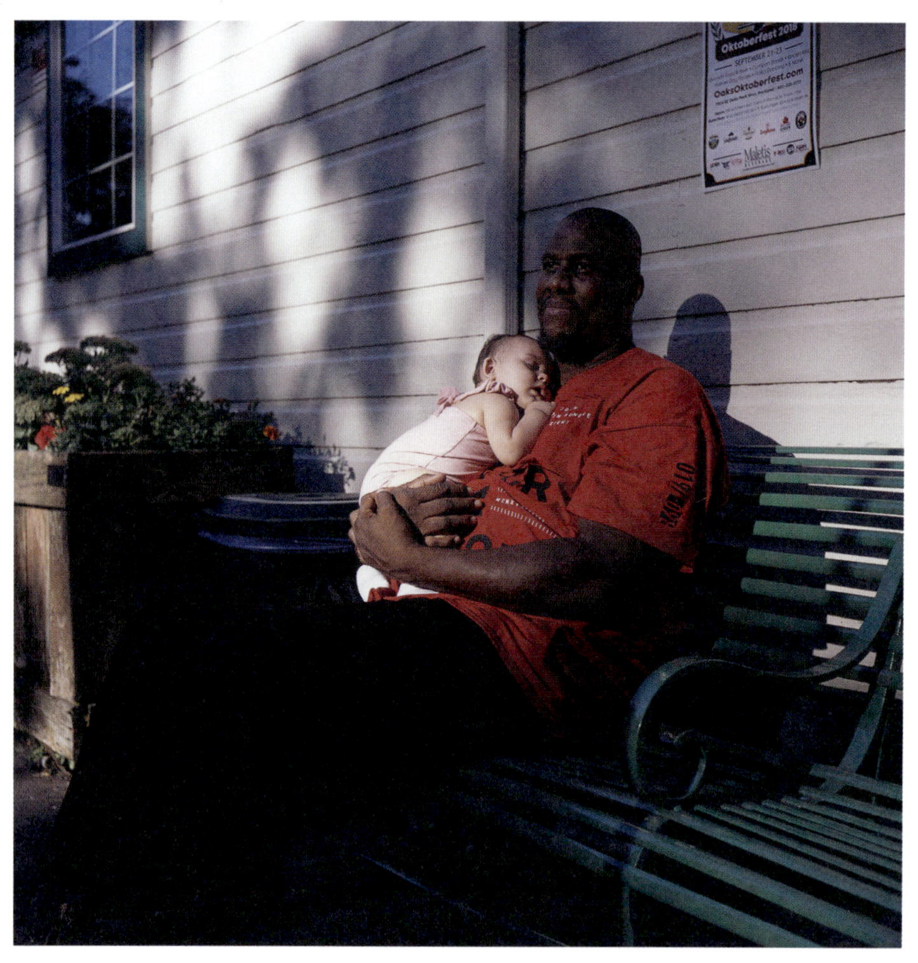

Grandbaby
by Lauren Hare
Portland, Oregon, USA

I met this man and his granddaughter
at Oaks Amusement Park. Chance meetings
with strangers sometimes yield the most intimate
moments, which I feel blessed to photograph.

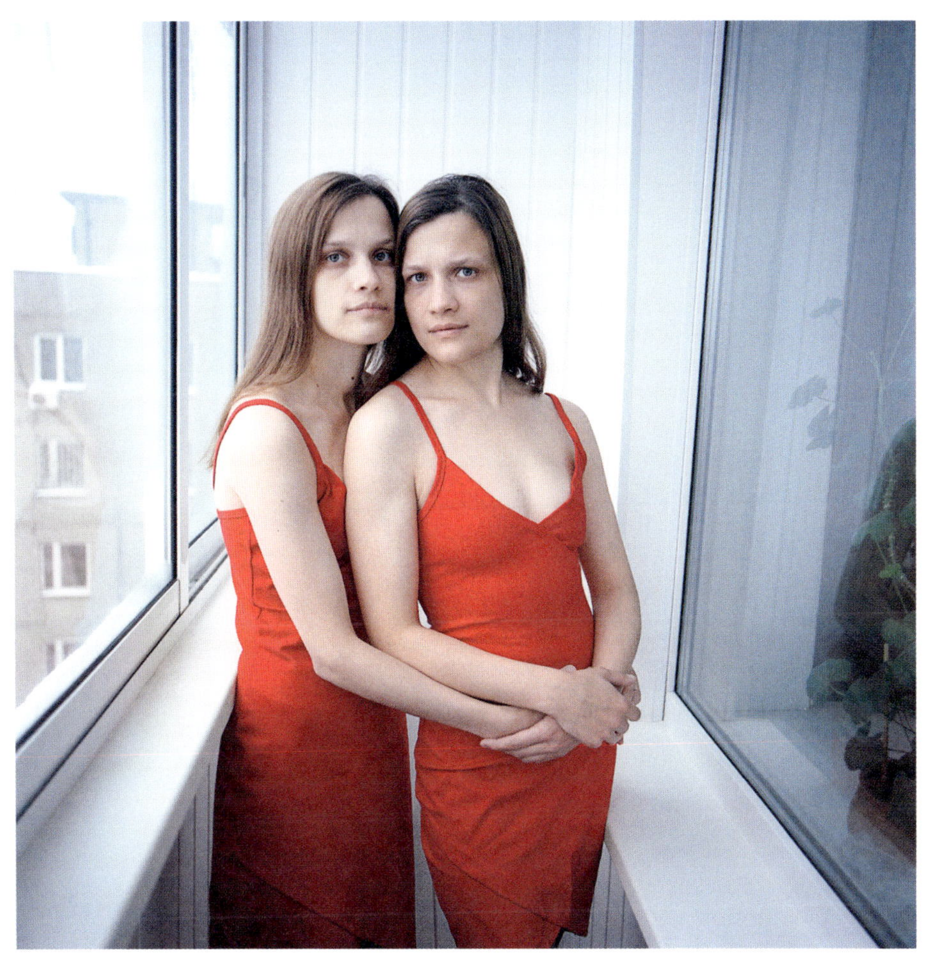

Alla and Claudia
by Snezhana von Buedingen
Perm, Russia

'The positive side of having a twin is you have
had your best friend with you since the day you were born.
My sister always supports me and never judges me
for my mistakes or wrong decisions. I feel like we're two
parts of a whole.' – Alla *(left)*

Boy

by Jon Wyatt
Ladakh, Northern India

The Nubra Valley in Ladakh is known as
'Ldumra' or 'the valley of flowers' – a green swathe
of fields on an arid, high altitude plateau. While
I was setting up my tripod in a meadow, a small boy
peered shyly around a mani wall, crept closer
and crouched down curiously behind me while I took
a photo. As I packed up my kit, I gestured to him
with the camera and took one frame.

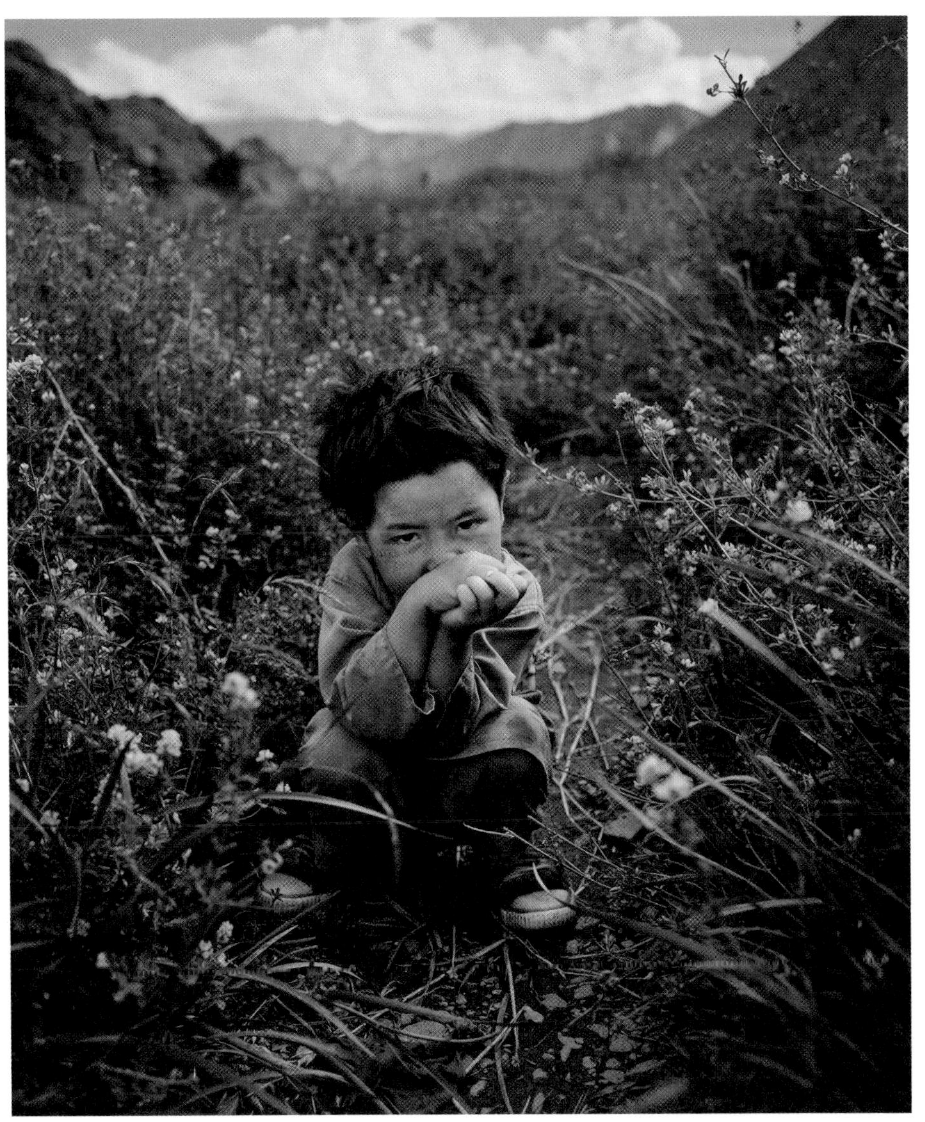

Index